The Nature of Rights at the American Founding and Beyond

Constitutionalism
And Democracy

GREGG IVERS AND
KEVIN T. MCGUIRE,
EDITORS

The Nature of Rights at the American Founding and Beyond

EDITED BY Barry Alan Shain

UNIVERSITY OF VIRGINIA PRESS CHARLOTTESVILLE AND LONDON

University of Virginia Press
© 2007 by the Rector and Visitors of the University of Virginia
"The History of Rights in Early America" © 2007 by Gordon S. Wood
All rights reserved
Printed in the United States of America on acid-free paper

First published 2007
First paperback edition published 2013
ISBN 978-0-8139-3446-4 (paper)

9 8 7 6 5 4 3 2 1

The Library of Congress has cataloged the hardcover edition as follows:

LIBRARY OF CONGRESS CATALOGING-IN-PUBLICATION DATA
The nature of rights at the American founding and beyond / edited by Barry Alan Shain.
    p.   cm. — (Constitutionalism and democracy)
    Includes bibliographical references and index.
    ISBN 978-0-8139-2666-7 (alk. paper)
    1. Constitutional history—United States. 2. Liberty—Political aspects—United
States—History. I. Shain, Barry Alan, 1950–
    KF4541.N38 2007
    342.7302'9—dc22

                                                                    2007017839

In memory of Joseph Hamburger, the late Pelatiah Perit Professor of Political and Social Science at Yale University—my teacher, my mentor, and a continuing inspiration as a scholar and a man.

CONTENTS

PART 3   Looking Backward and Forward: A Nation of Rights

ACKNOWLEDGMENTS

This volume of essays is based on a series of lectures on the nature of "Rights at the American Founding" delivered at Colgate University in 2000–2001. This lecture series was one that I proposed and directed along with two highly supportive colleagues, Professors Stanley C. Brubaker and Robert P. Kraynak. It was made possible by a generous grant from the John M. Olin Foundation's "Project on the Principles of a Free Society" and the support of Professor Jane Pinchin, then Colgate's Dean of the Faculty. The principal theme of the initial lecture series, as the title suggests, was the nature of rights as understood in late eighteenth-century America and how it differs, if at all, from today's understanding. In addition, in keeping with the goals of the Olin project, participants were asked to consider how such concepts have continued to shape and reshape the American experience of political liberty. Thus in their remarks speakers focused on particular issues but also spoke to broader themes. These broader concerns, in both the lectures and the chapters expressly written or revised for this volume, explore whether America at its foundation was predominantly individualistic or in important ways communal (for example, imitative of classically republican polities or still predominantly shaped by Reformed Protestantism).

These lectures provided Colgate students with a novel, even jarring, understanding of the debates surrounding the nature of rights during the American Revolution and Founding eras and a sense of the multiple streams of discourse carried within that inheritance. Indeed, like those first lectures, the essays in this volume help us understand whether rights at the Founding are best viewed in a libertarian sense that emphasizes personal fulfillment and freedom, as is so often assumed in high school and college texts, or as more recent historiography suggests, in a corporate sense that emphasizes the "people" as a group with individual civic duties and religious obligations.

Although holding to subtle differences on this and other issues, the volume's contributors all agree, and have made substantial strides toward demonstrating, that the nature of rights in America has been anything but constant and that the understanding defended in the late eighteenth century was some distance from that celebrated today. It is hoped these essays will provide for a broader audience much of the same sense of discovery experienced by many of Colgate's students present during the delivery of the initial lecture series.

This collection of essays, like most scholarly works, highlights the efforts of the authors while leaving in the background those individuals and organizations whose assistance, encouragement, and financial support made the volume possible. Not surprisingly, then, my debts as director of the lecture series and as editor and contributor to this volume are many.

Everything I put in print and much of what I think is immeasurably improved by the editing and critical scrutiny of my wife, Dr. Carolyn Nagase Shain. As well, she has been a constant source of emotional support and an inspiration to our daughter, Susan. All of these qualities have been on display from this project's inception in 1999. Similarly, Professor Rogers M. Smith, a teacher, friend, contributor, and coauthor of the introduction, provided much-needed guidance in the final stages of putting this volume together. Frequent conversations with three of my colleagues, Professors Stanley C. Brubaker, Robert P. Kraynak, and Joseph Wagner, even if rarely ending in agreement, have done much to refine my thought on the subject of this volume and any number of matters. Additionally, their encouragement helped to prevent me from abandoning this project when the difficulties seemed insurmountable. Much credit also must be given to my two research assistants, Jessica Lester and Vanessa N. Persico, most particularly Vanessa, who formatted and edited each essay and did much in helping create a coherent whole. Finally, I wish to thank all of the genuinely supportive individuals associated with the University of Virginia Press. They include the two anonymous reviewers of the manuscript whose helpful comments were important in shaping the introduction; my steadfast acquisitions editor, Richard Holway, who unfailingly continued to believe in this project; and Angie Hogan, Ellen G. Satrom, and Ruth Steinberg, who have helped shepherd the manuscript through the review and editorial process.

I also wish to thank a number of organizations that financially supported this project at various stages and, ultimately, made possible its completion. Indeed, each of these groups has previously supported my research at a critical time in my career, and thus I owe each of them my most sincere gratitude. Most importantly, I want to recognize and thank the Board of Directors and the Executive Director, James Piereson, of the John M. Olin Foundation for their support of this volume and the lecture series that preceded it. I also want to thank the Board of Directors of the Earhart Foundation for their support in the summer of 2002 of my first efforts at organizing this volume and soliciting and editing contributions. Colgate University helped fund the 2000–2001 lecture series, granted me a sabbatical leave in 2004 that allowed me to begin revising my contributions to this volume, and provided support for my two research assistants. Finally, I wish to acknowledge the support provided in 2005 by the National Endowment for the Humanities and its "We the People" Project, which permitted me to finish revising my contributions and to work with this volume's remarkable group of contributors so that the collection became a unified piece of scholarship.

Finally, my debt to Professor Joseph Hamburger, to whom this book is dedicated, is not one that I will ever be capable of repaying. He was a marvelous and unusually generous man who believed in and, when needed, protected me, and whose untimely death in 1997 left those who knew him with a deep and irreparable loss.

The Nature of Rights at the American Founding and Beyond

Introduction

BARRY ALAN SHAIN AND ROGERS M. SMITH

Since at least the Revolution, rights have always been an integral part of the language of American life and politics. This seems to be broadly accepted and recognized, even celebrated. Less thoroughly understood are the ways that dominant understandings of the meaning and status of rights have been transformed over time. In this volume we have sought to collect a range of views from leading scholars in several disciplines that together can serve to provide fresh insights on how rights came to be so prominent in early American political discourse and on the changes that have since occurred.

The contributors to this volume—historians, jurists, and political scientists—certainly do not agree in all matters concerning the history of American rights. John Phillip Reid, for example, minimizes more than some others the significance of the language of natural rights during the Revolutionary era. Gordon Wood places distinctive emphasis on how by the end of the Revolution the language of individual rights came to be a tool through which judges restrained popular majorities, rather than a rhetoric trumpeted by popular movements. Akhil Reed Amar contends that it was the Fourteenth Amendment's drafters—not, as some would have it, its twentieth-century interpreters—who made the national government, including the federal courts, responsible for protecting a wide range of individual rights against state violations. Readers will find other contrasts as well. These differences represent some of the most important historically grounded interpretations of American rights in contemporary scholarship, and one goal of this collection is to make these contrasting and alternative views readily accessible.

Still, it is notable that in their overarching historical accounts the level of agreement among these diverse contributors is surprisingly high. In opposition to older, "consensus" interpretations stressing the relatively unchanging character of American political thought, and particularly its focus on rights, this volume's contributors demonstrate that the history of American rights has gone through distinct stages, beginning with a pre-Revolutionary past in which modern conceptions of individual rights were rare. During each of the ensuing stages of "rights talk" in American history, new rights have been invented, while others have been retired or transformed. Perhaps the one constant is that, once the language of rights became prevalent, rights claims were then regularly used as politically valuable rhetorical tools, often but not always potent, whose meaning and application have been strenuously, even violently, contested.

In spite of their description as "natural," the history of the Revolution's famed "inalienable rights," rights that cannot be voluntarily surrendered, is one that several contributors trace back to religious rather than secular foundations, with Dutch and English Protestants serving as important intermediaries between Spanish Catholic natural-law thinkers and later secular theorists. More immediately, various contributors here suggest that the right of religious conscience (with its closely linked duty of religious devotion), as it developed in the English-speaking world, became the first individual right to be widely regarded as inalienable both outside and inside of civil society. This was a pathbreaking right, even if more limited in its scope than is now often understood. By the end of the eighteenth century, it helped generate radical changes in the moral and political standing of individuals, with the status of rights less subordinated to duties, and natural and civil rights more often treated as mutually definitive.

Most striking, though, is the agreement reached by the contributors in finding that culturally accepted seventeenth- and eighteenth-century rights claims, with the exception of religious conscience, were not primarily individualistic. They often were corporate in focus: appeals made on behalf of communities, corporations, colonies, states, "the people," not persons. This is not so surprising when one considers the lived character of eighteenth-century political and social life, in which most men (including slaves, indentured servants, debtors, the indigent, upland farmers, sailors, and urban mechanics) had, at best, limited social and political prerogatives, and women, particularly married ones, often had far less. Such features of early American national life deserve fair consideration in correctly assessing the dominant understandings of American rights claimed at the Founding and beyond.

The development of a potent language of natural rights at the end of the eighteenth century in America was, even as late as the beginning of the imperial crisis in 1764, anything but an inevitable outcome. As several contributors show, it was only at the end of that era, in late 1775 or early

1776, that many American political actors, particularly outside the New England colonies and Virginia, finally were willing to exploit in official state papers the language of natural rights free from any historical moorings in British constitutionalism (and the contributors differ on how significant this development was). This slowness in turning to natural-rights discourse is not hard to understand, no more than it would be for a contemporary litigant to make use of American legal precedents first, before turning in frustration to international legal codes or abstract moral philosophy in arguing his or her case before the Supreme Court.

Then as now, however, there were men who were unwilling to be so constrained, most likely because of closeness to British radicalism and its socially transformative goals, a deeply learned philosophical background, or alternatively a lack of legal training. Only in 1776 did the relatively few Americans who for several years had supported separation from Britain finally find others willing to use such language. This gave birth, in ways still not fully understood, to a new, unparalleled future for abstract individual rights, in which natural and civil rights became harder to distinguish and in which rights and duties no longer were so tightly or hierarchically linked.

It was not that natural rights were conceptually new when put forward by congressional delegates in 1776. No contributor here so contends. It is rather that in the context of America's War of Independence and its immediate aftermath, natural rights came to be treated as either definitive of or as capable of overriding civil rights, permitting abstract conceptions of rights to escape from the closets of philosophers, jurists, and theologians and to enjoy an active political presence on a world stage for the first time. Something new occurred with the American War for Independence and what many here see as its final explanatory language of natural rights. Heretofore, natural rights had been relegated to four extra-conventional legal conditions: presocial; between polities; for some, between generations; and for others, the individual right of emigration that rested on the corporate right of a people to be self-directing (even intolerantly so). Now these rights began to overlap with socially defined and heretofore alienable civil rights. The conflation of civil and natural rights, advanced by British and American radicals at the end of the eighteenth century, was an epochal event that characterized the close of America's momentous first stage in its history of rights.

Much of the early nineteenth century was then marked by the efforts of radical and socially marginal citizens—free blacks and abolitionists, workers, and women—to take advantage of the newly contested relationship between claims to inalienable natural rights and assertions of socially defined and usually limited civil ones. Similarly, during this same period, those who enjoyed political and social power and privilege, such as slaveholders, commercial and financial classes, and judges, sought to limit the reach of natural-rights discourse and to restore the distinction between hard-to-control natural-rights claims and more readily controlled and socially constrained civil ones. This period of conflict led to the Union victory at the end of the Civil War, with dramatic legal, political, and economic consequences, most importantly the passage of the Fourteenth Amendment and the birth of what some call a "second" Bill of Rights.

Far more than the original Bill of Rights, this second Bill is now seen as centered on individual rights in a radical new way. Yet in the aftermath of Reconstruction, ironically, those rights first came to be associated not with the claims of isolated individuals or oppressed groups so much as with the interests of powerful corporations and property holders. Thus, by the end of the century, and as a result of worldwide philosophical as well as domestic social and political movements, the language of natural rights declined among progressive political forces (at least among whites and the well educated). This period of severe challenge to the utility of the rhetoric of natural rights, for some a third stage in the history of rights in America, endured through much of the first half of the twentieth century.

A new ascendancy in the language of natural and inalienable rights followed in the aftermath of World War II and the horrors of National Socialism in Germany and Marxism in the Soviet Union, which some attributed to those regimes' legal and philosophical positivism. These political and philosophical experiments pushed authors and political actors in Western Europe and America back toward modified versions of the conceptions of natural rights and law that had prevailed in the previous century. Contentions for the existence of inalienable natural individual rights, now retitled as "human rights," began a trajectory that would sweep across the domestic politics of industrialized nations, and then across those of many developing ones. Those who defend this broad recognition of human rights are working today to achieve international protection for them under the auspices of newly empowered international organizations. Although the foundational language of nature is again under attack in certain philosophical circles, the forward movement of internationally recognized and advanced human rights, a process that can be traced back to the mixing of natural and civil rights that began during the American Revolution, continues to make impressive strides.

On this description of the overall pattern of historical transformations in American rights, the contributors here generally agree. The essays also display a common belief that it may well be instructive to revisit the American Revolutionary movement, when a new language of rights first came to political prominence, especially with similar movements afoot today in various parts of the world. This period of American history was deemed that of "the first new nation" by one "consensus" scholar, Seymour Martin Lipset. These years marked the beginning of the struggles that transformed terms frequently used to advance local and corporate concerns into resoundingly universalistic conceptions that many have since invoked on behalf of a wide range of individual and group causes. This is a trajectory of political development that arguably finds echoes in many more recently developed states. The less than smooth history of American rights, therefore, may in the end prove useful to those seeking to understand legal and political changes in many parts of today's world.

America's historical path of development now stretches across great distances. As this volume's authors find, the Declaration of Independence and Bill of Rights are today understood by many in ways that would have surprised most (though not all) Americans who gave sanction to them when they were issued at the end of the eighteenth century. Conflicting understandings are made all the more likely because the two men who drafted these documents likely viewed them differently than the other representatives of the bodies that issued them.

The contributors to this volume do not speak collectively to whether the original or more revisionist understandings of the Declaration of Independence, the Bill of Rights, and later rights statements are morally superior. Although no poll was taken of the contributors, it is likely that most share Madison's prescient understanding of the potential importance of rights in protecting individuals from intrusive majorities. It is this understanding that he brought to the editing of the Bill of Rights. But this volume's contributors take this stance while recognizing that Madison's individualistic goals, at the end of the eighteenth century, were anomalously progressive. It is this, the recognition that his understanding of rights was in important respects unusual and should not be taken as typical of late eighteenth-century American views, that demands notice. This and related historical clarifications form the common goal of this volume. Normative decisions concerning which America should be preferred are addressed by some contributors, but in the main are largely left to the reader. Getting right the historical story of American rights is a demanding enough task in itself, and it is one that will take more than this volume to complete. But with their distinctive contributions and their common themes, the essays collected here provide a useful start.

The first section, "Situating Rights," contains two essays, one more conceptual and the other more historical. Together, they introduce the concept of rights and an abbreviated history of them to the reader and present American rights in ways far less fixed and far more elusive than are commonly encountered.

Richard Primus, in "An Introduction to the Nature of American Rights," argues that our rights discourse, whatever else it does, has been a means of awarding certain moral stances with a privileged position and, as such, is a rhetoric that, without the necessity of offering reasons, possesses unusual normative power. But although the normative power that rights enjoy has long been present in America, the content has almost as constantly changed. Primus suggests in particular that our contemporary language of individual human rights has much to do with the ideological needs of a post–World War II world in which America sought to distinguish itself from its Cold War adversaries. To see these conceptions as always dominant in America is to misunderstand the past and to limit our access to a diversity of views that we may well find edifying or some day need.

But how did all this talk of rights get started? James H. Hutson's essay, "The Emergence of the Modern Concept of a Right in America: The Contribution of Michel Villey," takes the reader back into the medieval history of rights and argues that our current concept of rights did not enjoy significant standing until well into the seventeenth century. Widespread embrace of notions of "subjective rights," rights as powers legitimately wielded by subjects, came in most cases still later. Hutson traces the first glimmerings of such rights to sixteenth-century Spanish Scholastics—Vitoria, DeSoto, Vasquez, Molina, and Suarez—whose work was often mined by later English and Dutch Protestant thinkers. Still, Hutson claims that it was Hobbes who gave rights their first modern formulation. And it was not until the end of the eighteenth century that they achieved their full articulation in the French Declaration of Rights.

In British America, English legal conceptions of rights prevailed; subjective understandings were rare through most of the colonial period. When such views arose, Americans derived them not so much from Hobbes as from Reformed Protestant thought and practices. Though it was visible from the mid-eighteenth century on, not until near the end of the imperial crisis does Hutson find that something approaching a fully subjective meaning of rights began to gain sway, and in ways that would come to be unduly identified with the meaning of the American Revolution.

The second section, "The Nature of Rights at the American Founding," contains five essays. It focuses on understandings of rights in the years leading up to and immediately following the War of Independence for thirteen of Great Britain's two dozen or so North American colonies and on their formation first of a series of common governments, and then of a national Bill of Rights in 1791. The essays in this section thus move from the pre-Revolutionary notions of rights dominant in British North America in 1764 to the partly transformed views that shaped the Founders' Bill of Rights.

The first essay, "The Authority of Rights at the American Founding," by John Phillip Reid, rests on prodigious research to which many other contributors recur. Reid's focus is not on the content of rights, but their foundations. That is, he takes for granted the inherited English character of the actual rights being claimed on both sides of the imperial crisis and instead focuses on the grounds, the authority, advanced by American patriots (and many Loyalists) in defending their rights claims. Among the ten sources of authority to rights that he identifies, Reid focuses here on those of the original (colonial) contract, the English migration to America, the migration purchase and the duties it imposed on one generation to pass on its inherited rights to future ones, Englishness and its tradition of balanced government and jury trial, the equality of British peoples, customary usage, and among the two least important, nature and charters.

In making his case for the varied grounds upon which American (British) constitutional theorists rested their claims for exemption from parliamentary oversight and the protection of the colonists' rights to self-legislation and jury trials, Reid draws attention to the nearly impossible nature of the impasse that British theorists on both sides of the Atlantic then confronted. Under Whig theory, they had developed a set of institutions and principles that, through Parliamentary supremacy, had enabled a people to protect themselves from the arbitrary actions of a monarch. Yet they had not given sufficient consideration to the problem of a subordinate people wanting the same protection from Parliament under a constitution with entrenched protections from that body's actions. Only a new understanding of constitutionalism would solve this problem.

In the second essay, "Rights Natural and Civil in the Declaration of Independence," Barry Alan Shain, like Reid, argues that the dominant rights claims of the Declaration's main body were largely shaped by English tradition, and that the equality of greatest importance was that of British peoples. But the focus of this essay is on the Preamble's rights claims. Shain suggests that the most useful approach to understanding them is one that emphasizes why, at this late juncture in the imperial crisis, Americans were forced to shift from an argument that appealed to British constitutional law and civil rights to one that emphasized international law and natural rights. The reason for doing so in the summer of 1776 is not hard to comprehend: a majority of delegates had reluctantly concluded that they could no longer defend their corporate rights from within the First British Empire, and thus were forced to seek support and validation from the eighteenth-century international (read western European) community.

In so doing, Americans turned to the international language of rights, natural ones. Shain then seeks to discriminate between natural and civil rights and to show that the Preamble's international focus ensured that it would be written in the language of natural law and rights. But for most of the delegates who supported the Declaration, natural law and rights described a condition outside of civil society, and in their quickly changing world, this meant for most of them that such claims played a limited role in shaping the specific moral and political contours within society. But this distinction between natural and civil rights and the traditional close linkage between rights and duties were theoretical claims that, at the end of the eighteenth century, were beginning to be contested. The Preamble was written so that it could appeal to various audiences, but it seems likely that for most of them the meaning that they attributed to the Preamble was the traditional, not the newly radical, one.

The next essay, "The Creation, Reconstruction, and Interpretation of the Bill of Rights," by Akhil Reed Amar, reminds us that for much of early American history the Bill of Rights was of little importance. Amar argues, as do others, that there have effectively been not one, but two Bills of Rights. The first was a communal and localistic product of the War for Independence, that viewed central government as the dominant threat to liberty, and local and state governments as its guarantor. A second Bill, however, followed the Civil War. This one was national and individualistic, and understood state and local governments to be the preeminent threats to liberty and the federal courts its protector.

This view of the Bill of Rights was developed by Radical Republicans who, like Lincoln, reinterpreted the Founders' Bill of Rights as enunciating universal principles that could limit not only the federal government, but indeed all levels of government. But after the Civil War and the passage of the Fourteenth Amendment in 1868, their understanding would not soon come to guide the Supreme Court. Only in the early years of the twentieth century would the Court begin to "incorporate" the Bill of Rights so that the most relevant rights would apply equally to state and local as well as federal government.

Jack Rakove observes, in "The Dilemma of Declaring Rights," that if in the course of their Revolutionary struggles, many Americans had come to wield a significantly new language of natural rights sometimes claimed on behalf of individuals as well as communities, even proponents of such rights often disagreed on the wisdom of seeking to secure such rights through positive law. It may seem puzzling that James Madison, whom most of the contributors here see as a stronger champion of individual rights than many other early Americans, should have initially opposed calls to add a list of enumerated rights to the Constitution. Anti-Federalists accused Madison of simply wishing to avoid all restraints on national power. But while seeing Madison as indeed a nationalist, Rakove argues that Madison was duly concerned about the dangers that enumerating rights presented to the cause of securing rights. These dangers pose a "dilemma" of enduring significance for the increasingly popular and widespread enterprise of governance via written constitutions today.

The final essay in this section, "The Limited Horizons of Whig Religious Rights," by A. Gregg Roeber, emphasizes how distant and variegated the world of the Founders was from our own, in particular concerning religion. Recognizing that the handful of historically elevated, elite Founders, in the main occupied a significantly less religious space than did the vast majority of Americans, he nonetheless finds that they too lived within a political and moral landscape importantly shaped by Protestant categories of thought and historical concerns. Indeed, Roeber argues that these elite actors and thinkers were able to allow for increased religious latitude because they could rely on the certainty of a pervasive Protestant environment.

Additionally, at the core of the thinking of both elite and more popular religious forces was a shared antipathy to Roman Catholicism. But even if Catholicism was the most feared religion, it was not alone in winning the disdain of both elite and popular religiosity. Native Americans, African Americans, Jews, and from the mid-nineteenth century onward, Mormons, all were treated with common intolerance. Yet even with the rise of such challenges to Protestant hegemony, nationalist elites were free to support a relatively neutral national state. They could do so because they were able to rely on the continued Protestantism of the society and, in many instances, of state governments. In sum, Roeber finds that the defense of religious rights by the Founders was far more reliant on an assumed Protestant environment and far less progressive and "liberal" than is often assumed.

The third and final section, "Looking Backward and Forward: A Nation of Rights," contains four essays that offer a synoptic view of rights discourse as it developed in America, starting with its antecedent development in Britain and ending in contemporary rights talk.

The first essay, "The History of Rights in Early America," by Gordon S. Wood, focuses on how, across time, Americans developed a court-centered rights theory that attempted to resolve two dilemmas that challenged rights notions as they developed in the late eighteenth century. Wood shows first that Americans' understanding of rights only slowly came to grips with the tensions between the standing and the rights of popular legislatures, the people, and individuals. Although there was little uncertainty regarding the necessity of popular control over monarchical prerogatives, Whig-inspired political theory and practice were little prepared for the possibility that popular legislatures, and even the people, might prove equally destructive to the rights of individuals. As Wood notes, most eighteenth-century British, and British Americans before the imperial crisis, had trouble understanding how the subjects' Parliament could ever threaten rights.

The second dilemma that Wood highlights is the changing and often confusing delineation between private and public domains. He shows that American notions of this demarcation transformed rapidly during the late eighteenth century, in ways that were hard to sort out fully. The role played in these developments by republican theory and the changes wrought by the Revolution often had counterintuitive and ironic effects. In both instances, according to Wood, it was to the court system that early-national Americans turned to restore an orderly system of rights. And, "it is a conclusion that in our history we have reached time and time again."

The next essay, "Rights Consciousness in American History," by Daniel T. Rodgers, notes that rights talk is eminently American, but as has been noted by all other contributors as well, there has been much less consistency in our history regarding the content of such claims. Like other contributors, Rodgers divides this history into four epochs, often shaped around the different needs of various wars. Particular to Rodgers's account is his sense that two of the four periods were driven by insistent demands from social forces from both above and below the mainstream, while the other two were driven from below in one case and from above in the other. Rodgers finds that these social groupings produced different languages of rights, and that these elite- and populist-driven languages seem to find their moment of greatest innovation in the twentieth century, when responding to the threats and challenges offered by National Socialism, Communism, and the Cold War.

Unlike most of the previous essays, the focus of "The Diversity of Rights in Contemporary Ethical and Political Thought," by Leif Wenar and Stephen Macedo, is more philosophical than historical. While confirming the shifting nature of rights discourse in American history, Wenar and Macedo provocatively argue that this elasticity is philosophically defensible, and that such malleability, both in terms of rights claims and foundations, has become since World War II the leading view among rights theorists. In support of these claims, they explicate the rights language of the Universal Declaration of Human Rights (1948) and briefly summarize the varying positions taken over the past sixty years by leading rights theorists. They find that the Universal Declaration was intentionally promiscuous in its foundational language, allowing different audiences to select among varying justificatory schemes. Such diversity, they argue, is in keeping with a world of diverse philosophical and religious traditions, and, indeed, anything else would be self-defeating.

They also argue that the Universal Declaration's proto-answers to a number of core questions in ethical theory came to dominate postwar American rights theorizing. Among these questions are: Why do people have basic rights? Which rights do they have? Who is a rights holder? And what is the relation between rights and duties? Their discussion focuses in particular on how different groups of theorists have answered the "Why?" question. They find much of this perspective captured in John Rawls's account of basic political rights. As well, they report that among all the various schools of contemporary thought, there has been a growing tendency to avoid abstruse theological or metaphysical speculation in attempting to answer the question "Why rights?" In a manner linking contemporary theorists with their American antecedents and in opposition to numerous critics, Wenar and Macedo further insist that the post–World War II world has seen a return in the importance of group rights, including the hallowed one of a people to self-government. Similarly, they suggest that the altered linkage between rights and duties is better understood as one of change rather than of simple reduction. In sum, in keeping with the shifting nature of American rights claims, Wenar and Macedo, in their treatment of the last sixty years of theorizing, point to important changes in the grounding of rights and the linked and renewed, though modified, emphasis on communal rights and the centrality of duty.

In the final essay of the section, "The Politics of Rights Talk, Then and

Now," Rogers M. Smith conceives of rights and characterizes the different stages in the development of American rights language in ways that largely concur with the analyses of most of the other contributors to this volume. He is especially interested in why rights talk has so often been politically efficacious, as well as in why it has nonetheless never been sufficient to win legal and political struggles. He contends that rights language serves to confer a legitimating aura of ethical worth on political causes, thereby sometimes inspiring oppressed groups who might be intimidated by the enormous obstacles they face, and at other times protecting privileged groups against charges that their advantages have been unjustly acquired. Smith concludes that though rights talk has never been enough by itself to win political battles, its value in conferring high ethical standing to political causes means that it is likely to continue to be a major resource for participants in American processes of governance, as it has been throughout the nation's history. That is one of many reasons that it is worthwhile for scholars and citizens alike to consider the nature of rights at the American Founding and beyond.

Situating Rights | 1

An Introduction to the Nature of American Rights

RICHARD PRIMUS

The title of this book carries an important implication. If it makes sense to inquire into the nature of rights at the American Founding, then the nature of rights at the American Founding might not have been the same as the nature of rights at all other times and places. If rights were the same everywhere and at all times, there would be little need to write about their nature at one particular time and place, even if that time and place were as momentous as the American Founding. Nobody would write a book about the nature of carbon atoms at the American Founding, or at any other specific time and place, because the nature of carbon atoms is not dependent on particular historical settings.

This point is worth making because one strong tendency in thinking about rights is to imagine them as universal, a priori propositions. This approach goes by several different names. We speak sometimes of natural rights, sometimes of inalienable rights, and sometimes of human rights. Any of those rubrics encourages a vision of rights as propositions that are true for all people, everywhere and always. Often, the bite of that approach is to assert moral claims against tyrannical governments. When governments sanction oppression, positive law often affords no recourse, because the positive law is the creature of the government. In that situation the idea of universal, a priori rights invokes a higher authority as a way of opposing the government's law.

Whether and to what extent right and wrong exist prior to human conventions like positive law is a large philosophical question that this book does not attempt to answer. This book is an inquiry into the idea of rights, but it is not a work of moral theory. Instead, it examines the ways that political actors at certain times and places used the language of rights to express their normative ideas.

The plural in the previous sentence is important: Americans of the Founding generation thought about rights in varying ways, just as every generation since has done. But also like their successors in later generations, Americans of the Founding era did not use the category "rights" as a way of describing every normative proposition, every instance of right and wrong. They framed only a subset of their normative ideas as matters of rights, and the same is true for us today. The best way to understand an inquiry into the nature of rights, therefore, is as an inquiry into which kinds of normative propositions belong in that category. And different propositions have found their way into that category at different times.

In principle, the variation in what the category of rights has contained at different times could be due either to differences in people's normative views or to differences in their analytic conception of what kind of thing a right is. The case of normative variation over time is easy to imagine. If Roger says that black men have no rights and that white men need respect, but Martin says that every man has the right to be judged by the content of his character, the difference between them is likely to be a straightforward normative dispute about race and equality.

In other cases, though, conflicts about rights seem to reflect something different from this kind of normative disagreement. Some disputes appear to flow from analytic or even metaphysical disagreements about what rights are. For example, many thinkers have argued that rights can be predicated of individuals but not of groups. Suppose that this is Ronnie's view but not Lani's. Lani, unlike Ronnie, believes that we should sometimes think in terms of group rights. For example, groups might have rights to proportionate representation in a political system. One might understand this conflict between Ronnie and Lani as an analytic disagreement about the nature of rights: the question is whether rights can or cannot be held by groups. In principle, Ronnie and Lani might hold their respective answers without regard to their opinions on first-order normative issues, such as the issue of whether proportional representation of groups in politics is a good idea.

In the end, however, disputes about the nature of rights are almost always normative. The reason why lies in the actual practice of talking about rights. Rights claims are a powerful form of rhetoric, used to identify some normative propositions as especially important. If one side in a dispute has a right and the other side does not, the side with the right is likely to persuade the relevant audience that it should prevail. Accordingly, a dispute about whether groups as well as individuals can have rights is not just a dispute about the analytic nature of something called "rights," at least not in the way that a dispute about whether the number "1" is a prime number is a dispute about the analytic properties of prime numbers. The dispute about rights is partly analytic, but it is also normative, because the inevitable consequence of deciding that groups can or cannot have rights is to tilt political argument toward or away from practices like proportional representation in politics. Indeed, that is not just a consequence of the argument: it may also be its motivation. In other words, ostensibly analytic propositions about rights, like "Rights attach only to individuals and not to groups," are frequently offered, defended, rejected, or accepted because they will support certain normative propositions, not because they are more or less accurate in capturing some entity called "rights."

Outside of a few specialized contexts, however, claims of rights commonly fail to convey reasons why those normative claims should be honored. Arguments about rights appear to invoke authority, implying that some binding source of norms requires that a given conflict be resolved in a particular way. If I want something, you may or may not consent to give it to me, but if I have a right to that thing, you ought to give it to me even if you would prefer not to. Much of the time, however, the implicit authority on which a rights claim rests is left unspecified. The claim about rights announces the claimant's desire, indeed, often his strong desire, that his or her claim be respected. Announcing an attitude is not the same as supplying an argument. Nonetheless, claims of rights are often rhetorically powerful, at least before American audiences (and perhaps before English-speaking audiences more generally). If an audience can be brought to think that a rights claim supports some result, it often will endorse that result without asking about the underlying reasons that would justify the normative attitude that the rights claim announces.

Why rights language enjoys such rhetorical power is a fascinating question about the history of American political discourse. Moreover, it is a question with no clearly satisfying answer. To some extent the American language of rights descends from the English common-law tradition, which used (and still uses) the idea of rights to frame all sorts of legal relationships. The status of rights in American political rhetoric may also owe something to the early influence of social contractarians who, in the manner of John Locke, imagined government as an endeavor designed to protect natural or otherwise pre-political rights. It here bears notice that these sources of rights language differed from each other strikingly in their substantive approaches to rights: consider, for example, that common-law rights tend to look to traditional practice as authoritative, but that thinkers like Locke invoked natural rights as a way of rejecting traditional authority. Without regard to content, however, the practice of framing legal and political contentions in terms of rights was familiar to early Americans.

That said, none of this suffices to explain why the language of rights came to play its dominant role in American political rhetoric. For one thing, early American thought also had roots in discourses that did not much feature the idea of rights. Covenant theology is one example. Moreover, familiarity with the common law does not necessarily lead a society to elevate the idea of rights to a preeminent position, as should be obvious from the fact that American rights discourse has differed from that of England itself. In the end, we have no clear and complete explanation for why the language of rights has been especially powerful in American politics.

But although we cannot completely identify the historical reasons why rights discourse achieved its central place in American political life, we can confidently exclude one possible reason. It cannot be the case that American law and politics have privileged the idea of rights due to something inherent in the nature of rights themselves. Very little is inherent in the nature of rights: a dizzying variety of different kinds of claims can be intelligibly described in the language of rights, such that distinguishing valid rights claims from invalid ones is usually a matter of normative judgment. Indeed, since before the beginning of the Republic Americans have used the language of rights to express their normative commitments on virtually every side of every important political issue.

In the 1760s and 1770s the claimed rights of North American colonial legislatures clashed with the declared rights of the British Parliament to unlimited sovereignty. At the Constitutional Convention, the rights of large states clashed with the rights of small states. For decades thereafter, the rights of slaveholders clashed with the rights of people held as slaves, and—as is still true today—the rights of the national government clashed with the rights of states. Dominant issues of the late nineteenth and early twentieth centuries featured contests between the right to control one's private property and the democratic majority's right to regulate it in the public interest. During the 1950s, the right to racial equality clashed with the right of free association. A generation later, the divisive issue of abortion was framed as a conflict between the right to choose and the right to life. There is no reason to expect the pattern to end. The language of rights has proved extremely flexible, flexible enough to be used in the service of every significant agenda in American politics.

This tremendous flexibility of rights language may be part of what sends modern Americans back to the Founding with the hope of learning about the conceptions of rights that prevailed then and there. Even if most Americans implicitly agree that rights should be treated with great respect, that agreement does not help settle many contested issues, because we often disagree about which of the many different things that might be rights are the ones worthy of our normative approbation. It can be appealing, therefore, to identify criteria that will discriminate among all the possible ways of using the concept of rights, marking some but not others as the ones we approve. We could then adjudicate our disputes on the authority of those criteria. And one perennial candidate for a method of identifying which normative content should be poured into the flexible container of rights language is asking how rights were understood by the people who formed our republic.

The efficacy of that method is limited, though, by the fact that the Founders had many intramural disagreements about the content of rights. Accordingly, careful readings of Founding-era history may not be able to supply criteria limiting the scope of the nature of rights. Rebels and Loyalists, Federalists and Anti-Federalists, Hamiltonians and Jeffersonians all used rights language, and they all were able to deploy that language intelligibly against one another. They purported to derive rights from many different sources of authority, including nature, history, the common law, contract, right reason, and God. They attributed rights to a whole gamut of different kinds of rights holders, including not just individuals but also towns, communities, states, institutions, collective interest groups, and the people as a whole. Indeed, perhaps the signature right of the Founding era—the right of self-government—is best understood as a collective right rather than an individual right. When the Founders spoke of the right of self-government, they did not principally mean the right of an individual to make decisions for himself, which is to say that they were not naming the right that modern philosophers call the right of personal autonomy. They were referring to the idea that a community of people, like that of Boston or Virginia or the nascent United States as a whole, was entitled to make collective decisions without being subject to an outside power such as the Parliament of Great Britain.

Rarely, if ever, did eighteenth-century Americans contend that their political opponents misapprehended the nature of rights. There was relatively little argument, for example, about whether this or that source of authority could underwrite a claim of rights, or about whether groups as well as individuals could be rights holders. Rivals contradicted and argued against each others' views about the substance of rights, but they almost never charged that their opponents' rights-based arguments suffered from category mistakes by claiming as rights things that, in their nature, could not be rights at all. As a result, even if we were willing to be guided by the prevailing conceptions of the Founding era, looking to the discourse of that time would do little to limit the range of propositions that could be described validly as rights.

What, then, might we hope to gain from studying Founding conceptions of rights? One possibility is that such a study would explain the origins of particular rights that are important in American life today. In other words, perhaps we can examine conceptions of rights at the Founding in order to understand the roots of our prevailing normative ideas about free speech, individual equality, and so forth. And indeed we can learn something about the historical background of our present ideas from such an inquiry. That said, we must be modest about how much of the history of our ideas we can glean by studying the Founding. The rights discourse of that era is part of the historical development of our own ideas about rights, but it is only a small slice of that development. In substance, if not always in name, the rights at the center of modern American law and politics are more the products of the nineteenth and twentieth centuries than of the eighteenth. Freedom of speech was written into the Constitution in 1791, but with a narrow meaning. The substantive idea that within very broad bounds individuals must be immune from legal sanction for criticizing the powerful or offending the majority did not prevail in American law until much later in history. Only well into the twentieth century did that idea, denominated as the right to free speech, come to assume a central position in American political morality. Similarly, although the idea that people have a right to be treated as individuals without respect to ascriptive characteristics like ancestry or skin color has forerunners in the eighteenth century, that idea was obviously not honored then in the way that almost all Americans would insist upon it now. Nor did the changes from Founding conceptions of rights to our modern conceptions occur at a single moment. Instead, norms changed over a long period of history. Understanding the development of rights as we know them requires us to investigate widely through time. Some periods, like the Founding, capture the imagination more than others, but no one period tells the full developmental story. Indeed, if the goal is to understand where our modern political values come from, other periods of history are at least as important as the Founding.

Several times after the eighteenth century ended, Americans reacted to new problems by articulating new sets of rights. This dynamic marked the Founding as well, of course. Colonists subject to unwelcome taxation spoke of their right to be represented in the legislature that imposed taxes; colonists whose homes were searched on the authority of generalized search warrants began speaking of their rights against unreasonable searches and seizures; people tried in maritime Admiralty courts under Roman law were inclined to assert their right to trial by civilian juries under British common law. But the pattern whereby particular problems called forth specific claims of rights recurred in later history as well, with the substantive ground of rights argument shifting when the most salient social conflicts came to focus on issues other than those that marked the rebellion against King George. Thus, in the nineteenth century, people opposed to Southern slavery articulated a set of rights about free labor and certain limited kinds of racial equality. In the middle of the twentieth century, Americans confronting European totalitarianism articulated or strengthened their commitments to free speech, privacy, and racial egalitarianism, all of which mapped points of opposition to either Nazi Germany or the Soviet Union or both. Each crisis eventually receded, but the ideas about rights articulated in response to each often remained. What survived was a pastiche of rights shaped and reshaped by a series of different problems over time.

Many of the underlying norms animating claims of rights at each of these times antedated the actual crises, at least in part. In other words, part of why many Americans opposed certain practices of the British Empire, Southern slaveholders, or European totalitarians was that those practices conflicted with normative views that many or most Americans already held. (Some ideas about right and wrong were shaped in the conflicts themselves, but the conflicts were themselves precipitated in part by normative ideas.) Even when the norms underwriting the conflicts were preexisting, however, the specific features of each conflict affected their salience. People are likely to place a higher priority on racial equality, for example, when directly confronted with horrors like slavery and genocide than under circumstances in which racial discrimination is a problem only in the abstract, or when the damage it does can be discounted or ignored. And because almost any normative proposition will be articulated in terms of rights if it is considered sufficiently important, shifts in salience have produced shifts in the ways that Americans speak and think about rights.

This way of understanding how modern American ideas about rights emerged can help clarify the relationship between rights and individualism. As noted above, some leading theorists of rights have maintained that rights attach specifically and perhaps exclusively to individuals. In the terminology of political theory, this is a classically liberal view. In the latter years of the twentieth century, the idea that rights attach to individuals rather than to groups or to society at large was advanced both by liberal individualists who approved of rights so conceived and by nonliberals who intended to criticize rights-based argument by exposing its individualist cast. But the assumption that rights have a specific connection with individualist norms is an overgeneralization from the contingent circumstances of America in the decades after 1930. At that time and place, rights discourse was indeed heavily individualistic. The reasons why it was individualistic, however, do not lie in the nature of rights as such. They lie in the specific historical development of American political values.

The greatest transformation in American thinking about rights during the twentieth century occurred in reaction to the confrontations with Nazi Germany and the Soviet Union. European totalitarianism posed the most pronounced threats to the United States in the twentieth century, and American political thought evolved under the influence of that encounter. One important function of American political thought during the years of those confrontations was to provide, both for home consumption and for export, a moral distinction between the United States and its major adversaries. It is not hard to understand why the project of distinguishing America from Europe's totalitarianisms would draw heavily on the liberal-individualist strains within American norms.

To be sure, individualist norms already existed in American political culture. Long before Hitler and Stalin, liberal individualists could find much in American law, politics, and traditions that supported or vindicated their ideas. Like most complex political cultures, however, the political culture of the United States in the middle of the twentieth century contained elements of many different kinds of ideas, and those ideas often existed in tension with one another. Liberal individualism was an important part of American thought and practice, but so was white supremacism. The confrontation with European totalitarianism did not occasion the invention of American liberal individualism, but it did encourage mainstream Americans to accentuate the liberal individualism within their political culture and to downplay, marginalize, or reject certain other values that had also been present within American politics.

The emphasis on liberal individualism moved the rights associated with that set of ideas to the center of American rights discourse generally. Over time, the project of articulating political values distinguishing the United States from Nazi Germany and the Soviet Union brought many Americans to see the rights that carried the content of liberal individualism as the paradigm of the category of rights itself. Thus, American conceptions of rights late in the twentieth century were heavily individualistic not because the nature of rights is individualistic, but because individualism was a central substantive commitment of political norms at that time and place.

Once twentieth-century Americans assigned a high priority to individualism, it was both natural and easy for them to look back through history and find support for the idea that individualism had always been at the core of American rights. After all, American political culture did have a rich tradition of individualism, one that stretched back to the Founding and beyond. Because Americans have always used rights language to express their most important political commitments, much of their individualism had long been articulated through the framework of rights. It would thus not be difficult to discern a theme of individualist rights in the writings of, say, Paine, Adams, Jefferson, Emerson, and Lincoln, as well as within American culture more broadly. To do so, however, would be to see a part of American rights discourse and mistake it for the whole. For one could also assemble a compendium of writings by an overlapping set of prominent Americans—say, Adams, Jefferson, Marshall, Jackson, and Lincoln—showcasing a tradition of rights in which communities rather than (or in addition to) individuals are properly the bearers of rights.

Given that our modern substantive norms lead us to privilege individualism—and even if it is normatively desirable that we do so—there will be a tendency, when trying to uncover historical conceptions of rights, to overemphasize the individualist strains in rights thinking. For one thing, we are more likely to go looking for things where we expect to find them than in places where we do not expect to find them. Primed to think of rights as sounding primarily in individualism, we may look to the writings of more individualistically inclined thinkers for the history of rights theory, thus slanting the historical sources in favor of individualist uses of rights argument. An investigation of the nature of rights at the American Founding must take care to avoid this bias. Otherwise, it would risk portraying the ideas of the past as if they were the ideas of the present, just at an earlier time.

Fortunately, our awareness of this danger helps clarify what we, as modern Americans, can hope to get out of a book about the rights thinking of the Founding era. One of the reasons why we must be open to discovering that the rights discourse of the Founding was different from our own is that rights argument is extremely flexible. Indeed, it is flexible enough that many different kinds of political movements have been able to use the rhetoric of rights for widely varying agendas. Once we recognize that ideas about rights have exhibited great variability, we should be more receptive to the fact that no single conception of rights prevailed among the Founders. We cannot look to their thoughts and arguments to determine the true nature or content of rights, or even of rights in the American context. But we can examine their ideas to appreciate the rich diversity of American political thought, even among a relatively small and homogenous group during one small slice of time, and even when the ideas we examine all purport to be about something called "rights."

The Emergence of the Modern Concept of a Right in America

The Contribution of Michel Villey

JAMES H. HUTSON

In recent decades French social historians—members of the so-called Annales School—have been widely read in the United States. Their influence is evident in many areas of American scholarship, especially in the writing of the history of colonial America.[1] French legal historians, on the other hand, are virtually unknown in this country. Dealing with a legal order radically different from the Anglo-American system, their work is rarely relevant to the problems that interest American scholars.

The one French legal historian who has come to the attention of American writers in recent years is Michel Villey (d. 1990), whose arguments, according to a critic writing in 1997, have been "widely and uncritically accepted."[2] Villey's specialty was Roman law, on which he wrote prolifically during a long academic career at the University of Strasbourg and later at the Sorbonne.[3] His particular interest was the Roman definition of right (*jus*) and the evolution of the concept from the time of Gaius to Grotius, from imperial Rome to seventeenth-century Europe. Villey had only a passing acquaintance with the jurisprudence of the United States and never tried to fit his ideas into an American context. Those ideas are nevertheless applicable to issues in American legal history. It is the argument of this essay that Villey's theories can correct a major misconception about the development of rights in this country and can offer new insights into the meaning of rights during the Founding period (ca. 1763–89) and beyond.

One theme—complaint might be a better word—runs through Villey's writings: lawyers in their professional capacity are inhospitable to history. The French legal mind, as Villey described it, is ahistorical, in the sense that it takes fundamental concepts as it finds them and is not inquisitive about the extent to which they may have changed over time. Rights are approached in this spirit, a point Villey illustrated by citing the eminent law school dean Gabriel Le Bras, who asserted in 1953 that the definition of a right then current in France was "as old as Adam and Eve." Villey mentioned other French scholars, who claimed that the understanding of a right had not changed since "cuneiform" times. French law itself assumed the static character of a right, for Villey pointed to a right called the "proprieté à la Romaine," whose name presumed that it had existed since the days of Caesar Augustus.[4]

Villey vigorously contested this assumption that the definition of a right was changeless. Although the Romans and their successors used the term *jus* profusely, Villey insisted that a "modern" definition of a right was not articulated in Europe until the fourteenth century and did not obtain a significant following until well into the seventeenth century. As a result, Villey argued, for more than a millennium and a half of the Christian era, *jus* meant something far different than it does today. So much, then, for Adam and Eve and the immutability of right.

The attitude of American students of rights is similar to that which Villey encountered among his countrymen. Americans, no less than the French, consider the concept of a right as immutably embedded in their history. They assume that the people who stepped off the *Susan Constant* and the *Mayflower* brought with them the idea of a right and understood the concept much as we do today. In a typical scholarly assessment, two constitutional experts claimed in 1987 that "from the beginning, it seems, the language of America has been the language of rights"; in 1991 a government commission took the same position, boasting that "America has always been about rights," rights which another scholar—in the manner of Dean Le Bras—claimed in 1992 to be links in an "indissoluble chain of liberty that stretched back to ancient Greece and continued through the Roman Republic . . . to the thirteen colonies."[5]

In affirming the immutability of rights, American scholars seem to have been influenced by the authority of the leaders of the Revolution, who from 1764 onward aggressively asserted that American rights had descended to their countrymen intact from the remote reaches of English history through the first settlers of the colonies. Many colonial leaders insisted, even when they knew that the early charters mentioned only liberties and privileges (and thus were possessed more insecurely), that their ancestors had carried with them documents that put them in "full Possession of the Rights of Englishmen." "By removing themselves hither," a patriot declared in 1768, the first settlers "brought with them every right which they could or ought to have enjoyed had they abided in England." Political parsons went even further and assured their flocks that their rights could be traced back to apostolic times (if not to Adam and Eve), since

Saint Paul was a "strong advocate for the just rights of manhood."[6] By making these assertions, the Revolutionary leaders were initiating a well-honed strategy, practiced by English popular leaders from the reigns of the Stuarts onward, of enhancing the status of rights—even freshly minted ones—by investing them with great antiquity.[7] In accepting such claims for the immutability of rights, contemporary American scholars have unwittingly passed off patriot propaganda for historical fact.

A recently published volume of essays, *The Bill of Rights and the States*, is a striking example of the American scholar's penchant for attributing rights to distant generations. The first settlers of South Carolina are said to have received "specific rights" from Charles II's charter of 1663, yet an inspection of that charter reveals that the term "rights" never appears. Similarly, North Carolinians are said to have obtained "certain individual rights" from the Fundamental Constitutions of Carolina of 1669, yet once again, an inspection of that instrument does not disclose the presence of the term "rights." A similar claim, that the Georgia charter of 1732 set forth the "general rights" of the colonists, is equally without substance. The southern charters are not the only early documents on which rights are boldly superimposed. A scholar has called the preamble to a 1650 Connecticut legal code a "Declaration of Rights"; when the said "Declaration" is read, it is found to contain no mention of the term "rights."[8]

Uncomfortable, perhaps, with these casual ascriptions of rights to the first generation of Americans, A. E. Dick Howard, in an introductory essay to *The Bill of Rights and the States*, enclosed "the rights of Englishmen" in quotation marks when describing what appeared to be libertarian language in the early colonial charters. Professor Howard's caution seems well advised, for the existence of anything approaching the contemporary concept of a right is difficult to document in early America. Benjamin F. Wright, for example, found rights "very rarely" discussed in the seventeenth century. Lawrence Leder observed that seventeenth-century Americans did not "catalog" their rights. Although John Phillip Reid took issue with Leder's statement, he himself called attention to the "vagueness" of the talk about rights in colonial America.[9]

The current presumption that the idea of a right was an unchanging feature of American society "from the beginning" conflicts with evidence that at the dawn of American history a "modern" understanding of rights was absent, and that a substantial period of time elapsed before a "modern" definition emerged. Villey found the same situation in tracing the history of rights in Europe. His work, therefore, provides a model through which the development of rights in America is usefully viewed.

Villey asserted that Western civilization has known only two conceptions of a right. One was classical natural right ("droit natural classique"),
which he also called objective right ("droit objectif"). Rooted in Aristotle
and refined by the lawyers of imperial Rome, classical natural right maintained its ascendancy over the European mind for centuries and began to
lose its grip only in the seventeenth century, when it was challenged by its
modern successor, subjective right ("droit subjectif"). According to Villey,
subjective right is the "master word" of modern judicial thought, a concept
even more fundamental to modern jurisprudence than positivism.[10] Subjective right, Villey contended, is what contemporary writers have in mind
when they project the concept of a right back across the centuries to create the illusion of the unchangeable meaning of a right in Western history.

How do classical natural right and subjective right differ? Villey explained that when the Romans and their successors used the term "right"
(*jus*), they meant, in the broad sense, the just: "la res justa, l'objectum jus-
titiae, l'id quom justum est."[11] The specific meaning of the term stemmed,
Villey asserted, from the classical world's view of what was "natural." The
Greeks and Romans believed that civil society itself was "natural" and that
man was "naturally social and even political." A right, therefore, was a "social phenomenon," which must be discerned in the complex web of relationships between people.[12] The good society would "give to everyone his
right." This phrase, a translation of Ulpian's well-known dictum, *suum jus
cuique tribuere,* Villey regarded as a key to understanding classical natural
right.[13] To give someone his right (*suum jus*) meant in the classical world
to give him "what he deserved," "his due."[14] What was due to the individual in society? His just share ("le part juste," "le bon partage").[15] Here,
said Villey, was the meaning of classical natural right: a just share for every
individual member of society of its benefits and burdens.

Who, in the classical world, was the arbiter of right? Who decided what
individual's just share was? The task, Villey explained, fell not to philosophers and "theoricians in chambre," but to the courts, where judges in
consultation with lawyers—"practiciens (ou jurisprudents)"—reached
their decisions on a case-by-case basis.[16] Classical natural right, Villey argued, was fluid, was "souplesse même,"[17] and therefore could be ascer-
tained only by the consideration of the various and peculiar facts at issue
in each case. Judges could not know the "just solution . . . in advance," for
that solution was "mutable, as it ought to be if it results from the nature
of changing things."[18]

An unusual feature of classical natural right, as described by Villey, was
its association with burdens or duties. The contemporary mind does not

consider rights as imposing burdens on their possessors, but Villey insisted that what he variously called "charges" and "peines" were important aspects of classical natural right.[19] Villey did not mean to belittle the importance of benefits: for the Romans this was always the most important feature of a right. A plot of land, for example, could confer several different benefits, all of which could be described as rights (*jura*): a right of usage, of passage, of habitation, of drawing water, and so on. But the same piece of property might also be encumbered by the burdensome right of not raising the height of an existing structure (*jus non altius tollendi*).[20] The *jus civitatis* was another burdensome right, for it obliged its possessor to perform military service.[21]

Whether burdensome or beneficial, a right, Villey asserted, was considered by classical jurisprudence as a *res incorporales*. Rights were "things, institutions, which owed an artificial existence to the invention of jurists."[22] As a "thing, an object," or more precisely, a share or "fraction" of a thing or object, a classical right was by definition "objective."[23] It was objective in another sense as well, being a product, Villey explained, of the Aristotelian worldview that held that "Nature" or "universal reason" imposed on all animate and inanimate beings a just and harmonious order. Under these circumstances the just share of an individual in a given society was objectively established, and the "objective natural right" of each person could be discerned by the human mind.[24] Classical natural right was objective, then, in a double sense: it was a share of an object and a standard fixed by a superintending wisdom.

The Birth of Subjective Rights

One of the most controversial aspects of Villey's work was his theory about the sudden appearance ("eclosion") in the fourteenth century of subjective right. Villey asserted that subjective right was invented by the Franciscan monk and philosopher William of Ockham, who enunciated the concept in his book, *Opus nonaginta dierum* (1332). The occasion for Ockham's foray into jurisprudence was the quarrel over Franciscan poverty. Saint Francis founded his order on a commitment to poverty, but as its reputation grew, its admirers showered it with gifts of real estate, money, and so on. A sympathetic papacy devised a legal fiction that permitted the Franciscans to retain both their gifts and their vows. According to papal lawyers, the Franciscans merely had the use of the property donated to their order; the "jus, proprietas [and] dominium" over their goods were vested in the Bishop of Rome. An opponent of the Franciscans, Pope John XXII refused to abide by his predecessors' accommodations with the order and, early in the fourteenth century, "undertook to generalize the regime of property and to impose it on the Franciscan community"; that is, John XXII attempted to compel the order to admit that it had property rights in the goods it administered. The Franciscans took refuge in the old "artifice" that they had the use of, but not the right to, property. Their spokesman, Ockham, gave the formula a new twist, however, by redefining "right" to show its incompatibility with his order's ideals. A right, Ockham announced, was a power ("potesta licita"), and power, however defined, was anathema to the Franciscans.[25]

Right as power! Here, according to Villey, was a "Copernican moment" in jurisprudence, the advent of a new way of thinking which eventually carried all before it. The Romans, Villey observed, "naturally knew the idea of powers of the individual, but without giving to these powers a juridical quality, without calling powers rights." By uniting the two concepts, Ockham created subjective right. This new species of right was subjective because power, its essence, was part of the individual subject. Villey hammered this point home. Subjective rights were "qualities," "faculties" of the individual, "the forces which radiated through his being."[26] A subjective right was a power "drawn from the being itself of the subject, from his essence, from his nature." A subjective right was an "attribute of the subject," a power that "appertained to his essence, that was inherent in him."[27] The difference between classical or objective natural right and the new subjective right was stark: the former was the share of some external object; the latter was power inherent in an individual.

The source of the individual's power, Ockham assumed as a matter of course (he was, after all, a member of a religious order), was God. For Ockham and thinkers of his era, subjective right was "an indication of the absolute power of God which was partially conferred upon man, created in his image."[28] Therefore, subjective right, as understood by its creators, was grounded in religion, although "its dependence . . . on Christian morality" was a fact, Villey ironically noted, that the "majority of our contemporaries had difficulty acknowledging."[29]

Villey considered Ockham the obvious candidate to introduce a new concept of rights because of his prowess as a philosopher. Villey was guided by the principle that the idea of a right was the creation of philosophy and that philosophy inexorably invaded the law. As a product of Aristotelianism, classical natural right flourished as long as its philosophical underpinnings held firm. These crumbled under the onslaught of the "via moderna," the new philosophical system of nominalism that Ockham helped to create. Nominalism rejected the "universal" categories of Aristotelianism and asserted that reality could only be found in individuals.[30] The emphasis on individuals and the power inherent in them led to the new definition of right. Nominalism became, then, "the mother of subjective right."[31] "All philosophy," Villey explained, "is 'tentaculaire' . . . its spirit obliges [mankind] to see the whole world from its perspective. It was inevitable that modern individualistic philosophy would impose its definition of right, not merely by destroying the old classical concept of right, but by replacing it."[32]

The process of replacement, if sure, was nevertheless slow. Ockham's formulations were too recondite for the ordinary jurist, and for more than two centuries the new concept of subjective right, like the mystery of an ancient cult, was in the custody of a coterie of philosophers. From Ockham, Villey traced the new concept to the French nominalists, Pierre d'Ailly and Jean Gerson. He regarded Gerson as a particularly important figure, who not only furnished a definition of subjective right "en forme" in his book, *De Vita Spirituli Animae* (1402)—"jus est facultas seu potestas propinqua conveniens alicui"—but also served as a link to the Spanish Scholastics of the sixteenth century, whose importance in the formation and transmission of the idea of a subjective right could not, in Villey's opinion, be overestimated.[33]

The sixteenth century, Villey reminded us, was the "era of Spanish preponderance," a period in Europe when the influence of Spain's thinkers matched the power of its kings. The authority of the Spanish Scholastics (by whom Villey meant the Dominicans Vitoria, DeSoto, and Banez, and the Jesuits Vasquez, Molina, and Suarez) imposed itself with "particular force" in Germany and the Netherlands, where even staunch Calvinists "pillaged" their writings.[34] According to Villey, the new concept of subjective right became the "doctrine courante" of the Spanish school, and he quoted statements like Vitoria's "jus est potestas" to prove his point.[35] Yet the Spaniards continued to use the old vocabulary of classical natural right and integrated the old and new ideas of right so awkwardly that even the works of luminaries like Suarez, who called a right a "moral power," conveyed the impression of being "an undigested and incoherent mixture, the product of a mediocre eclecticism."[36]

Villey argued that the "honor" of formulating the first thoroughly modern definition of subjective right, stripped of all residues of Roman law, was reserved for Thomas Hobbes, whose major works—*Elements of Law, De Cive,* and *Leviathan*—appeared in the mid-seventeenth century. In common with all who, from Ockham forward, had cultivated the concept of subjective right, Hobbes was a philosopher. His "great definitions in form" of subjective right, which were influenced by the Spanish Scholastics,[37] appeared in all of his principal writing, as, for example, in *Leviathan:* a right "is the liberty each man hath to use his own power, as he will himself, for the preservation of his nature."[38] Hobbes's lucid, uncompromising definitions "sealed the decisive victory" of subjective right over its venerable rival, classical natural right. "Philosophy had," Villey concluded, "as it ordinarily does, preceded the jurists on the revolutionary path."[39]

Whatever his strengths as an expositor of philosophical ideas, Hobbes was a poor proselytizer for subjective right because his reputed atheism repelled potential readers (this was especially true in America). Whether because of Hobbes's reputation or an innate conservatism, large numbers of "jurists" recoiled at the introduction of the new concept of a right into the law. Villey describes this recalcitrant majority as "technicians of the judicial art," traditionalists, and ordinary members of the bar. "These jurists," he said, "resisted for a long time, being essentially attached to tradition. A good part of the authors of the ancien régime continued to reproduce and apply Roman law and customs without transforming them." Subjective right gained a foothold in the law only in the seventeenth century through the agency of attorneys "capable of a certain culture," lawyers with intellectual interests who could also act as "philosophical jurists, publicists, and professors of legal philosophy."[40] Foremost among this group was the Dutch master, Hugo Grotius, saluted by Villey as "one of the most efficacious mediators that history has ever known between a philosophical vision of the world and the science of law."[41]

In his great work, *De Jure Belli ac Pacis* (1625), Grotius offered a definition of subjective right as a moral power, a "qualitas moralis personae," a "potestas . . . in se," and a "potestas . . . . in alios."[42] Yet he also paraphrased Ulpian's classic dictum about right—"the obligation of rendering what is owing"—and reverted to the old definition of right as the just.[43] Grotius, in fact, employed so many elements of classical natural right in his work that, like Suarez's writings, which seem to have influenced him, his treatise was "not exempt from embarrassment and contradictions."[44] Therefore, Grotius could not, in Villey's judgment, be credited with conceiving "subjective right in a perfectly firm manner." Only toward the end of the seventeenth century did Villey discover lawyers who were in "full possession of the idea of subjective right."[45]

Villey's energies seemed to flag as he reached the eighteenth century, and he spent little time with familiar subjective-rights publicists like Wolff and Burlamaqui. Villey saw subjective right gradually insinuating itself into the minds of the most obdurate traditionalists and finally "triumphing towards the end of the eighteenth century."[46] In his view, a famous document like the French Declaration of the Rights of Man of 1789 testified to its ascendancy. "The rights of man," Villey claimed, "are precisely subjective rights."[47]

Reflecting on the victory of subjective rights, Villey observed that "the moderns had repudiated Right . . . and substituted the natural Rights of the individual."[48] Villey considered the distinction between *droit* (right) and *droits* (rights) as significant. He held that a speaker or author using the singular, right, meant classical, objective right, while the use of the plural, rights, indicated subjective rights. Although this rule frequently falls afoul of the vagaries of spelling in colonial America—one encounters "Ryght" and "rites" as well as "right" and "rights"—it can sometimes be a useful diagnostic tool.

Villey's argument for a medieval origin of the modern, subjective definition of a right has been accepted by scholars, although it received some criticism when it first appeared. In 1954, for example, the Italian jurist Giovanni Pugliese asserted that the Romans had, in fact, possessed a concept of subjective right,[49] and a few years later the distinguished German Romanist Helmut Coing professed to have found the word *jus,* in a "subjective sense," in certain Roman legal texts. Nevertheless, Coing endorsed Villey's view that "subjective right played for classical Roman jurisprudence no decisive role."[50] Other critics took issue with Villey for identifying William of Ockham as the inventor of subjective right. Reinhold Schwartz argued that the credit for the first clear formulation of the concept should go to Jean Gerson,[51] whom Villey regarded as no more than a conduit for Ockham's ideas. Brian Tierney, on the other hand, believed that subjective right preceded Ockham and that it could be found as far back as the twelfth century, in the writings of canonists like Rufinus and Huguccio.[52]

England's Competing Rights Languages

With the exception of Thomas Hobbes and John Locke (to whom Villey devoted some attention), all of the protagonists of subjective right who appeared in his pages were continental Europeans. So, too, with a few exceptions, were the commentators on and critics of his work. The term "subjective right" itself was Continental, having been coined by the German jurists Windscheid, Puchta, and Savigny in the nineteenth century.[53] How, then, does subjective right relate to Great Britain and, by extension, to America, with their systems of common-law jurisprudence, so different from the civil (i.e., Roman) law context in which subjective right took root on the Continent? A British lawyer, Frederick Lawson, claimed that the term "subjective right" would be incomprehensible to most practitioners in his country. "An ordinary English jurist," he wrote in 1959, "would not know whereof one spoke if you would use in a conversation with him the technical expressions (*fachausdrucke*) objective right and subjective right. Even if one would explain to him their significance, it would still be very difficult for him to understand why right was designated as objective on the one hand and subjective on the other." Commenting on Lawson's observations, a German specialist, Konrad Zweigert, stressed the "bewegende Nichtverstehenwollen" of the common law, as compared to the "luziden Dogmengeschichte" of subjective right on the Continent.[54] The resistance of British legal discourse to the term "subjective right" does not mean, however, that the idea it represented was absent in England, nor does it mean that Villey's thesis is inapplicable in an English context. Villey's ideas appear, in fact, to work as well in England as they do on the Continent, as an examination of writings as far back as Bracton will indicate.

In Bracton's great treatise, *On the Laws and Customs of England,* compiled in the middle of the thirteenth century, there is no sign of an acquaintance with a modern, subjective definition of right. This is unsurprising, since Bracton was a civilian, deeply immersed in Roman law, who introduced "almost five hundred different sections of the Digest and Code" into his opus.[55] For Bracton, right meant justice, the characteristic feature, in Villey's view, of classical natural right. "Right is thus called justice," Bracton wrote, "because all right is included in justice. Right likewise, is derived from justice and it has various significations." One of Bracton's significations, lifted directly from Roman sources, equated right with the process of law; right, he explained, could mean a court ("the place where justice is awarded"), actions at law, or various kinds of law: civil, natural, or praetorian. Bracton quoted Celsus's definition of a right, "ars boni et aequi," as well as Ulpian's even more celebrated definition, "jus suum cuique tribuere."[56] By using this phrase, Bracton appeared to indicate that he understood right in the way Villey considered to be its purest classical form: an individual's "juste partage," his just share.

Bracton's reliance on Roman sources can be misleading, however, for early English lawyers did not appropriate wholesale the classical concept of right; they developed a distinctive understanding of the term which revealed itself in the operation of the *breve de recto,* the writ of right. The writ of right was a "cluster" or "group" of writs: the writ of right patent, the *praecipe in capite*, and the little writ of right.[57] Of "great antiquity"— in use at least two centuries before Bracton wrote—the writ of right served to "originate actions for land in a feudal court." Although a writ of right could relate to all kinds of property, it was associated in the English mind with land to the virtual exclusion of all else. Writs of right were "orders to do justice." They enjoined courts, feudal and royal, to assure that justice was done between rival claimants to land. Typically, each claimant would assert that his right—by which he meant his title—to a piece of land was superior to his adversary's. The writ of right required the court to decide "quis habeat major jus" in the disputed land.[58] The successful claimant would obtain ownership and usually, although not always, possession (*seisin*) of the land. A right, then, in medieval England, was a title which, if validated by a court, conferred ownership of land.[59]

English right was similar in many ways to classical natural right as formulated on the Continent. In both places, courts defined right on a case-by-case basis. In both places, right was considered the handmaiden of justice. And in both places, right was held to involve incorporeal things— titles to land, according to Holdsworth, being viewed in medieval England as incorporeal.[60] The principal difference between the two concepts was the severe constriction of the meaning of right in England, where it was almost exclusively identified with real property. Right in medieval England can be considered, therefore, as a derivative of classical natural right, differentiated only by its real property bias.

Right underwent little change in meaning from Bracton's time to the reign of the Tudors. Examination of the law dictionaries which began to be published in sixteenth-century England illustrates this point. The earliest English law dictionary, if St. Germain's *Doctor and Student* is excluded from consideration, was John Rastell's *Termes de la ley*, published in French in 1527. The *Termes de la ley* enjoyed remarkable popularity, being reprinted with occasional changes in title seven times in the sixteenth century, at least twelve times in the seventeenth century, and appearing in a new edition as late as 1812.[61] Rastell defined right (he used the French word *droit* for more than a century and a half) by reference to the writ of right. Through the 1575 edition, right was described as a writ that "lyethe where a man claymeth any landes or tenements and aledgeth no title but only that one of his auncestoures in olde tyme was seized." The 1579 edition gave a new definition, modeled on the writ of right praecipe, which asserted, as a basis for litigation, that land had been wrongfully taken.[62] The work now defined right as the "challenge or claime" of the victim to have the validity of his title upheld. This definition was expanded in 1624 with the addition of language from Coke's *Reports*. It was not altered thereafter.

The next important dictionary, John Cowell's *The Interpreter: or the Booke Containing the Significations of Words*, was published in 1607, and despite being burned at the order of the House of Commons for its alleged absolutist bias, was reissued three times during the seventeenth century. *The Interpreter* followed Rastell in defining right by reference to the writ of right, observing, "Whereas other writs in real actions, be only to recover the possession of land, or tenements in question . . . this aimeth to recover both the seisin . . . and also the propertie of the thing."[63]

The publication in 1628 of Sir Edward Coke's *Institutes of the Laws of England* had a major influence on the definition of right, not because the great lawyer changed the meaning of the term—he used without apology the traditional definition—but because Coke's treatise established an immediate authority over English lawyers, who obediently quoted him when describing a right. Coke offered two definitions of a right. One asserted that a right could be considered not simply as a title to land, but as "the estate in esse," a position that Coke's rival, Francis Bacon, had taken in his *Reading on the Statute of Uses* (1600).[64] More popular with legal writers was Coke's second definition: "*Jus* or right, in general signification includeth not only a right for which a writ of rights doth lie, but also any title or claime, either by force of a Condition, Mortmaine or the like, for which no action is given by law, but only an entrie."[65] This definition was used, with slight alteration, by William Sheppard, who "published something like an official law dictionary during the Protectorate";[66] by Thomas Blount in his *Nomo-Lexikon* (1691); and in later editions of Cowell's *Interpreter*. In *The Compleat Lawyer* (1651), Charles I's attorney general, William Noy, also used Cokean language in differentiating between "naked" and "cloathed" rights, perpetuating in the process the medieval distinction, which was becoming obsolete, between possession (*seisin*) and ownership. A "cloathed" right, Noy explained, combined ownership and possession of land; a "naked" right separated the two.[67] Coke had made the same distinction in his *Institutes:* "There is a *jus proprietatis*, a right of ownership, a *jus possessionis*, a right of *seisin* or possession and *jus proprietatis* and *possessionis*, a right of both propertie and possession: and this is anciently called *jus duplicatum* or *Droit droit*." In a less pedantic passage, Coke explained simply that "every right is a title . . . and signifieth the means whereby a man commeth to land."[68]

In the hands of the House of Commons, this venerable definition of right underwent a remarkable transformation during the reign of James I, so remarkable that it is no exaggeration to say that the Parliamentarians confronting the first Stuart king invented "civil" rights just as deliberately as Ockham, in Villey's view, invented subjective right, and to assert that they did it in a "tentacular" way by extending the reach of the real property concept of right to enclose in its protective grasp various endangered elements in English public life.

James I ascended the English throne in 1603 with exaggerated ideas of royal power and disdain for the political aspirations of his subjects. In his view, popular freedoms were nothing more than revocable royal favors. As James informed his first Parliament, in 1604, the people "derived all matters of privilege from him and by his grant," an opinion the king repeated in 1621, lecturing Parliament in that year that "your privileges were derived from the grace and permission of our ancestors and us."[69] The Stuarts and their spokesmen took this position for as long as they ruled. Charles I's chaplain claimed in 1637 that since kings gave the people their liberties, they could withdraw them at will. Robert Filmer described parliamentary privileges as "liberties of grace from the king" that were "derived from the bounty or indulgence of the monarch."[70] After the Restoration, royalist writers, following Filmer, argued that "all the liberties of Englishmen, owed their being to the will of the King [who] might revoke any of them." In James II's reign, Robert Brady's historical studies purported to prove that "all the Liberties and Privileges the people can pretend to were the Grants and Concessions of the King," nothing more than a "pure gift" of the monarch, as one of Brady's cronies argued.[71]

Parliament's response to Stuart efforts to trivialize popular liberties was consistent throughout the seventeenth century. James I's first House of Commons considered it imperative to respond to the new king's denigration of the country's freedoms and staked out the popular position in their "Form of Apology and Satisfaction," of June 20, 1604. Parliament's strategy was simple: it denied that the king had any control over popular freedoms and asserted that, on the contrary, Englishmen owned their liberties and privileges by a right or title as incontestably as they owned their lands. "We must truly avouch," the Apology asserted, "that our privileges and liberties are our right and due inheritance, no less than our very lands and goods."[72] The same sentiments were expressed in subsequent Parliaments. In 1621, for example, in response to James's contention that popular liberties were royal favors, Sir Randolph Crew responded: "We have our privileges of right not of grace. This [James's claim] were to make us from freeholders of inheritance to make us Copiholders ad placitum, or rather, tenants at will."[73] Extending the idea of titled ownership of land to such incorporeal matters as were at issue between the king and Parliament in 1604—the members' exemption from imprisonment during sessions of Parliament, their liberty to speak freely in Parliament—created a wholly new category of nonproperty rights involving freedom to conduct civic affairs. It is in this sense that Parliament can be said to have invented civil rights in 1604. Challenged by an aggressive monarch, the members appropriated the most invulnerable tenure conceivable to the seventeenth-century mind—ownership of land by good title—to protect their liberties. James I's confrontational tactics sowed dragons' teeth, for if Parliament could assimilate to land activities as dissimilar as speech and criminal justice, there was no limit to what might be considered—to the detriment of monarchical pretensions—as a right. The new understanding of civil rights, strengthened in constant combat with the Stuarts, would in the course of the seventeenth century become known by the familiar phrase "rights of Englishmen," conveying the idea of the impregnability of rights, owned and possessed, like choice lands, by an unassailable title.

It is necessary to insist on the novelty, the inventiveness, of Parliament's actions of 1604 in extending rights of land ownership to the political and civic arenas. Despite the assertions by the seventeenth-century English popular leaders of the antiquity of the various rights they were claiming, before 1604 the use of the term "right" seems to have been confined to discussions about and litigation over land. The published proceedings of Elizabeth I's Parliaments reveal, for example, the absence of the term from political discourse.[74] The members repeatedly requested that the queen respect their liberties and privileges, not their rights. "Liberty" was the traditional English word for popular freedoms. Liberty, however, had liabilities as a weapon in a forensic contest with arbitrary rulers. In medieval England, it had been enjoyed by groups, "organized collectivities" like towns and guilds.[75] Medieval liberties were exclusive and discriminatory. Groups who possessed them, always as a favor from the monarch, used them to collect tolls from their fellow subjects or to monopolize certain trades and industries to the exclusion of other Englishmen. By James I's time, liberties were being conceived individualistically, but as Coke himself admitted, they were still considered as gifts from the monarch.[76] Parliament was sensitive to this fact, and lest they be considered as begging the king for favors when their Speaker petitioned the monarch at the beginning of each session for accustomed liberties and privileges, they affirmed, in the Apology of 1604, "that our making of request in the entrance of Parliament to enjoy our privilege is an act only of manners, and doth weaken our right no more than our suing the King for our lands by petition."[77]

Well into the seventeenth century, "liberties" and "privileges" remained the terms of choice for Englishmen discussing their freedoms. The process by which "right" eventually displaced these words is clear enough. In debates on impositions in 1610, the House of Commons used the phrase, "the fundamental right of the liberty of Parliament" to free speech, which in the context of the recent expansion of the term meant Parliament's ownership of the liberty of speech.[78] As the seventeenth century progressed, such locutions began to seem tautological, and in the interest of economy of speech, "liberty" dropped out in favor of the stronger term "right," just as over the course of the century possessive adjectives disappeared from phrases like "God his Throne on earth," used by James I in his *Trew Law of Free Monarchies* (1598), and yielded to apostrophes.[79]

Rights, it must be emphasized, achieved no easy or immediate ascendancy, as the drafting of the Petition of Right of 1628 demonstrates. Coke and many of his allies who drafted the petition had been active in the Parliament of 1604, but preferred to use older, more familiar language in making their case against Charles I. According to Conrad Russell, the Parliament of 1628 displayed an "obsessive concentration on issues of liberties," not rights.[80] One contemporary called the Petition of Right "the ancientist . . . way" of dealing with the monarch, and claimed that such petitions were at least as old as Magna Carta. The Petition of Right was a demand by Parliament for justice from the king. The petition recited the laws of England as they related to the issues in dispute between the king and the people (taxation, the administration of criminal justice, and quartering), gave examples of royal malfeasance, and demanded that the laws be obeyed. The king's answer, "Let right be done as is desired," conveyed his intention to do "justice," as James I had promised in reply to a petition of right in 1604.[81] Justice would be done by royal obedience to the law. A government of law would be established (or reestablished), and the benefits conferred by the rule of law would be considered the people's "rights." By presenting rights as benefits of the rule of law or as the law itself, Parliament gave the Petition of Right a strong classical flavor, for it employed one of the principal Roman definitions of rights: right as law.

The Petition of Right was a temporary accommodation between the king and Parliament that failed to contain the tensions that burst into civil war in the 1640s. The English Civil War is considered by scholars to have been a boom time for rights; a few even argue that it was the occasion for the introduction into England by the Levellers of the concept of subjective right.[82] It is true that rights as titled ownership—or as the rights of Englishmen, as they were being called by the 1640s—flourished during the Civil War, but the role of the Levellers as promoters of subjective right becomes questionable under close scrutiny. The Levellers' objective, as their spokesmen indicated at the Putney Debates in the fall of 1647, was to secure the people's "birthrights." They intended, said Sexby, "to recover our birthright and privileges as Englishmen. . . . There are many thousands of us soldiers that have ventured our lives; we have had little propriety in the kingdom as to our estates, yet we have had a birthright."[83] Birthrights, or "native rights," as they were also called during the Civil War, were not subjective rights; rather they were a special kind of title by which land was owned. An Elizabethan case, *Willons v. Berkeley,* had given land acquired by birth or inheritance specific immunity from royal intervention, and therefore these titles enjoyed a prized status.[84] By emphasizing birthrights, popular leaders during the Civil War were trying to invest their claims to a wider suffrage and to other shares in the political process with strength superior to ordinary rights. Also unfavorable to claims that Levellers were innovators in rights was the tendency of leaders like John Lilburne to present his group's demands as claims for liberties, not rights.[85] Richard Tuck has argued, in addition, that the Levellers had an ambivalent attitude toward rights, holding at times the medieval view that rights, like liberties, were "collective."[86]

Tuck has pointed out that Grotius, in Villey's view the principal seventeenth-century conduit for subjective rights, was read by "many of the more important radical theorists" during the Civil War, and that these radicals may have given England its first taste of the new theory of rights.[87] Grotius asserted that the individual could exert his subjective right, the power inherent in him, over external objects as well as over his own person. Self-empowerment could manifest itself in the free choice of religion, and it is possible, as a few commentators have asserted, that the claims for the right to religious freedom made by the Levellers and other dissenting groups can be considered as expressions of subjective right. This question requires much more study, but what we do know is that after the Restoration, England was fatigued by what it regarded as the tiresome agitation by fringe groups for religious rights. It was not until the close of the century that Locke, a philosopher and apostle of subjective right, obtained a respectful hearing from a broad audience for the right of religious conscience, serving thereby as the channel through which subjective right passed in England from the world of philosophy to the world of law and public affairs. Locke's role is consistent with developments on the Continent, where Villey discerned toward the end of the seventeenth century subjective right migrating from philosophy to law and acquiring among lawyers champions such as Pufendorf, Feltman, and Thomasius.[88]

The new, modern concept of subjective right was not instantly adopted by English statesmen, as the Bill of Rights of 1689 demonstrates. Save for the "right of the subjects to petition the King," and for Protestants to bear arms, there was little in that document concerning the exercise of power by individuals. The Bill of Rights resembled nothing so much as the Petition of Right of 1628; "many members," Lois Schwoerer explained, "intended it to be closely identified with that time honored device." Like the Petition of Right, the Bill of Rights contained a list of illegal royal actions which Parliament enumerated for the purpose of "vindicating and asserting their ancient rights and liberties." On February 13, 1689, the Bill (at this time, the Declaration) of Rights was presented to William and Mary along with the offer of the English crown. In accepting the Crown, William declared, less explicitly than Charles I had done sixty years earlier, but in words whose meaning could not be mistaken, that he "would preserve the nation's rights."[89] Since rights had been presented to the king as a list of violations of the law, preserving rights meant to William and his Parliament the observing of the law. In 1689, as in 1628, rights could still be defined, without arousing objections, in the classical sense as benefits of the rule of law or as the law itself.

The status of rights at the end of the seventeenth century in England was unsettled, a persistence, in fact, of the "eclecticism" that Villey criticized a century earlier, during the period of Spanish intellectual hegemony: new and old conceptions of rights coexisted and were mutually employed by individuals who seemed to be unaware of, or untroubled by, their apparent incompatibility.

Consider, in this respect, the libertarian language of William Penn, the founder of Pennsylvania. As a religious leader, lobbyist, entrepreneur, and friend of kings, Penn was at the center of English public life for a half century, from the 1660s to the 1710s. Penn was a close friend of savants like Sidney and Locke and studied law at Lincoln's Inn. He kept abreast of the fresh currents in British and Continental intellectual circles and incorporated into his own tireless advocacy of rights the latest thinking on the subject. Penn explicitly repudiated classical natural right in its objective sense by describing Ulpian's dictum, "jus suum cuiq; tribuere," as an "excellent principle" which was irrelevant to the debate in late seventeenth-century England.[90] From Locke and his circle, Penn absorbed the new idea of subjective rights, defining a right as a power "born with" an individual.[91] But contrary to Villey's paradigm, the philosophers' conception of subjective right did not imperiously impose itself on Penn or other Englishmen schooled in the common law. From Coke, whose principles he absorbed in the Inns of Court, and the parliamentary opponents of the Stuarts, Penn acquired the idea of a right as "an ownership, and undisturbed possession."[92] That Penn understood ownership in terms of land is evident from his repeated assertions that an Englishman was "estated" in his rights, had an "entail" of them, and that no one could "disseise or dispossess" him of them.[93] In Penn, as in other well-informed contemporaries, the philosophical and common-law definitions blended to create a new, peculiarly English, "possessive" definition of a right: an inherent power, owned by its possessor by a title as unassailable as one to freehold property.[94]

Penn was not a proselytizer for Anglicized, subjective rights. In fact, in his writings he employed venerable terms like "liberty" and "privilege" as synonyms for the new concept. Where one would expect to find natural rights, Penn used "natural privileges," "natural and civil common privileges," "paramount privileges," or phrases such as the "grand pillars of English liberty" and "fundamental vital Privileges."[95] Penn's libertarian writings are, therefore, a jumble of terms—rights, liberties, privileges—which indicate that in England at the end of the seventeenth century, the new idea of subjective rights was far from being distinguished from its older rivals that continued to thrive in the vocabularies of both the learned and the common people.

The Language of Rights in Seventeenth-Century America

Penn is an obvious link to the American colonies, even though Pennsylvania was not founded until 1682, three-quarters of a century later than Virginia and Massachusetts. The first settlers of those jurisdictions had no acquaintance with the philosophers' idea of subjective rights, which did not emerge in the mother country until a half century after they crossed the Atlantic. The great majority of the colonists were equally unacquainted with the new practice of defining rights by applying titled ownership to incorporeal objects, such as parliamentary immunities that began about the time of their emigration from England. As a result, libertarian language in the colonies initially had an antiquated, even medieval quality.

This fact has been obscured by historians who attribute to the first settlers modern concepts of rights. These scholars have been misled by the "individualist illusion," failing to realize that life in seventeenth-century

America was communal in nature, which resulted in the "subordination of the person to the collectivity." Individual rights and individualism itself (the word did not appear in America until the nineteenth century) could not put down roots in such a climate.[96] Historians of Virginia have been cheerleaders for primordial rights, motivated by a desire to establish a genealogy of rights that will connect settlers at Jamestown to Jefferson's generation. Thomas J. Wertenbaker, for example, contended that the first Virginia Company charter of 1606 was a beacon that Virginians followed "throughout the entire colonial period [as] they contended for all the rights of native Englishmen." Wertenbaker assailed Gates's Laws of 1610 as being "in open violation of the rights guaranteed to the settlers in their charters" of 1606 and 1609. Alexander Brown, who believed that "Give me liberty or give me death was the inspiration of our foundation as well as the battle cry of our Revolution," extolled the charter of 1609 for granting "liberal charter rights."[97] In fact, neither the charter of 1606 nor that of 1609 mentions the rights of the settlers of Virginia. The charters conferred upon the colonists merely "Liberties, Franchises, and Immunities,"[98] boilerplate language borrowed from the numerous trading company charters issued by the English government in the late sixteenth and early seventeenth centuries. James I certainly did not consider that, in issuing charters to Englishmen departing for the New World, he was creating rights, for the "plain truth is," he informed his advisers, "we cannot with patience endure our subjects to use such anti-monarchical words to us concerning their liberties." Just how fragile Virginia's freedoms were became apparent in James's policy toward the lottery that he gave the settlers the "Liberty and License" to establish in 1612. Nine years later, the king peremptorily abolished the lottery, demonstrating that in Virginia liberties were nothing more than revocable royal favors.[99]

A standard work, Richard Morton's *Colonial Virginia,* published in 1960, followed the lead of Brown and Wertenbaker. Morton described the "Great Charter of 1619," which authorized a representative assembly in Virginia, as conferring "all the rights of Englishmen," when, in fact, the document does not mention rights. The members of the first assembly, on July 31, 1619, thanked authorities in England, not for granting rights, but for extending "privileges and favours."[100] Morton then called attention to laws passed by the newly constituted Assembly, in 1623–24, "to protect their [the peoples'] rights."[101] But none of these statutes mention rights, individual or corporate.

The term "rights," it should be understood, was not absent from public discourse during the Virginia Company's tenure, 1607–24. The third

Virginia charter, of 1612, stipulated that certain new investors should enjoy full benefits of membership in the Virginia Company, and included "Right" in a list of "Interests . . . Profits and Commodities." In the same spirit, the first Massachusetts charter, issued a few years later, listed "Rightes" among an array of shareholders' benefits that included "Landes and Groundes, Soyles, Woods and Wood Grounds."[102] Here, "right" was obviously being used in its old, narrow sense as a title to land. Virginia Company officials certainly understood the term in this way.[103] In 1617, Captain Samuel Argall pledged to support the inhabitants of Bermuda Hundred in a land dispute, assuring them that he would "not Infringe their rights." On July 20, 1619, Governor George Yeardley wrote to a friend, expressing the hope that "I may not be wronged in that which is my deu and Ryght, I mean my Land of Weyonock." And on April 6, 1626, the governor and Council of Virginia sent an address to the English Privy Council, thanking Charles I's government for recognizing the validity of the land titles that the settlers had purchased in good faith from the defunct Virginia Company, whose charter had been revoked two years earlier. Virginians rejoiced, the local authorities asserted, at "his majesties gratious assurance that every man should have his particular right preserved."[104]

From 1624 until the advent of the Civil War in England, Virginia records reveal little, if any, use of the term "rights." A sudden and modern-sounding claim for rights appeared in a Declaration of April 5, 1647, in which the governor, Council, and House of Burgesses protested against rumors that Parliament intended to exclude Dutch merchants from Virginia, and denounced proponents of the anti-Dutch laws as "Oppugners of our undoubted rights." Edmund S. Morgan's belief that Governor William Berkeley wrote this manifesto is plausible because Berkeley had been in England in the 1640s and would have been exposed to the "rights talk" that emerged during the Civil War.[105] An autocratic royalist, Berkeley was certainly no tribune of the people—the beneficiaries of the rights he was claiming would have been a coterie of wealthy planters—and when Virginia capitulated to parliamentary forces in 1652, he negotiated a settlement that granted the citizenry "freedomes and priviledges," not rights. Rights of the extended sort that Parliament began claiming in 1604 are first encountered in Virginia in the 1653 acknowledgment by an acting governor of the "right of Assemblies in the free choice of a speaker." Yet the ancient royal property definition of rights appears in 1674, when a court ordered one Anthony Vauson to assign "all his rights" in an escheated estate to a certain Peter Starke.[106]

However defined, rights were infrequently asserted in Virginia before

Bacon's Rebellion of 1676. That upheaval demonstrated how shallow the roots of rights were in the Old Dominion a century before the American Revolution. Bacon claimed to be seeking to establish the colony's "liberties,"[107] not rights, and none of the literature generated by his followers mentions rights. Bacon's Rebellion, as Professor Morgan observed, produced "no revolutionary manifesto, not even any revolutionary slogans."[108] More striking still are the reports of the royal commissioners sent to Virginia in the wake of Bacon's Rebellion to investigate the causes and consequences of the turmoil. The commissioners visited all the counties in the colony and collected reports on the popular mood, based on interviews with local officials. The citizens related numerous grievances, but in none of the reports is there any mention that rights had been violated.[109] It was as if the concept of rights had not yet entered popular consciousness.

Rights did not play a significantly greater role in seventeenth-century New England than they did in Virginia. New England was a network of towns in which a communitarian ethic based on shared religious beliefs was particularly strong. A society organized on these principles was inhospitable to the aggressive individualism of subjective rights. Rights, to be sure, were occasionally mentioned in the first decades of New England, especially in a celebrated legal code, the Body of Liberties, written in 1641 by Nathaniel Ward. The document, which was titled a "Coppie of the Liberties of the Massachusetts Collonie in New England," is a list of the liberties—the term is used repeatedly—of the citizens of Massachusetts to do everything from appealing a court decision to electing deputies to the legislature. A long instrument, consisting of ninety-eight sections, some with subsections of twelve articles, the Coppie of Liberties mentions "Rites" just four times and explicitly subordinates rights to the more familiar term "liberty"; in the words of section 96, "The above specified rites, freedomes, Immunities, Authorities and priveledges, both Civil and Ecclesiastical are expressed only under the name and title of Liberties."[110]

New England's coolness to rights surfaced in the conflict with Dr. Robert Child in 1645. A Presbyterian, Child claimed that the Congregational establishment in Massachusetts was persecuting him because of a difference of opinion over religion. Like Governor Berkeley, Child borrowed from the mother country the Civil War rhetoric of rights to argue his case, claiming that "natural rights, as freeborne subjects of the English nation" were being violated by the intolerant Puritans. The authorities in Boston rebuffed Child and drove him from the colony. Massachusetts then steeled itself in a policy of "doctrinaire intolerance."[111] The author of the Body of Liberties cheered the colony's officials on. Ward detested "polypiety" and railed against the "Toleration of divers Religions, or of one Religion in Segregant Shapes."[112] In the 1650s and 1660s Massachusetts displayed its contempt for the rights of minorities by hanging Quakers in the name of religious uniformity.

Arguments for rights occasionally cropped up in the political arena after the restoration of Charles II. On June 10, 1661, a committee of the Massachusetts General Court, responding to reports that the new king meant to alter their government, used "right" in the old sense of the rule of law; the charter of 1629, claimed the assembly, granted in good faith by Charles I and still in force, guaranteed them immunity from the new king's innovations. "We conceive," declared the committee, "any imposition prejudicial to the country contrary to any just lawe of ours . . . to be an infringement of our right."[113] Four years later, the town of Northampton submitted what a recent scholar has called a "commonwealth petition" to the General Court, urging it to oppose the machinations of royal commissioners sent to the colony in 1664, and "to maintain our former and ancient rights, liberties and privileges, both in church and commonwealth."[114] Rights in this context, although undifferentiated from liberties and privileges, have a modern sound, but the Bay Colony's response twenty years later to the Dominion of New England shows that in Massachusetts, as in Virginia, "right" was not yet the term of choice for most participants in political and legal controversies.

The Dominion was a shotgun wedding, a union imposed on the New England colonies by the government of James II. A military man, Sir Edmund Andros, was appointed governor in 1686 and ruled without a representative assembly. Andros's regime proceeded to tax New Englanders, raising precisely the issue that helped precipitate the American Revolution: the taking of property without consent. Although a few New Englanders protested Andros's actions "as a violation of the Common Rights, which all Englishmen justly count themselves born unto,"[115] many more, including the most notable dissidents, John Wise and his Ipswich followers, did not invoke the language of rights at all. At an Ipswich town meeting, August 23, 1687, Wise "made a Speech . . . and said we had a good God, and a good King, and should do well to stand for our Privileges." The Ipswich selectmen then voted that "it was against the common Privileges of English Subjects to have money raised without their consent in an Assembly or Parliament." Imprisoned for their defiance, Wise and his compatriots were denied a writ of habeas corpus and were tried under irregular circumstances in Boston. At the trial, the prisoners once again asserted "the privilege of Englishmen not to be taxed without their consent," and also claimed the "privileges of English law."[116] The absence of the term "rights" in protesting taxation without representation indicates that the concept of rights was as unfamiliar in Ipswich as it was to a committee of Bostonians who, seeking to describe a written guarantee of rights allegedly promised to Increase Mather by James II, could find no better phrase than "a certain Magna Charta" to designate a document that later generations would have automatically called a bill of rights.[117]

If dealings about land are excepted, a right was a rather exotic concept in the 1680s in both New England and Virginia. Rights became, of course, a major component of political and legal discourse in eighteenth-century America. What catalyst raised rights consciousness in the colonies from its dim seventeenth-century level? Beyond doubt, it was the Glorious Revolution and its enduring testament, the Bill of Rights of 1689. Americans regarded the Bill of Rights as a talisman that patriots had wielded to save England from "Popery and Arbitrary Power," and perceived that they, no less than citizens of the metropolis, could wield rights to defeat autocrats in their midst.[118] What increased America's interest in rights was the appealing way—the integration of rights with religion—in which the concept was presented by Locke and his Continental contemporaries, such as Samuel Pufendorf. Pufendorf's impact on colonial American thought is just beginning to be appreciated. Recently, a scholar has observed that Grotius and Pufendorf were "omnipresent in the eighteenth century" and that Pufendorf was "required reading in . . . many English dissenting academics and American colleges."[119] When John Wise wrote his *Vindication of the Government of New England Churches* in 1717, it was Pufendorf rather than Locke upon whom he relied for his discussion of "the civil being of man." "I shall," Wise advised his readers, "principally take baron Pufendorf for my chief guide and spokesman."[120]

Both Locke and Pufendorf defined a right as a power: "The several kinds of Power have . . . a particular Name . . . we have thought it convenient to give it the name Right."[121] They also insisted, in opposition to Hobbes but in conformity with writers stretching back to Ockham, that a right was a moral power. The iconoclast as usual, Hobbes had argued that a right was "absolute," "unlimited" power, restrained by no considerations of justice, religion, or morality.[122] In his view, men had a "Right to everything, even to one another's body."[123] This "aberration" was corrected by Locke, Pufendorf, and others, "who restored the moral content" to right.[124] Pufendorf was "preoccupied with . . . moral power conceived as right,"[125] and so was Locke. John Dunn, who has stressed that Locke's concept of rights must be understood in the "context of his religious belief," has asserted that "for Locke all the rights humans have . . . derive from, depend upon and are rigidly constrained by a framework of objective duty: God's requirement for human agents."[126] Villey explained that in deriving rights from duties, Locke was following Grotius. Paraphrasing Grotius's and Locke's argument, Villey wrote: "Had God not given to each man by the natural law (confirmed in the Holy Scriptures) a duty to preserve himself, to increase and multiply? Man therefore must have received the means to increase and prosper, that is, the rights indispensable to the exercise of these duties."[127]

Rights in Eighteenth-Century America: Changing and Contested

Here, Villey was describing the correlative character of rights and duties that became such an important feature of the discussions of rights by members of the eighteenth century's "natural law–based moral philosophy" school: Burlamaqui, Vattel, Wolff, Rutherforth, and participants in the Scottish Enlightenment, among whom Francis Hutcheson had the widest following in America. Hutcheson insisted that a right was a "moral quality," while Vattel declared it was "nothing more than the power of doing what is morally possible."[128] They were especially keen on emphasizing the correlation between rights and duties that Burlamaqui explained, saying that rights were powers bestowed by God and "have a natural connection to our duties and are given to man only as a means to perform them."[129] The moral philosophers argued that through the law of nature, God prescribed for each individual moral duties (the foremost being self-preservation) that must be discharged by employing moral rights or powers, the exercise of which imposed moral duties on others to permit the rights holder to act without interference. The hand-glove relationship between rights and divinely dictated duties explains why in the 1790s John Adams could dismiss Rousseau's claim that Americans had invented the "science of the rights of man" with the rejoinder that they had "found it in their Religion."[130] And it explains why a Continental expert on subjective rights, George Jellinek, could assert that the idea of "inalienable, inherent and sacred rights of the individual is not of political but religious origin."[131]

A religious society, as eighteenth-century America was, opened its arms to natural or subjective rights, presented as moral power inherent to individuals. Ministers of the gospel, as Edmund S. Morgan has shown,[132] were enthusiastic proponents of subjective rights, and lawyers displayed none of the aversion to the new concept that Villey discovered among their eighteenth-century European brethren. Still, subjective right was no more successful in sweeping the field of its rivals than it had been in England. In fact, during the first decades of the eighteenth century, many American political leaders continued to speak in the language of Coke and his contemporaries. In 1711, for example, the New Jersey assembly presented an address to Governor Robert Hunter, complaining about the arbitrary conduct of his predecessor, Lord Cornbury, who was accused of taking "Daring and Violent Measures, to subvert the Liberties of this Country." Cornbury was repeatedly assailed for undermining the colony's "liberties." The assembly used the term "right," but only in its ancient sense as a title to land, as when it censured Cornbury for invading the "Rights" of the former proprietors of the colony, those "Rights" being their "Title to their Lands and Rents, violently and Arbitrarily forced from them."[133] In Boston, a decade later, young Benjamin Franklin revealed the continuing disinclination of colonial Americans to differentiate rights from related concepts. "I am naturally very jealous," wrote Franklin, "for the Rights and Liberties of my Country; and the least appearance of an Incroachment on those invaluable Priviledges is apt to make my Blood boil."[134]

By the 1730s, subjective rights, at times described as natural rights, began finding their way into the public discourse. Commenting on the Zenger trial in 1737, James Alexander warned opponents of freedom of speech and of the press that "whoever attempts to suppress either of those our natural rights, ought to be regarded as enemies to liberty and to the constitution."[135] The Great Awakening of the 1740s promoted the use of subjective rights because the "New Lights," dissenters from the established order, adopted the customary tactics of English religious minorities in claiming the "inaliable Right" to practice religion as they saw fit. One of their principal spokesmen, Elisha Williams, insisted on a "Christian's natural and unalienable right of private judgment in matters of religion," and cited as his authority "the celebrated Mr. Lock in his *Treatise of Government* . . . in which it is justly to be presumed all are agreed who understand the natural rights of mankind."[136] Some New Lights insisted that the "inherent natural Rights of Englishmen" be applied in the political as well as in the religious sphere.[137] During the French and Indian War, 1755–63, natural/subjective rights were invoked to protest the British military's practices of impressment and quartering.[138]

By the end of the French and Indian War, subjective rights had taken their place, as they had in William Penn's England, among an array of overlapping and often incompatible libertarian concepts that Americans had not until then been obliged to sort out. Throughout the colonies, older concepts such as liberties and privileges and miscellaneous notions such as franchises and immunities jostled with the new idea of rights for pride of place. The result was that on the eve of the conflict with Britain, many Americans found the concept of a right to be indistinct and incoherent.

This was not a new problem. William Penn had observed in 1687 that it "may reasonably be supposed that we shall find in this part of the world [America] many men, both old and young, that are strangers, in a great measure, to the true understanding" of rights. The concept of a right, Penn knew, had been formulated by intellectuals whose writings were likely to be inaccessible to ordinary people with neither the means nor the leisure "to read large volumes" and "Law-Books."[139] The situation had improved only marginally by the middle of the eighteenth century. Even those who had the inclination and opportunity to master the meaning of rights were challenged by an extensive and often impenetrable literature. Some experts—Pufendorf, for example—explicated subjective rights in the "antique vocabulary" of Roman law.[140] Others used a highly technical language, loaded with phrases like "adventitious rights which are either real or personal" and "natural rights which are of the imperfect sort."[141] Many—and not merely those of "inferior condition" and education— were confounded by this jargon.

Consider the case of William Bollan, agent to London for Massachusetts. "A learned man of indefatigable research," Bollan, in 1762, proposed to write a book "establishing . . . the native equal and permanent rights of the colonists against all Opponents," but he found that "the facts and arguments necessary on this occasion . . . are so numerous and various, and many of them so difficult in their nature, that the completion of a work of this kind" was beyond his capacity.[142] Bollan might have been consoled by experts like Francis Hutcheson, who admitted in 1755 that "our notion of right is a complex conception,"[143] or by public officials like Massachusetts governor Thomas Hutchinson, who testified to the abundant confusion about rights among practicing politicians. As a young member of the Massachusetts assembly in the 1740s and 1750s, Hutchinson affected "to catechize . . . about English rights," but he subsequently admitted that "no precise idea seems to have been affixed" to the phrase "natural rights of an English man."[144] In 1765, John Adams attributed the problem of comprehension to his countrymen's intellectual diffidence, to their "reluctance to examine into the grounds of our privileges." Years later, Adams conceded that rights might not, after all, be "definable."[145] Recent scholars, too, have commented on America's perplexity over rights. John Phillip Reid described "vagueness" in their discussion of the subject, an absence of a "precision of definitions."[146] Knud Haakonssen concluded that in discussing rights few Americans "understood exactly what they were talking about," a judgment that echoed James Wilson's contention in 1787 that "there are very few who understand the whole of these rights."[147]

The dispute with Britain, beginning with the Sugar Act of 1764, improved, if it did not perfect, America's understanding of rights. Americans, declared the First Continental Congress in 1774, "were animated by a just love of our invaded rights."[148] Making rights the principal issue in the contest with Britain compelled the colonists to strive for a common definition and to differentiate rights from superficially similar concepts. Leading patriots investigated rights with the "utmost precision," a postwar writer boasted.[149] As early as 1765, James Otis warned his countrymen against confounding "the terms rights, liberties, and privileges, which in legal as well as vulgar acceptation denote very different ideas."[150] A year earlier the General Assembly of New York anticipated Otis's admonition when it informed Parliament that a British legislature in which Americans were unrepresented could not compel them to pay taxes. "The People of this Colony," the assembly declared, "nobly disdain the thought of claiming that Exemption as a Privilege. They found it on a Basis more honourable, solid and stable; they challenge it and glory in it as their Right."[151] In 1766 Governor Stephen Hopkins of Rhode Island made the distinction Otis demanded. "Americans," said Hopkins, "do not hold those rights as privileges granted them, but possess them as inherent and indefeasible."[152]

Stressing the "inherent" nature of rights, as Hopkins did, became increasingly common during the Revolutionary era, a sign that some Americans were using "rights" in the subjective sense, as powers intrinsic in a person. Yet individuals did not suddenly stop indulging their old habit of stringing together, as though they were equivalents, "Rights, Franchises, Immunities, and Liberties."[153] Precision of definition eluded the First Continental Congress, which considered its principal business to be the drafting of a bill of rights to guide its constituents in their resistance to British authorities. Published on October 27, 1774, the congressional Bill of Rights asserted, to be sure, colonial rights, but also included claims to "immunities and privileges" and, in the manner of Coke and the opponents of the early Stuarts, declared the "common law of England" to be a right.[154]

The bills of rights drafted by the new states after 1776 were a hodgepodge of every kind of libertarian language then available. Scholars have been struck by the "sporadic and confused" nature of these documents. Gordon Wood observed that they contained a "jarring but exciting combination of ringing declarations of universal principles with a motley collection of common law procedures." Leonard Levy reproved the drafters for proceeding "in an incredibly haphazard fashion that verged on ineptitude," omitting one fundamental right after another, as though they were ignorant of what rights were or should be.[155]

Repeated testimony about the influence of experts suggests that from 1774 onward, American leaders took a crash course in their writings as a means of explicating the rights that they had declared to be the principal matter at issue with the mother country. In October 1774, James Madison received a report about the debates in the First Continental Congress, noting that "Vattel, Burlamaqui, Locke, and Montesquieu seem to be the standard to which they refer when settling the rights of the colonies." The next year, in *The Farmer Refuted*, Alexander Hamilton recommended "Grotius, Pufendorf, Locke, Montesquieu and Burlamaqui" to the perusal of his opponent. Ten years later, Elbridge Gerry, while serving in the Continental Congress, asked a friend to send him "Vattel's Law of Nations, Burlamaqui's principles of natural and political law . . . and a translation of Grotius on War and peace." Surveying experts on rights, James Wilson in 1787 observed that "all political writers, from Grotius and Puffendorf down to Vattel, have treated on this subject." The next year, John Adams offered the following advice to his son John Quincy, a fledgling lawyer: "To Vattel and Burlamaqui, whom you say you have read, you must add Grotius and Puffendorf."[156] In the nineteenth century legal commentators with views as diverse as St. George Tucker and Joseph Story continued to cite these writers with approval.[157] Their influence, together with that of the Scottish moral philosophers and other, lesser figures who shared their views, produced by 1776 among some well (and not so well) informed Americans the ascendancy of subjective right and created the intellectual climate in which Thomas Paine, writing in a Pennsylvania newspaper in 1777, could be understood when he offered this quintessentially subjective definition of a right: "A natural right is an animal right, and the power to act it, is supposed, either fully or in part, to be mechanically contained within ourselves as individuals."[158]

Independence brought two developments that are often said to have influenced the American approach to rights. Because Americans were no longer subjects of the British king, a favorite phrase, the "rights of Englishmen," disappeared from the national vocabulary. But Americans did not repudiate the legal system that had spawned the phrase and continued to incorporate into their concept of rights the venerable English notion of ownership by unassailable title. In the United States today, one of the core, if unarticulated, meanings of a right is inviolable ownership.

The other significant post-1776 development was the enthusiastic

American embrace of republicanism. A generation of recent writers has described this philosophy as inhospitable to assertions of individual interests or rights claims, which republican ideologues demanded be subordinated to the public or common good.[159] But the strong moral content with which the Revolutionary generation invested rights dissolved any conflict, real or apparent, between rights and republicanism. After 1776 as before, Americans believed, as Jefferson stated in his *Notes on the State of Virginia,* that for their rights "we are answerable . . . to our God."[160] From one end of the continent to another, Americans, when discussing rights, acknowledged the "divine authority from whence they sprung."[161] The divine authority, acting through the law of nature, dictated duties that, no one doubted, served the common good. By exercising rights/powers to discharge these duties, citizens served the common good, the objective of republicanism. Rights and republicanism were, therefore, considered congruent by the Revolutionary generation.

Conclusion

The voluminous literature generated by the conflict over the ratification of the Constitution in 1788 demonstrates the firmness with which subjective right had established itself in the new American nation. The exchanges between Federalists and Anti-Federalists teem with the concept of right as power.[162] Similarly, two years later, in his polemic against the "rights of man," *Reflections on the Revolution in France,* Edmund Burke called the British public's attention to the dual definitions of a right that had emerged by 1790. According to the "theorists," whom Burke cited with his customary sneer, "the right of the people is almost always sophistically confounded with their power." Burke was pleased, on the other hand, to remind his readers that the traditional English understanding of a right was very different; it was an "entailed inheritance," "an estate specifically belonging to the people."[163] Americans had comfortably combined these two definitions, something that Burke and his fellow British conservatives could never do. Sealing the victory of subjective right (as Villey might have said) was a pronouncement from the U.S. Supreme Court at the end of the eighteenth century. "When I say that a right is vested in a citizen," declared Justice Chase in *Calder v. Bull* (1798), "I mean that he has the power to do certain actions."[164]

Achieving a definition of a right did not resolve the question of limits or appropriate ends. How many rights were there? What exercise of power could legitimately be called a right? Locke and the moral philosophers popular in Revolutionary America were of little help here, for they did not attempt to compile an authoritative catalog of rights. They tended to assume, however, that rights were fewer rather than greater in number, circumscribed as they must be by the law of nature and attendant duties. But in the new American republic, the law of nature itself appeared to be expansive. If, for example, the fundamental duty imposed by the law of nature was self-preservation, why should fishing and hunting not be considered basic rights, as Pennsylvania Anti-Federalists proposed in 1788? Self-preservation might require mobility. Should an individual not, therefore, have "a natural right to emigrate from one state to another," as the Pennsylvania Bill of Rights of 1776 declared?[165] It was the individual's duty, as some state bills of rights affirmed, to worship God. Why, then, should those who officiated at such services—Congregational ministers in New England, for example—not have a "natural and unalienable right" to have their salaries paid by the state legislature?[166] And was it too much of a stretch to claim that in the interest of protecting true religion, "one of the natural and civil rights of a free People" was to limit public office holding to Protestants?[167] And on and on it went.

An expansive conception of rights has persisted and is, in fact, triumphant in the United States today. The continuity with the Founding period, evident here, has been severed elsewhere in recent decades by writers, principally philosophers (as Villey would have predicted) and legal theorists, who have cut rights/powers adrift from their ancient anchor in Christian norms, thereby divorcing varying notions of rights from Christian morality. Many commentators conceive a right to be a species of power, possessed absolutely by an individual (in the old English legal title sense). This power they regard as being vested in a person, whose function is not to discharge divinely ordained moral duties but to gratify more or less unrestrained personal ambitions and appetites in the name of vindicating individual autonomy. As long as rights and their correlative duties were consistent with a moral consensus, created by the country's widely shared Christian convictions, they were regarded, even in their most expansive mode, as a positive force in national life. But rights/powers indulged to fulfill autonomous personal goals that transgress traditional moral boundaries have for some become controversial.

Recent efforts to separate rights from Christian—more properly, Judeo-Christian—morality mark a radical new step in the evolution of the concept of subjective rights, a step that would have been welcomed by few of the Founders of the American republic and by fewer still in the line of distinguished thinkers stretching back at least to the fourteenth century.

Perhaps Thomas Hobbes alone would have approved this development. Whether rights can retain their prestige in American society, as the populace at large comes to appreciate that certain recent promoters conceive them to be little more than the exercise of self-directed individual power, will be one of the interesting intellectual and public-policy questions of the twenty-first century.

Notes

An earlier version of this article appeared in the *American Journal of Jurisprudence* 39 (1994): 185–224.

1. See, e.g., Henretta, "Social History as Lived and Written," 1293–1322.

2. See Tierney, "Villey, Ockham, and the Origin of Individual Rights," 1–31; Tierney, *Idea of Natural Rights*, 14. The gravamen of Tierney's complaint against Villey is the French scholar's failure to recognize that subjective right was conceived and articulated by canon lawyers in the twelfth century, not invented by William of Ockham two centuries later (ibid., 13–77). For the proceedings of a colloquium on Villey's influence on the debate over the origin of the concept of subjective right in which both Villey and Tierney are criticized for not recognizing the importance of Thomas Aquinas, see Tierney, "Natural Law and Natural Right: Old Problems and Recent Approaches," 389–420.

3. Most relevant for this essay were Villey's *Leçons d'histoire de la philosophie du droit* (1957); *La formation de la pensée juridique moderne* (1968); *Seize essais de philosophie du droit* (1969); and *Philosophie du droit* (1978).

4. Villey, *La formation*, 226, 231–32; "Droit subjectif, I," in Villey, *Seize essais*, 147, 150.

5. Kurland and Lerner, *Founders' Constitution*, 424; Commission on the Bicentennial of the United States Constitution, *Bill of Rights and Beyond*, foreword; Kaminski, "Liberty versus Authority," 214.

6. Hyneman and Lutz, *American Political Writing*, 46, 98, 427.

7. On this point see, among others, Elton, *Parliaments of England*, 337–38; Hexter, "Parliament, Liberty, and Freedom of Elections," 43; Schwoerer, *Declaration of Rights*, 283.

8. Conley and Kaminski, *Bill of Rights and the States*, 400, 426, 444, 101.

9. Ibid., 4–5; Wright, *American Interpretations of Natural Law*, 7; Leder, *Liberty and Authority*, 126; Reid, *Authority of Rights*, 4, 10–11, 93.

10. Villey, *La formation*, 225, 262.

11. "La nature des choses," in Villey, *Seize essais*, 24.

12. "Droit subjectif, II," ibid., 182; Villey, *Philosophie*, 74.

13. See "Droit subjectif, I," in Villey, *Seize essais*, 148, 152–53; "Droit subjectif, II," ibid., 182–83; "Les origines de la notion de droit subjectif," in Villey, *Leçons*, 262; Villey, *La formation*, 229, 234, 236, 546.

14. Villey, *La formation*, 365; Sandars, *Institutes of Justinian*, 6.

15. Villey, *La formation*, 381, 650; "Le humanisme et le droit," in Villey, *Seize essais*, 69; Villey, *Philosophie*, 150.

16. "La nature des choses," in Villey, *Seize essais*, 150.

17. "Une definition du droit," ibid., 27.

18. "La nature des choses," ibid., 51.

19. Villey, *Philosophie*, 77, 115, 144.

20. "Les origines de la notion de droit subjectif," in Villey, *Leçons*, 261.

21. Villey, *Philosophie*, 150.

22. "Les origines de la notion de droit subjectif," in Villey, *Leçons*, 261.

23. "Droit subjectif, I," in Villey, *Seize essais*, 153.

24. "Les origines de la notion de droit subjectif," in Villey, *Leçons*, 256, 276.

25. "Droit subjectif, I," in Villey, *Seize essais*, 158, 168, 159, 161, 166.

26. Villey, *La formation*, 261, 232, 230.

27. "Droit subjectif, I," in Villey, *Seize essais*, 144–45.

28. Villey, *La formation*, 653.

29. Villey, *Philosophie*, 116.

30. Ibid., 137–39; Villey, *La formation*, 209–10, 652; "Droit subjectif, II," in Villey, *Seize essais*, 184–85.

31. Villey, *La formation*, 253.

32. Villey, *Philosophie*, 143.

33. "Les origines de la notion de droit subjectif," in Villey, *Leçons*, 272; Villey, *La formation*, 365, 381.

34. Villey, *La formation*, 341, 351.

35. "Les origines de la notion de droit subjectif," in Villey, *Leçons*, 273; Villey, *La formation*, 364.

36. Suarez quoted in White, *Philosophy of American Revolution*, 145; Villey, *La formation*, 393.

37. Villey, *La formation*, 654.

38. "Droit Subjectif, II," in Villey, *Seize essais*, 188.

39. Villey, *La formation*, 650; "Les origines de la notion de droit subjectif," in Villey, *Leçons*, 272.

40. "La pensée moderne et le systeme juridique actuel," in Villey, *Leçons*, 66.

41. Villey, *La formation*, 598.

42. "Les origines de la notion de droit subjectif," in Villey, *Leçons*, 249.

43. Tuck, *Natural Rights Theories*, 74.

44. Villey, *La formation*, 654.

45. "Les origines de la notion de droit subjectif," in Villey, *Leçons*, 250, 274–76.

46. "La pensée moderne et le systeme juridique actuel," ibid., 66.

47. Villey, *Philosophie*, 69.

48. "Les origines de la notion de droit subjectif," in Villey, *Leçons*, 277.

49. Tierney, "Villey, Ockham, and the Origin of Individual Rights," 1–31.

50. Coing, "Zur Geschichte des Begriffs 'subjectives Recht,'" in Zweigert, *Das subjektive Recht*, 11.

51. Tierney, "Origins of Natural Rights Language," 624.

52. Ibid., 630–37.

53. "Droit subjectif, I," in Villey, *Seize essais*, 144.

54. Zweigert, *Das subjektive Recht*, 24, 5.

55. Thorne, *Bracton*, xxxvi.

56. Ibid., 24; Twiss, *Henri de Bracton*, 16–18.

57. Maitland, "History of the Register of Original Writs," 139; Holdsworth, *History of English Law*, 5–6.

58. Van Carnegem, *Royal Writs in England*, 212, 195, 313–15.

59. At the least it conferred "a sort of ownership." Milsom, *Historical Foundations*, 120.

60. Holdsworth, *History of English Law*, 3.

61. The title of the 1567 edition changed to *Exposisions of the terms of the laws of England*, and until 1624 the several editions were published with slight variations upon this title. In 1624 *Les termes de la ley* was resurrected as the title and used throughout the remainder of the volume's publishing history. Early editions contain no pagination; until the 1667 edition, the definition of a right must be sought under "droit." All editions consulted are in the Rare Book Section, Law Library, Library of Congress.

62. For an explanation of the writ of right praecipe, see Van Carnegem, *Royal Writs*, 234–38.

63. Cowell, *Interpreter*, s.v. "Right Rectum."

64. Coke, *First Part of Institutes*, ed. Hargrave and Butler, 3.11.650. Bacon asserted that "there are but two rights. . . . The one is an estate, which is Jus in re." Bacon, *Works of Francis Bacon*, ed. Spedding, 287.

65. Coke, *First Part of Institutes*, ed. Hargrave and Butler, 3.8.445.

66. Sheppard, *Epitome of Common and Statute Laws*, 466–67.

67. Noy, *Compleat Lawyer*, 82–83.

68. Coke, *First Part of Institutes*, ed. Hargrave and Butler, 3.8.447, 3.11.650.

69. Tanner, *Documents of Reign of James I*, 204, 286.

70. Hexter, *Parliament and Liberty*, 81.

71. Pocock, *Ancient Constitution*, 213, 218.

72. Tanner, *Documents of Reign of James I*, 94.

73. Notestein, *Commons Debates, 1621*, 334–35.

74. See Hartley, *Proceedings in Parliaments of Elizabeth I*.

75. Hexter, *Parliament and Liberty*, 93.

76. Ibid., 94; Coke, *Second Part of Institutes*, 47.

77. Tanner, *Documents of Reign of James I*, 221.

78. Ibid., 246.

79. Peck, *Mental World*, 73.

80. Russell, *Parliaments and English Politics*, 359.

81. Foster, "Petitions and the Petition of Right," 24, 34.

82. See Peck, *Mental World*, 63; Tierney, "Origins of Natural Rights Language," 623.

83. Woodhouse, *Puritanism and Liberty*, 69, 445.

84. Hexter, *Parliament and Liberty*, 139.

85. Macpherson, *Political Theory of Possessive Individualism*, 137.

86. Tuck, *Natural Rights Theories*, 149.

87. Ibid., 144.

88. "Les origines de la notion de droit subjectif," in Villey, *Leçons*, 274–76.

89. Schwoerer, *Declaration of Rights*, 16, 258–60.

90. Penn, *Select Works*, 2:273.

91. "Each man having a Fundamental Right born with him," in Kurland and Lerner, *Founders' Constitution*, 432.

92. Penn, *Select Works*, 2:120, 273.

93. Kurland and Lerner, *Founders' Constitution*, 433; Penn, *Select Works*, 2:133, 285.

94. C. B. Macpherson has described the seventeenth century as a period of "possessive individualism" in which human beings were conceived to be owners of their "persons

and capacities," including their rights, which they exchanged in a market setting. Macpherson appears to understand the idea of the ownership of rights and capacities as arising in a Marxist fashion from impersonal economic forces. See Macpherson, *Political Theory of Possessive Individualism*. It is the argument of this essay that the idea of a right as a title to ownership was developed as a defensive political strategy against the arbitrary political pretensions of the Stuarts.

95. Penn, *Select Works*, 2:196, 201; Kurland and Lerner, *Founders' Constitution*, 432.

96. Shain, *Myth of American Individualism*, 56, 73, 86–95.

97. Wertenbaker, *Virginia under the Stuarts*, 34, 23; Brown, *English Politics*, 13.

98. Swindler, *Sources and Documents*, 10:22, 34.

99. Tanner, *Documents of Reign of James I*, 287; Kingsbury, *Records of Virginia Company*, 3:434.

100. Morton, *Colonial Virginia*, 58; Kingsbury, *Records of Virginia Company*, 3:161.

101. Morton, *Colonial Virginia*, 104.

102. Swindler, *Sources and Documents*, 10:40, 5:34.

103. The gadfly Captain John Bargrave occasionally invoked the term, as when he charged in 1621 that "all the rights privileges and liberties together with the government of law is laid aside" by the company's monopoly of trade, but it is doubtful that Bargrave understood *right* in a modern subjective sense, since on another occasion he defined the term *right* by reference to Aristotle. Kingsbury, *Records of Virginia Company*, 3:519, 4:410.

104. Ibid., 3:76, 152, 571.

105. "Declaration concerning the Dutch Trade," in Morgan, *American Slavery*, 247; ibid., 147n.

106. Billings, *Old Dominion*, 241, 65, 59.

107. Webb, *1676*, 67.

108. Morgan, *American Slavery*, 269.

109. PRO, CO 1/39, 244 ff., Library of Congress microfilm copies.

110. Swindler, *Sources and Documents*, 5:46, 66.

111. Miller, *New England Mind*, 121, 122.

112. *DAB*, s.v. "Ward, Nathaniel."

113. Hall, Leder, and Kammen, *Glorious Revolution in America*, 13.

114. Bliss, *Revolution and Empire*, 156.

115. Whitmore, *Andros Tracts*, 3:194.

116. Ibid., 1:82, 85, 2:6.

117. Ibid., 1:17.

118. Ibid., 1:75.

119. Haakonssen and Lacey, *Culture of Rights*, 19–61.

120. Wise, *Vindication*, 23.

121. Pufendorf, *Law of Nature and Nations*, 11–12. For Locke's equating of right and power, see Simmons, "Inalienable Rights," 2, 46, 49.

122. Villey, *La formation*, 230, 660–61.

123. Hobbes, *Leviathan*, 91.

124. Tierney, "Origins of Natural Rights Language," 622.

125. White, *Philosophy of American Revolution*, 188.

126. Kloppenberg, "Virtues of Liberalism," 16n.

127. Villey, *Philosophie*, 155.

128. Haakonssen and Lacey, *Culture of Rights*, 35; Vattel, *Laws of Nations*, x.

129. White, *Philosophy of American Revolution*, 140, 189–90.

130. John Adams to Thomas Boylston Adams, 18 March 1794, in Adams Papers, microfilm, reel 377, Library of Congress.

131. Shain, *Myth of American Individualism*, 126, 194.

132. In the sense that they dispensed Locke's ideas, see Morgan, "American Revolution Considered," 176.

133. Morris, *Papers of Lewis Morris*, 115, 116, 125, 130.

134. Franklin, *Silence Dogood, II* (April 1722), 13.

135. Alexander, *Case and Trial of John Peter Zenger*, 190.

136. Williams, "Seasonable Plea," 59, 85.

137. Bonomi, *Under the Cope of Heaven*, 156.

138. Rogers, *Empire and Liberty*, 84–85.

139. Kurland and Lerner, *Founders' Constitution*, 121, 431, 432.

140. "La pensée moderne et le systeme juridique actuel," in Villey, *Leçons*, 73.

141. Hutcheson, *System of Moral Philosophy*, 303, 340.

142. Washburn, *Collections*, 28–29.

143. Hutcheson, *System of Moral Philosophy*, 258.

144. Rogers, *Empire and Liberty*, 84–85; Morgan, *Prologue to Revolution*, 123.

145. Adams, "Dissertation on the Canon and Feudal Law" (1765), 123, and John Adams to Thomas Boylston Adams, 18 March 1794, in Adams Papers, microfilm, reel 377, Library of Congress.

146. Reid, *Authority of Rights*, 10, 11, 93.

147. Haakonssen and Lacey, *Culture of Rights*, 61; Jensen, *Documentary History*, 2:470.

148. Hutson, *Decent Respect to the Opinions of Mankind*, 66–67.

149. Jensen, *Documentary History*, 8:375.

150. Otis, *Vindication of the British Colonies* (1765), 558.

151. Morgan, *Prologue to Revolution*, 10.

152. Reid, *Authority of Rights*, 108.

153. Hyneman and Lutz, *American Political Writing*, 457.

154. For the Bill of Rights and List of Grievances, see Hutson, *Decent Respect to the Opinions of Mankind*, 50–57.

155. Wood, *Creation of the American Republic*, 271; Levy, *Legacy of Suppression*, 281.

156. William Bradford to James Madison, 17 Oct. 1774, in *Papers of James Madison*, 126; Hamilton, *Papers of Alexander Hamilton*, 86; Elbridge Gerry to Timothy Pickering, 15 Oct. 1785, in Gerry Papers, Library of Congress; Jensen, *Documentary History*, 2:470; John Adams to John Quincy Adams, 23 Jan. 1788, in Adams Papers, microfilm, reel 371, Library of Congress.

157. Tucker, *Blackstone's Commentaries* (1803), appendix to vol. 1, pt. 1, pp. 64–73, 332, 382; Story, *Commentaries*, 3:538, 722.

158. "Ludlow," *Pennsylvania Journal*, 4 June 1777.

159. Shain, *Myth of American Individualism*, 32–38, 121–22.

160. Jefferson, *Notes on the State of Virginia*, 159.

161. Jensen, *Documentary History* 8:353.

162. Cooke, *Federalist*, 8; Storing, *Complete Anti-Federalist*, 4:22, 5:177; Jensen, *Doc-*

umentary History, 1:335, 2:388, 430, 570; Elliot, *Debates in Several State Conventions,* 3:3, 598, 650, 4:145, 238.

163. Burke, *Reflections on Revolution in France,* 180–81, 210.

164. 3 Dallas 394. For a lawyer who has treated the right-power relationship perceptively, observing that "rights and powers are two sides of the same coin," see McAffee, "Original Meaning of the Ninth Amendment," 1226.

165. Brennan, "Natural Rights and the Constitution," 1003, 1004n.219.

166. "Irenaeus," *Boston Gazette,* 27 Nov. 1780.

167. Handlin, *Popular Sources of Political Authority,* 904.

Bibliography

Adams, John. *The Papers of John Adams,* ed. Robert Taylor et al. Cambridge, MA, 1977–.

———— to John Quincy Adams, 23 Jan. 1788, reel 371, and to Thomas Boylston Adams, 18 March 1794, reel 377, Adams Papers, microfilm, Library of Congress.

Alexander, James. *Brief Narrative of the Case and Trial of John Peter Zenger,* ed. Stanley N. Katz. Cambridge, MA, 1963.

Bacon, Francis. *Works of Francis Bacon,* ed. James Spedding et al. Boston, 1861–64.

Billings, Warren M., ed. *The Old Dominion in the Seventeenth Century: A Documentary History of Virginia, 1606–1689.* Chapel Hill, NC, 1975.

Bliss, Robert. *Revolution and Empire.* Manchester, UK, 1990.

Bonomi, Patricia. *Under the Cope of Heaven.* New York, 1986.

Brennan, Terry. "Natural Rights and the Constitution: The Original 'Original Intent.'" *Harvard Journal of Law and Public Policy* 15 (1992): 1003.

Brown, Alexander. *English Politics in Early Virginia History.* Rept. New York, 1968.

Burke, Edmund. *Reflections on the Revolution in France.* Rept. New York, 1909.

Coke, Edward. *First Part of the Institutes of the Laws of England,* ed. Francis Hargrave and Charles Butler. 7 vols. London: E & R Brooke, 1794.

————. *Second Part of the Institutes of the Laws of England.* London: Printed for A. Cooke, 1669.

Commission on the Bicentennial of the United States Constitution. *Bill of Rights and Beyond.* Washington, DC, 1991.

Conley, Patrick T., and John Kaminski, eds. *The Bill of Rights and the States: The Colonial Revolutionary Origins of American Liberties.* Madison, WI, 1992.

Cooke, Jacob E., ed. *The Federalist.* Middletown, CT, 1961.

Cowell, John. *The Interpreter; or the Booke Containing the Significations of Words.* Cambridge: Printed by Iohn Legate, 1607.

"Declaration concerning the Dutch Trade." *Virginia Magazine of History and Biography* 23 (1915): 247.

Elliot, Jonathan, ed. *Debates in the Several State Conventions on the Adoption of the Federal Constitution.* 2d ed. Philadelphia, 1896.

Elton, G. R. *Parliaments of England.* Cambridge, 1986.

Foster, Elizabeth Read. "Petitions and the Petition of Right." *Journal of British Studies* 14 (1974): 24.

Franklin, Benjamin. *The Papers of Benjamin Franklin,* ed. Leonard W. Labaree et al. New Haven, 1959–.

Gerry, Elbridge, to Timothy Pickering, 15 Oct. 1785, in Gerry Papers, Library of Congress.

Haakonssen, Knud, and Michael J. Lacey, eds. *Culture of Rights: The Bill of Rights in Philosophy, Politics, and Law—1791 and 1991*. Cambridge, 1991.

Hall, Michael G., Lawrence H. Leder, and Michael G. Kammen, eds. *The Glorious Revolution in America: Documents on the Colonial Crisis of 1689*. Chapel Hill, NC, 1964.

Hamilton, Alexander. *The Papers of Alexander Hamilton*. Vol. 1. Ed. Harold C. Syrett et al. New York, 1961.

Handlin, Oscar and Mary, eds. *The Popular Sources of Political Authority: Documents on the Massachusetts Constitution of 1780*. Cambridge, MA, 1966.

Hartley, T. E. *Proceedings in the Parliaments of Elizabeth I*. Vol. 1. *1558–1581*. Wilmington, DE, 1981.

Henretta, James A. "Social History as Lived and Written." *American Historical Review* 84 (1979): 1293–1322.

Hexter, J. H., ed. *Parliament and Liberty from the Reign of Elizabeth to the English Civil War*. Stanford, CA, 1992.

Hobbes, Thomas. *Leviathan*, ed. Richard Tuck. Cambridge, 1991.

Holdsworth, William S. *History of English Law*. London, 1923.

Hutcheson, Francis. *A System of Moral Philosophy*. Vol. 1. London: Sold by A. Millar, 1755.

Hutson, James, ed. *A Decent Respect to the Opinions of Mankind: Congressional State Papers, 1774–1776*. Washington, DC, 1975.

Hyneman, Charles, and Donald Lutz, eds. *American Political Writing during the Founding Era, 1760–1805*. Indianapolis, 1983.

"Irenaeus." *Boston Gazette*, 27 Nov. 1780.

Jefferson, Thomas. *Notes on the State of Virginia*, ed. William Peden. Chapel Hill, NC, 1955.

Jensen, Merrill, et al., eds. *The Documentary History of the Ratification of the Constitution*. Madison, WI, 1976–.

Kaminski, John. "Liberty versus Authority: The Eternal Conflict in Government." *Southern Illinois University Law Journal* 16 (1992): 214.

Kingsbury, Susan M., ed. *The Records of the Virginia Company of London*. Washington, DC, 1906–35.

Kloppenberg, James. "Virtues of Liberalism: Christianity, Republicanism, and Ethics in Early American Political Discourse." *Journal of American History* 74 (1987): 16n.

Kurland, Philip B., and Ralph Lerner, eds. *The Founders' Constitution*. Chicago, 1987.

Leder, Lawrence. *Liberty and Authority: Early American Political Ideology*. Chicago, 1968.

Levy, Leonard W. *Legacy of Suppression: Freedom of Speech and Press in Early American History*. Cambridge, MA, 1960.

"Ludlow." *Pennsylvania Journal*, 4 June 1777.

Macpherson, C. B. *The Political Theory of Possessive Individualism: Hobbes to Locke*. New ed. New York, 1989.

Madison, James. *Papers of James Madison*. Vol. 1. Ed. William T. Hutchison and William M. E. Rachal. Chicago, 1962.

Maitland, F. W. "History of the Register of Original Writs." In *Collected Papers of Frederic William Maitland, Downing Professor of the Laws of England*, ed. H. A. L. Fisher. Cambridge, 1911.

McAffee, Thomas. "Original Meaning of the Ninth Amendment." *Columbia Law Review* 90 (1990): 1226.

Miller, Perry. *The New England Mind: From Colony to Province.* Cambridge, MA, 1953.

Milsom, S. F. C. *Historical Foundations of the Common Law.* 2d ed. London, 1981.

Morgan, Edmund S. "American Revolution Considered as an Intellectual Movement." In *Causes and Consequences of the American Revolution,* ed. Esmond Wright. Chicago, 1966.

———. *American Slavery, American Freedom: The Ordeal of Colonial Virginia.* New York, 1975.

———. *Prologue to Revolution: Sources and Documents on the Stamp Act Crisis, 1764–1766.* Chapel Hill, NC, 1959.

Morris, Lewis. *The Papers of Lewis Morris.* Vol. 1. Ed. Eugene R. Sheridan. Newark, NJ, 1991.

Morton, Richard Lee. *Colonial Virginia.* Chapel Hill, NC, 1960.

Notestein, Wallace, et al., eds. *Commons Debates, 1621.* New Haven, CT, 1935.

Noy, William. *Compleat Lawyer: or, A Treatise Concerning Tenures and Estates. . . .* London: Printed by W.W., 1651.

Otis, James. *Vindication of the British Colonies.* 1765. In *Pamphlets of the American Revolution, 1750–1776,* ed. Bernard Bailyn. Cambridge, MA, 1965.

Peck, Linda Levy, ed. *The Mental World of the Jacobean Court.* Cambridge, 1991.

Penn, William. *Select Works of William Penn.* Rept. New York, 1971.

Pocock, J. G. A. *The Ancient Constitution and the Feudal Law: A Study of English Historical Thought in the Seventeenth Century.* Rept. Cambridge, 1987.

PRO, CO 1/39, 244 ff. Library of Congress microfilm copies.

Pufendorf, Samuel. *The Law of Nature and Nations.* 5th ed. London: J. & J. Bonwicke, 1749.

Reid, John Phillip. *Constitutional History of the American Revolution: The Authority of Rights.* Madison, WI, 1986.

Rogers, Alan. *Empire and Liberty: American Resistance to British Authority, 1755–1763.* Berkeley, CA, 1974.

Russell, Conrad. *Parliaments and English Politics, 1621–1629.* Oxford, 1979.

Sandars, Thomas. *The Institutes of Justinian.* Westport, CT, 1970.

Schwoerer, Lois G. *The Declaration of Rights, 1689.* Baltimore, 1981.

Shain, Barry. *The Myth of American Individualism: The Protestant Origins of American Political Thought.* Princeton, NJ, 1994.

Sheppard, William. *An Epitome of All the Common and Statute Laws of this Nation, Now in Force.* London: n.p., 1656.

Simmons, A. John. "Inalienable Rights and Locke's *Treatises.*" In *Locke,* ed. John Dunn and Ian Harris. Cheltenham, UK, 1997.

Storing, Herbert, ed. *The Complete Anti-Federalist.* Chicago, 1981.

Story, Joseph. *Commentaries on the Constitution of the United States.* Boston, 1833.

Swindler, William F., ed. *Sources and Documents of United States Constitutions.* Dobbs Ferry, NY, 1973–79.

Tanner, J. R., ed. *Constitutional Documents of the Reign of James I, A.D. 1603–1625.* Cambridge, 1930.

Thorne, Samuel E., ed. *Bracton on the Laws and Customs of England.* Cambridge, MA, 1968.

Tierney, Brian. *The Idea of Natural Rights: Studies on Natural Rights, Natural Law, and Church Law, 1150–1625.* Atlanta, 1997.

———. "Natural Law and Natural Right: Old Problems and Recent Approaches." *Review of Politics* 64:3 (Summer 2002): 389–420.

———. "Origins of Natural Rights Language: Texts and Contexts, 1150–1250." *History of Political Thought* 10 (1989): 624.

———. "Villey, Ockham, and the Origin of Individual Rights." In *Weightier Matters of the Law,* ed. John Witte and Frank Alexander, 1–31. Atlanta, 1988.

Tuck, Richard. *Natural Rights Theories: Their Origin and Development.* Cambridge, 1979.

Tucker, St. George. *Blackstone's Commentaries.* 1803. Rept. Union, NJ, 1996.

Twiss, Sir Travers. *Henri de Bracton de Legibus et Consuetudinibus Angliae.* London, 1878.

Van Carnegem, R. C. *Royal Writs in England from the Conquest to Glanvill.* London, 1959.

Vattel, Emer de. *The Laws of Nations, or Principles of the Law of Nature.* London, 1811.

Villey, Michel. *La formation de la pensée juridique moderne: cours d'histoire de la philosophie du droit.* Paris, 1968.

———. *Leçons d'histoire de la philosophie du droit.* Paris, 1957.

———. *Philosophie du droit.* Washington, DC, 1978.

———. *Seize essais de philosophie du droit, dont un sur la crise universitaire.* Paris, 1969.

Washburn, Charles G. *Collections.* Boston, 1918.

Webb, Stephen Saunders. *1676: The End of American Independence.* New York, 1984.

Wertenbaker, Thomas J. *Virginia under the Stuarts, 1607–1688.* Rept. New York, 1959.

White, Morton Gabriel. *The Philosophy of the American Revolution.* New York, 1978.

Whitmore, W. H., ed. *Andros Tracts.* Boston, 1868–74.

Williams, Elisha. "A Seasonable Plea for the Liberty of Conscience, and the Right of Private Judgment." In *Political Sermons of the American Founding Era, 1730–1805,* ed. Ellis Sandoz. Indianapolis, 1991.

Wise, John. *A Vindication of the Government of New England Churches.* Boston: John Boyles, 1772.

Wood, Gordon S. *The Creation of the American Republic, 1776–1787.* Chapel Hill, NC, 1969.

Woodhouse, A. S. P., ed. *Puritanism and Liberty: Being the Army Debates (1647–49) from the Clarke Manuscripts.* London, 1986.

Wright, Benjamin F., Jr. *American Interpretations of Natural Law.* New York, 1962.

Zweigert, Konrad, ed. *Das subjektive Recht und der Rechtsschutz der Personlichkeit.* Frankfurt/M., 1959.

The Nature of Rights at the American Founding

2

The Authority of Rights at the American Founding

JOHN PHILLIP REID

During the colonial period, when the British ruled North America, there was general agreement among constitutional theorists and lawyers that the colonists derived their rights from the mother country and that they possessed the same rights as those possessed by the people of the home islands, particularly by the English and the Welsh. In the legal language of the eighteenth century, it was a matter of "inheritance" as well as equality. "The British subjects in America have equal rights with those in Britain," Rhode Island's governor Stephen Hopkins wrote when claiming that one right belonging to all American colonials was the right to what Hopkins called British rights, though what he meant was English rights.[1] "They do not hold those rights as a privilege granted them, nor enjoy them as a grace and favor bestowed, but possess them as an inherent, indefeasible right, as they and their ancestors were freeborn subjects, justly and naturally entitled to all the rights and advantages of the British constitution." Hopkins postulated a constitutional theory with which all colonial constitutionalist theorists agreed. It is also likely most imperialists did too, perhaps even most common lawyers, including Sir William Blackstone.[2]

Writing about American claims to English constitutional rights, the Scottish theologian John Erskine defined the concept of a civil right in terms much the same as the legal theory articulated by Governor Hopkins. "A civil right," Erskine explained, "is that which law and constitution confer, not that which may be derived from the arbitrary bounty of those in authority." The proposition was stated frequently by contemporary students of British politics who had no interest in American constitutional rights. "The privileges of Englishmen are not a matter of grace and favour, but of rights," Joseph Towers argued. Urging his countrymen to take advantage of the Volunteer movement and "restore" the "original" constitution, an Irishman cited the same principles. "The *privileges* we claim are not the *grants* of *Princes,* they are ORIGINAL Rights, conditions of the original CONTRACTS, co-equal with *prerogative,* and coeval with our government."[3] Colonial civil rights, in short, were not conferred but inherent.

To a surprising extent, there was even general agreement among British and North American constitutional lawyers in the eighteenth century as to what rights people possessed. The point over which many British constitutionalists and lawyers differed from most of their American counterparts was the way they defined the constitutionality or the authority for the claim that rights were inherent. British constitutionalists in the late eighteenth century tended to think of civil rights as originating from the Glorious Revolution and the Revolution Settlements. According to Whig political theory, rights most importantly protected citizens from the Crown. That the people might also possess rights against Parliament hardly ever entered their arguments. Most American constitutionalists adhered to an older tradition. Civil rights protected citizens from the exercise of arbitrary power of any origin. That distinction caused Americans to put greater emphasis than did the British on the question of how rights existed and from what authority a person could claim them against the government. The authority upon which rights were based was the most discussed issue, until the establishment of American independence, in colonial constitutional jurisprudence. It is the focus of this study.

Richard Henry Lee showed how intuitively American colonists writing on constitutional topics turned to the question of the authority for rights when, in the preface of the Virginia edition of John Dickinson's *Letters from a Farmer in Pennsylvania to the Inhabitants of the British Colonies,* he praised Dickinson for "contending for our just and legal possession of property and freedom. A possession that has its foundation on the clearest principle of the law of nature, the most evident declarations of the *English* constitution, the plainest contract made between [the] Crown and our forefathers, and all these sealed and sanctified by the usage of near two hundred years."[4] It would be well to consider closely just what Lee wrote. He was not claiming rights or defining them. Rather, he was stating the central grounds or authority for rights; that is, he was delineating part of the constitutional explanation of why Americans claimed the rights they did. The rights were British rights and were well known. Why Americans were entitled to them was more controversial and more complicated than what the rights were or how they were defined. Lee identified five sources or authorities for rights: possession (or ownership), natural law, the British (or English) constitution, colonial charters, and immemorial custom. These were among those most often claimed, although eighteenth-century Americans relied on many more authorities than these five.

When American constitutional writers made such claims and asserted rights, they did not do so to advance theoretical hypotheses, but to oppose particular British manifestations of authority. Essentially, London had three legal justifications for its constitutional pretensions: (1) parliamentary authority to tax the colonies; (2) parliamentary authority to bind the colonies by legislation in all cases whatsoever; and, a less important claim, (3) ministerial authority to govern by executive instructions. Colonial constitutionalists and lawyers interposed the doctrine of rights in opposition to these claimed powers. They said they were immune from imperial taxation and asserted the privilege of legislating for and governing themselves by virtue of constitutional rights derived from known sources and supported by known British constitutional authorities. In so doing, they went beyond the five bases noted by Lee and included as many as ten in their list of authorities for their rights, including: (1) the original contract;[5] (2) the emigration contract; (3) their rights as English subjects; (4) equality with other British peoples, especially Protestants in Great Britain and Ireland; (5) the customary American constitution; (6) natural law; (7) colonial charters; (8) the original colonial contract;[6] (9) the emigration purchase;[7] and (10) the principles of the British constitution.

As with the rights themselves, the claim to constitutional authority for American rights could be and often was grounded on different foundations at different times. It was a matter of rhetoric as well as legal theory. For example, in a set of resolutions denigrating the jurisdiction of the vice-admiralty courts and the taking of property by parliamentary statutes to which Americans never consented, the House of Burgesses complained that Virginians were being deprived "of those great and fundamental Rights, which, until lately, they have constantly enjoyed, and which they and their Forefathers have ever claimed as their inalienable Rights as Men, their Constitutional Rights as Subjects of the British Empire, and their Right by Charters granted to the first Settlers of this Distant Country by his Majesty's Royal Ancestors, *Kings of England.*" Yet six days later the Burgesses petitioned George III "to secure to us the free and uninterrupted Enjoyment of all those Rights and Privileges, which from the Laws of Nature, of Community in general, and in a most especial Manner from the Principles of the *British* Constitution, particularly recognized and confirm'd to this Colony by repeated and express Stipulations . . . in common with all the rest of your Majesty's Subjects, under the same Circumstances." In the resolutions, the Burgesses claimed rights on the authority of fundamental law, custom, inheritance, natural law, constitutional law, charter, and contract. In the petition to the king, the authorities relied on were natural law, the British constitution, contract, and equality with other British subjects.[8]

A consideration that must be stressed is that American constitutional writers employed rather peculiar expressions when identifying the authority for the rights they claimed. They spoke, for example, of privileges that were "the Purchase of the People" obtained with "valuable Considerations," "the Purchase of their Ancestors, as a gracious and royal Reward of the Merit and Services of their Forefathers, and as one of the best Inheritances they left to their Children," and of "those rights and immunities which were purchased for us, by the lives and blood of our worthy ancestors, and secured to us by solemn stipulation (or contract) with our late majesties King William and Queen Mary."[9] Such expressions may strike the uninformed reader as American bombast, the language of politics rather than of law, used to invent bogus rights for which there was no constitutional authority, and which at best could be supported by contrived boasts or passionate pleas. The language, however, was the same vocabulary Britons employed to delineate legal rights and to explain the constitutional authority for rights. A favorite word on both sides of the Atlantic was "blood." A frequently cited authority for rights, for example, was that "our ancestors redeemed" those rights "with their blood," "sealed with their blood," "purchased for us with their blood," or "purchased with seas of blood, to entail upon their posterity."[10]

Such language was not limited to political pamphlets or polemicists. It was standard usage in official resolutions and in petitions to Parliament. London's Common Council, for example, warned the king of "the desperate Attempts which have been, and are too successfully made . . . to subvert those sacred Laws which our Ancestors have sealed with their Blood." And in words reminiscent of many American petitions, the East India Company protested that legislation intruding upon corporate management was "subversive of those rights which they held under their charter; the original privileges of which, and the continuation thereof, have been purchased by their predecessors from the public for a valuable consideration, and repeatedly confirmed by several acts of parliament." The constitutional principle was that rights had been acquired by "purchase" and were grounded on the authority of implied contract and prescriptive custom. That was the meaning William Pitt, the Earl of Chatham, intended to convey to the House of Lords when he spoke of America's "dear-bought privileges," and what London's Council meant when it told the

House of Commons that the East India bill, if enacted, would destroy "the most sacred rights of the subject, purchased for valuable consideration, and sanctioned by the most *solemn charters* and *acts of parliament.*"[11]

Significance of the Original Contract

The authority for rights most frequently argued for and relied upon on by both sides, British as well as American, was not the authority of custom, and certainly not the authority of nature. The authority most often cited was the authority of the original contract.[12] The specificity with which a constitutional contract was argued may be surprising to people who think in twenty-first-century legal terms.

Writing in 1777 on Canadian affairs, Francis Maseres, former attorney general of Quebec and an official in the English judiciary, outlined the constitutional consequences resulting from the fact that eighteenth-century lawyers perceived the original contract to be an actual contract. "All civil powers are ultimately founded on compacts," he explained, "and every *question of right* will, if traced to its fountain-head, appear to be in reality *a question of fact*, that is, an inquiry concerning an ancient fact, to wit, the intention of the parties between whom the question arises, or of their ancestors and predecessors, at a time when the case, concerning which it has arisen, began to exist." That was why lawyers could think the original contract a firm reality. For them, the constitution, although unwritten, like the original contract, was an actual document, and so was the original contract, for the original contract was very close to being the constitution itself.[13]

In fact, some of those who in the eighteenth century wrote about the original contract equated it with the constitution. A typical example is provided by "A Freeholder" writing in the *Maryland Gazette* in 1748: "Our *Constitution* is plainly an *original Contract* betwixt the *People* and their *Rulers;* and as many Jests as have been broke on this Expression, we might safely venture to defy the warmest Stickler for arbitrary Power to produce any one Point of Time, since which we know any Thing of our *Constitution,* wherein the whole Scheme of it would not have been one monstrous Absurdity unless an *original Contract* had been suppos'd." Another example was the Earl of Abingdon. In a magazine article entitled "Great Outlines of the English Constitution," Abingdon asked, rhetorically, what the constitution was. "I would say, that *Constitution* signified *Compact,*" Abingdon answered. "I define *Constitution* then to be, those *Agreements* entered into, those *Rights* determined upon, and those *Forms* prescribed by and between the members of any society in the first settlement of their union, and in the frame and mode of their government."[14]

The new American version (novation) of the original contract, that is, the original colonial contract, was considered a real, actual contract by even the leading Loyalist, Governor Thomas Hutchinson, who asserted that "the agreements made with the Subjects who went into the Colonies were known to all the world." What was known? Another New England governor furnished one answer. "Before their departure," Stephen Hopkins wrote of the first settlers, "the terms of their freedom, and the relation they should stand in to the mother country, in their emigrant state were fully settled; they were to remain subject to the king, and dependent on the kingdom of Great Britain. In return they were to receive protection, and enjoy all the rights and privileges of freeborn Englishmen."[15] Hopkins said what is pertinent for us to know: among the various terms of the original colonial contract, the stipulations generally singled out and mentioned with the greatest frequency were the rights of freeborn Englishmen.

The voters of Roxbury, Massachusetts, boasted that their ancestors "had the promise of the King for himself and Successors, that they and theirs should enjoy all the Liberties and Immunities of natural-born Subjects within the Realm of England." It was a specific promise made for a specific purpose. "Our Ancestors," the governor and Company of Rhode Island told George III, "removed and planted here under a royal promise that, observing and fulfilling the conditions enjoined them, they and their children after them forever, should hold and enjoy equal rights, privileges and immunities with their fellow subjects in Britain."[16] For that specific promise, the king received specific consideration. It was an exchange of promises, according to Gilbert Burnet, Bishop of Salisbury, who told Increase Mather that the first settlers "promised the King to inlarge his dominions on their owne charges, provided that they and their posterity after them might enjoy such and such privileges." Decades later, Moses Mather repeated much the same facts. "These original compacts," he wrote, "were made and entered into by the King, not only for himself, but expressly for his heirs and successors on the one part, and the colonies, their successors and assigns on the other."[17]

Mather employed the word "expressly," as did many other observers when describing the original colonial contract. Its terms had been "expres[s]ly stipulated, between the King and People."[18] Some participants in the pre-Revolutionary argument even specified when the original contract had been negotiated. Samuel Adams said the negotiation occurred "immediately after their Arrival here," when the first settlers "solemnly recog-

niz[e]d their Allegiance to their Sovereign in England, & the Crown gra-
ciously . . . declared them & their Heirs for ever entitled to all the Liber-
tys & immunitys of free & natural born Subjects of the Realm." Nine
years later an anonymous writer was just as certain that the transaction had
taken place on the other side of the Atlantic, although agreeing with
Adams about the terms of the contract. "It was the same thing as if both
King and people had assembled upon the sea shore, and the one had
sworn to govern them according to the laws of the land, and the other to
obey him in *America* as subjects within the realm."[19] Equally wonder-
ful was the certitude of commentators on the terms of the original contract. They not only knew what the contract provided, but referred to the
"words" and even claimed that they had "read" them.[20] With such confidence, Americans found in the "original contract" a trusted authority
upon which to rest their constitutional rights. But it was only the first of
numerous others.

The English Migration to America

There is one authority for rights that has been consistently overlooked
by scholars. The fact is surprising, for if we consider the colonial side of
the imperial controversy, few authorities for rights were cited more frequently. In fact, if we take Patrick Henry's Virginia resolutions opposing
the Stamp Act to be the beginning of the colonial side of the controversy,
then this claim of authority was the very first American defense made.
"*Resolved*," the preamble of Henry's resolutions provided, "that the first
Adventurers and Settlers of this his Majesty's Colony and Dominion of
Virginia brought with them, and transmitted to their Posterity, and all
other his Majesty's Subjects since inhabiting in this his Majesty's said
Colony, all the Liberties, Privileges, Franchises, and Immunities, that
have at any Time been held, enjoyed and possessed, by the people of *Great
Britain*." Rights were claimed in that opening statement of the colonial
argument, and the first authority asserted for those rights was not the British constitution or equality of British peoples, but migration.[21]

There were numerous explanations for why migration was an authority for rights. The simplest, stated by the First Continental Congress and
Georgia's Commons House of Assembly, was that the migrants to the
North American colonies had enjoyed certain, known, and well-defined
rights in the mother country, and had not lost them by leaving the kingdom for another part of the realm. They resolved, "That, by the emigration, they by no means forfeited, surrendered, or lost any of those rights,

but they were, and their descendants now are, entitled to the exercise and enjoyment of all such of them as their local and other circumstances enable them to exercise and enjoy." Or, as the attorney general of Quebec told a Montreal jury when opening a capital prosecution, "Every Set of *English* Planters, upon their first occupying and settling a new Colony, have carried with them the Laws of *England* then in Force at the Time of their leaving it to go to the new Colony."[22]

Property was another means of giving the theory expression, by describing civil rights as part of the baggage the migrants took from the Old to the New World. It "followed" from the principles of the British constitution, New York's General Assembly explained to the House of Lords, that "the Colonists carried with them all the rights they were entitled to in the country from which they migrated." That is, the Pennsylvania General Assembly pointed out, the first settlers brought with them at migration "those constitutional Rights and Liberties which were inseparately annexed to their Persons," rights "now vested in their Descendants, as an Inheritance the most important and valuable."[23] A third way to speak of the authority of migration was to stress what was called "the nature of their migration," to argue that the first English settlers did not come to enjoy fewer rights than they had possessed in England, but had anticipated obtaining, if not more rights, at the least the same rights better secured. As Governor Hopkins suggested, "There would be found very few people in the world, willing to leave their native country, and go through the fatigue and hardship of planting in a new uncultivated one, for the sake of losing their freedom."[24] The migration principle was not sui generis to the American colonists, but an old established doctrine in the British constitution.[25]

The imperialist side of the Revolutionary debate attempted to nullify the claim to rights by migration by appealing to a rule of Roman law that a country conquered in war was at the will and pleasure of the conqueror and had to accept whatever laws, rights, and privileges the conqueror decreed. The reverse side of the Roman-law rule was that countries not conquered but settled by the British received the English common law unaltered. A factual dispute running throughout colonial history, accordingly, was whether British North America had been settled or conquered. The colonists maintained that, except for New York and Jamaica, they were never conquered, sometimes arguing that if anyone had been conquered, it was the Indian natives, and that they, the settlers, had been the conquerors. "Some of the Plantations, 'tis true, came to *England* by Conquest. But must the Conquerors themselves be look't upon as a conquered People," the Barbadian Edward Littleton asked in 1689. "It were very strange, if those that bring Countries under the Dominion of *England*, and maintain the possession, should by doing so lose their own *English* Liberties."[26]

There are three important concepts that must be kept distinct. The first concerns what laws the original settlers carried with them. The generally accepted rule was that they took only so much English law as was applicable to their situation and the conditions of an infant colony. The other two deal with rights specifically and are easily confused. The first is the right of British migrants going from the home kingdom to a territory, not conquered, which they were settling, to carry with them the common law and English constitutional civil rights. Although there were lawyers who questioned special applications of this right, there was remarkably uniform authority supporting the right.[27] The other distinct right was the right to migrate. This right rested on less-convincing authority, and whether it was a right that had existed in the seventeenth century, at the time of the first settlements, was quite important, due to the counterargument that if there was no such right, then migration was an "indulgence" granted to the original colonists on terms set by the government. One of the terms, after all, could have been that the settlers did not carry their English rights with them, or carried only those rights the sovereign permitted.[28]

There was much ambiguity in the eighteenth century whether migration was a self-executing civil right, an indulgence granted by the rulers, or as claimed by Richard Bland and Thomas Jefferson, a natural right. The natural right of migration was neither an American original nor a radical doctrine, but one that long had been a staple in the legal literature of Europe. Burlamaqui stated the rule just as positively as did Jefferson, even adding that "the subjects of a state cannot be denied the liberty of settling elsewhere, in order to procure the advantages which they do not find in their native country."[29] The historian's difficulty, therefore, is that the right appears to have been a natural right, not a positive civil right, and therefore may not have existed at common law.

During the era of the first settlements, the Earl of Strafford had maintained that the right to migrate was not recognized in English law; he claimed that the Crown had authority to issue the writ of *ne exeat regno*, restraining any subject or group of subjects from departing the country.[30] By the second half of the eighteenth century, though, that authority had been weakened considerably. The writ probably was limited to being issued on petition of private persons seeking to keep parties to a civil action within a court's jurisdiction, and Parliament sometimes forbade named individuals, such as the South Sea directors, from leaving the kingdom.

Former Massachusetts governor Thomas Pownall, writing about the North American colonies, stated positively that there was no right to migrate, but the legal author Francis Plowden was just as positive that there was.[31] The better view is that there was not a positive right, but there was an implied right by acquiescence of the government. Whether or not that acquiescence carried conditions, restricting other rights or curtailing what law the settlers carried with them, was the question that was most often under dispute, not whether there was a natural right of migration.

The American principle that their English ancestors' migration was an authority for the rights they, the Americans, claimed to possess was generally stated as an assumed obvious fact, one they did not expect to be disputed. Usually the discussion was supported by a physical depiction of the first settlers carrying their rights with them as part of their migration across the Atlantic. There were even explanations of what they did to "carry" those rights. One was that the first settlers had possessed rights in England and, on leaving, simply took them along, just as they took their other movable property.[32] A more legalistic explanation was that no English rights were diminished or in any way affected by the migration, as it was a constitutionally neutral undertaking. Going from the European part of the empire to the American part was, in constitutional law, no different than moving from Canterbury to York.[33] A third explanation was the theory that common law followed the subject, for as counsel argued in 1693 in *Dutton v. Howell,* when "Subjects of *England,* by Consent of their Prince, go and possess an uninhabited desert Country, the Common Law must be supposed their Rule, as 'twas their Birthright, and as 'tis the best, as so to be presumed their Choice; and not only that, but even as Obligatory, 'tis so."[34]

In several legal opinions, counsel to the Board of Trade, as well as the attorney and solicitor generals of England advising the Privy Council, had upheld the doctrine that some but not all law had been carried to the New World by the migration. "The Common Law of England is the Common Law of the Plantations," Richard West ruled in 1720. "Let an Englishman go where he will, he carries as much of law and liberty with him, as the nature of things will bear."[35] That was precisely the point that was in dispute. How much could and did the nature of things bear? The chief British position, never clearly defined, was basically that no matter what rights migrated to the colonies, they were subject to the supreme authority of Parliament. American constitutionalists, by contrast, not only claimed all rights existing in the mother country, but derived from the authority of the migration additional rights, or at least extra protection for their various rights.

The Migration Purchase

American constitutionalists extended the protections that the authority of migration provided for civil rights when they supplemented the doctrine of migration with the well-established English constitutional principle of "rights purchased." The initial argument came from the imperial side of the debate when defenders of parliamentary supremacy claimed that the American colonies were in Great Britain's debt, as the mother country had financed their settlement, furnished their population, and protected them from foreign enemies. The right to have this debt repaid provided Great Britain with the constitutional authority both to tax the colonies and, for purposes of imperial supervision, to exercise some police power curtailing what otherwise would have been autonomous American civil rights. The colonies answered the taxation part of this argument by pleading what have been called settlement and commercial contracts,[36] contending that the constitution provided methods of paying London other than by submission to parliamentary rule. To defend their claim to rights, they also recited the facts of migration, most particularly the theme that the migration was a purchase by which they had resecured or reenforced title to the rights they already possessed.

The constitutional doctrine was that American civil and religious rights had been secured by purchase. In an extreme statement of the theory, the people of Gloucester, Massachusetts, reasoned that the travails of migration alone, without conferring benefits on Great Britain, was sufficient to prove the purchase and provide adequate authority for colonial rights. "The first settlers of this country," they voted, "left their native land and came into this, when a wild and uncultivated wilderness, inhabited by no human creatures except Savages, and suffered extreme hardships, risqued their lives and spent their fortunes, to obtain and secure their civil and ecclesiastical liberties and privileges."[37]

The factual dispute was not complicated. Imperialists maintained that the settlement of North America had been costly to England in lost population, protection expended, and many expensive services rendered, most particularly financial aid. That settlement debt gave Great Britain, in the 1760s, a claim on the colonies, including the constitutional authority to order and enforce repayment. The American patriot answer was that no colonies except Georgia and Nova Scotia had received any aid, whether monetary or military, at the time of settlement. New York had been obtained from the Dutch in exchange for Surinam, and those three instances, Americans said, were the only financial claims Great Britain had on the colonies, except for assistance in war and protection at sea for their trade, two items the colonists paid for by permitting Parliament to regulate trade under what has been called the commercial contract.[38] "Nor have these colonies since [the conquest of New York] been any expence to the crown, either for support of their governments, or inhabitants," Connecticut's Moses Mather contended in a frequently repeated argument. "And the Americans have had no enemies but what were equally the enemies of Great-Britain; nor been engaged in any war, but what the nation was equally engaged in, except the wars with the Indians; which they carried on and maintained themselves."[39]

It must be emphasized that what may look like a constitutional argument about historical data and their interpretation was not concerned with history at all. The dispute was about law. It is quite possible that the question of fact might easily have been resolved had it not been for the conclusion of law that it supported. To sustain the conclusion that they sought to establish, the disputants assumed or prejudged the facts—or "history"—and there could never have been agreement about the history, even in the few arguments when the history was pertinent. After all, resolution of the facts would have been of no importance except for the constitutional principle each side sought to establish as law.

An example comes from Joseph Warren's 1775 Boston Massacre oration:

> The crown of England looked with indifference on the contest; our ancestors were left alone to combat with the natives. Nor is there any reason to believe, that it ever was intended by the one party, or expected by the other, that the *grantor* should defend and maintain the *grantees* in the peaceable possession of the lands named in the patents. And it appears plainly, from the history of those times, that neither the prince, nor the people of England, thought themselves much interested in the matter. They had not then any idea of a thousandth part of those advantages which they since *have*, and we are most heartily willing they should *still continue* to reap from us.[40]

Warren's argument would have made little sense had London not been claiming that it was owed a settlement debt. Why did he bother claiming that the mother country gave the colonies no protection, and why did he admit that Great Britain was entitled to reap the unanticipated "advantages" from the commercial contract? These questions would have had no point had Warren been explaining the history of Massachusetts Bay rather than arguing forensic history, that is, arguing "facts" supporting the migration purchase of rights.[41]

There is no need to go further into the factual dispute. It is the legal conclusion that interests us. From the historical record, as they interpreted it, American colonials drew two constitutional conclusions. The first was that the colonies owed Great Britain nothing "for any defence or protection from the first planting the country to this moment, but on the contrary, a balance is due to us from our exertions in the general cause." The second was articulated by the town meeting of Wallingford, Connecticut, during the Stamp Act crisis. "It appears from the ancient records and other memorials of incontestable validity," Wallingford voted, "that our ancestors with a great sum purchased said township: at their only expence, planted, with great peril possessed and defended the same." Or, in a more elaborate form, the claim was to a purchase that became an inheritable property. That claim was asserted eight years later in the Suffolk Resolves: "Whereas this, then savage and uncultivated desert, was purchased by the valor and blood of those, our venerable progenitors, who bequeathed to us the dear bought inheritance, who consigned it to our care and protection; the most sacred obligations are upon us to transmit the glorious purchase, unfettered by power, unclogged with shackles, to our innocent and beloved offspring."[42]

One more point must be stressed, one that has to be made only because so many writers on the pre-Revolutionary era have assumed that most American arguments were original with the colonists. Few were, and that fact is certainly true for the legal concept of purchased rights. It came straight out of British constitutional thought. Ever since the days of Lord Coke, if not earlier, the English talked and wrote of purchasing rights and liberties. A 1648 declaration of the County of Dorset asserted that "our Liberties" were the "purchase of our ancestors' blood," and in 1768 a pamphleteer called upon his fellow British subjects to defend "their liberties, which their fore-fathers purchased with seas of blood."[43]

Eighteenth-century constitutional theory also imposed duties on those to whom rights by purchase had descended. Every literate person knew that collectively and individually Britons had the duty to transmit such rights to their posterity, to preserve them for the generations yet unborn, and to defend them against those who would weaken or destroy them. William Pitt, the Earl of Chatham, referred to this duty when he told the House of Lords, in 1774, "that the principal towns in *America* are learned and polite, and understand the constitution of the empire as well as the noble Lords who are in office, and consequently, they will have a watchful eye over their liberties, to prevent the least encroachment on their hereditary rights." Three months later, a majority of North Carolina's Convention concluded that it was time for Americans to shoulder that duty, urging the Continental Congress "to take such measures as they may deem prudent to effect the purpose of describing with certainty the rights of *Americans;* repairing the breaches made in those rights, and for guarding them for the future."[44]

The duty to preserve, defend, and bequeath rights was entailed on the possessors of rights not only by the tenure of ownership but by having received rights, including those of purchase, through inheritance. In part, it was a debt, a matter of honoring and repaying the forebears who had suffered and bequeathed the legacy of rights. "Should we, or any succeeding age, despise our *liberty,* so dearly bought, what do we, but trample upon our fathers' dust, and disturb the ashes of our godly ancestors, who purchased this land for us at so great expense?" Amos Adams asked in preaching the 1768 Thanksgiving sermon at Roxbury, Massachusetts. The North Carolina Convention, six years later, thought the duty was not just to transmit, but, if possible, to improve, and thereby not to disgrace the heritage of those to whom so much was owed: "It is the duty, and will be the endeavour of us as *British Americans,* to transmit this happy Constitution to our posterity in a state, if possible, better than we found it; and that to suffer it to undergo a change which may impair that invaluable blessing, would be to disgrace those ancestors, who, at the expense of their blood, purchased those privileges which their degenerate posterity are too weak or too wicked to maintain inviolate." The duty, most importantly, could be rationalized or made even stronger by tying it to the migration purchase. People "should keep a jealous eye" on their rights, Charles Chauncy asserted in the Massachusetts election sermon of 1747, "and think no cost too much to be expended, for the defence and security of them: Especially, if they were the purchase of wise and pious ancestors, who submitted to difficulties, endured hardships, spent their estates, and ventured their lives, that they might transmit them as an inheritance to their posterity."[45]

The duty owed to ancestors to preserve gifts they had bequeathed was a concept that colonial constitutionalists shared with their fellow constitutionalists in Great Britain. In 1768, a London pamphleteer commenting on the Wilkes controversy urged his readers "to shew themselves Britons, and to stand up in defence of their birthright; their liberties, which their fore-fathers purchased with seas of blood, to entail upon their posterity."[46]

Both Chauncy and the British pamphleteer described a similar assumed fact: that after purchasing these rights, their ancestors had entailed those rights on their descendants.

That vesting of rights gave rise to a second explanation why there was a duty to defend rights, for with the transmission of rights from previous generations came the duty to transmit them to future ones. "Our Rights are our own to keep but not to relinquish," the Whig divine Samuel Johnson observed in 1694, for "we are but Tenants for Life; and as they were transmitted to us by our Forefathers oftentimes sealed with their Blood, so we ought to leave them, Dry at least, to our Posterity."[47] The concept was expressed in a variety of ways in both America and Great Britain.

In New Jersey, people in Essex County spoke of "the [incalculable] privileges of Englishmen [that] have not only been handed down to us, but committed to our Care & improvement, as well for our own, as the felicity of our remotest posterity." Farther south, Richard Henry Lee urged Virginians "to hand down to your children, the liberty given you by your fathers." Across the Atlantic, John Shebbeare had told Britons to "deliver the Constitution to your Sons as you received it from your Fathers," and the author of the *Guide to Rights* argued that as "our great and generous Forefathers" took care to secure "every Man in the quiet Possession of his Rights, Liberties and Properties; I think it incumbent on us, who are their Successors, to be very watchful over so precious a Jewel, and to take Care that so glorious an Inheritance may descend whole, and intire to our Posterity."[48] Even William Blackstone had written that the British had the duty of protecting and transmitting to their descendants rights purchased by their ancestors. "The protection of the LIBERTY of BRITAIN," he wrote in the best summary of the doctrine, "is a duty which they owe to themselves, who enjoy it; to their ancestors, who transmitted it down; and to their posterity, who will claim at their hands this the best birthright, and the noblest inheritance of mankind."[49]

The Rights of Englishmen

Throughout the colonial period, American constitutionalists insisted, consistently and from various vantage points, that their rights were English rights. When the ailing James Otis retired to the country on the advice of his physician, the people of Boston, assembled in their town meeting, voted him thanks "for his undaunted Exertions in the Common Cause of the Colonies, from the Beginning of the present glorious Struggle for the Rights of the British Constitution." To use the word "British" rather than

"English" in the phrase, "Rights of the British Constitution," was unusual but not ambiguous. The Stamp Act Congress, in its petition to the king, a document that Otis helped to draft, had spoken of "securing the inherent Rights and Liberties of your Subjects here, upon the Principles of the *English* Constitution." Although one might object that there was in 1765 no such thing as an English constitution, this claim could not be misunderstood. What was sought was both English and British: English rights under the then current British constitution. Quite often colonial leaders professed to be defending American rights, as when the Stamp Act Congress asserted "the most Essential Rights and Liberties of the Colonists," and when the people of Lebanon, Connecticut, wrote of "the rights of America." Although the language was less precise than we would like, the meaning was clear. Colonial writers might speak of American rights, but they were thinking of English rights guaranteed to Americans by the British constitution.[50]

Not surprisingly, then, from the beginning of the imperial crisis to its end, colonists defended their rights, not as American, but as English rights. The first official list of claimed rights, drafted during the earliest period of the Revolutionary controversy, was Patrick Henry's resolves, adopted by Virginia's House of Burgesses in May 1765. Passed in response to the Stamp Act, they were limited to threats posed to rights by that act, yet they presaged all the claims that the American side would later make. Henry asserted three rights. The first was the English right to equality, in this case, equality between the American and European subjects of George III. The colonists, the Virginia resolves insisted, were entitled to "all the Liberties, Privileges, Franchises, and Immunities, that have at any time been held, enjoyed, and possessed, by the people of *Great Britain*"; that is, "all Liberties, Privileges, and Immunities of Denizens and natural Subjects, to all Intents and Purposes, as if they had been abiding and born within the Realm of *England*." The second English right asserted was the one most directly imperiled by the Stamp Act, the English right to be taxed by representation and only by representation. The third, closely related to the second, was the English right to government by consent: "the inestimable Right of being governed by such Laws, respecting their internal Polity and Taxation, as are derived from their own Consent."[51]

Much the same language would be advanced months later, this time in New York. The New York Assembly, too, enunciated the basic constitutional principles upon which colonial constitutionalists would make their final stand when it resolved that Americans "owe Obedience to all

Acts of Parliament not inconsistent with the essential Rights and Liberties of *Englishmen,* and are intitled to the same Rights and Liberties which his Majesty's *English* Subjects both within and without the Realm have ever enjoyed."[52] In the numerous declarations and petitions to follow, the same constitutional theory would continue to shape fundamental American constitutional claims.

Compare these early statements to the Declaration of Rights, promulgated by the Continental Congress nine years later, when all American grievances had been identified and colonial constitutionalists were becoming apprehensive that parliamentary denial of some of their rights might cause civil war. Although the Declaration was the most comprehensive statement of claimed colonial privileges made during the eighteenth century, it continued to rest its arguments principally on the English rights of the colonists. In contrast to Henry's Resolves, which were concerned with the single grievance of internal taxation without consent, the later Declaration listed all the rights Americans were claiming, with only a few omissions such as the right to have judges serving at good behavior rather than at the Crown's pleasure. Nine significant rights were asserted.

The first, a major legacy of English constitutional history, traceable to the earliest origins of the common law, was the right to life, liberty, and property. The colonists "are entitled to life, liberty and property: and they have never ceded to any sovereign power whatever, a right to dispose of either without their consent." The second right was equality, stated in terms of the migration contract. The first English settlers, on migrating to North America, had carried all English privileges with them, and they and their descendants continued to possess them to the extent that "their local and other circumstances enable them to exercise and enjoy." This was both a claim to a right—the right to equality—and an assertion to a source or authority for having rights: equality with the people of the mother country. Another example of a source of rights stated by the Continental Congress as a right was a resolution claiming that "these, his Majesty's colonies, are likewise entitled to all the immunities and privileges granted and confirmed them by [British] royal charters, and secured them by their several codes of provincial laws." Third was the English right of representation. It was, as usual, coupled with a denial that Americans were represented in the British parliament. Rather, as the Delaware Convention had explained two months earlier, "the only lawful Representatives of the freemen in the several Colonies are persons they elect to serve as Members of the General Assembly thereof." From that principle of British constitutionalism, it followed that it was "the just right and privilege of the said freemen to be governed by laws made by their General Assembly in the article of Taxation and internal police."[53]

The fourth, fifth, and sixth rights claimed were "the common law of England" (which meant the constitutional law of England, not necessarily of Great Britain), the "inestimable privilege" of trial by jury (the main institutional bulwark of English common law), and "such of the English statutes, as existed at the time" of colonization. Many Americans thought of jury trial not merely as a right to defense against a criminal indictment, but as the guarantee that rights would be preserved. As the Connecticut House of Representatives expressed it, the people had a right "not to be disseized of their liberties or free customs, sentenced or condemned, but by lawful judgment of their peers."[54]

The seventh right claimed was the English right of petition, and the eighth was to be free of standing armies "without the consent of the legislature of that colony in which the army is kept." Two auxiliary rights, attached to the last, were claimed in the Declaration of Independence, when George III was indicted for affecting "to render the military independent of and superior to the civil power" and for conspiring to quarter "large bodies of armed troops among us." And Congress's last asserted right was broadly concerned with free government. Free government, according to then current British constitutional theory, was balanced government, under which the branches of the legislature were mutually independent.

Guarding the American right to English rights was a central objective of the colonial side in the imperial debate until its close in 1776. Clearly, among the most important to eighteenth-century British and their North American fellow subjects was the civil and criminal jury. For them the right to trial by jury was the most essential element of their understanding of how restrained government functioned. Juries were expected to check official power, ensuring that government was not arbitrary or, at least, was less arbitrary. Trial without jury, Maryland legislators explained during the Stamp Act crisis, "renders the Subject insecure in his Liberty and Property." The Earl of Chatham told the House of Lords that the jury was the bulwark of an Englishman's "personal security and property"; the New York Assembly agreed that the jury was "essential to the Safety" of the "Lives, Liberty, and Property" of British subjects, and Virginia's House of Burgesses asserted that it was "the surest Support of Property."[55] Juries secured the rights to property by providing determiners of facts who (1) were disinterested and not associated with the Crown, and (2) shared with the litigant a community interest in the security of all property.

Their presence alone precluded secret trials and furnished the citizenry with a shield against venal jurists, purchased testimony, dependent officials, and partial judgments.[56]

A still more significant British right which juries guarded, even more priceless than the right to property, was liberty and its enjoyment. Eighteenth-century literature lauding British liberty was filled with pages explaining how citizens and dissenting groups of people could utilize the right to trial by jury to preserve their liberty.[57] One needs only read the political platitudes bandied about during the era of the American Revolution to discover the close association between the right to jury trial and the existence of liberty in the minds of people living in the various common-law jurisdictions. To London's Common Council, jury trial was "that sacred Bulwark of *British* Liberty," and to a New York grand jury it was "the very foundation of *British* liberty." It was "the grand Bulwark of LIBERTY" to the Maryland House of Representatives, and "that inestimable privilege and characteristic of English liberty" to the Massachusetts General Court.[58] On both sides of the Atlantic, any deprivation of trial by jury was decried as diminishing liberty.

A special American affection for juries arose from the colonial worry about English common lawyers, appointed by London to preside over colonial courts, who, it was feared, had a greater attachment to imperial rule than to impartial justice. It was a matter of intra-empire balance, of preserving the autonomy of the periphery from the strength of the center, not unrelated in constitutional practice to the check that seventeenth-century common law had fastened on prerogative courts. The judge might be sent out from the mother country to promote the interests of the empire, but if the judge was unable to function without a jury of the neighborhood, imperial legislative and judicial mandates might have to be tempered to meet a local constitutional consensus. For that reason, New England, where most judges had always been native sons, not placemen, felt particularly menaced when it became known that violations of the Stamp Act were to be prosecuted in vice-admiralty—that is, not at common law—and before a Crown-appointed judge sitting without a jury. Taking away the ancient right of being judged only by one's peers, the voters of Boston protested, "deprives us of the most essential Rights of *Britons,* and greatly weakens the best security of our Lives, Liberties and Estates; which may hereafter be at the Disposal of Judges who may be Strangers to us, and perhaps malicious, mercenary, corrupt and oppressive."[59] This was a loss of equality North American British colonists could not accept.

The Equality of British Peoples

"The excise has been lately extended in this country," Richard Hussey, barrister and bencher of the Middle Temple, was quoted as telling his colleagues in the House of Commons, but he believed that "no Minister would dare to propose to take away the trial by jury in all cases relating to the revenue. We should be shocked at this proposal here; why should the honest Americans be more submissive?" For us in the twenty-first century, Hussey appears to be talking politics, and he was, but any Americans listening to his speech would have said he was also talking constitutional law. He stated a constitutional right, the right to equality, a right of special interest as it was one in which American constitutional theory diverged from that of the mother country. The divergence was not in the definition of the right, but in emphasis.[60]

The concept of equality was expanding in North American jurisprudence, largely in reaction to the imperial relationship, and was emerging as a right utilized to protect other rights. Consider, for example, its use by "about 1200 Freemen and Freeholders of New York City," who argued that to be deprived of the right to trial by jury meant they were not treated equally with other British subjects. "Without these Bulwarks our Fellow Subjects in England would not think themselves either safe or free; nor can we see any Reason why American Subjects should not set an equal Value upon these Privileges, which are equally essential to both."[61]

Of course, the same complaint could be directed against vice-admiralty jurisdiction. Voters of Boston were disturbed to find in Parliament's statute reforming the vice-admiralty:

"... that all Penalties and Forfeitures which shall be incurred in Great Britain, shall be prosecuted Sued for and recovered, in any of his Majesty's Courts of Record in Westminster, or in the Court of Exchequer in Scotland respectively." Here is a Contrast that stares us in the Face! A partial distinction that is made between the Subjects in *Great Britain* and the Subjects in America! the Parliament in one Section guarding the People of the Realm and securing to them the benefit of a tryal by Jury and the Law of the Land, and by the next Session [*sic*] depriving Americans of the same important Rights.[62]

The grievance was twofold: Americans were denied a British constitutional right, and were not treated equally. "We are unhappily distinguished from our fellow subjects in Britain," the government of Rhode Island complained.[63] "Why are not His Majesty's good Subjects in *Great Britain* thus treated?" the voters of Cambridge, Massachusetts, asked. "Why must we in *America* . . . be thus discriminated?"[64]

Inequality was proven by facts, and American apprehensions that they were being treated unequally were disputed by facts. The imperial side pointed out that in Great Britain stamp duties and most excises were prosecuted by the government without juries; indeed, most revenue matters were tried in the mother country without juries.[65] Unlike so many other disputes of facts, this contention of fact drew little argument from American constitutional writers. They thought it largely irrelevant, because they argued that both the right to trial by jury and the right to equality were, according to other facts, violated. The right to trial by jury was no less a constitutional right because it was denied in some other parts of the empire. And although in Great Britain the government prosecuted some tax questions without juries, generally they were tried before justices of the peace or other common-law judges by common-law procedures, and not in civil (i.e., according to Roman) law, the law of the vice-admiralty court—the jurisdiction in which the imperial government prosecuted laws such as the White Pines Act and where it had planned to enforce the Stamp Act. The denial of common law in these cases made Americans unequal with their fellow subjects and was per se a denial of their right to equality.

The concept of equality was stated in two ways during the eighteenth century. One was to speak of equality not as a constitutional right, but as a source of rights. Because all British people were equal, they shared equality in rights, making the rights of one the rights of all. If the English, Scots, or Irish claimed a particular privilege, the principle of equality gave a claim of equal validity to Carolinians, New Yorkers, and Jamaicans. The other way of stating equality was as a constitutional right itself. Most often, the right of equality was asserted to secure a right already possessed by the British on the grounds that Americans had a right to equality, or, to state the principle most strictly, a right to an equality of rights.

John Dickinson's legal principles remained consistent through the Revolutionary controversy. "If," he wrote at the beginning of the controversy, "the Colonies are equally intitled to Happiness with the Inhabitants of Great-Britain, and Freedom is essential to Happiness, they are equally intitled to Freedom." It was a central thesis of Dickinson's constitutional jurisprudence that "the inhabitants of these colonies are entitled to the same rights and liberties WITHIN these colonies that the subjects born in *England* are entitled to WITHIN that realm."[66] Focus attention on these two statements by Dickinson. In them he mentioned two different aspects of the equality principle. In the second quotation, he asserted that the Americans were entitled to the same rights as those possessed by the British. That was the right to equality, the right Lord Shelburne had in mind when saying that during his tenure as secretary of state in charge of colonial affairs, his practice toward the Americans had been "to hold them as countrymen, fellow-subjects, and Englishmen."[67]

In his first statement, Dickinson was also concerned with equality, but his emphasis concentrated on another aspect. The right he claimed was freedom—happiness through freedom—and equality was the source of that right. It was because the colonists were equal with their fellow subjects that they could claim freedom. The distinction between the right to equality and equality as an authority for rights is blurry and was not made explicitly by Americans, but it was made implicitly frequently enough to merit attention in a study on rights at the time of the national Founding.

As the right to equality was frequently claimed by Americans during the constitutional debate with Great Britain, so the claim to equality in rights was repeated over and over during the decade and a half before the Battle of Lexington. The right to equality was more than a civil right; it was also a source of rights. Americans were equal to the British, and therefore, the Pennsylvania Convention resolved, they "are entitled to the same rights and liberties within these colonies that the subjects born in England are entitled to within that realm."[68] The constitutional justification was explained by the Massachusetts House of Representatives. "All the free subjects of any kingdom," the House told the Earl of Shelburne, "are entitled equally to all the rights of the constitution; for it appears unnatural and unreasonable to affirm, that local, or other circumstances, can justly deprive any part of the subjects of the same prince, of the full enjoyment of the rights of that constitution, upon which the government itself is formed."[69]

The constitutional criterion for making equality an authority for rights was much the same as the criterion for the right to equality itself. "The benefit of the constitution, and of the laws," Samuel Cooke explained in 1770, "must extend to every branch, and each individual in society, of whatever degree; that every man may enjoy his property, and pursue his honest course of life with security." Cooke was unusual in speaking of individuals. Generally, the emphasis was not on persons but on imperial corporate subdivisions. "Since the constitution of the State, as it ought to be, is fixed," the Massachusetts House told the colonial secretary, "it is humbly presumed that the subjects in every part of the Empire, however remote, have an equitable claim to all the advantages of it." This is another argument that deserves close attention, for it holds the answer for what most eighteenth-century authors meant by the concept of equality.[70]

We must avoid defining the values of the American past by the values of the American present, something easily done when dealing with the word "equality." We find colonial political and constitutional writers using the word, and it looks, sounds, and seems to be defined much like today's word "equality." But when eighteenth-century British spoke of equality, were they speaking of equality of individuals? Of course there were references to personal equality—not to social leveling or to property redistribution, but to peoples being legally equal. However, we must ask how they were equal, and when we examine the definitions behind the rhetoric, one conclusion becomes inescapable: the eighteenth-century meaning of equality of individuals was isonomic. Persons were entitled, as Rhode Island's governor Stephen Hopkins said, to "the advantage of just and equal laws," or, as Edmund Burke phrased it, "to equal rights, but to equal rights to unequal things."[71] The role of equality as an authority for rights in the eighteenth century, therefore, is best approached from the imperial perspective. That perspective finds the meaning of eighteenth-century constitutional equality not so much an equality of individuals as an equality of peoples. As a collective people, a separate and distinct division of the British Empire, colonials insisted on equality with the peoples of Britain and, to some extent, with the Protestants of Ireland. The town meeting of Providence stated the American goals. "We are willing, and even desirous, of a Continuance of Connection between the Colonies and Britain, if it may be had upon Terms in any Measure equal."[72]

Colonial constitutionalists did not argue that all individuals, as individuals, were equal. What they claimed was that the American people were equal to the British people. To make a claim to possession of the right to representation on grounds of equality, for example, the probative fact was that the British people possessed that right. It was immaterial that in some colonial assemblies certain people were not represented or that in other assemblies representation was unequal. This is an aspect of the American constitutional argument easily misinterpreted. It was not a probative fact in the imperial controversy that there were groups within the colonies demanding equality as a local American right: the Baptists who wanted an equality of taxation with the Congregationalists, and the Anglicans who pleaded their right to a North American bishopric on the grounds that the Moravians and the Quebec Catholics had bishops. For the Americans to demand equality with the British yet ignore requests for equality in the colonies was not constitutional hypocrisy. "The question," Governor Hopkins explained, "is not whether all colonies, as compared one with another, enjoy equal liberty, but whether all enjoy as much freedom as the inhabitants of the mother state."[73] The equality issue as it was debated during the imperial controversy did not concern local American rights. It concerned American equality, that is, Americans collectively enjoying the same rights that the British possessed as a people.

David Griffith, rector of Shelburne Parish, Virginia, came as close as anyone during the pre-Revolutionary debates to stating clearly the importance of the right to equality between peoples in different divisions of the British Empire. He also explained—as we look forward a few months to a far more famous description of equality in the Declaration of Independence—why separate peoples within the empire were entitled to equality with one another:

> The colonists . . . contend that their fellow subjects in Britain are but their equals: That the power ordained of God; that the share of power that exists in the people, is, equally, the privilege of every individual subject: They insist that a Briton cannot boast a single blessing from the constitution, but what an American is, equally, entitled to: They say the claim of the commons of Britain is an innovation; that is unnatural, unjust and oppressive; and destructive of that equal justice and liberty which, by the constitution, was meant to be secured to all.

Americans, Griffith concluded, were "contending with their equals, only; [that is,] with those who are ordained to have no greater share of power than themselves."[74]

Customary Use and Possession

Although language can occasionally be found from eighteenth-century arguments explaining rights as grants from the sovereign,[75] we usually cannot tell whether these statements reflected serious legal theory or were written without fully considering their constitutional implications. Even if serious statements of law, they reflected a minority view. The dominant legal doctrine went back at least to Sir Edward Coke and the first Stuarts. James I tried to establish the contrary principle when he told the Commons that its rights "grow from precedents which shews rather a toleration than inheritance." His son, Charles I, had to retreat, however, acknowledging that Parliament's liberties "are not of grace, but of right."[76] Repetition of that theme over the following decades gave substance to what would evolve as constitutional legal theory, a theory reflected in the way that Magna Carta was generally viewed. Every authority stressed that Magna Carta had not been a grant of rights newly recognized by the Crown.

Rather it had been a summary of ancient common-law privileges, "recognitions," as Lord Chancellor Somers explained, "of what we have reserved to ourselves in the original institution of our government, and of what had always appertained unto us by common law and immemorial customs."[77]

When the Earl of Chatham, defending the right of the County of Middlesex to elect John Wilkes to the House of Commons, told the House of Lords that rights were "as old as the constitution itself; the liberties of the people in the original distribution of government, being the first provided for," he was stating a thesis of constitutional law, not a lesson from history.[78] The point bears repeating. Arguments such as the one by Chatham were not contentions for law based on the proven facts of historical scholarship, but rather they sought to project current constitutional principles onto a presumed past. It might be more descriptive, although not quite accurate, to think that we are considering a legal fiction. It was believed that rights were immemorial; those existing today have existed from a time before there were kings to grant them, and the only evidence to prove immemoriality was that they exist today. Yet immemoriality was not a trivial allegation: it was the best, the strongest proof of constitutionality.[79] "Whatever are the Rights of Man *in this Age,* were their Rights *in every Age;* for, Rights are independent of *Power,*" one of Robert Walpole's newspapers had explained on behalf of an administration that is generally thought to have traced rights back no further than the Glorious Revolution. "The People have *originally all Right in themselves:* They *receive* none from *Governors;* but Governors *receive* all from them."[80] It was insignificant that the thesis could not be proven historically. What mattered was that it was a defensible statement of what the writer wanted to be current law.

Ironically, the very acts of kings in seeming to grant rights—as in Magna Carta, the Petition of Right, the Bill of Rights—strengthened the legal theory, for in law, when a right that previously existed in less definite precision is defined, it is added to, and one attribute added to it is a reinforced presumption of immemoriality. "The object of the Bill of Rights was to assert those parts of the Laws and Constitution which had been violated in act, or of which doubts were entertained," John Brand explained at the relatively late date of 1796. "Those liberties, when they were fully and completely regained, were then as securely ours as law, in the turbulent state of society which then obtained, could render them, and the explicit acknowledgment of some pre-existing laws and their principles cannot be considered as even a change of them; it cannot amount to a new-modelling a Constitution."[81] This theory of jurisprudence was law; it was not history;

it was as easily supported by historical hypothesis as it was by pseudohistory. "Had King WILLIAM," Richard Price conjectured about the Prince of Orange, "instead of coming over by invitation to deliver us, invaded us; and, at the head of an army, offered us the BILL OF RIGHTS, we should, perhaps, have spurned at it; and considered LIBERTY itself as no better than SLAVERY, when enjoyed as a boon from an insolent conqueror."[82]

When Americans stated the authority for claiming rights, they almost always did so in the alternative, that is, in constitutional alternatives, as for example in the Connecticut resolutions of June 1774. The colonists, Connecticut's Assembly resolved, claimed "the rights, liberties and immunities of free-born Englishmen, to which they were justly intitled by the law of nature, by the royal grant and charter of his late Majesty King Charles the Second, and by long and uninterrupted possession."[83] It is indicative of how our legal assumptions and constitutional words have changed since the eighteenth century that most lawyers today would dismiss the last-mentioned source of rights as the least important. Yet of those cited—natural law, royal grant, charter, and possession—the last was the strongest claim in eighteenth-century law, at least if "uninterrupted possession" meant not just prescription but also ownership and custom. Certainly in the eighteenth century, as Arthur Lee demonstrated, long possession was a stronger claim than a charter.[84] The legal fact could be stated in various ways: "uninterrupted possession," "uninterrupted Practice and Usage," "venerable by long Usage," "constant usage."[85] But the evidence proving the right and the authority for the right were found in usage and custom. It was not a political boast but a statement of constitutional law to say that rights had been "sanctified by long usage, a uniformity of principle and practice for ages past."[86] The theory was not only that *long Possession* gives a Title in Law, or at least enforces it . . . so the *publick Rights of Mankind* acquire Strength by *long Prescription*,"[87] but also, as explained by Oxford's Vinerian Professor of Law, that immemorial usage was "evidence of common acquiescence and consent."[88]

To say that rights were known by usage was to say they were established by the conventions of civil society—conventions comprising both the practice of the rulers and acceptance by the ruled. For Americans, these conventions were proven by evidence from the English, British, and colonial constitutional past. To learn the law, both the ways of rulers and the expectations of the ruled, one had only to study the century and a half of colonial home rule. Again note: the appeal was to law, not history. Custom was changeless time, a view of the past in which civil rights existed in a timeless infinity, a frozen history without origins, without transmission, and without change, an unmeasurable duration during which there were no manifestations of sovereign will except for the implied consent of habitual acquiescence.

It was from custom—from receiving its authority from custom—that the eighteenth-century concept of rights obtained much of the theoretical base making it so different from today's notions of personal rights. The old, customary theory of rights was confining when compared to the theory that would emerge in both British and American constitutional law during the nineteenth century. Rights in the eighteenth century were thought of as restraints on arbitrary government rather than as liberating individuals. The offspring of a static legality that encased government in a timeless, changeless constitution, the eighteenth-century concept of rights was torn between the ideal of freeing human subjectivity and the reality of confining human subjectivity within the restrictive mores of a customary society.

Rights and Nature

The search for the authority for rights does not stop with learning that the colonists believed themselves inheritors of an original contract, of rights derived from emigration and consequent sacrifice, of English civil rights enjoying equality with other British peoples, and of long-followed precedent. Beneath lay another source—nature—that James Otis described as the "origin" and "author" of rights. John Dickinson too claimed that rights "are created in us by the decrees of Providence."[89] Yet we must be careful, for earlier generations of historians have made far too much of the law of nature. To realize that nature was one authority for the validity of rights is quite different from saying that nature defined rights, determined which rights were enjoyed by British subjects, or provided for the enforcement of rights. The chief utility of nature as a source of rights was to give civil rights an authority independent of human creation. "Kings or parliaments could not *give* the *rights essential to happiness*," Dickinson explained. "We claim them from a higher source—from the King of kings, and Lord of all the earth. . . . They are born with us; exist with us; and cannot be taken from us by any human power, without taking our lives."[90]

Another, less frequently utilized aspect of natural-law authority for rights was that no higher authority existed. It was supposedly the highest source, creating rights not only beyond the reach of positive law, but also beyond positive law. "Resolved," some North Carolina freeholders voted in 1774, "that those absolute rights we are entitled to as men, by the immutable Laws of Nature, are antecedent to all social and relative duties whatsoever." Nature was also cited as the authority for particular rights such as the right to be taxed only by consent of representation, and for certain all-embracing rights, such as that to "liberty." Even Alexander Hamilton, as a youthful college student, in an uncharacteristically extreme argument, succumbed to the great ease of attributing liberty—and therefore, rights—to the authority of nature.[91]

Elected legislative bodies, most particularly in New England, were also prone to cite nature as an authority for the right to rights. "The natural Rights of the Colonists" were the same as those of "all Mankind," the Massachusetts House boasted three years before the Revolutionary controversy even began. "The principal of those rights is to be 'free from any superior power on Earth, and not to be under the Will or Legislative Authority of man, but to have only the Law of Nature for his Rule.'" Although statements such as this have had much made of them by twentieth-century constitutional historians, they were much less significant than has been commonly believed. The rhetoric was memorable, but the constitutional principle was fantasized and was void of any practical legal application.[92]

There are several theories to explain why nature was a constitutional authority establishing the right to rights. One was God. John Selden labeled the law of nature the "law of God" or "God and Nature," with or without revelation.[93] A second was the universal assumption of the perfect freedom and the extensive rights people would possess if living in the state of nature, as some believed people had in prehistoric times, before governments were formed. Closely related to that assumption was the legal theory of natural rights, which were those rights belonging to humans as humans, rights to which an individual is entitled from his God-given nature and which were deduced from the great plan of nature. A final explanation was reason. Natural law was not only reasonable, it was reason, law "founded in Natural Reason."[94] Three other attributes, often mentioned as part of natural law, were also generally described as giving authority to natural rights. They were that natural law, and therefore natural rights, were universal, immutable, and inalienable.[95]

Not to be overlooked is that few eighteenth-century rights came within any of these natural-law meanings. Certainly they were not universal. Almost no one living in other nations possessed the right of representation, to taxation by consent, to a jury of their peers, to judges serving at tenure of good behavior, or even to the right of petition. Yet it was common practice for eighteenth-century political theorists to claim that such British constitutional rights were "natural." In truth, few British civil rights fit any of the various eighteenth-century definitions of natural law. The possession of property may have existed in the state of nature, but certainly no one believed that true of security of property. It is likely that there was only one right that everyone agreed was "natural," the right to self-defense.

It cannot be denied, though, that natural law was an important eighteenth-century legal and constitutional concept. Lawyers as well as constitutionalists boasted of natural rights and even cherished them. But if one reads carefully what was written, it is evident that with the exception of the right to self-defense, natural rights turn out to be broad generalities, not specifics that could be legally enforced. Robert Hall seems to have been as specific as any eighteenth-century political theorist, yet he did not get any more concrete than asserting that it "can scarcely be doubted" that "there are *natural rights*." Indeed, he stated, "every man must have a natural right to use his limbs in what manner he pleases, that is not injurious to another. In like manner he must have a right to worship God after the mode he thinks acceptable; or in other words, he ought not to be compelled to consult any thing but his own conscience. These are a specimen of those rights which may properly be called *natural*."[96] Hall's "rights" were not actualities, but the shared platitudes of the educated that could neither serve as standards for controlling government conduct nor be applied to enforce legal rights.

Yet Hall's claims are no less precise than what every other eighteenth-century exponent of natural rights produced when compiling a list of working specifics. Even the very careful William Paley, in his influential treatise on moral and political philosophy, was no more helpful. He was absolutely confident that natural rights existed—"Natural rights are such as belong to a man, although there subsisted in the world no civil government whatever"—yet when enumerating them he provided no definitions that could have guided a court in protecting them. "*Natural rights* are a man's right to his life, limbs, and liberty; his right to the produce of his personal labour, to the use, in common with others, of air, light, water. If a thousand different persons, from a thousand different corners of the world, were cast together upon a desert island, they would from the first, be every one entitled to these rights."[97]

It is especially revealing that during the American Revolutionary controversy, few imperialists bothered to dispute colonial claims to natural rights. One conclusion may be that the concept of natural rights had such a hold on eighteenth-century legal thought that everyone accepted that they existed and that the colonists not only possessed them, but possessed a right to them. An opposite conclusion is that everyone appreciated that natural rights were so nebulous that there was no reason to quarrel about them.

There were, however, some imperial officials and ministerial writers who questioned colonial claims to the authority of nature and to natural rights. Anthony Bacon, a member of Parliament and a former Maryland storekeeper, made good eighteenth-century sense and raised sound constitutional doctrine when he pointed out that natural rights "have no meaning; for men are born members of society, and consequently have no rights, but such as are given by the laws of that society to which they belong. To suppose any thing else, is to suppose them out of society, in a state of nature." John Lind was a ministerial pamphleteer who believed that the colonists' claim to inherent rights was based on natural, not British constitutional, law. "The terms of *natural* and *inherent* rights . . . are to my understanding, perfectly unintelligible," he wrote. "The *Citizen* is to look for his *rights* in the laws of his country." Bacon's and Lind's arguments both made use of widely accepted views of rights, both natural and positive.[98]

Keep in mind that we are considering only the extent to which natural law provided an authority for civil rights. Three points need to be understood: (1) that natural law was almost always cited as an alternative authority for rights; (2) that, in the context of rights, natural law was equated with British constitutional and positive law and with English common law; and (3) that natural rights based on the authority of nature alone, and not also said to have a more positive authority, were rarely argued during the years leading up to independence. Indeed, there was little support among eighteenth-century legal theorists for the proposition that nature could serve as an authority for converting natural rights into positive rights. And, in fact, if one forsakes the history books and goes back to the arguments of the colonists as they made them, it is undeniable that the American colonists, in the vast majority of cases, were claiming positive constitutional rights, not abstract natural rights.

In some political pamphlets and anonymous newspaper articles, however, claims were made to rights on the authority of nature alone. Such claims were not found in official colonial petitions, resolutions, or declarations. Rather, just as claims to natural law were stated in the alternative to claims to constitutional and charter laws, so claims to natural rights were stated as alternative or extra authority. For example, the Lyme, Connecticut, town meeting in 1766 claimed that the colonists possessed a natural right to civil rights, that is, "an inviolable Right by the God of Nature," but "as well as [by] the English Constitution, (and is unalienable even by ourselves) to those Principles and Immunities which by the Execution of the Stamp Act we shall be forever stript and deprived." The authority cited for this right to rights is nature, true enough, but it is added to that of the British constitution. And the authority of nature is an alternative authority, as it is in almost all Revolutionary-era resolutions passed by representative bodies. When nature is cited as an authority, it is always cited along with the authority of the common law, prescription, grant, purchase, contract, custom, or, more broadly, the British constitution. Even in the Massachusetts Resolves of 1765, containing arguably the strongest statement supporting the authority of natural law made by any colonial assembly, the claim is to constitutional rights with nature cited as an alternative authority for those rights.[99]

On every important occasion when American Revolutionaries gathered to claim rights or state grievances about their deprivation, nature was rejected as the sole authority. The only exceptions were the Boston declaration of November 20, 1772, and the Preamble of the Declaration of Independence—just the Preamble, the rhetorical, decorative flourish, and not the indictment or substantive part of the Declaration listing the rights violated, none of which are natural rights. Natural law was not even the authority for claiming the right to independence. British violations of the constitution were the principal justification for this claim. We should not be surprised. The English-speaking peoples of the eighteenth century believed in the existence of natural law and made claims about natural rights, but they realized that there were practical considerations preventing the ideal from being transformed into positive reality.

The Evidence of Colonial Charters

Commentators crediting colonial charters, whether royal or proprietary, as authority for American rights were even fewer than those crediting nature. After all, to claim the charters as the authority for their rights would have been the same as admitting that civil rights were granted rather than inherent. For that reason, it is doubtful whether charters were ever seriously claimed as a prominent authority for rights. Rather, charters were valued primarily as evidence of rights, not as grants originating or even guaranteeing rights. A charter was evidence of the terms of the original contract.

The constitutional theory that a charter was a contract provided Americans with stronger arguments defending civil rights than would have been the case had the charter been interpreted as a unilateral grant from the Crown. The charter that Massachusetts Bay received from William and

Mary, the colony's executive council told Governor Thomas Hutchinson, "contained certain Rights and Privileges granted to this People as an inheritance." Any infraction of those rights "would be unjustifiable and in Violation of the mutual Compact." From this constitutional perspective, in addition to all the other authority for American civil rights, there was also what the Connecticut town of Pomfret called the "solemn Charter Compact." Seen in terms of a contractual theory, the authority followed from the fact that the charter had been negotiated on such a high level of the government, for such inestimable consideration, which had been paid beyond anything that the original contractors could have imagined, "that it ought to be kept Sacred and Inviolated by each Party and . . . cannot in any Respect be varied or altered by one Party only, without a most Criminal Breach of Faith."[100]

The argument that charters should be honored because they were executed contracts of the most solemn nature was as far as Americans went in contending that charters provided constitutional support for their rights. It is true that sermons and pamphlets written by private individuals speaking only for themselves contain claims or suggestions that charters were an authority for rights.[101] But official statements issued by colonial representative bodies made no such claims or suggestions. The most that official colonial papers claimed was that rights had been obtained "by several charters of compact from the crown" or that the British constitution "was covenanted to us in the charter of the province." More typical were assertions making charters authorities of lesser standing than the higher categories of "constitutional" or "fundamental," such as the Pennsylvania Assembly's equation of its charter with mere statute law when it said that the charter was "of the same Validity, with respect to the Rights thereby granted to the People here, as the Laws and Statutes of *England,* with regard to the Privileges derived under them, to the People of *England.*"[102]

The general understanding of the relationship between colonial charters and civil rights was summed up by two South Carolinians. The rights that Americans claimed equally with the British, William Henry Drayton pointed out, were "of infinitely more importance, than the Colony Charters from the Crown." And Christopher Gadsden warned that "confirmation of our essential and common rights as Englishmen may be pleaded from charters safely enough, but any further dependence upon them may be fatal."[103] In other words, because charters were so vulnerable, Gadsden contended that they should not be cited as the authority for rights; if a charter was the authority, then rights would be equally vulnerable.

There were good legal reasons for not making much of the authority of charters. One was the weakness of the contract argument. "The assertion that these charters are not charters, but *Pacta conventa,* is brim full of absurdity," Allan Ramsay pointed out. "The whole sovereign power could not, by the nature of things, enter into any indefeasible compact of that sort."[104] Ramsay's law may or may not have been valid in the seventeenth century when most charters had been granted, but it was constitutional law when he wrote in 1769, and it was the later law that would have decided the matter had the question been put to a judicial test. A second reason was that not every colony had a charter and, as well, the charters of Pennsylvania and Maryland had been granted to their proprietors, not to their original settlers. A third reason not to depend on a charter as an authority for rights was the risk of the counterargument that if rights came from a charter, they were limited by a charter. "The colonies have no rights independent of their charters; they can claim no greater than those give them," Martin Howard had argued during the Stamp Act crisis. "What were the privileges originally granted by the crown to the colonies?" John Lind asked. "A review of the charters is the only means of answering this question."[105] The fourth reason was the most important. Charters could not secure rights, for they were revocable. They were not organic acts, they were not immutable, but were instead vague grants of power to municipal corporations that the superior legislative power could alter, revise, amend, or revoke at any time. Subject to the sovereign's whim and caprice, charters offered little protection for civil rights.

Protecting Rights, and British and American Constitutionalism

If it were possible to establish constitutional security of rights within the separate divisions of the eighteenth-century British Empire, the solution was never taught to the leaders of the British government. In some respects that fact is unsurprising. After all, there was a universal given, held inviolable on both sides of the Atlantic, that the British constitution was not only the finest in the world, it was the best that ever could be devised by human ingenuity. There was a time when Americans of all political persuasions put their complete trust and faith in that constitutional tradition. Events that occurred between 1765 and 1774 taught most of them, at least legalists, that even the best unwritten constitution was not safely secure. In 1765, the administration of George Grenville forever altered American constitutional perceptions by imposing a constitutional innovation that American imperialists as well as American Whigs had supposed to be constitutionally impossible and that most Americans believed was unconstitutional: internal taxation for the purpose of raising revenue.

In 1773, the administration of Lord North passed the East India tea tax, an external duty that was intended to raise revenue, not to regulate trade. It was clear that American rights were far more precarious than they had appeared to be before 1765. The constitutional dilemma was parliamentary sovereignty; one British parliament, no matter how solemnly its honor was pledged, could not bind subsequent parliaments. One session of a parliament could not even bind another session of the same parliament. Passage of the Stamp Act had been the great constitutional awakening. If Parliament was now sovereign over law and the constitution, no rights were immutable.

The American dilemma that arose because rights were no longer secure against the whims of sovereignty was complicated by the fact that American constitutionalists and British constitutionalists adhered to two different constitutions. One constitution, defended by Americans, was the old English constitution of custom, prescription, and contract, with rights secured as property, both inherited and inherent, from the arbitrary capriciousness of government power. The other, that of the British ministry, was a newer British constitution, the emerging constitution of the nineteenth century—of sovereign command and of arbitrary parliamentary supremacy.

The tension between the two constitutions can be sensed by considering the thinking of James Duane at the First Continental Congress. "It is now," he told his fellow members of the committee on rights, "essential to place our Rights on a broader & firmer Basis to advance and adhere to some solid and Constitutional Principle which will preserve Us from future Violations—a principle clear & explicit and which is beyond the Reach of cunning, & the Arts of oppression." Duane was thinking of the constitution of parliamentary command when seeking security from "future Violations"; he was thinking, that is, of the new emerging constitution of parliamentary sovereignty. After all, he was saying that American rights had to be put "above the Reach" of parliamentary supremacy: that is, they had to be somehow entrenched in the constitution. Duane apparently spoke from a written text, for we have his own version of what he said. "I shall only observe that their Charters are to be esteemed Compacts," he told the committee, referring to the colonies, "that they have long been acquiesced in, and if exceptionable in their origin can not now be violated by oppression."[106] Again, he was thinking of the American future, of trying anew to entrench rights.

Like many other Americans, Duane had come to realize that the lawyers of the mother country now accepted the principle that rights could be violated by the sovereign power, though those lawyers would have preferred another verb, such as "modified," "redefined," or "changed." Like most other American colonial leaders of the 1770s, he stared sovereignty in the face and drew back in fear. "If the subject is bound by a Law to which he does not assent, either personally or by his Representative, he is no longer free but under an arbitrary power, which may oppress him or ruin him at pleasure."[107] Duane surely did not realize that he was describing two existing British constitutions, the old English constitution in which rights existed independent of sovereign will and pleasure, and the newer British constitution in which the "arbitrary power" of parliamentary command could, at its pleasure, "oppress" the subject by ignoring or changing or obliterating "rights." In 1774, Duane's concerns still had constitutional meaning in London almost as much as they did in Philadelphia. In this fact lay the dilemma making the security of rights almost a constitutional impossibility under the emerging British constitution of the nineteenth century.

None of the American statesmen, lawyers, or politicians searching for a solution devised a usable plan, perhaps because they thought of Parliament in the old ways, as the Parliament of customary, prescriptive, contractual authority, and not as the sovereign Parliament of arbitrary will and pleasure. Duane's solution made much more sense to the generation of 1774 than it would have to John Austin and the British of 1850. The first migrants had made a contract with the king, Duane contended, and they owned rights that could not be forfeited or altered by moving from one part of the empire to another: "The priviledges of Englishmen were inherent. They were their Birth right and of which they cou[l]d only be deprived by their free Consent. Every Institution legislative and Juridical, essential to the Exercise & Enjoyment of these Rights and priviledges in constitutional Security, were equally their Birth right and inalienable Inheritance. They cou[l]d not be with held but by lawless oppression and by lawless oppression only can they be *violated*."[108] Duane's solution can be understood only in the context of the two constitutions. He relied on the old customary, prescriptive, contractual constitution of inherited and inherent rights vesting at birth.

It was the Cokean constitution in which law was right, not a command, and because law, not Parliament, was sovereign, it made constitutional sense to speak of Parliament's command as "lawless oppression." The prevailing legal theory was still based on the concepts of the old English constitution: limited government, customary restraints, and inherited birthrights beyond the discretionary power of legislative authority. The constitutional bugbear that stirred most constitutional fears remained as it had been throughout English history: arbitrary power. British lawyers, statesmen, and politicians, reluctant to acknowledge in the late eighteenth century that arbitrary power was creeping into British constitutionalism, were unwilling to come to grips with the possibility that the threat of arbitrary authority lay at the center of the imperial crisis; they were unwilling to face directly the American constitutional challenge.

No plan could have been devised to secure rights sufficiently under the eighteenth-century British constitution to quiet the apprehensions of American constitutionalists. Constitutional thought in the English-speaking world was at a crossroads, and Americans were drawing forever apart from their fellow subjects of George III. The British were looking ahead to a constitution of parliamentary command, in which government was entrusted with arbitrary power and civil rights were grants from the sovereign. What remained was to make the sovereign truly representative of society, so that government, even though arbitrary, would be government by consent. The Americans were looking backward to government by the rule of law, to the constitution of John Hampden and the ship-money controversy, to a sovereign that did not grant rights but was limited by rights, a sovereign that was, like rights, created by "law," the guardian of civil rights. What remained was to devise an instrument to limit government when it threatened rights, so that rights, not government, would be secured.

Writing their own constitutions, Americans would demonstrate their concern with entrenching rights constitutionally beyond even the reach of themselves, the republican majority—beyond the power of the political process to abrogate. In 1777, they were not thinking yet of how to accomplish the feat. When experience, joined with experiment and necessity, demonstrated the utility of the independent judiciary guided by the concept of the rule of law, a new constitutional consensus would emerge. The instruments for protecting the entrenched rights—the independent judiciary and the rule of law—were inherited from the ideals of the old English constitution, but the new constitutional consensus was an American consensus; it would never be a British one.

Notes

The material for this essay is derived largely from Reid, *Constitutional History of the American Revolution: The Authority of Rights* (1986).

1. As will be explained below, it is necessary to distinguish between the English, Scots, and Irish constitutions.

2. Hopkins, *Rights,* 9; Willman, "Blackstone and the 'Theoretical Perfection' of English Law in the Reign of Charles II," 45.

3. [Erskine], *Reflections on the Rise, Progress, and Probable Consequences,* 40; [Towers], *Observations on Public Liberty,* 16; *Rights of the People Asserted,* 52.

4. Lee, "Preface to Williamsburg Edition," 290.

5. See Reid, *Authority of Rights,* 132–38.

6. Ibid., 139–45

7. Ibid., 124–31.

8. "Resolution of 21 June 1770," 12:85; and "Petition of 27 June 1770," 12:102.

9. [Fitch, Ingersoll, Silliman, and Wyllys], *Reasons Why British Colonies in America, Should not be Charged with Internal Taxes,* 26; "Non-Conformist," *Massachusetts Gazette and Boston News-Letter,* 30 March 1775, p. 2, col. 1.

10. *Fair Trial of Important Question,* 75; Johnson, *Notes Upon the Phoenix Edition,* 61; *Observations Upon Authority, Manner, and Circumstances,* 33; *Short Examination into Conduct of Lord M[ans]ff[iel]d,* 4–5.

11. "Petition of 24 June 1769," 6, 22; "East India Petition to the House of Commons," 14 Dec. 1772; "Speech of Lord Chatham," Lords Debates, 26 May 1774, 1:167; "Petition of Lord Mayor, *et al.,* to House of Commons," 28 May 1773.

12. For the constitutional theory of the original contract and the distinction between the original contract and the social contract (which played no role in the American Revolutionary dispute), see Reid, *Authority of Rights,* 132–58.

13. [Maseres], *Canadian Freeholder,* 453.

14. *Maryland Gazette,* 16 March 1748, p. 2, col. 1; Willoughby Bertie, Earl of Abingdon, *Town and Country Magazine* 9 (1977): 453.

15. The Hutchinson essay on colonial rights is contained in Morgan, "Thomas Hutchinson and the Stamp Act," 482; see also [Hopkins], *Grievances,* 8.

16. "Roxbury Declaration," 14 Dec. 1772; "Petition of Governor and Company of Rhode Island to King," 29 Nov. 1764, 415.

17. "Autobiography of Increase Mather," 327; [Moses Mather], *America's Appeal,* 25.

18. [Bancroft], *Remarks,* 7.

19. Samuel Adams to John Smith, 19 Dec. 1765, in *Writings of Samuel Adams,* 1:45; *Argument in Defence of the Exclusive Right,* 95.

20. Johnson, *Remarks on the New Essay of the Pen[n]sylvanian Farmer,* 42.

21. "Virginia Resolves," June 1765, 47.

22. "Resolves of Congress," 14 Oct. 1774, 97; "Georgia Resolves," January 1775, 1:156–57; Disney, *Trial of Daniel Disney, Esq.,* 15.

23. "New York Memorial to the House of Lords," 25 March 1775, 1316; "Address Read at a Meeting of Merchants to Consider Non-Importation," in Dickinson, *Writings,* 411.

24. [Hopkins], *Grievances,* 10.

25. Whatever Americans claimed under the migration principle, the Irish had also claimed. See Reid, *Authority of Rights,* 117.

26. [Littleton], *Groans of the Plantations*, 16.

27. *Campbell v. Hall*, 20:239, 265, 269 (King's Bench, 1774); *Lloyd v. Mansell*, 2:73, 74–75 (1722); Blackstone, *Commentaries*, 106–7.

28. Smith, "English Criminal Law in Early America," 12–22; [Phelps], *Rights of the Colonies*, 9.

29. Jefferson, *Summary View of the Rights of British North America*, in *Papers of Thomas Jefferson*, 1:121; Rossiter, *Political Thought of the American Revolution*, 110; Burlamaqui, *Principles of Politic Law*, 119.

30. [Wentworth], *Briefe and Perfect Relation*, 32; Wynne, *Eunomus*, 4:198.

31. Wynne, *Eunomus*, 2:198–99; Pownall, *Administration of British Colonies*, 2:22–23; Plowden, *Jura Anglorum*, 68.

32. "Declaration of Rights," 14 October 1774, 60; "Petition from Jamaica to King."

33. "Instructions of Massachusetts to Jasper Mauduit," 1762, in *Jasper Mauduit: Agent in London*, 40–41; "Petition of General Assembly to House of Lords," 16 April 1768, 1:57.

34. Smith, "English Criminal Law in Early America," 12.

35. Chalmers, *Opinions of Eminent Lawyers*, 206.

36. For the theory of the original colonial contracts, see Reid, *Authority of Rights*, 132–58.

37. "Declaration of 6 July 1775, 92–93"; "Gloucester Resolves," 27 March 1770.

38. For the British claim, see Allen, *American Crisis*, 16; and [Galloway], "A Letter Signed Americanus," 6–7. For the American answer, see Franklin, *Letters to the Press, 1758–1775*, 88; *South Carolina Gazette*, 27 July 1767, p. 1, col. 1; *Boston Post-Boy & Advertiser*, 22 June 1767, p. 1, col. 1; Bland, *Enquiry into the Rights*, 13–14; and *Necessity of Repealing American Stamp-Act*, 7–9.

39. [Moses Mather], *America's Appeal*, 53.

40. *Orations Delivered at the Request of the Inhabitants of the Town of Boston*, 60.

41. For the most important debate on the facts, forensic history, and law of the migration purchase, see Governor Thomas Hutchinson, "Address of January 1773"; James Bowdoin, "Answer of the Council," 25 January 1773; and John Adams, "Answer of the House of Representatives," 26 January 1773, all in *Briefs of the American Revolution*, 15–16, 34–36, and 54–58, respectively.

42. [Downer], *Discourse Delivered in Providence*, 9; "Wallingford Resolves," 13 Jan. 1766; "Suffolk Resolves," 9 Sept. 1774, 601.

43. "Dorset Declaration," 15 June 1648, 207; *Short Examination into Conduct of Lord M[ans]f[iel]d*, 4–5.

44. "From another Gentleman, London" (letter), 11 Feb. 1766, 1:168; "Speech of Lord Chatham," Lords Debates, 26 May 1774, 1:735; "Resolutions of the North Carolina Convention," 27 Aug. 1774, 1:735.

45. Adams, *Religious Liberty*, 50–51; "Resolutions of the North Carolina Convention," 27 Aug. 1774, 1:736; Chauncy, *Civil Magistrates must be just*, 32–33.

46. *Short Examination into Conduct of Lord M[ans]f[iel]d*, 4–5.

47. "Suffolk Resolves," 9 Sept. 1774, 602; Johnson, *Notes on Pastoral*, 61.

48. "Essex County Resolves," 11 June 1774, 1:17; "To the Good People of Virginia," 1776, 1:39; [Shebbeare], *Fifth Letter*, 52–53; [Somers], *Guide to Rights*, iii.

49. [Keld], *Essay on Polity of England*, 434 (quoting Blackstone).

50. "Boston Resolves," 8 May 1770; "The Petition of the King [of the Stamp Act Congress]," in Morgan, *Prologue*, 64; "Letter of Lebanon Town Meeting," 13 June 1768.

51. "Virginia Resolves," June 1765, 47–48.

52. "New York Resolves," 18 December 1765, 807.

53. "Declaration of Rights," 14 October 1774, 60–63; "Resolves of the Delaware Convention," 2 August 1774, 1:667–68.

54. "Resolves of Connecticut Representatives," May 1774, in 14:348.

55. "Maryland Resolves," 28 September 1765 [I], 53; "Speech of Lord Chatham," Lords Debates, 17 June 1774; "New York Resolves," 14 Dec. 1765; "Resolves of 21 June 1770, 12:85."

56. Hale, *Common Law*, 249–61; "Quebec Petition to the House of Commons," 12 November 1774, 257; Wright, *Speech of John Wright*, 2; Patten, *Discourse Delivered at Halifax*, 14.

57. [Care], *English Liberties*, 220–27; [Somers], *Guide to Rights*, 200–214.

58. "Remonstrance to the King," 15 December 1770, 25; "Address of Grand Jury to Justices," 10 February 1775, 1:1227; "Maryland Resolves," 28 September 1765 [II], 10; "Answer to Governor Francis Bernard," 3 November 1764, 18.

59. "Instructions of Boston," 18 Sept. 1765.

60. "Speech of Richard Hussey," Commons Debates, 3 February 1766, 22:271.

61. "Instructions of New York Freemen," 26 Nov. 1765.

62. "Instructions of 8 May 1769,", 287.

63. "Petition of Governor and Company of Rhode Island to King," 29 Nov. 1764, 6:415.

64. "Instructions of Cambridge," 14 Oct. 1765.

65. "Lords Second Protest," 17 March 1766; [Whately], *Considerations on Trade and Finances*, 227; [Hutchinson], *Strictures*, 23–24; [Dalrymple], *Address of People of Great-Britain*, 39.

66. "Address to Friends and Countrymen," in Dickinson, *Writings*, 202; [Dickinson], *New Essay [By the Pennsylvania Farmer]*, 4.

67. *Boston Evening-Post* (supplement), 23 July 1770, p. 2, col. 1.

68. "Pennsylvania Resolutions," 15 July 1774.

69. "Letter from Massachusetts House to Earl of Shelburne," 15 January 1768, 13.

70. Cooke, *Sermon Preached at Cambridge*, 15; "Letter from Massachusetts House to Henry Seymour Conway," 13 Feb. 1769.

71. Hopkins, *Rights*, 507; Kronenberger, *Kings and Desperate Men*, 41 (quoting Burke).

72. "Providence Resolves," 19 Jan. 1774.

73. Hopkins, *Rights*, 510.

74. Griffith, *Passive Obedience*, 21.

75. [Howard], *Letter from a Gentleman at Halifax*, 535; Lockwood, *Worth and Excellence*, 10.

76. Ashton, "Tradition and Innovation in the Great Rebellion," 211 (quoting James); "Speech of Lord Keeper to Both Houses" (speaking for Charles), 28 April 1628, 3:172.

77. "Meeting of 22 March 1782," 9 (quoting Somers), published by the Society for Constitutional Information. Two publications of the society, without title, imprint, or binding, are in the Huntington Library, San Marino, CA, numbered rare books 310802 and 305204.

78. "Speech of the Earl of Chatham," Lords Debates, 2 February 1770.

79. For a recent study of this theory of forensic history and its importance to the

development of political liberty, see Reid, *The Ancient Constitution and the Origins of Anglo-American Liberty*.

80. *Daily Gazetteer*, 5 July 1735, p. 1, col. 1.

81. Brand, *Defence of the Pamphlet*, 66, 62–63.

82. Price, *Additional Observations*, 86.

83. "Connecticut Resolutions," June 1774, 1:116.

84. [Lee], *Virginia Gazette* [Rind], 24 March 1768, p. 1, col. 1.

85. "Instructions of Providence," 13 Aug. 1765; *Journal of Votes and Proceedings of the General Assembly of the Colony of New-York,* 770; "Resolves of Virginia's Richmond County," 29 June 1774, 1:492; "Resolves of Caroline County," 14 July 1774, 1:540.

86. [Hawley], "To the Inhabitants," 13 April 1775, 2:332.

87. *Craftsman* 466 (7 June 1735): 2.

88. Wooddeson, *Elements of Jurisprudence*, 35–36.

89. [Otis], *Vindication of the British Colonies*, 563; "Address to the Committee of Correspondence in Barbados," 1766, in Dickinson, *Writings*, 262.

90. *To Barbados*, in Dickinson, *Writings*, 262.

91. "Granville County Resolutions," 15 August 1774, 9:1034; *Farmer Refuted: or A more impartial and comprehensive View of the Dispute between Great-Britain and the Colonies,* in *Papers of Alexander Hamilton*, 1:104.

92. Manduit, *Jasper Mauduit: Agent in London*, 39.

93. Selden, *Table Talk*, 69; [Sheridan], *Observations on the Doctrine*, 32.

94. [Drayton], *Letter From Freeman of South-Carolina*, 40; "Resolves of 13 September 1768," 261.

95. Wynne, *Eunomus*, 1:66; "Massachusetts Instructions to Agent," 1768; [Robinson-Morris], *Considerations*, 7–8; Blackstone, *Commentaries*, 1:54; Tucker, *Treatise concerning Civil Government*, 235–36; *Hibernia Magazine* 5 (1775): 790; *Gentleman's Magazine* 46 (1776): 450.

96. Hall, *Apology for Freedom of Press*, 49.

97. Paley, *Principles*, 75.

98. [Bacon], *Short Address*, 5; [Lind], *Remarks on the Principal Acts of the Thirteenth Parliament of Great Britain*, 1:191n.

99. "Lyme Resolves," January 1766; "Massachusetts Resolves," 29 October 1765, 56.

100. "Message from the Massachusetts Council to Governor Hutchinson," 5 April 1771; "Pomfret Resolves," 25 Dec. 1765,; "Hampshire County Resolves," 23 Sept. 1774.

101. Haven, *Sermon*, 45; [Otis], *Vindication of the British Colonies*, 558–59; [Dulany], *Considerations on Imposing Taxes*, 15–16.

102. "Resolves of Albermarle County," 26 July 1774, 1:119; "Suffolk Resolves," 9 Sept. 1774, 602; "Instructions to Richard Jackson," 22 September 1764, 183.

103. [Drayton], *Letter from Freeman of South-Carolina*, 30; *Writings of Christopher Gadsden*, xx.

104. [Ramsay], *Thoughts on the Origin and Nature of Government*, 53.

105. [Howard], *Letter from a Gentleman at Halifax*, 535; [Lind], *Thirteenth Parliament*, 86.

106. *Letters of Delegates to Congress*, 1:52.

107. Ibid.

108. Ibid., 53.

Bibliography

Adams, Amos. *Religious Liberty.* Boston: Kneeland & Adams for Leverett, 1768.

Adams, Samuel. *Writings of Samuel Adams.* Ed. Harry Alonzo Cushing. New York, 1904.

"Address of Grand Jury to Justices," 10 February 1775. In vol. 1 of *American Archives,* 4th ser., ed. Peter Force. Washington, DC, 1837–53.

Allen, William. *American Crisis: A Letter, Addressed by Permission to the Earl Gower, Lord President of the Council, &c. &c. &c. On the Present Alarming Disturbances in the Colonies.* London, 1774.

"Answer to Governor Francis Bernard," 3 November 1764. In *Speeches of the Governors of Massachusetts From 1765 to 1775; And the Answers of the House of Representatives to the Same; with their Resolutions and Addresses for that Period,* [by Alden Bradford]. Boston: Printed by Russell and Gardner, 1818.

Argument in Defence of the Exclusive Right Claimed by the Colonies to Tax Themselves. . . . London, 1774.

Ashton, Robert. "Tradition and Innovation in the Great Rebellion." In *Three British Revolutions: 1641, 1688, 1776,* ed. J. G. A. Pocock, 208–23. Princeton, NJ, 1980.

[Bacon, Anthony]. *Short Address to the Government, the Merchants, Manufacturers, and the Colonists in America, and the Sugar Islands, On the present State of Affairs.* London: Printed for G. Robinson, 1775.

[Bancroft, Edward]. *Remarks on the Review of the Controversy Between Great Britain and Her Colonies.* . . . London: Printed for T. Becket and P. A. DeHondt, 1769.

Bertie, Willoughby, Earl of Abingdon. *Town and Country Magazine* 9 (1777): 453.

Blackstone, William. *Commentaries on the Laws of England.* Vol. 1. Oxford: Printed at the Clarendon Press, 1765.

Bland, Richard. *Enquiry into the Rights of the British Colonies, Intended as an Answer to the Regulations lately made concerning the Colonies, and the Taxes imposed upon them considered.* Williamsburg, VA, 1766.

Boston Evening-Post (supplement), 23 July 1770, p. 2, col. 1.

Boston Post-Boy & Advertiser, 22 June 1767, p. 1, col. 1

"Boston Resolves," 8 May 1770. *Boston-Evening Post,* 14 May 1770, p. 3, col. 2.

Brand, John. *A Defence of the Pamphlet Ascribed to John Reeves, Esq. and Entitled, "Thoughts on the English Government."* London: Printed for T. N. Longman and J. Owen, 1796.

Briefs of the American Revolution: Constitutional Arguments between Thomas Hutchinson, Governor of Massachusetts Bay, and James Bowdoin for the Council and John Adams for the House of Representatives. Ed. John Phillip Reid. New York, 1981.

Burlamaqui, Jean Jacques. *Principles of Politic Law: Being a Sequel to the Principles of Natural Law.* London: Printed for J. Nourse, 1752.

Campbell v. Hall. In vol. 20 of *Complete Collection of State Trials and Proceedings for High Treason and Other Crimes and Misdemeanors From the Earliest Period to the Year 1783. With Notes and Illustrations,* comp. T. B. Howell. London, 1816–28.

[Care, Henry]. *English Liberties; or, the Free-Born Subject's Inheritance Etc.* 2d ed. London, 1691.

Chalmers, George. *Opinions of Eminent Lawyers on Various Points of English Jurisprudence, Chiefly Concerning the Colonies, Fisheries, and Commerce of Great Britain.* Burlington, VT: C. Goodrich and Co., 1858.

Chauncy, Charles. *Civil Magistrates must be just, ruling in the fear of God. A Sermon Preached before His Excellency William Shirley, Esq; . . . May 27, 1747. Being the Anniversary for the Election of His Majesty's Council for the said Province.* Boston, 1747.

"Connecticut Resolutions," June 1774. In vol. 1 of *Revolutionary Virginia: The Road to Independence,* comp. William J. Van Schreeven, ed. Robert J. Scribner. Charlottesville, VA, 1973.

Cooke, Samuel. *Sermon Preached at Cambridge, in the Audience of his Excellency Thomas Hutchinson, Esq.* Boston: Printed by Edes and Gill, 1770.

Craftsman 466 (7 June 1735): 2.

Daily Gazetteer, 5 July 1735, p. 1, col. 1.

[Dalrymple, John]. *Address of the People of Great-Britain to the Inhabitants in America.* London: Printed for T. Cadell, 1775.

"Declaration of Rights," 14 October 1774. In *Journal of the Proceedings of the Congress, held at Philadelphia, September 5, 1774.* Philadelphia, 1774.

"Declaration of 6 July 1775." In *Documents of American History,* ed. Henry Steele Commager. New York, 1934.

[Dickinson, John]. *A New Essay (by the Pennsylvania Farmer) on the Constitutional Power of Great-Britain Over the Colonies in America.* London: Printed for J. Almon, 1774.

———. *The Writings of John Dickinson,* ed. Paul Leicester Ford. Philadelphia, 1895.

Disney, Daniel. *The Trial of Daniel Disney, Esq.* Quebec: Printed by Brown and Gilmore, 1767.

"Dorset Declaration," 15 June 1648. In *Revolt of the Provinces: Conservatives and Radicals in the English Civil War, 1630–1650,* by J. S. Morrill. London, 1976.

[Downer, Silas]. *Discourse Delivered in Providence, in the Colony of Rhode-Island, upon the 25th Day of July 1768. At the Dedication of the Tree of Liberty, From the Summer House in the Tree.* Providence: Printed and sold by J. Waterman, 1768.

[Drayton, William Henry]. *Letter from Freeman of South-Carolina, to the Deputies of North-America, Assembled in the High Court of Congress at Philadelphia.* Charleston, 1774.

[Dulany, Daniel]. *Considerations on the Propriety of Imposing Taxes in the British Colonies, For the Purpose of raising a Revenue, by Act of Parliament.* 2d ed. Annapolis: J. Green, 1765.

"East India Petition to the House of Commons," 14 Dec. 1772. *Scots Magazine* 35 (1773): 122.

[Erskine, John]. *Reflections on the Rise, Progress, and Probable Consequences, of the Present Contentions with the Colonies. By a Freeholder.* Edinburgh, 1776.

"Essex County Resolves," 11 June 1774. In vol. 1 of *The Papers of William Livingston,* ed. Carl E. Prince. Trenton, NJ, 1979.

A Fair Trial of the Important Question, or the Rights of Election Asserted. London: J. Almon, 1769.

[Fitch, Thomas, Jared Ingersoll, Ebenezer Silliman, and George Wyllys]. *Reasons Why the British Colonies in America, Should not be Charged with Internal Taxes, by Authority of Parliament; Humbly offered, For Consideration. In Behalf of the Colony of Connecticut.* New Haven: B. Mecom, 1764.

Franklin, Benjamin. *Letters to the Press.* Ed. Verner W. Crane. Chapel Hill, NC, 1950.

"From another Gentleman, London" (letter), 11 Feb. 1766. In vol. 1 of *American Archives*, 4th ser., ed. Peter Force. Washington, DC, 1837–53.

Gadsden, Christopher. *Writings of Christopher Gadsden, 1746–1805.* Ed. Richard Walsh. Columbia, SC, 1966.

[Galloway, Joseph]. "A Letter Signed Americanus." *New York Gazette*, 15 Aug. 1765. Rept. in *Americanus Examined, and his Principles compared to those of the Approved Advocates for America, by a Pennsylvanian*, ed. Anonymous. Philadelphia, 1774.

Gentleman's Magazine 46 (1776): 450.

"Georgia Resolves," January 1775. In vol. 1 of *American Archives*, 4th ser., ed. Peter Force. Washington, DC, 1837–53.

"Gloucester Resolves," 27 March 1770. *Boston Evening Post*, 16 April 1770, p. 4, col. 1.

"Granville County Resolutions," 15 August 1774. In vol. 9 of *Colonial Records of North Carolina, Published under the Supervision of the Trustees of the Public Libraries*, ed. William L. Saunders. Raleigh, 1890.

Griffith, David. *Passive Obedience Considered: In a Sermon Preached at Williamsburg, December 31st, 1775.* Williamsburg: Printed by A. Purdie, [1776].

Hale, Sir Matthew. *History of the Common Law of England.* 2d ed., corrected. London: J. Walthoe and J. Walthoe Jr., 1716.

Hall, Robert. *Apology for the Freedom of the Press, and for General Liberty.* London: Printed for G. G. J. and J. Robinson, 1793.

Hamilton, Alexander. *The Papers of Alexander Hamilton*, ed. Harold C. Syrett et al. New York, 1961.

"Hampshire County Resolves," 23 Sept. 1774. *Massachusetts Gazette & Boston Post-Boy*, 10 Oct. 1774, p. 1, col. 1.

Haven, Jason. *Sermon Preached before His Excellency Sir Francis Bernard, Baronet, Governor: His Honor Thomas Hutchison, Esq.: Lieutenant-Governor, The Honorable His Majesty's Council, and the Honorable House of Representatives, of the Province of the Massachusetts-Bay in New-England.* Boston: Printed by Richard Draper, 1769.

[Hawley, Joseph]. "To the Inhabitants," 13 April 1775. In vol. 2 of *American Archives*, 4th ser., ed. Peter Force. Washington, DC, 1837–53.

Hibernia Magazine 5 (1775): 790.

[Hollis, Thomas]. *True Sentiments of America: Contained in a Collection of Letters Sent from the House of Representatives of the Province of Massachusetts Bay to Several Persons of High Ranks in this Kingdom.* London: Printed for J. Almon, 1768.

Hopkins, Stephen. *Rights of the Colonies Examined.* Providence: Printed by W. Goddard, 1765.

[————]. *Grievances of the American Colonies Candidly Examined.* London: Reprinted for J. Almon, 1766.

[Howard, Martin, Jr.]. *Letter from a Gentleman at Halifax.* 1765. In *Pamphlets of the American Revolution*, ed. Bernard Bailyn, 535. Cambridge, MA, 1965.

[Hutchinson, Governor Thomas]. *Strictures Upon the Declaration of Congress at Philadelphia; In a Letter to a Noble Lord, &c.* London, 1776.

"Instructions of 8 May 1769." In *Report of the Record Commissioners of the City of Boston, Containing the Boston Town Records, 1758 to 1769* (16th Report). Boston, 1881–1905.

"Instructions of Boston," 18 Sept. 1765. *Massachusetts Gazette and Boston New-Letter*, 19 Sept. 1765, p. 2, col. 1.

"Instructions of Cambridge," 14 Oct. 1765. *Boston Post-Boy & Advertiser*, 21 Oct. 1765, p. 2, col. 1.

"Instructions of New York Freemen," 26 Nov. 1765. *Boston Post-Boy & Advertiser*, 9 Dec. 1765, p. 2, col. 3.

"Instructions of Providence," 13 Aug. 1765. *Boston Evening-Post*, 19 Aug. 1765, p. 2, col. 2.

"Instructions to Richard Jackson," 22 September 1764. In *Letters and Papers of Benjamin Franklin and Richard Jackson, 1753–1785,* ed Carl Van Doren. Philadelphia, 1947.

Jefferson, Thomas. *Papers of Thomas Jefferson.* Ed. Julian Boyd. Vol. 1. Princeton, NJ, 1950.

Johnson, Samuel. *Notes Upon the Phoenix Edition of the Pastoral Letter.* Pt. 1. London: Printed for the author, 1694.

Johnson, Samuel. *Remarks on the New Essay of the Pen[n]sylvanian Farmer; and on the Resolves and Instructions Prefixed to that Essay. . . .* London: Printed for T. Becket, 1775.

Journal of the Proceedings of the Congress, held at Philadelphia, September 5, 1774. Philadelphia, 1774.

Journal of Votes and Proceedings of the General Assembly of the Colony of New-York. Begun the 8th Day of November, 1743; and Ended the 23d of December, 1765. Vol. 2. New York: Printed by H. Gaine, 1766.

Journals of Each Provincial Congress of Massachusetts in 1774 and 1775, and of the Committee of Safety, with an Appendix, Containing the Proceedings of the County Conventions—Narratives of the Events of the Nineteenth of April, 1775. Boston, 1838.

[Keld, Christopher]. *Essay on the Polity of England.* London, 1785.

Kronenberger, Louis. *Kings and Desperate Men: Life in Eighteenth-Century England.* St. Paul, MN, 1942.

[Lee, Arthur]. *Virginia Gazette* [Rind], 24 March 1768, p. 1, col. 1.

———. "Preface to Williamsburg Edition." In *Writings of John Dickinson: Political Writings, 1764–1774,* ed. Paul Leicester Ford, 290. Philadelphia, 1895.

"Letter 'From Another Gentleman, London,'" 11 Feb. 1766. *South-Carolina Gazette*, 16 June 1766, p. 2, col. 2.

"Letter from Massachusetts House to Earl of Shelburne," 15 Jan. 1768. In *True Sentiments of America: Contained in a Collection of Letters Sent from the House of Representatives of the Province of Massachusetts Bay to Several Persons of High Ranks in this Kingdom,* by [Thomas Hollis]. London: Printed for J. Almon, 1768.

"Letter from Massachusetts House to Henry Seymour Conway," 13 Feb. 1769. *Boston Post-Boy & Advertiser*, 28 March 1768, p. 2, col. 1.

"Letter of Lebanon Town Meeting." *South-Carolina Gazette*, 13 June 1768, p. 2, col. 2.

Letters of Delegates to Congress, 1774–1789. Ed. Paul H. Smith. Vol. 1. Washington, DC, 1976.

[Lind, John]. *Remarks on the Principal Acts of the Thirteenth Parliament of Great Britain: Vol. I Containing Remarks on the Acts Relating to the Colonies With a Plan of Reconciliation.* London: Printed for T. Payne, 1775.

[Littleton, Edward]. *Groans of the Plantations: or a True Account of their Grievous and Extreme Sufferings by the Heavy Impositions upon Sugar, and other Hardships. . . .* London: Printed by M. Clark, 1689.

Lloyd v. Mansell. In vol. 2 of *Reports of Cases Argued and Determined in the High Court of Chancery.* 5th ed. London, 1793.

Lockwood, James. *Worth and Excellence of Civil Freedom and Liberty Illustrated. . . .* New London, CT, 1759.

"Lords Second Protest," 17 March 1766. *Boston Evening-Post* (supplement), 16 June 1766, p. 1, col. 1.

"Lyme Resolves," January 1766. *Massachusetts Gazette* (supplement), 23 Jan. 1766, p. 2, col. 2.

Maryland Gazette, 16 March 1748, p. 2, col. 1.

"Maryland Resolves," 28 September 1765 [I]. In *Prologue to Revolution: Sources and Documents on the Stamp Act Crisis, 1764–1766*, ed. Edmund S. Morgan. Chapel Hill, NC, 1959.

"Maryland Resolves," 28 September 1765 [II]. In *Votes and Proceedings of the Lower House of Assembly of the Province of Maryland, September Session, 1765. Being the First Session of this Assembly.* Annapolis: Printed by Jonas Green, printer to the province, [1766].

[Maseres, Francis]. *Account of the Proceedings of the British, And other Protestant Inhabitants of the Province of Quebeck, In North America. In order to obtain An House of Assembly In that Province.* London: Sold by B. White, 1775.

[———]. *The Canadian Freeholder: In Two Dialogues Between an Englishman and a Frenchman, Settled in Canada.* Vol. 1. London, 1777.

"Massachusetts Instructions to Agent," 1768. *Scots Magazine* 30 (1768): 463–64.

"Massachusetts Resolves," 29 October 1765. In *Prologue to Revolution: Sources and Documents on the Stamp Act Crisis, 1764–1766*, ed. Edmund S. Morgan. Chapel Hill, NC, 1959.

Mather, Increase. "Autobiography of Increase Mather." Ed. M. G. Hall. *Proceedings of the American Antiquarian Society* 71 (1961): 327.

[Mather, Moses]. *America's Appeal to the Impartial World. . . .* Hartford: Printed by Ebenezer Watson, 1775.

Mauduit, Jasper. *Jasper Mauduit: Agent in London for the Province of the Massachusetts Bay, 1763–1765.* Boston, 1918.

"Message from the Massachusetts Council to Governor Hutchinson," 5 April 1771. *Boston Evening-Post*, 8 April 1771, p. 2, col. 1.

Morgan, Edmund S. "Thomas Hutchinson and the Stamp Act." *New England Quarterly* 21 (1948): 459–92.

The Necessity of Repealing the American Stamp-Act Demonstrated: Or, a Proof that Great-Britain must be injured by that Act. London: J. Almon, 1766.

"New York Memorial to the House of Lords," 25 March 1775. In vol. 1 of *American Archives*, 4th ser., ed. Peter Force. Washington, DC, 1837–53.

"New York Resolves," 14 Dec. 1765. *Boston Post Boy and Advertiser*, 6 Jan. 1766, p. 2, col. 1.

"New York Resolves," 18 Dec. 1765. In *Journal of Votes and Proceedings of the General Assembly of the Colony of New-York. Begun the 8th Day of November, 1743; and Ended the 23d of December, 1765*, vol. 2. New York: Printed by H. Gaine, 1766.

"Non-Conformist." *Massachusetts Gazette and Boston News-Letter*, 30 March 1775, p. 2, col. 1.

North Carolina (Colony). *Colonial Records of North Carolina, Published under the Supervision of the Trustees of the Public Libraries.* Ed. William L. Saunders. Vol. 9. Raleigh, 1890.

Observations Upon the Authority, Manner, and Circumstances of the Apprehension and Confinement of Mr. Wilkes. Addressed to Free-Born Englishmen. London: Printed for J. Williams. . . , 1763.

Orations Delivered at the Request of the Inhabitants of the Town of Boston, to Commemorate the Evening of the Fifth of March, 1770; When a Number of Citizens were Killed by a Party of British Troops, Quartered Among them, in a Time of Peace. Boston: Printed by Peter Edes, in State-Street, 1785.

[Otis, James]. *Vindication of the British Colonies, against the Aspersions of the Halifax Gentleman* [1765]. In *Pamphlets of the American Revolution*, ed. Bernard Bailyn, 554–79. Cambridge, MA, 1965.

Paley, William. *Principles of Moral and Political Philosophy*. London: Printed for R. Faulder, 1785.

Patten, William. *Discourse Delivered at Halifax in the County of Plymouth, July 24th 1766. . . .* Boston, 1766.

"Pennsylvania Resolutions," 15 July 1774. *Gentleman's Magazine* 44 (1774): 438.

"Petition from Jamaica to King." *Gentleman's Magazine* 45 (1775): 617n.

"Petition of 24 June 1769." In *Addresses, Remonstrances, and Petitions; Commencing the 24th of June 1769, Presented to the King and Parliament, from the Court of Common Council, and the Livery in Common Hall Assembled, with his Majesty's Answers*. London, [1778].

"Petition of 27 June 1770." In *Journals of the House of Burgesses of Virginia*, [vol. 12,] *1770–1772*, ed. John Pendleton Kennedy. Richmond, 1906.

"Petition of General Assembly to House of Lords," 16 April 1768. In vol. 1 of *Revolutionary Virginia: The Road to Independence*, comp. William J. Van Schreeven, ed. Robert J. Scribner. Charlottesville, VA, 1973.

"Petition of Governor and Company of Rhode Island to King," 29 Nov. 1764. In vol. 6 of *Records of the Colony of Rhode Island and Providence Plantations in New England*, ed. John R. Bartlett. Providence, RI, 1856.

"Petition of the Lord Mayor, *et al.*, to the House of Commons," 28 May 1773. *London Magazine* 43 (1774): 417.

[Phelps, Richard]. *The Rights of the Colonies and the Extent of the Legislative Authority of Great-Britain, Briefly Stated and Considered*. London: Printed for J. Nourse, 1769.

Plowden, Francis. *Jura Anglorum: The Rights of Englishmen*. Dublin: Printed by G. Bonham, 1792.

"Pomfret Resolves," 25 Dec. 1765. *Massachusetts Gazette and Boston News-Letter*, 9 Jan. 1766, p. 1, col. 2.

Pownall, Thomas. *Administration of the British Colonies*. 6th ed. London: Printed for J. Walter, 1777.

Price, Richard. *Additional Observations on the Nature and Value of Civil Liberty, and the War with America. . . .* 3d ed., 1776. In *Two Tracts on Civil Liberty, the War with America, and the Debts and Finances of the Kingdom: with a General Introduction and Supplement*. 1778. Rept. New York, 1972.

"Providence Resolves," 19 Jan. 1774. *Boston Evening-Post*, 31 Jan. 1774, p. 3, col. 1.

"Quebec Petition to the House of Commons," 12 November 1774. In *Account of the Proceedings of the British, And other Protestant Inhabitants of the Province of Quebeck, In North America. In order to obtain An House of Assembly In that Province*, [by Francis Maseres]. London: Sold by B. White, 1775.

[Ramsay, Allan]. *Thoughts on the Origin and Nature of Government Occasioned by the Late Disputes between Great Britain and her American Colonies*. London: Printed for T. Becket, 1769.

Reid, John Phillip. *Constitutional History of the American Revolution: The Authority of Rights.* Madison, WI, 1986.

————. *The Ancient Constitution and the Origins of Anglo-American Liberty.* DeKalb, IL, 2005.

"Remonstrance to the King," 15 December 1770. In *Addresses, Remonstrances, and Petitions of the Common Council to the King, On his Majesty's Accession to the Throne, and on various other Occasions, and his Answers . . . Agreed to between the 23d October, 1760 and the 12th October 1770.* London, [1770].

Report of the Record Commissioners of the City of Boston, Containing the Boston Town Records, 1758 to 1769. Vols. 1–10. Boston, 1881–1905.

"Resolution of 21 June 1770." In *Journals of the House of Burgesses of Virginia,* [vol. 12], *1770–1772,* ed. John Pendleton Kennedy. Richmond, 1906.

"Resolutions of the North Carolina Convention," 27 Aug. 1774. In vol. 1 of *American Archives,* 4th ser., ed. Peter Force. Washington, DC, 1837–53.

"Resolves of Albermarle County," 26 July 1774. In vol. 1 of *Revolutionary Virginia: The Road to Independence,* comp. William J. Van Schreeven, ed. Robert J. Scribner. Charlottesville, VA, 1973.

"Resolves of Caroline County," 14 July 1774. In vol. 1 of *American Archives,* 4th ser., ed. Peter Force. Washington, DC, 1837–53.

"Resolves of Congress," 14 Oct. 1774. In U.S. House, *Commemoration Ceremony in Honor of the Two Hundredth Anniversary of the First Continental Congress, in the United States House of Representatives, September 25, 1974.* 93d Cong., 2d sess., H. Doc. 93-413.

"Resolves of Connecticut Representatives," May 1774. In vol. 14 of *The Public Records of the Colony of Connecticut [1636–1776],* ed. Charles J. Hoadly. Hartford, CT, 1881–90.

"Resolves of the Delaware Convention," 2 August 1774. In vol. 1 of *American Archives,* 4th ser., ed. Peter Force. Washington, DC, 1837–53.

"Resolves of 13 September 1768." In *Report of the Record Commissioners of the City of Boston, Containing the Boston Town Records, 1758 to 1769* (18th Report). Boston, 1881–1905.

"Resolves of 21 June 1770." In *Journals of the House of Burgesses of Virginia,* [vol. 12], *1770–1772,* ed. John Pendleton Kennedy. Richmond, 1906.

"Resolves of Virginia's Richmond County," 29 June 1774. In vol. 1 of *American Archives,* 4th ser., ed. Peter Force. Washington, DC, 1837–53.

Rights of the People Asserted, and the Necessity of a More Equal Representative in Parliament Stated and Proved. Dublin, 1783.

[Robinson-Morris, Matthew, Second Baron Rokeby]. *Considerations on the Measures Carrying on with Respect to the British Colonies in North America.* 2d ed. London: Sold by R. Baldwin, [1774].

Rossiter, Clinton. *Political Thought of the American Revolution.* New York, 1963.

"Roxbury Declaration," 14 Dec. 1772. *Boston Evening-Post,* 21 Dec. 1772, p. 1, col. 2.

Selden, John. *Table Talk of John Selden.* Ed. Frederick Pollock. London, 1927.

[Shebbeare, John]. *Fifth Letter to the People of England, on the Subversion of the Constitution: And, The Necessity of its being restored.* 2d ed. London: Printed for J. Morgan, 1757.

[Sheridan, Charles Francis]. *Observations on the Doctrine laid down by Sir William Blackstone, Respecting the extent of the Power of the British Parliament, Particularly with relation to Ireland.* 2d ed. London, 1779.

Short Examination into the Conduct of Lord M[ans]f[iel]d, through the Affair of Mr. Wilkes. London, 1768.

Smith, Joseph H. "English Criminal Law in Early America." In *English Legal System: Carryover to the Colonies: Papers Read at the Clark Library Seminar, November 3, 1973.* Los Angeles, 1975.

[Somers, John Barton, Baron]. *A Guide to the Knowledge of the Rights and Privileges of Englishmen.* London: Printed for J. Scott, 1757.

"Speech of the Earl of Chatham," Lords Debates, 2 February 1770. *Parliamentary History* 16: 818.

"Speech of the Lord Chatham," Lords Debates, 26 May 1774. In vol. 1 of *American Archives,* 4th ser., ed. Peter Force. Washington, DC, 1837–53.

"Speech of Lord Chatham," Lords Debates, 17 June 1774. *Scots Magazine* 36 (1776).

"Speech of Lord Keeper to Both Houses" (speaking for Charles), 28 April 1628. In vol. 3 of *Complete Collection of State Trials and Proceedings for High Treason and Other Crimes and Misdemeanors From the Earliest Period to the Year 1783. With Notes and Illustrations,* comp. T. B. Howell. London, 1816–28.

"Speech of Richard Hussey," Commons Debates, 3 February 1766, reproduced in "Parliamentary Diaries of Nathaniel Ryder, 1764–7." In *Camden Miscellany XXIII,* ed. P. D. G. Thomas. Camden 4th ser., no. 7. London, 1969.

"Suffolk Resolves," 9 Sept. 1774. In *Journals of Each Provincial Congress of Massachusetts in 1774 and 1775, and of the Committee of Safety, with an Appendix, Containing the Proceedings of the County Conventions—Narratives of the Events of the Nineteenth of April, 1775.* Boston, 1838.

"To the Good People of Virginia," 1776. In vol. 1 of *Memoir of the Life of Richard Henry Lee, and His Correspondence with the Most Distinguished Men in America and Europe, Illustrative of their Characters, and of the Events of the American Revolution,* by Richard Henry Lee. Philadelphia, 1825.

[Towers, Joseph]. *Observations on Public Liberty, Patriotism, Ministerial Despotism, and National Grievances. . . .* London: Printed for J. Towers, 1769.

Tucker, Josiah. *Treatise Concerning Civil Government, In Three Parts.* London: T. Cadell, 1781.

U.S. House. *Commemoration Ceremony in Honor of the Two Hundredth Anniversary of the First Continental Congress, in the United States House of Representatives, September 25, 1974.* 93d Cong., 2d sess. H. Doc. 93-413.

Van Doren, Carl, ed. *Letters and Papers of Benjamin Franklin and Richard Jackson, 1753–1785.* Philadelphia, 1947.

Van Schreeven, William J., comp., and Robert J. Scribner, ed. *Revolutionary Virginia: The Road to Independence.* Vols. 1, 2. Charlottesville, VA, 1973, 1975.

"Virginia Resolves," June 1765. In *Prologue to Revolution: Sources and Documents on the Stamp Act Crisis, 1764–1766,* ed. Edmund S. Morgan. Chapel Hill, NC, 1959.

Votes and Proceedings of the Lower House of Assembly of the Province of Maryland, September Session, 1765. Annapolis, MD, n.d.

"Wallingford Resolves," 13 Jan. 1766. *Massachusetts Gazette and Boston News-Letter,* 6 Feb. 1766, p. 3, col. 1.

[Wentworth, Thomas]. *Briefe and Perfect Relation, of the Answeres and Replies of Thomas*

Earle of Strafford: To the Articles Exhibited against him, by the House of Commons on the thirteenth of April, An. Dom. 1641. London, 1647.

[Whately, Thomas]. *Considerations on the Trade and Finances of this Kingdom, and on the Measures of Administration, with Respect to those great National Objects since the Conclusion of the Peace.* 3d ed. London: Printed for J. Wilkie, 1769.

Willman, Robert. "Blackstone and the 'Theoretical Perfection' of English Law in the Reign of Charles II." *Historical Journal* 26 (1983): 39–70.

Wooddeson, Richard. *Elements of Jurisprudence, Treated of in the Preliminary Part of a Course of Lectures on the Law of England.* Dublin: J. Moore, 1792.

Wright, John. *The Speech of John Wright, Esq.; One of the Magistrates of Lancaster County, to the Court and Grand-Jury, on his Removal from the Commission of Peace at the Quarter-Sessions held at Lancaster for the said County in May 1741.* [Philadelphia, 1741].

Wynne, Edward. *Eunomus, or, Dialogues Concerning the Law and Constitution of England with an Essay on Dialogue.* 2nd ed. 2 vols. London, 1785.

Rights Natural and Civil in the Declaration of Independence

BARRY A. SHAIN

Since the early nineteenth century, the American Declaration of Independence has been at the center of numerous controversies.[1] Many of these have concerned its original meaning, its originality (or lack thereof), its eighteenth-century significance, and its lasting importance. My interest here is in exploring the rights language in the Preamble and how it was likely understood by most of its eighteenth-century authors and readers.[2] This task has been made more difficult because, as Thomas Jefferson recalled forty years after the fact, all of the Declaration's "designs and discussions, having been conducted by Congress with closed doors, and no member, as far as I know, having made notes of them, these [questions concerning the meaning and intent of the Declaration], which are the life and soul of history must for ever be unknown."[3] Indeed, no member of the Second Continental Congress who supported the Declaration's adoption commented in diaries or personal correspondence on his understanding of it. Nonetheless, this document has not wanted for interpreters of its authentic meaning. Certainly the most famous was Abraham Lincoln, who in 1857 characterized the Declaration in a manner that likely changed how it subsequently came to be viewed, and in the process transformed Americans' self-understanding. He did so not in isolation, but with the support of some and the opposition of others,[4] most importantly, his nemesis, Stephen Douglas.

Lincoln believed that "the authors of that notable instrument intended to include *all* men," and it is clear in his presentation that when he spoke of "all men" he meant that African Americans were to be included. Lincoln further explained, however, that equality for the Founders was not all-expansive, but was limited to "'certain inalienable rights, among which are life, liberty, and the pursuit of happiness.'" Thus, he restricted the Declaration's equality claim while holding that its individual rights were fully inalienable; that is, in the dominant moral theorizing of the eighteenth and nineteenth centuries, they were so closely linked to absolute duties to God and one's family and country that they could not be surrendered. As Lincoln's contemporary, A.T. Bledsoe, explained in 1856, following the well-accepted logic of the prominent mid-eighteenth-century Genevan natural-law and moral theorist, J.J. Burlamaqui, "an inalienable right is a right coupled with a duty; a duty with which no other obligation can interfere."[5] But far less expected was Lincoln's claim that "the assertion that 'all men are created equal' was of no practical use in effecting the separation from Great Britain; it was placed in the Declaration not for that, but for future use."[6]

Lincoln thus held that one of the central planks of the Declaration's Preamble—that all men are created equal—was meant to include and apply to the chattel slaves of African origin, "the property" of the delegates to the Continental Congress who wrote the document, and their constituents, and that it was intentionally placed there to act as an intellectual time bomb that would go off at some undisclosed point in the future. In opposition to Lincoln's view, the history of the Revolution suggests that the implicit and explicit claims for corporate and individual equality were not subversive depth charges, but were necessary elements of Americans' international brief for, and in defense of, its separation from Britain under the canons of natural and international law. As Charles McIlwain noted, the Declaration was "addressed to the world, not to Great Britain, and naturally the ground of such a protest will be one understood by a world that knows little of the British constitution and cares less: it will be based on the law of nature instead of the constitution of the British Empire."[7]

Lincoln made this claim while responding to what he took to be the partisan posturing of Stephen Douglas, who also had sought to make sense of the Declaration and its authors' intentions. In contrast to Lincoln, though, Douglas held that "no man can vindicate the character, motives, and conduct of the signers of the Declaration of Independence, except upon the hypothesis that they referred to the white race alone, and not to the African."[8] He pleaded that it could not have made sense for them to have argued otherwise.

Douglas would have been pleased to know that one of the Founders, a most prominent one at that, Edmund Randolph, in his manuscript history of Virginia, written in 1809–10, left us his thoughts on the subject and provided Douglas a measure of support. Looking back on the comparable natural-rights language in the June 12, 1776, Virginia Declaration of Rights that served as a template for the July Declaration of a few weeks later,[9] Randolph wrote: "The declaration in the first article in the bill of rights, that all men are by nature equally free and independent, was opposed by Robert Carter Nicholas, as being the forerunner of pretext or civil convulsion. It was answered, perhaps with too great an indifference to futurity, and not without inconsistency, that with arms in our hands, asserting the general rights of man, we ought not to be too nice and too much restricted in the delineation of them." But then he presciently added, as if looking forward to Lincoln's understanding, that "the slaves not being constituent members of our society could never pretend to any benefits from such a maxim."[10] Although he did not claim and may not have believed, as Douglas did, that the claim of equality, in nature, failed to encompass African slaves, Randolph was categorical in denying them inclusion in civil society, and thus civil rights, to say nothing of civil equality. And it is on this contested ground, between a long-held traditional distinction between natural and civil rights and a new emerging radical conflation of them,[11] that the debate concerning the Preamble is usefully and rightly situated.

Douglas may have been close to getting it substantially right when he held that, practically speaking and in contrast to Lincoln, "when they declared all men to have been created equal . . . they were speaking of British subjects on this continent being equal to British subjects born and residing in Great Britain; [declaring] that they were entitled to the same inalienable rights." According to Douglas, the claim of equality was not a secret teaching to take effect in the distant future, but an integral component in the indictment against George III that the Continental Congress brought before the international court of world opinion. For, as Douglas further explained, "the Declaration was adopted for the purpose of justifying the colonists in the eyes of the civilized world in withdrawing their allegiance from the British crown, and dissolving their connection with the mother country."[12] In opposition to Lincoln, Douglas argued that the equality claim was primarily corporate in intent, asserting the equality of British North Americans with those in the United Kingdom, and that the Declaration, in appealing to nature rather than a common superior, was using a logic readily understandable in international law.[13] Rather than a work in political philosophy introducing an as yet unaccepted novel doctrine of rights in which individual natural rights were equally inalienable out of and in civil society, the Declaration from this perspective was an international legal brief that invoked commonplace eighteenth-century British and Continental legal and moral standards.[14]

Lincoln argued that the central importance and thus the principal meaning of the Declaration lay in its future defense of individual human rights, not in its 1776 defense of Americans' corporate political rights. Indeed, he asked his nineteenth-century audience if they were "willing that the Declaration shall thus be frittered away . . . shorn of its vitality and practical value, and left without the germ or even the suggestion of the individual rights of man in it."[15] Lincoln's concern almost certainly was not with correct exegesis of a historical text, but rather with the normative power that the Declaration had and would increasingly come to possess.[16] Douglas, however, argued instead that the Declaration's central aim had been contemporaneous with political concerns of its day and that it had been written, not implausibly, to explain to the world the grounds for one people's political independence from another. Accordingly, its rhetorically brilliant elliptical exposition in the Preamble of the individual natural rights of life, liberty, and the pursuit of happiness was a syllogistic means toward a corporate end rather than, as Lincoln contended,[17] a radically individualistic one.

Reading the Declaration

The interpretations of Lincoln and Douglas appeal to different constructions of the document; each rests on different understandings of the claim to natural equality and, by close association, the linked rights of the Preamble. To evaluate the accuracy of their respective appeals, it is necessary to place the Preamble in context within its internationally focused ends and the personal lives of the delegates to the Continental Congress. Without constructing such an overarching framework within which to understand it, the artfully constructed meaning of the Preamble's rights claims is likely to be misunderstood. In particular, this is truest of those natural rights that the Declaration holds as inalienable. If such rights, like that of religious conscience, are understood to be equally inalienable in and out of society, it paints the Declaration in colors that are out of keeping with late eighteenth-century American political and social practices and dominant Anglo-American and Continental patterns of thought.

It is essential, then, to understand that well into the nineteenth century, full inalienability was generally reserved only for the rarest of rights, most particularly the individual right of religious conscience. As one speaker in the 1835 North Carolina constitutional convention noted, government could "restrict the rights of individuals for the good of the whole . . . [so that] all must surrender some of their natural rights on entering society," yet "the liberty of conscience is a natural right, inviolable, and inalienable. No man, by his engagement with society, can surrender it, or absolve himself from the obligation to exercise it freely and without restraint, in the discharge of his duty to his God."[18] Such an understanding of inalienability was not at variance with internationally accepted eighteenth-century standards. As Burlamaqui had written, inalienable rights in fact limit as well as protect individual freedom because they "have a natural connection with our duties, and are given to man only, as means to perform them. To renounce this sort of rights would, be therefore renouncing our duty, which is never allowed."[19] Inalienability of rights was intimately tied to the enormity of certain obligations or duties, and therefore few individual rights were understood to be inalienable and the same within and outside society.

Reading this document in a radically individualistic way that ignores the unique standing of the individual right of religious conscience is all the more difficult to accept when one considers that its authors were in the main highly educated men, many of them lawyers, trained to view language carefully.[20] It seems reasonable to begin by assuming that they would not sanction the use of words in the Preamble that readily defied a widely accepted eighteenth-century understanding that closely tied rights to duties. As another highly influential Genevan legal theorist,[21] Emmerich Vattel, wrote, "A right is nothing else but the power of doing what is morally possible, that is to say, what is good in itself and conformable to duty, [and thus] it is clear that right is derived from duty." The even more popular Burlamaqui had taught a decade earlier that "right therefore and obligation are, as logicians express it, *correlative* terms; one of these ideas necessarily supposes the other."[22] Yet it is exactly this kind of inattention to the linguistic norms of the eighteenth and even nineteenth centuries that seems to guide too many interpreters of the Preamble's rights claims.[23]

When such historical analysis is ignored, Lincoln's and Douglas's differing perspectives provide interested scholars with distinct normative frameworks within which to work.[24] More pointedly, they present contrasting visions of what was then (and, for many, continues to be) America's "true" or dominant political tradition. Lincoln, with little apparent concern for the historical meaning of concepts in the 1776 text, looked forward to America becoming a land that supports the inalienable civil rights of all men. This land of individualism he then projected backward into the eighteenth century. Douglas, however, began by looking backward to a communal people defending before the world their inalienable corporate right to majoritarian self-government and corporately defined, historically determined, and alienable individual civil rights. In a mirror image to Lincoln's projection backward, Douglas projected forward his view of

America's past. In short, both men were guilty of manipulating America's past and future in advancing their contrasting visions of the Declaration's essence. Many, possibly even most, contemporary Americans may well agree on which vision is the more appealing, but the historiography of students of the late eighteenth century should not be controlled by such normative preferences. American history need not possess the power to shape the future, but to maintain its own integrity it must avoid endorsing false but pleasing illusions.[25]

Often, though, interpreters of the Declaration's Preamble seem all too ready to follow Lincoln's brilliant lead rather than working to uncover the dominant eighteenth-century meaning(s) of the Preamble. For example, many authors have insisted that one need only attend to the thought of its principal draftsman,[26] Thomas Jefferson, and not to the intention of its numerous authors—"the representatives of the UNITED STATES OF AMERICA, in General Congress assembled"—who issued the Declaration "in the name, and by the authority of the good people of" the American states.[27] What the young but eloquent and often idiosyncratic Jefferson might have thought about rights must not be the primary issue, for the Declaration is a public document, and as James Madison later insisted, one must distinguish "the binding public intention of the state from the private opinions of any individual or group of individuals."[28] Jefferson should serve, then, as one of the most closely connected and insightful reporters of events associated with the drafting of the Declaration and, in addition, as a significant participant in the shaping of the underlying American political thinking of the period, but no more.[29]

Still more difficult to commend is the singular emphasis that some interpreters place on the thought of the seventeenth-century English philosopher John Locke, because of the close fit between the language of his *Second Treatise of Government* and that of the Preamble.[30] Without a demonstration that its authors understood the Preamble's language in the same way that some contemporary scholars believe Locke would have, an emphasis on Locke's still contested seventeenth-century view of such matters offers little to advance our comprehension of the late eighteenth-century meaning of the Declaration's Preamble.[31] Whatever Locke may have meant a century earlier,[32] it is the thought of the 1776 congressional delegates that matters most in understanding the Preamble's rights claims.

In short, privileging the views of Locke or those of Jefferson, mostly recorded after his long stay in France and in his old age,[33] is not especially helpful in uncovering the meaning of this congressional declaration. Freed from undue reliance on the thought of either Jefferson or Locke, scholars can focus instead on explicating the Declaration's natural-right claims in the context of America's international audience and its aspiration for recognition as a distinct people in international law; on the broadly held eighteenth-century understanding of the proper differences between natural and civil rights; and on widespread American social and political practices. Even then, given the artful ambiguity of the Preamble's language and the likelihood that different men with distinct political aspirations and normative commitments almost surely understood it differently, there is much to do.

The Declaration's International Aims and Audience

Jefferson and his colleagues claimed in the Declaration that their most important motivation for making the case for independence was "a decent respect to the opinions of mankind" that required "that they should declare the causes which impel them to the separation." They further stated that it had become "necessary for one people to dissolve political bands which have connected them with another, and to assume, among the powers of the earth, the separate and equal station to which the laws of nature and of nature's God entitle them." Here, Jefferson apparently followed Vattel,[34] who counseled that once "the political bonds between a sovereign and his people are broken, or at least suspended, they must be considered as two distinct parties, and since both are independent of all foreign authority, no one has the right to judge them . . . [so that] the two parties must be allowed to act as if possessed of equal right."[35] According to such internationally accepted thought, supportive delegates declared that they were a separate people and thus deserved to be awarded all the internationally recognized rights associated with being a free and independent nation. By their own admission, the Declaration was not principally written for internal American consumption, nor, accordingly, was it primarily concerned with municipal law and civil rights, but rather it was written for an international audience with an appropriate focus on international and natural law and rights. This was to be expected of a document intended primarily to persuade others in the international community of the propriety of the colonies' separation from Britain. A decade of arguing British constitutional law, while seeking to be accepted, like Scotland, as a dominion of the king, we must remember, had proven fruitless.[36]

Indeed, as copious ancillary materials demonstrate, it was the certain intent of Congress to shape world opinion when its members asked a committee of five to draft an appropriate declaration that would explain their actions to the world and facilitate the forging of necessary commercial, diplomatic, and military relations with European bankers and nations.[37] The soon-to-be-famous English radical, Thomas Paine, had urged as much in arguing that "were a manifesto to be published and dispatched to foreign Courts, setting forth the miseries we have endured, and . . . declaring at the same time, that not being able any longer to live happily or safely, under the cruel disposition of the British Court," such that we are forced to declare our independence, it "would produce more good effects to this Continent, than if a ship were freighted with petitions to Britain."[38] And a few months later, in mid-May 1776, a Virginia resolution directed Richard Henry Lee to propose that the Congress declare independence (as it did on July 2, 1776). More particularly, Lee was instructed to give "the assent of this Colony to such declarations, and to whatever measures may be thought proper and necessary by the Congress for forming foreign alliances."[39] Thus, one recent commentator feels confident in concluding that the Declaration, when issued, was above all else a "foreign-policy statement."[40] The Declaration did serve important domestic functions, in particular raising the stakes in negotiating a return to British sovereignty with a high-level British delegation on its way to New York.[41] But it was more a document in foreign affairs than one that addressed the domestic political situation or novel philosophical matters.[42]

In the best record we have of the congressional debate, Jefferson recalled that it centered on the need to facilitate foreign contacts and aid, and on selecting the most propitious time for declaring independence in order to meet this need. He wrote "that a declaration of Independence" was necessary because it "alone could render it consistent with European delicacy for European powers to treat with us, or even to receive an Ambassador from us."[43] The two most essential architects of American independence, Richard Henry Lee and Samuel Adams, agreed with Jefferson, the Revolution's most valued penman (once that role was ceded by its first possessor, John Dickinson).[44] Writing to Joseph Hawley on April 15, 1776, Adams argued that "no foreign Power can consistently yield Comfort to Rebels, or enter into any kind of Treaty with these Colonies till they declare themselves free and independent." As Stephen Lucas has pointed out, Adams thus stated his realization that "the crucial factor in opening the way for foreign aid was the act of declaring independence. . . . The Declaration reinforced the perception that the conflict was not a civil war." Similarly, Lee too knew the rules of international relations, in writing on June 2, 1776, that "it is not choice then but necessity that calls for independence as the only means by which foreign alliance can be obtained."[45]

Again, with these ends in mind, we must expect that the central rights claims of the Declaration would be couched in the rights language of international relations and (extra-conventional) law, that is, natural law and rights, rather than that of British common law and constitutionalism—the realm of municipal law and civil rights to which Americans had forcefully clung for over ten years.[46]

In the Declaration, the American perspective was to be described for its primary international and secondary domestic audiences in the "proper tone and spirit called for by the occasion."[47] But, as Perry Miller explained, with politically influential Europeans as its principal audience, it was "necessary for the official statement to be released in primarily 'political' terms—the social compact, inalienable rights, [and] the right of revolution," rather than in the Reformed Protestant language of sin, contrition, and sacrifice that the Congress regularly used in addressing "the ranks of militia and citizens."[48] The delegates wished to convince those in Britain still well disposed to them (who included some Whigs and most radicals) of the propriety and necessity of their separation,[49] and bankers, diplomats, and the political powers in France, Holland, and Spain of their resolve and sovereignty. It was necessary, therefore, that the language, using natural rather than civil rights, highlight the British violation of internationally accepted political norms and long-held contractual arrangements. And it is in the light of such intentions that the Declaration's rights discourse must be read if it is not to be anachronistically misunderstood.

Nevertheless, it is also true that Americans believed that if a government abused or failed to protect the civil rights legitimately held by a people, the rights for which men had theoretically sacrificed their natural liberty, a "majority of the community hath an indubitable, inalienable, and indefeasible right to reform, alter, or abolish it."[50] And Americans claimed that, as a people, they were in just such a revolutionary situation vis-à-vis the British government. British North Americans under their "original colonial contract" had exchanged natural rights to equality and absolute independence for the protected and limited civil rights of life, liberty, and the pursuit of happiness. The British monarch had failed to protect these rights, as outlined in the Declaration's remarkably traditional set of twenty-eight indictments issued against the king. Thus, according to an internationally accepted logic that began with natural equality between the peoples of the British Empire, the British monarchy had abrogated its explicit contract with the American people to provide protection in exchange for loyalty. This was the same act that many on both sides of the Atlantic believed the English king had committed previously in the seventeenth century during the English Civil War and then later in the Glorious Revolution.[51] Americans collectively could therefore justify to themselves and, more importantly, before the court of world opinion, their decision to withdraw their allegiance from the British king, both on historical English constitutional grounds and according to an emerging body of Vattelian international law that legitimated their separatist aspirations.[52]

Natural and Civil Rights

Still, a focus on the preeminently international aims of the Declaration leaves unclear the exact meaning and nature of the Preamble's rights claims. Does, for example, the Preamble assert that Americans possess individual rights that are morally preeminent before a legitimately constituted democratic majority, as our contemporary understanding would suggest? Or was it the case, instead, that the natural rights of life, liberty, and the pursuit of happiness were fully inalienable only under a limited number of circumstances that did little to determine the extent and power of matching civil rights?[53] Such questions can be answered with reasonable confidence, but only when the Declaration is read as part of an extended text.[54] Such an examination indicates that for most, though likely not all, delegates, the focus of the Preamble was on natural rather than civil rights, that the rights of life, liberty, and the pursuit of happiness were limited in their range of application, and that civil rights were by almost all accounts alienable and subordinate to the public's corporate needs and the people's fully inalienable rights.[55]

Such a reading is in keeping with the most common eighteenth-century understanding of natural and civil rights, in which men, upon entering society, surrendered their equality and almost all of their capacious natural rights for more limited, but more secure alienable civil rights. According to Vattel, civil rights result from each member yielding "certain of his rights to the general body," with the agreement "that there should be some authority capable of giving commands." Thus, for the natural-law theorist Burlamaqui, unlike natural rights, civil rights "are founded on the express or tacit permission, received from the sovereign or the law."[56] James Wilson, following Burlamaqui, described the related concepts of natural and civil liberty: "Civil liberty is nothing else but natural liberty, divested of that part which constituted the independence of individuals, by the authority, which it confers on sovereigns, attended with a right of insisting upon their making a good use of their authority."[57] The Reverend Moses Hemmenway similarly lectured in a 1784 election sermon that "though the *natural rights* of men may, in general, seem much alike, they being, in this respect, 'all FREE and EQUAL;' yet it is in different degrees that they are permitted to use them. According to the different civil constitutions which men are under, their *civil liberty* is larger, or more restricted."[58]

Civil rights (and closely related but distinct and less powerful privileges, liberties, and immunities), unlike natural rights, were protected by a polity within the limits set by historical precedent and public need, not the absolute, though inexact and unenforceable, standards of natural law. Even Jefferson accepted that "every man, and every body of men on earth, possesses the righ[t] of self-government: they receive it with their being from the hand of nature. Individuals exercise it by their single will: collections of men, by that of the majority; for the law of the *majority* is the natural law of every society of men . . . [and] natural rights, may be abridged or modified in its exercise, by their own consent, or by the law of those who depute them."[59] Zephaniah Swift of Connecticut was even more emphatic in lecturing that "natural and civil rights cannot be enjoyed at the same time. We must give up the one to attain the other."[60]

Understanding that the individual rights advanced as inalienable in the Preamble were natural allows the reader to recognize that for most of the delegates these rights were not inalienable when viewed from within civil society.[61] Gouverneur Morris, later the Constitution's draftsman, explained that "Natural Liberty absolutely excludes the Idea of political [civil] Liberty since it implies in every man the Right to do what he pleases. So long, therefore, as it exists Society cannot be established. And when Society is established natural Liberty must cease. . . . He who wishes to enjoy natural Rights must establish himself where natural Rights are admitted. He must live alone."[62]

As with Morris, individual natural liberty and rights were understood by most at the time as fully inalienable only under a limited number of conditions—most importantly: (1) as Morris described, when an individual lives outside of society, in what was most frequently understood to be a presocial setting; (2) as the Declaration characterized, the relation between Americans and Parliament, that is, when one people or nation attempts to legislate for another, thus depriving it of the right to govern itself; (3) as the Virginia Bill of Rights counseled, when one generation tries to "deprive or divest their posterity" of them; or (4) as Vattel noticed, when an individual wishes to depart (emigrate) from an environment in which the morally or religiously intrusive vision of the majority is at odds with his own.[63] Individual natural rights, in sum, were important conceptual "trumps," but only in a restricted number of circumstances outside of ordinary legal ones.[64]

Jefferson not only endorsed the natural right of emigration (number 4 above),[65] but emphatically emphasized two others (numbers 2 and 3), writing that natural rights are dominant "between society and society, or generation and generation [in situations where] there is no municipal obligation, no umpire but the law of nature. We seem not to have perceived that, by the law of nature, one generation is to another as one independent nation to another."[66] In a manner still often overlooked, but one that Jefferson was especially keen to highlight,[67] the inalienable character of intergenerational natural rights, which dictated that one generation must not surrender the rights of a future one, was of central importance to the logic of colonial resistance. This is captured in the assertion of the Virginia Declaration of Rights that "all men are by nature equally free and independent, and have certain inherent rights, of which, when they enter society they cannot by any compact, deprive or divest their posterity; namely, the enjoyment of life and liberty, with the means of acquiring and possessing property, and pursuing and obtaining happiness and safety." American Revolutionary-era pamphleteers, in opposition to those who would come to defend written constitutions, emphasized that the current generation was not free to surrender the natural rights of their descendants; it was their duty to protect their children's rights to life, liberty, and property and to pass on to them these rights undiminished.[68]

Given their circumstances, not surprisingly, American essayists rarely emphasized so-called Lockean individual rights that men possessed presocially. Edmund Randolph pointedly found such claims misplaced, in that "a preamble [in this case to the Constitution] seems proper not for the purpose of designating the ends of government and human polities— This business, if not fitter for the schools . . . *is* unfit here; since we are not working on the natural rights of men not yet gathered into society, but upon those rights, modified by society, and . . . [interwoven with] the rights of states."[69] The international nature of America's dispute with Britain made presocial rights of interest only to those locked in internal disputes within particular states where some hoped that with independence from Britain, the people had returned to a state of nature with presocial natural rights. Such truly revolutionary claims, often resting on an effort to radicalize natural rights and to undermine the distinction between them and civil ones, were little countenanced by responsible political actors.[70]

On Individual and Corporate Natural Equality and Individual Civil Inequality

In the Declaration's Preamble Jefferson wrote for his colleagues that "we hold these truths to be self-evident, that all men are created equal," and that, accordingly, they were "endowed by their Creator with certain in-alienable rights; that among these, are life, liberty, and the pursuit of hap-piness."[71] Moreover, "to secure these rights, governments are instituted among men." Jefferson thus began the Preamble stipulating that he and his fellow Americans held all men to be created equal. Here—despite the ar-gument of those who find something remarkable in the Congress defend-ing natural equality for all men (quite possibly, they assert, *pace* Douglas, Jefferson and many of his colleagues meant to include women and non-Europeans, including Africans)—Jefferson was advancing a standard eighteenth-century commonplace that had been frequently advanced in earlier legal, political, and religious thought.[72]

In so doing, he provided an important ground for the implied contract between a people and their government, or, less obvious today, between distinct nations or peoples, or between connected generations of one people. This description of equality in human creation, by the canons of accepted eighteenth-century thought and practice and in the more expan-sive language of Virginia's Declaration of Rights, was one in which all men are "by nature equally free and independent."[73] There should be little doubt that the Preamble's "assertion that 'all men are created equal,' which became a prominent part of the document's moral message, had originally referred to men in a state of nature, that is, before government existed."[74] As controversial and radical as this claim would become in the future, when written, it was utterly conventional in holding that human beings are all equally free in discrete situations governed by natural-law dictates rather than statutory, common, or constitutional law and civil rights.

But, similarly evident, it is difficult to envision any number of Amer-icans sent as delegates to Congress—be they slaveholding Southern plant-ers, slave-importing Northern merchants, or avaricious and ambitious law-yers from the middle colonies—who would have defended, in contrast to an indeterminate natural equality, an equality of talents; an equality of group political or civil standing; or an equality of individual civil rights, be they political, social, economic, racial, or sexual.[75] For, as Alexander Hamilton pointed out, although "men are naturally equal," as soon as they enter society, they "agree to depart from the natural Equality of man—this is done in every Society."[76] Here, Hamilton followed standard eighteenth-century authorities, such as Pufendorf, who consistently held that "in becoming a citizen, a man loses his natural liberty and subjects himself to an authority whose power includes the right of life and death," or, put differently, the state necessarily determines "what remains of each man's natural liberty, or how each must reconcile the enjoyment of his own rights with the tranquility of the state."[77] Metaphysical natural equality was not understood by most men in the eighteenth-century English-speaking world to carry over to civil society.[78]

Of special interest, as Douglas would argue, was the claim—implicit in the Preamble and explicit in the body of the Declaration, in almost every previous congressional state document, and in very numerous pamphlets—of Americans' corporate equality with their British brethren. This equality was claimed to exist between North American British and those living in the United Kingdom, all of whom, according to many, possessed the same rights.[79] Americans thus began pressing their case against the British ministry by arguing "that all individuals who belong to a single community . . . ought to be considered as equals within it."[80] Well before a handful of radicals in Massachusetts and Virginia had begun to entertain the idea of independence, most Americans were confident that they were a part of the British state and nation and, as subjects in good standing, had done nothing to warrant losing their British civil and constitutional rights. They should be able to enjoy their inherited corporate and individual civil rights equally with their British brethren. According to many in Britain and America, "No man will deny that the provincial Americans have an inherent, *unalienable Right* to all the Privileges of British Subjects."[81] Unfortunately, this position was not accepted by William Blackstone, the Crown, or by the majority in Parliament, who viewed America, along with Ireland (which at least could not be directly taxed by Parliament), as a conquered dominion of the Crown (rather than of the king) and thus subject to parliamentary control.[82]

The ministry's and Parliament's refusal even to consider their closely argued petitions challenging Parliament's sovereignty forced American spokesmen, still holding tight to their membership in the British state and nation, to conceive of themselves as a separate British people living apart, but under the umbrella of a still to be fully worked out British imperial constitution. It was this vision that gave form to much of American political writing during the ten years of the imperial crisis, 1765–75.[83] Either way, though, it was the right to equality with the king's subjects in England, to possess "equal rights with those in Britain," that Americans adamantly claimed as their own.[84]

Parliament persisted in dismissing these evolving claims of corporate equality between the North American British and those at home, and in holding Americans to be a conquered people without a legitimate claim to British political corporate and even individual common-law rights. As a result, politically active Americans began aggressively to move toward a more ready use of the language of natural law and rights, unmixed with that of British constitutionalism.[85] At the same time, they took a more independent-leaning stance that held "that any one people, considered collectively as a self-identified group, possesses in that capacity the same rights as other people."[86] Of course, it was this slow and late-to-develop position embracing a naturalistic defense of heretofore British constitutional corporate rights that eventually culminated in America's declaring independence. This was when Americans argued before the world that they and the British were separate and equal peoples and that each should enjoy equal rights to natural corporate sovereignty and autonomy under international law. According to Burlamaqui, "The natural state of nations . . . [is] a state of equality and independence, which establishes between them a right of equality." This was a position even more emphatically endorsed by Vattel, who made this a central theoretical claim.[87]

Even as late as 1774, in keeping with a wholly consistent line of argument, Jefferson, in writing his *Summary View of the Rights of British America,* continued to believe that Americans and Britons were conjoined equal peoples and that "the true ground on which we declare these [parliamentary] acts void is, that the British Parliament has no right to exercise authority over us." The king, Jefferson counseled, must "no longer persevere in sacrificing the rights of one part of the empire to the inordinate desires of another; but deal out to all equal and impartial right."[88] It would prove but a surprisingly short step from this intermediate position of civil equality between British peoples, in which the Parliament was severely limited in its rights, to that of the Declaration's view of Americans' corporate right to a natural equality with their former British brethren, though by then it would be as a separate people outside of the protection of the British monarch and constitution.[89]

American defenders of the separation from Britain thus could and did cogently defend a natural equality of all men (and peoples) and a civil equality between varying branches of the British people, while consistently arguing that most people living in British North America did not possess equal individual political or civil rights. In short, individual natural equality did not preclude the principled existence of civil inequality between groups and individuals living in British North America.

Lived Ideas—Pervasive Social and Political Practices

That such limitations existed accords with the social and political practices of late eighteenth-century America, in which men were legally but forcibly impressed for naval duty against their will, regularly imprisoned for religious infractions of strict moral codes and for debt or vagrancy,[90] and, more generally, intrusively policed regarding sexual matters, including the continued public shaming of adulterous women. Congressional and state delegates were men who endorsed the same and more: the limitation of political and certain civil rights to property-owning adult males; the denial of most property rights to married women; in many instances, the owning of chattel slaves; the rampant, wholesale, and enthusiastic dispossession, either by force or legalized theft, of the property of Native Americans; the grievous underenfranchisement of the majority of property-owning adult males in the western portions of many states; the suppression of equal religious rights for minority groups, most particularly in New England (excepting Rhode Island), where religious establishments would be maintained until well into the nineteenth century; and the maintenance or strengthening of religious-based barriers, including the supposedly radical Pennsylvania constitution that debarred all but Trinitarian Protestants, and most particularly Catholics, from elected state office (thus preventing them, at the end of the century, from being federal senatorial electors and, in many instances, presidential electors). In light of such ubiquitous practices, must we assume, as one must who assigns to the natural equality and rights language of the Preamble a radical understanding that applies equally in and outside of society, that the two or three dozen men who endorsed the Declaration were the boldest of liars and hypocrites?

If not, it is unreasonable to believe that the majority of these same men knowingly collapsed natural and civil equality and rights, thus endorsing a radically individualistic understanding of the Preamble's natural rights of life, liberty, and the pursuit of happiness, while denying all political and many civil rights, even the most basic, to the vast majority of residents in British North America.[91] These severe limitations, of course, at the time were applied also to men of vast property, high social standing, and great learning who were suspected of loyalty to their legal governors. Such men were regularly denied even the most basic British individual freedoms of speech, publication (as was true also of publishers who, beginning in 1764, dared publish opposition tracts), association, and movement, to say nothing of pursuing their happiness. Of course, it also should be remembered that little done by a Congress in which they were unrepresented (as the colonists were in Parliament) enjoyed their assent.

Congress in 1774, in fact, created the Association that came dangerously close to fostering arbitrary and intrusive rule throughout the nation by populist minorities. This congressionally sponsored organization allowed for committees of (often self-appointed) men to harass, interrogate, intimidate, and incarcerate those suspected of holding unpopular political and, indirectly, religious views (most Episcopal ministers, like many Quakers, were Loyalists). Even for those fellow British subjects not suspected of such views, these committees kept close tabs on their social, political, and economic lives. These illegal committees of questionable representative quality also did their utmost to "discourage every species of extravagance and dissipation, especially horse-racing, and all kinds of gaming, cock-fighting, exhibitions of shews, plays, and other expensive diversions." Evidence of the low priority delegates awarded the protection of established British common-law individual rights thus demands careful consideration in assessing how the Declaration's admittedly ambiguous equality and rights claims were likely understood by the majority of congressional delegates.[92]

Extant social and political practices demonstrate that, absent inviolable individual rights capable of overriding corporately determined civil ones, those rights recognized in society were "not absolute, and they are circumscribed directly and formally by the rights of the people to self-government."[93] James Wilson critically observed that "in the Establishment of society every man yields his life, his liberty, property & Character to the society." But then, he continues, "Indeed we have seen the Legislatures in our own Country deprive the citizen of Life, Liberty, & property [and] we have seen Attainders, Banishment, & Confiscation."[94]

With a clear absence of anything approaching civil equality and with rights-denying enactments regularly directed at them, the Loyalists were especially keen to remind their fellow subjects that if they had been concerned with securing individual equality and civil rights rather than corporate equality and political rights, they would have never declared independence from their lawful sovereign and begun experimenting with more popular and unbalanced (i.e., not free or moderate) forms of government.

Such governments, according to the Loyalists and the historical accounts that they believed to be dispositive, were the most intolerant of individual claims to freedom from oversight by legally constituted majorities.[95] One of the most articulate Loyalists reminded his readers that Britain was "by the Confession of the wisest Men in Europe, the freest and the noblest Government, of the Records of History."[96] What he surely had in mind was the unequaled range of individual civil rights enjoyed by British subjects,[97] rights that had been lost in the mid-seventeenth century under an extra-constitutional English government frighteningly similar to that which Loyalists found encircling them in eighteenth-century North America. But the American patriots were unconcerned with such matters; by all appearances they were primarily concerned with protecting the corporate right to self-government that many Americans believed the centralizing imperial ministries of the British Parliament intended to deny them. Not surprisingly, then, the rights in question, as debated in pamphlets and newspaper editorials, were, on the patriot side, solely political and constitutional—that is, corporate and communal rather than private and individual.[98]

We know that the Preamble's vaunted claims of equality and inalienable individual rights failed to guarantee even the most minimal of individual protections, not only to Loyalists, but to many others as well. The Declaration's authors showed so little sensitivity to such concerns that they even publicly castigated the king in the penultimate indictment of the Declaration for having his representative, Lord Dunmore, in November 1775 offer freedom to the slaves of Virginia, including those of Thomas Jefferson and his fellow delegates: the first American emancipation proclamation was condemned by Congress in defending America's separation from England.[99] The claim of natural equality advanced in the Preamble was of no immediate relevance to Congress in opposing Dunmore's manumission of black chattel slaves in Virginia. By the standards then current, such an act was a violation of the more important civil right of property.

Dr. Johnson observed in 1775 how strange it was that "if slavery be thus fatally contagious, how is it that we hear the loudest yelps for liberty among the drivers of negroes?"[100] John Lind (and Jeremy Bentham), responding to the Declaration, asked how is it that "his Majesty's Governors excite domestic insurrection," before answering: "They offered *freedom* to the *slaves* of these assertors of liberty. . . . It is their boast that they have taken up arms in support of these their own *self-evident truths*—'that all men are *equal*.'. . . Is it for *them* to complain *of the offer of freedom* held out to these wretched beings? of the offer of reinstating them in that *equality*, which, in this very paper, is declared to be the *gift of God to all.*"[101] In this matter Loyalists on both sides of the Atlantic noted that Americans seemed particularly unconcerned with either natural equality or hallowed British individual civil rights.

Because of the paucity of contemporary writings offering insight into the thinking of congressional delegates on abstract matters, most particularly regarding their understanding of the Preamble's defense of natural equality, students of the Declaration are unable to answer with complete confidence what this claim meant to those who voted for it. Still, we have compelling evidence from their lived political and social practices that most delegates were comfortable with high degrees of civil inequality. There is no extant evidence that there existed among the delegates widespread opposition to civil inequality and, instead, broad support for egalitarian changes to elite-dominated American colonial politics.[102]

Instead, based on social and political practices, it seems clear that the goal of most delegates as they entered the struggle with the British ministry, as Carl Becker first articulated in 1909,[103] was to protect their capacity to rule at home, not to change the nature of home rule by challenging long-accepted, and for their purposes essential, civil distinctions between men and women, children and adults, black and white, educated and uneducated, churched and unchurched, and, of course, rich and poor. That, in spite of their best intentions, the Revolution would change much, as wars almost always do, is not at issue.[104] It is their understanding of the Preamble's use of concepts like equality and rights that demands attention.

Individuals and the Natural Rights of Peoples

Indeed, the majority of the delegates to Congress had arrived hoping to defend Americans' corporate civil rights under British constitutional law, with its traditional naturalistic tinge and little else. Accordingly, in what they characterized as their Bill of Rights of 1774, they argued that Americans "have never ceded to any foreign power whatever, a right to dispose of either [life, or liberty and property] without their consent . . . [therefore, their rights] cannot be legally taken from them, altered or abridged by any power whatever, without their own consent, by their representatives in their several provincial legislatures."[105] The rights language of the First Continental Congress is instructive: the corporate right of self-government was inalienably held by a people or their legally constituted representatives, who were duty-bound to defend it against the usurpations of another people or their legislature. As McIlwain observed, for the Irish and the Americans the fundamental ground upon which their opposition rested was the same. It was that "the Parliament of *England* hath no more jurisdiction in *Ireland,* than it hath in *Scotland;* in general, that 'it cannot stand either in law or common reason, that one body politick should be subordinate or subject to the controul of the other.'"[106] For the majority of delegates, in a manner not always appreciated in a post-Lincolnian world, individual civil rights were clearly capable of being legally and morally denied to individuals and distinct groups by the "people" or their legitimate representatives, but the same right did not exist in another people's legislature, that is, for Americans in the British Parliament.

Many American authors went even further than had Congress, challenging the antecedents of individualism that would soon come to be associated with the teachings of John Locke and defending the ready transfer of natural individual rights to civil communities,[107] thus assigning "free and independent states" those rights often associated with "Locke's 'free and independent' individuals."[108] This was in keeping with standard treatments of such matters by Vattel, who had shown that "liberty and independence belong to man by his very nature, . . . [but] citizens of a State, having yielded them in part to the sovereign, do not enjoy them to their full and absolute extent. But the whole body of the Nation, the State, so long as it has not voluntarily submitted to other men or other Nations, remains absolutely free and independent."[109] Accordingly, in eighteenth-century thought it was most frequently states (not individuals), perpetually in a natural condition vis-à-vis other states, that remained free and equal.

Joseph Clark explained that "EQUALITY and INDEPENDENCE are the just claim, the indefeasible birth-right of men: In a state of nature, as individuals; in society, as states or nations."[110] The traditional understanding of this transfer was not limited to those we might today describe as conservative. Jefferson's friend and intellectual guide, Richard Bland, wrote of "the *Rights* of a people," and stated that these "*Rights* imply *Equality*" for them, not as individuals, but collectively.[111] The most important sense of equality defended by men like the congressional delegates, then, was that of "constitutional governing bodies" rather than "the social equality of persons."[112]

Among the defenders of this common understanding was the future Anti-Federalist, Luther Martin, who explained it as fully as anyone else. In Philadelphia, he carefully reasoned:

> The first principle of government is founded on the natural rights of individuals, and in perfect equality. Locke, Vattel, Lord Somers, and Dr. Priestly, all confirm this principle. This principle of equality, when applied to individuals, is lost in some degree, when he becomes a member of society, to which it is transferred; and this society . . . is, with respect to others, again on a perfect footing of equality—[and its people enjoy a perfect] right to govern themselves as they please. Nor can any other state, of right, deprive

them of this [national] equality. . . . We must treat as free states with each other, upon the same terms of equality that men originally formed themselves into societies. Vattel, Rutherford and Locke, are united in support of the position, that states, as to each other, are in a state of nature.[113]

Here, Martin covered the central elements of the political and legal thinking of the time concerning the relationship between individual natural equality and, upon the rise of civil societies, the national equality awarded to states, not individuals. Again, this was an internationally accepted norm, and Americans in the Preamble were appealing to the international community.[114]

From the end of the eighteenth century, from a world already greatly different from that of a few decades earlier, James Wilson looked back ruefully on the Revolutionary era's conception of rights with this widely accepted trade-off in mind. In particular, he rejected the long-accepted exchange that the individual was said to have made between natural equality and rights and limited civil ones. He observed that such an unequal exchange meant that "the right of individuals to their private property, to their personal liberty, to their health, to their reputation, and to their life, flow[s] from a human establishment, and can be traced to no higher source. The connexion between man and his natural rights is intercepted by the institution of civil society . . . [and] he can claim nothing but what the society provides."[115] To Wilson's dismay, most Americans in 1776 (and many in 1790 and beyond) viewed civil rights as dispossessing the individual of natural liberty and rights,[116] and offering in their stead civil liberty and rights as determined by popular legislatures. For many men from the middle states, liberal-conservative in a traditional aristocratic way like Wilson,[117] such an insecure foundation for rights, resting on fickle popular will, was not reassuring.

America's Evolving Dilemma: British vs. Natural Rights of Self-Government

The intellectual background that framed the meeting of the delegates to the First Continental Congress makes clearer why most sought to avoid the use of any mention of natural rights—that is, because of its implication of American national autonomy—and why for the same reason some felt compelled to make use of such claims.[118] Thus, in the debates leading to Congress's first public declaration, its October 1774 Bill of Rights, or Declaration and Resolves, we can see with unusual clarity the tensions accompanying a turn to natural rather than constitutional law in America's defense of its corporate political rights in the evolving imperial conflict. The Continental Congress made a calculated gamble when it declared that in accord with "the immutable laws of nature, the principles of the English constitution, and the several charters or compacts . . . the inhabitants of the English colonies in North-America . . . have the following RIGHTS . . . they are entitled to life, liberty and property." At this still relatively early juncture, in 1774, it was well understood that the modest inclusion of natural grounds along with copious civil ones in defense of American corporate rights was a risky maneuver that was sure to embolden domestic and overseas radicals and offend many suspicious members of Parliament with its extra-constitutional and thus necessarily separatist innuendos. Not surprisingly, the mere mention of natural law (to say nothing of rights) in this document deeply divided Congress.[119]

It did so principally because the delegates were formally committed by their instructions to seek a reconciliation with the king and his ministers (under the colonists' admittedly atavistic and monarchical understanding of the British imperial constitution).[120] Any use of the language of natural law or rights—the words closely linked in the eighteenth century with international claims of national sovereignty—they knew could only lessen that possibility. As Adams reported, on September 22, the grand committee considering America's rights, unable to decide whether to include any mention of natural rights, asked the Congress as a whole for its opinion. And "two days afterwards it was determined, against the views of Mr. Adams, that nothing should be said, at that time, of natural rights. This is said to have been caused by the influence of the conservative Virginia members, still anxious to avoid stumbling-blocks in the way of a possible return of good feeling between sovereign and people."[121] In a debate still circumscribed by British constitutional claims on both sides, with Americans seeking in fact to resurrect a monarchical form of constitutionalism that placed them in opposition to British Whigs,[122] making use of natural law or rights seemed to a majority of delegates dangerously premature, even in late 1774, likely to alienate the king and ultimately to lead to separation, and thus unwarranted and undesirable.

The sober New Yorker James Duane, for instance, greatly preferred "grounding our Rights on the Laws and Constitution of the Country from whence We sprung and Charters, without recurring to the Law of Nature—because this will be a feeble support. . . . Privileges of Englishmen were inherent, their Birthright and Inheritance, and cannot be deprived of them." The independence-seeking Virginian with close ties to British radicalism, Richard Henry Lee, with different goals and a much more ambitious agenda in mind, took the still precocious position that "Life and Liberty, which is necessary for the Security of Life, cannot be given up when We enter into Society." In effect, he was radicalizing natural rights in a manner more common in Britain than America and denying the still widely accepted distinction between natural and civil rights.[123]

To this, the future Loyalist Joseph Galloway, a longtime ally of Benjamin Franklin, responded: "I have looked for our Rights in the Laws of Nature—but could not find them in a State of Nature, but always in a State of political Society. I have looked for them in the Constitution of the English Government, and there found them. We may draw them from this Source securely." Splitting the difference between radical and conservative positions, John Adams remembered that he "was very strenuous for retaining and insisting on it [natural law], as a Resource to which We might be driven by Parliament much sooner than We were aware."[124] His position, neither a bold claim like Lee's endorsement of inviolable individual rights incapable of being civilly limited, nor a wholesale reliance like that of Duane or Galloway on British constitutionalism, was initially rejected. Then, after Congress changed the proposed language from that of natural rights to that of natural law, it came to embody the moderate position eventually adopted by a majority of the delegates. The inclusion of a grounding of rights in natural law, though, was inflammatory to those in Parliament who opposed colonial claims to extra-constitutional rights. Still, in the end, Adams proved prescient in forecasting that Americans, on the march toward independence, soon would have need of such intellectual ammunition, even if this result was in large part because of the efforts expended by John and his cousin.

In the summer of 1776, a majority of congressional delegates decided they were unable to depend any longer on the promise of protected political rights under British constitutional law and came to believe that only with independence would the American right to self-governance be protected. They reluctantly abandoned the safety of the still highly regarded British constitution, its attendant civil rights, and the comfort it provided as they moved into unexplored territory. Only when constitutional institutions were no longer available or binding and the constitutional substructure of civil society had collapsed were Americans' duly limited British civil rights to life, liberty, and happiness recast, in international forms, as natural and inalienable ones. Indeed, even Locke had claimed as much in recognizing that "those who are united into one Body, and have a common establish'd Law and Judicature to appeal to, with Authority to decide

Controversies between them, and punish Offenders, *are in Civil Society* one with another."[125] But, still, for most of the ten years of the conflict, American authors and the politically active had fought as Britons to enjoy equal civil rights with the king's subjects at home or elsewhere in the British Empire.

Ultimately, but reluctantly and with fear on the part of many, and enthusiasm and excitement on the part of only a few, America as a newly minted nation did defend its rights as natural in international law before the court of world opinion. As a separate and equal people, they believed themselves legally justified, under an already dated understanding of international law,[126] in breaking off their relations with Britain, repulsing its aggression, and declaring themselves a fully sovereign and independent nation. The powerful effects of having exploited natural rights in separating from Britain would only slowly come to be understood.[127] For, as John Phillip Reid reminds us, the eighteenth century's original "theory of rights was confining when compared to the theory that would emerge in both British and American constitutional law during the nineteenth century. Rights in the eighteenth century were thought of as restraining arbitrary government rather than as liberating the individual."[128]

Two Fully Inalienable Rights—One Individual, One Corporate

In the minds of most eighteenth-century Americans who left a record of such, it seems that the traditionally restrictive range of natural rights comes close to capturing their understanding of them, rather than an emerging radical one in which natural rights remained fully inalienable and inviolable in and out of civil society. With the exception of the right of religious conscience,[129] most authors understood that natural individual rights lost their inalienable status when individuals moved into civil society. Recall that natural rights were fully inalienable only in a limited number of cases: in a presocial state of nature, or, more apposite here, vis-à-vis another people, following the logic of Vatellian international law; between an intrusive and often intolerant majority and a dissatisfied emigrating individual; or, too often forgotten, between generations (this understanding would, in a world of written constitutions, prove particularly inconvenient).[130] In keeping with such standards, the "Federal Farmer" declared that only a few rights "are natural and unalienable, of which even the people cannot deprive individuals"—most particularly the individual right of religious conscience and the corporate right of popular self-governance. Most others were constitutional and could be altered or abolished by the people in express legislative acts. Among these were such important legal rights as "the trial by jury, the benefits of the writ of habeas corpus, etc.," while still other laws "are common or mere legal rights, that is, such as individuals claim under law."[131]

The New Hampshire bill of rights views matters in much the same way. It explains that upon entering society, people surrender their natural liberty and equality and certain rights, "to insure the protection of others." Only a few rights are "unalienable, because no equivalent can be given or received for them. Of this kind are the rights of conscience."[132] According to the legal historian Philip Hamburger, the 1782 New Hampshire constitutional convention, when introducing that state's bill of rights to their constituents, explained that they had "endeavor'd therein to ascertain and define the most important and essential natural rights of men. We have distinguished betwixt the alienable and unalienable rights: For the former of which, men may receive an equivalent; for the latter, or the RIGHTS OF CONSCIENCE, they can receive none."[133] Similarly, Samuel Stillman, one of the few Baptist ministers to be well regarded in Massachusetts, noted that "some of the natural rights of mankind are unalienable, and subject to no control but that of the Deity. Such are the SACRED RIGHTS OF CONSCIENCE. Which in a state of nature, and of civil society are exactly the same. They can neither be parted with nor controled, by any human authority whatever."[134] Other than the right of religious conscience, no other natural right regularly followed the individual into society and could inviolably protect him from legislative restriction of civil rights.

Hamburger has described the well-known Presbyterian minister, William Tennent, as acknowledging "that individuals could give government the power to regulate the rights often described as inalienable—the only exception being in matters of religion." Thus, "I can communicate to my representative, a power to dispose of part of my property . . . but, cannot . . . communicate to any man on earth, a right to dispose of my conscience, and to lay down for me what I shall believe and practice in religious matters."[135] Among individual civil rights only the liberty of religious conscience was tied, in correlative fashion, to an inalienable duty and guiding moral end particular to human beings. For this reason, unlike all other natural individual rights, it could not be transferred, not even to one's legitimate representatives. Only the right of conscience claimed "an entire Exemption from all human Jurisdiction: because its Ends, Offices, and Interests, are superior to all the Ends of Civil Association; and subjecting it to the Power of Man, is inconsistent with the very Being of Religion."[136] No other individual civil right, excepting possibly that of parental control over children,[137] was comparably tied to inalienable duties that could never be legitimately surrendered, not even to one's political sovereign. By the middle of the eighteenth century, then, only one natural right was viewed as fully inalienable: the right of religious conscience was the first and, at the end of the century, still the only individual right consistently viewed as such.[138]

The dominant eighteenth-century American understanding of the differences separating natural and civil rights was especially well described in 1778 during the ratification struggle over the Massachusetts constitution. In their returns, the citizens of the villages of western Massachusetts ardently defended the inalienability only of an individual's right to religious conscience and of a people's corporate right to form or abolish its government. The then and future radical citizens of Berkshire County affirmed that "the people at large are endowed with alienable and unalienable Rights. . . . Those which are unalienable, are those which belong to Conscience respecting the worship of God and the practice of the Christian Religion, and that of being determined or governed by the Majority in the Institution or formation of Government." Only these two were fully inalienable. "The alienable are those which may be delegated for the Common good, or those which are for the Common good to be parted with."[139] From this established American perspective, the individual was fully free in serving God and family, and in joining himself to the common will of his community, but in little else.[140] And in western Massachusetts, this view of the limited character of inalienable rights was advanced by one of the most radical populations in America.

One might object for this very reason that such an understanding of the limitations imposed on natural rights was not a common sentiment, except among rural, and still largely religious, radicals in western Massachusetts. Yet the historical record indicates that such a view was not unique to them. Throughout the colonies respectable public voices defended comparable opinions regarding the elevated standing of the individual's singularly inalienable right to worship God as he or she believed pleasing to Him. Even progressive thinkers such as Jefferson and Madison adhered to similar views. Jefferson wrote that "Our rulers can have authority over such natural rights only as we have submitted to them. The rights of conscience we never submitted, we could not submit. We are answerable for them to our God."[141] Madison, in keeping with dominant attitudes, described the inexorable relationship that then still existed between rights and duties, most especially concerning those that were inalienable, and claimed that the right of religious conscience was uniquely inalienable, for it was "the duty of every man to render to the Creator such homage, and such only, as he believes to be acceptable to him. This duty is precedent both in order of time and degree of obligation, to the claims of Civil Society." Therefore, "in matters of Religion, no man's right is abridged by the institution of Civil Society, and that of Religion is wholly exempt from its cognizance."[142] Even for the remarkably progressive Madison, inalienable rights were viewed as much as a restraint on individual freedom as an individual liberty that must be corporately protected from the intrusive pressures of others.

Almost as often lauded in America was the complementary inalienable corporate right and correlative duty of a people to govern itself. Here too, it was not only Berkshire radicals who claimed this right as inalienable. Respected men like the Reverend Jonas Clark held that the right of political self-determination resides "in the people, whether emerging from a state of nature, or the yoke of oppression, [and] is *an unalienable right.*"[143] Nathaniel Whitaker similarly concluded, in a manner that recalls any number of congressional declarations, that "no power on earth" was free to intervene against the people. "The freedom of a society or State consists in acting according to their own choice, within the bounds of the law of nature, in governing themselves, independent of all other States. This is the Liberty wherewith God hath made every State free, and which no power on earth may lawfully abridge, but by their own consent."[144] In Rhode Island, the lawyer and activist, Silas Downer, concurred that the "essence of the *British* constitution [is] that the people shall not be governed by laws, in the making of which they had no hand, or have their monies taken away without their own consent." This, he claimed, is both an inherited right and one that is also "a natural right which no creature can *give* [thus, inalienable], or hath a right to take away [inviolable]."[145]

Radicals of western Massachusetts, progressives like Jefferson and Madison, and even relatively conservative pastors were typical in holding that the natural rights of religious conscience and corporate self-determination were unusual in being equally inalienable both in and out of society. No other paired duties and rights matched the existential centrality and imposing responsibilities tied to individual religious conscience and corporate self-governance as divine "gifts of God" demanding unequaled inalienable status.[146] The divinely grounded rights of individual religious conscience and corporate governance would, in the most Godly obsessed part of America,[147] become the first inalienable rights with equal status in and outside of society.[148] Not surprisingly, the divine foundations of each shared little with the secular outlooks of those in Europe most readily associated with enlightened political aspirations.[149] Yet future secular authors nonetheless would exploit the moral standing of these epoch-changing claims, stripping them of their divine foundation and linkage to meta-physical and extra-personally defined duties and ends.[150]

Conclusion

America's Declaration of Independence defends the corporate right of a people to self-government and of individuals to important natural rights that they cannot deny to their descendants and that, as inalienable natu-ral rights, could not be surrendered to another people or legislature that sought to legislate for them illegitimately. Indeed, this principle is at the very heart of the imperial struggle that led to America's separation from Britain.[151] No extant evidence suggests that the Preamble can be properly understood as describing a radical philosophy holding that natural rights *"cannot* be given up by individuals in the name of some transcendent public good or in the name of anything else."[152] Although it is impossible to know what was inside the mind of each individual delegate when he agreed to the language of the Preamble, nothing supports a common read-ing of the Declaration that implies or asserts that the majority of endors-ing delegates were radicals committed to tearing down traditional British North American social and political practices by reading inalienability into rights civilly awarded in lieu of surrendered natural ones.[153] Most particularly, the views of the middle and southern state moderates who re-fused on July 1 to support R. H. Lee's independence proclamation—the majority of delegates from South Carolina, Delaware, Pennsylvania, and New York—should not be in doubt.

As Jefferson claimed fifty years after drafting the Declaration, its cen-tral goal was to explain to the world America's reasons for declaring inde-pendence. He wrote that Americans had believed that "when forced . . . to resort to arms for redress, an appeal to the tribunal of the world was deemed proper for our justification. This was the object of the Declara-tion of Independence."[154] He emphasized that it had not been their goal to proclaim to a skeptical world of bankers and diplomats a bold new un-derstanding of individual rights. It was, he recalled, "not to find out new principles, or new arguments never before thought of, not merely to say things that had never been said before; but to place before mankind the common sense of the subject, in terms so plain and firm as to command their assent, and to justify ourselves in the independent stand we are com-pelled to take." Thus, the individual natural rights of the Preamble are best understood in view of the Declaration's explanatory role as a listing of grievances, rather than as an original philosophical treatise laying out a novel theory of individual rights.[155] It had been the delegates' intention in 1776, Jefferson continued, "to give expression of the American mind," without "aiming at originality of principle or sentiment."[156]

The intention of the Declaration's authors was not to claim for Americans anything theoretically new. Rather, it was to set forth in an internationally acceptable language their standing as a free and sovereign people. It is not surprising, therefore, that in the late eighteenth century, the Declaration was not taken by American and European audiences as advancing a revolutionary theory of individual rights.[157] In fact, the Preamble's rights statement was viewed as so pedestrian that it was hardly attended to at all.[158] There may have been some, radicals like Samuel Adams and Richard Henry Lee, who did understand the rights language of the Preamble as advancing a new liberal philosophy of individual rights in which the distinction between the inalienability of natural rights and the alienability of civil ones collapsed and the dependence of rights on antecedent duties was rejected. All evidence from the words and even more from the delegates' deeds, however, suggests that such men were few. Still, the Preamble's artfully chosen language permitted different men to comprehend in it different things. Men of moderate political sympathies, almost certainly the majority of the congressional delegates, could read it as a traditional declaration of natural rights with appropriately deferential references to the Divine, while men of more progressive sympathies might see in its language something closer to their liking.[159] Either way, such studied ambiguity was part of its genius.

In defending the corporate rather than individualistic intentions of the Declaration and its differentiation between the inalienable but circumscribed role of natural rights, and the alienable but more pervasive one for civil rights, Stephen Douglas was closer to getting the 1776 Declaration historically right. It was Lincoln, though, who, in defending an expansive view of the inalienable individual rights of all human beings, captured the future in his noble but creative act of mythmaking at Gettysburg. As the popular historian Gary Wills has noted, by altering the Declaration and appealing to what he believed to be its spirit rather than what its substantive content described, Lincoln "performed one of the most daring acts of open-air sleight-of-hand ever witnessed by the unsuspecting. Everyone in that vast throng of thousands was having his or her intellectual pocket picked. . . . Lincoln had revolutionized the Revolution, given people a new past to live with that would change their future indefinitely."[160] But now, we must ask, "Should we continue to look the other way, or should the quest for truth impel us, in opposition to compelling reasons counseling silence, to report this theft?"

Notes

1. See Calhoun, "Speech on the Oregon Bill," 27 June 1848, 565–67; Hazelton, *Declaration of Independence;* and more recently and among the most polemical, Breen, "Lockean Moment."

2. In spirit, I follow Friedenwald, *Declaration of Independence,* 152–53: "The Declaration of Independence . . . is the least comprehended of all the great documents produced as a result of our political development . . . [because its authors left] no precise interpretation of the commonplaces which they comprehended so clearly as to lead them to believe that all who came after must understand with like readiness. . . . My task will be, therefore, to endeavor to put before the reader of these pages something of the aspect that the Declaration had in 1776."

3. Jefferson, *Adams–Jefferson Letters,* 452.

4. For other examples of the two sharply contrasting accounts of rights offered by Lincoln and Douglas, see Adams, *Selected Writings,* 398–99, and Winthrop, *Centennial of Independence* (4 July 1876), 302–5.

5. Cited by Wright, *American Interpretations of Natural Law,* 231–32. See also Burlamaqui, *Principles of Natural Law* (1763), 1:52; White, *Philosophy of the American Revolution,* 196–97: "Let me say at once, therefore, that the term 'unalienable' does not refer to what cannot be *taken away* but rather to what cannot be *transferred* to another."

6. Lincoln, *Life and Writings,* 422–23.

7. McIlwain, *American Revolution,* 191. See also Black, "Ethics of the Declaration," 81; Friedenwald, *Declaration of Independence,* 78–79; Lucas, "Stylistic Artistry of the Declaration," 30; Armitage, "Declaration of Independence and International Law."

8. Lincoln, *Life and Writings,* 423 (citing Douglas).

9. See Dana, "Political Principles of the Declaration," 110; Malone, *Jefferson and His Time,* 1:221; Chinard, *Apostle of Americanism,* 74: "It is no longer a question of analogy, or similarity of thought—the very words [in the Declaration of Independence] are identical . . . [indeed] it was clearly Jefferson's role and duty as a delegate from Virginia to incorporate in the Declaration as much as he could of the 'Bill of Rights.'"

10. Randolph, "Edmund Randolph's Essay," 45.

11. See Bryce, "Law of Nature," 508–9; Maine, "Modern History of the Law of Nature," 88, 92.

12. Lincoln, *Life and Writings,* 423 (citing Douglas).

13. See Maine, "Modern History of the Law of Nature," 107: "The theory of International Law assumes that commonwealths are, relatively to each other, in a state of nature . . . [and] if there be a higher power connecting them, however slightly and occasionally . . . the notion of positive law is [reintroduced and] the idea of a law natural [is excluded]."

14. See Reid, "Irrelevance of the Declaration," 83, asking that the central points of Wills, *Inventing America,* be heeded: "Three lessons are taught [by Wills]. One is that the Declaration's purpose was to lay the legal foundation for an alliance with France. A sec-

ond is that the Declaration, and especially its Preamble, was not regarded as important during the Revolution. And third, the Declaration was not, and was never intended to be, either a statement of philosophy or political theory. It was, pure and simple, a legal document."

15. Lincoln, *Life and Writings*, 425.

16. See Maier, *American Scripture*.

17. See Lucas, "Justifying America," 88.

18. Cited by Wright, *American Interpretations of Natural Law*, 189.

19. Burlamaqui, *Principles of Natural Law* (1763), 1:52.

20. See Hawke, *Transaction of Free Men*, 203.

21. The list of world-class theorists resident in what was then a village is most impressive. At the minimum, one must include Rousseau, Burlamaqui, Vattel, Lolme, and Constant. And, of course, although not a Genevan, Voltaire was a longtime resident.

22. Vattel, *Law of Nations*, 3; Burlamaqui, *Principles of Natural Law*, 1:50. Concerning the high regard awarded Burlamaqui and, then, Vattel by Revolutionary-era Americans, see Wright, *American Interpretations of Natural Law*, 6–8.

23. The confusion regarding the meaning of *inalienable* (and *inviolable*) and the indifference to the distinction between natural and civil rights are among the most egregious errors.

24. See Bradford, *Better Guide than Reason*, 39–40; Commager, "Declaration of Independence," 185–86; Jaffa, "Human Rights," 77; Kendall, "Equality," 30; Zuckert, *Natural Rights Republic*. See also Wills, *Lincoln at Gettysburg*, 39, describing those, like Bradford and Kendall, who opposed Lincoln's reading of the Declaration as "suicidally frank."

25. See Butterfield, *Whig Interpretation of History;* Maier, *American Scripture*, 208: "Lincoln and those who shared his convictions . . . felt the need for a document that stated those values in a way that could guide the nation, a document that the founding fathers had failed to supply. And so they made one, pouring old wine into an old vessel manufactured for another purpose, creating a testament whose continuing usefulness depended not on the faithfulness with which it described the intentions of the signers but on its capacity to convince and inspire living Americans."

26. See Maier, *American Scripture*, 98–99, 124–26: "The story of how the Declaration was written—is reasonably clear. It includes not a single talented writer but a group of men working under tight time constraints. . . . Jefferson had been appointed not as an author in the modern sense but as a draftsman."

27. For his thoughtful exploration of these issues, see Zyskind, "How to Read the Declaration." See also Reid, "Irrelevance of the Declaration," 82–83: "The document was not adopted and made official by Jefferson. It was adopted and made official by a majority of the congressional membership. If its meaning is to be found it must be from their understanding and their intent." Both Lincoln and Douglas, as is evident in the above citations, recognized the multiple authorship of the Declaration. See also Edmund Pendleton's nearly contemporary 22 July letter to Jefferson, in Hazelton, *Declaration of Independence*, 148: "I expected you had in the Preamble to our form of Government [Virginia's constitution], exhausted the Subject of complaint ag. Geo. 3d & was at a loss to discover what the Congress would do for one to their Declaration of Independence without copying, but find you have acquitted your selves very well on that score."

28. Cited by Powell, "Original Understanding of Original Intent," 937–38. See also Lutz, *Origins of American Constitutionalism*, 113; Evans, *Theme Is Freedom*, 231.

29. Straussian theorists, in particular, seem to have difficulty in discriminating between the public work of a representative body and the private philosophical views of an individual. For a number of essays suffering from this methodological confusion, see Engeman and Zuckert, *Protestantism and the American Founding*.

30. One of the earliest and most prominent scholars making this argument was Becker who, in his 1922 *Declaration of Independence*, may have been following Friedenwald's 1904 *Declaration of Independence* (see p. 197). There is no shortage, though, of more recent interpreters who have followed this path. Among the most polemical and substantively lacking is Breen, "Lockean Moment." Others in agreement with the position taken here include Reid, "Irrelevance of the Declaration," 70–71, and Wills, *Inventing America*, 173. See Warren, "Fourth of July Myths," 271, noting that the charge that Jefferson had copied the Declaration from Locke resulted from an early nineteenth-century smear campaign mounted by Jefferson's opponents.

31. See Zyskind, "How to Read the Declaration," 178–79: "Either the Declaration's general propositions are unclear in meaning or the meaning must be sought in interpretation. The propositions do not sufficiently explain themselves. How can the search proceed? One method would be to look for the origin of the ideas. For example, the fact is well known that Jefferson took many of his ideas from Locke's *Of Civil Government* (second essay). . . . But how do we know that Jefferson interprets Locke's meaning as we do? How do we account for the places where Jefferson in the Declaration seems deliberately to alter Locke's phraseology (Jefferson omits the vital term *property*)? And even if we could discover from such outside sources what Jefferson believed, how do we know that the signers of the Declaration meant what Jefferson meant?"

32. See Waldron, *God, Locke, and Equality*.

33. See Vossler, *Jefferson and the American Revolutionary Ideal*; Palmer, "Neglected Work."

34. See Vattel, *Law of Nations*, editor's Intro, xxix–xxx: with the War for Independence, Americans "turned to European publicists. Charles W. F. Dumas, a Swiss living in Holland, and an ardent republican . . . brought out a new edition [of Vattel] with notes inspired by recent events, and sent three copies of it to Franklin. Vattel, replied Franklin [December 1775], came at the right time. . . . From 1776 to 1783, the more the United States progressed, the greater became Vattel's influence. In 1780 his *Law of Nations* was a classic, a *text book* in the universities."

35. Ibid., 131; see also Grotius, *Rights of War*, 2:569–70, 674.

36. See McIlwain, *American Revolution*, 1–2: "The Americans stoutly insisted during the whole of their contest with Parliament to the summer of 1776 that the resistance was a constitutional resistance to unconstitutional acts."

37. Bemis, *Diplomacy of the American Revolution*, 31–32, 43.

38. Paine, *Common Sense* (January 1776), 445.

39. Schwartz, *Roots of the Bill of Rights*, 2:236. For a list of similar instructions issued by other state conventions, see Wills, *Inventing America*, 326. He concludes that "independence *had* to be declared to get foreign aid; and a league had to be formed to negotiate that aid." Of course, it was primarily regarding the timing and sequencing of such matters that the congressional delegates long disagreed.

40. Dull, *Diplomatic History of the American Revolution*, 52.

41. The timing of congressional action and the near-simultaneous arrival of the Howes on Long Island must not be viewed as coincidental.

42. In regard to any number of secondary goals, see Ginsberg, "Declaration as Rhetoric," 219: one may also "speak to the enemy, warning that the fight is in earnest; one may speak to sympathetic elements among the enemy to gain them over to the rebellion's cause; one may address the people in one's own ranks hesitant to fight against the mother country." Yet in each instance the "address must be made with an eye to the primary audience," which in this instance was internationally influential states in western Europe, i.e., the "international" community.

43. Jefferson, "Autobiography," 6 Jan. 1821], in *Writings*, 16. See also Evans, *Theme Is Freedom*, 235; Hazelton, *Declaration of Independence*, 42–43; Hutson, "Partition Treaty and the Declaration," 877; Pencak, "Declaration of Independence," 225–26.

44. See Wright, *American Interpretations of Natural Law*, 76, correcting Tyler, who had described Dickinson as "the penman of the American Revolution," by noting that "he was really the penman of the period between 1765 and 1774." I would push the later date to 1775 when he and Jefferson began to share overlapping responsibilities.

45. Lucas, "Stylistic Artistry of the Declaration," 28 (citing Adams); Wills, *Inventing America*, 325 (citing Lee).

46. See McIlwain, *American Revolution*, 7.

47. Jefferson, *Writings*, 16.

48. Miller, "From the Covenant to the Revival," 333.

49. See Jefferson, *Writings*, 18: "The pusillanimous idea that we had friends in England worth keeping terms with, still haunted the minds of many"; Guttridge, *English Whiggism and the American Revolution*.

50. Perry, *Sources of Our Liberties*, 311.

51. See Lucas, "Rhetorical Ancestry of the Declaration of Independence," 157: "The men who led America out of the British empire were devoted students of history who consciously modeled their revolution on those that had occurred in England during the 1640s and 1680s."

52. See Vattel, *Law of Nations*, 130–34, 174; cf. Grotius, *Rights of War*.

53. See Wishy, "John Locke and the Spirit of '76," 419, asking if the Declaration asserts "fully and unambiguously a doctrine of human rights that amounts to the supremacy of the individual conscience or does it establish a doctrine of popular sovereignty?"

54. See Lutz, *Preface to American Political Theory*, 32–48, 62–71; Dana, "Political Principles of the Declaration," 106, arguing that the document's lack of "originality is of the first importance in one aspect. It does not isolate the Declaration of Independence from all other state-papers, and make the Declaration itself the sole source of authoritative interpretation. It leaves open the whole body of contemporary history, as, also, the literature of the times, to clear up ambiguities, or to supply omissions. This is a most essential point."

55. See Palmer, "Liberties as Constitutional Provisions," 65–66; Peters, *Massachusetts Constitution of 1780*, 79, 155–56; Adams, *First American Constitutions*, 137–38; Lutz, *Origins of American Constitutionalism*, 98–99.

56. Vattel, *Law of Nations*, 9a; Burlamaqui, *Principles of Natural Law*, 1:72; see also Shain, *Myth of American Individualism*, 277–82, 285.

57. Cited by Wright, *American Interpretations of Natural Law*, 85; see also Burlamaqui, *Principles of Natural Law*, 2:20.

58. Cited by Hamburger, "Equality and Diversity," 308; ibid., 312: "Americans did not

typically consider most other natural rights [excepting religious conscience]—even 'inalienable' natural rights—immune from government restraints."

59. Jefferson, *Papers of Thomas Jefferson*, 17:195; see also Chinard, *Apostle of Americanism*, 80–81, describing Jefferson writing of the distinction between civil and natural rights.

60. Cited by Hamburger, "Natural Rights," 932.

61. See Kendall and Carey, *Basic Symbols*, 69–70, 121–22; Adams, *First American Constitutions*, 169, 174; Lutz, *Origins of American Constitutionalism*, 80.

62. Morris, "Political Enquiries, 1776," 330; Farrand, *Records*, 2:666; see also Lind [and Bentham], *Answer to the Declaration*, 120, writing similarly, in opposition to America's declaration of independence, that some Americans "perceive not, or will not seem to perceive, that nothing which can be called Government ever was, or ever could be, in any instance, exercised, but at the expence of one or other of those rights. That, consequently, in as many instances as Government is ever exercised, some one or other of these rights, pretended to be unalienable, is actually alienated."

63. See Vattel, *Law of Nations*, 90: "If the majority of a Nation, or the sovereign who represents it, seek to establish laws in matters to which the compact of society can not oblige all citizens to submit, those to whom the laws are repugnant have the right to withdraw from the society and settle elsewhere."

64. There were also a number of other specialized instances that under certain conditions, most importantly including self-defense and necessity, invoked inalienable natural rights.

65. See Wright, *American Interpretations of Natural Law*, 86–87: like Bland, Jefferson in his *Summary View* defended the argument that Americans "possessed a right which nature has given to all men, of departing from the country in which chance, not choice, has placed them."

66. Jefferson, *Writings*, 962.

67. The protection of a future generation from the political impositions of an earlier one was of special importance to Jefferson. See, e.g., his extensive development of this idea and his discrimination between associated natural and civil rights in *Portable Thomas Jefferson*, 444–51, esp. 449: "No society can make a perpetual constitution, or even a perpetual law. . . . The constitution and the laws of their predecessors [are] extinguished then in their natural course with those who gave them being."

68. Thus, we find *inalienable being* defined as "that which cannot be legally alienated or made over to another," such as the dominions of the king or "the estates of a minor," in *Encyclopedia Britannica* (1771), s.v. "Inalienable."

69. Randolph, in Farrand, *Records*, 2:137.

70. For these internal controversies within various states, see Jensen, *Articles of Confederation*, 16–103.

71. An apparent linkage between the claims of equality and rights is still clearer in the language originally used by Jefferson. There, as reported in Hazelton, *Declaration of Independence*, 308, he wrote that "We hold these Truths to be self-evident; that all Men are created equal and independent; that from that equal Creation they derive Rights inherent and unalienable." Still, one should read Lucas, "Justifying America," 86, for his intriguing exploration of varying ways that the linkage between the equality and rights claims might reasonably be read.

72. See Mullett, *Fundamental Law and the American Revolution*, 18; Wright, *Ameri-*

can Interpretations of Natural Law, 52, 54, 60, 65, 85. E.g., Wright notes that John Wise in his *Vindication* (1717) "quotes Ulpian as having said that 'by natural right all men are born free.'" For similar claims among Sophists, see Gurvitch, "Natural Law," 11:285–86; in Roman and late medieval law, Sigmund, "Late Medieval Roots of Liberal Theory"; more generally, Bryce, "Law of Nature," 599, noting that what was so remarkable was "that which had been for nearly two thousand years a harmless maxim, almost a commonplace of morality, became in the end of eighteenth century a mass of dynamite"; Maine, "Modern History of the Law of Nature," 90–91, describing the doctrine as having had little influence "until it passed out of the possession of the lawyers into that of the literary men of the eighteenth century."

73. See Ginsberg, "Declaration as Rhetoric," 232–33, considering why Jefferson, in subsequent drafts of the Declaration, may have rejected, on prudential grounds, this language found in the seminal Virginia Declaration of Rights of 12 June 1776.

74. Maier, *American Scripture*, 155.

75. See Lucas, "Justifying America," 86: "One thing we can be sure of is that neither the Continental Congress nor contemporary readers of the Declaration would have taken 'all men are created equal' to mean all people possess equal physical or intellectual endowments, or are entitled to equal social status and material conditions regardless of their abilities and achievements."

76. Farrand, *Records*, 1:477. For similar views, see, among numerous others, Ginsberg, *Casebook on the Declaration*, 6; Maxcy, *An Oration* (1799), 1048, 1229.

77. Pufendorf, *Duty of Man and Citizen*, 132–33, 139.

78. See Adams, *Adams–Jefferson Letters*, 355.

79. See Adams, *First American Constitutions*, 169–74; Black, "Ethics of the Declaration," 81; Dana, "Political Principles of the Declaration," 106; Friedenwald, *Declaration of Independence*, 78–79; Ginsberg, "Declaration as Rhetoric," 232–33; Greene, *All Men Are Created Equal*, 34; McDonald, *Novus Ordo Seclorum*, 53–55.

80. Pole, "Loyalists, Whigs, and Equality," 73.

81. *Considerations upon the Rights* (1766), 12.

82. See McIlwain, *American Revolution*, 78–80; Blackstone, *Commentaries* (1765)], 1:105, claiming that "our American plantations are principally of this latter sort [conquered or ceded lands] . . . and therefore the common law of England, as such, has no allowance or authority there . . . they are subject however to the control of parliament."

83. See Adams, *Political Ideas of the American Revolution*.

84. Jensen, *Tracts of the American Revolution*, 47, 24–27, 66–67, 170–72, 360; [Johnson], *Some Important Observations* (1766), 34–35; Thacher, *Sentiments of a British American* (1764), 490–92; Morgan, *Prologue to Revolution*, 47–48, 62–67; Patten, *Discourse Delivered at Hallifax* (1766), 13–14. See also Dana, "Political Principles of the Declaration," 117: "The Colonists spoke for, and in the name of, themselves, as British subjects, the equals, in all respects of those native-born within the kingdom. The instances of this character are so numerous as almost to defy recapitulation."

85. See Wright, *American Interpretations of Natural Law,* 36–37, making clear that before 1760, and in fact not until 1774, it was not common for colonial spokesmen to make any mention of natural law or rights. In this earlier period "only a very few persons, other than the clergy of New England colonies, made any very important use of natural law arguments. . . . And even in such literature as was produced the natural law concept ap-

pears but rarely." McIlwain, *American Revolution*, 7, argues that the shift only occurred in May 1776.

86. Pole, "Loyalists, Whigs, and Equality," 73.

87. Burlamaqui, *Principles of Natural Law*, 2:10; see also Vattel, *Law of Nations*, 3–9.

88. Jefferson, *Writings*, 110, 121; see also Conrad, "Putting Rights Talk in Its Place," 269.

89. See McIlwain, *American Revolution*, 152, for his depiction of a four-stage evolution of the American position with three resting on constitutional law and a final one on natural law.

90. Consider, e.g., Vermont's 1797 "welfare" legislation which allowed towns to "'build, purchase or hire a house of correction or workhouse, in which to confine and set their poor to work.'. . . There were sections in the law which permitted officials to 'fetter, shackle or whip, not exceeding twenty stripes, any person confined therein who does not perform the labor designed to him or her, or is refractory or disobedient to lawful commands.'" Cited by Bryan and McClaughry, *Vermont Papers*, 203.

91. See Mahoney, "Declaration of Independence," 60, contending, like most Straussian theorists, without evidence, that "the Declaration rejects . . . that men on entering society and submitting to government yield their natural rights and retain only 'civil' rights."

92. See Ginsberg, "Declaration as Rhetoric," 233: "*All Men are created equal* is as commanding an utterance as men may make. It is pious, philosophic, fraternal. Who would not hesitate to go on record against *Life, Liberty, and the Pursuit of Happiness*? These stirring words beg to be filled in with particular meanings by the hearers, establishing agreement with the speaker. They are rhetorical *commonplaces* rather than philosophic *terms*."

93. Peters, *Massachusetts Constitution of 1780*, 51.

94. Farrand, *Records*, 1:172.

95. Many of the conservatives who, in the end, supported separation were concerned to protect individual constitutional freedoms from popular oversight. Their fears ultimately found expression in their successful movement to create a new government under the federal Constitution that was able to hold state governments and popular majorities in check.

96. [Boucher], *Letter From a Virginian* (1774), 25; see also Wesley, *Calm Address to Our American Colonies* (1775), 417.

97. See Lolme, *Constitution of England*, 176, for his passionate defense of the British protection of individual rights and his distinction between essential civil rights and unessential political ones.

98. See [Allen], *American Alarm* (1773), essay 3, pp. 2, 7; and in agreement regarding the central nature of the conflict, though from the Loyalist perspective, see Howard, *Letter from a Gentleman* (1765), 66–67.

99. See Quarles, "Lord Dunmore as Liberator."

100. See Johnson, *Taxation No Tyranny* (March 1775), 132; see ibid., 130, where in direct reference to Dunmore's emancipation proclamation, he wrote that "it has been proposed, that the slaves should be set free, an act which surely the lovers of liberty cannot but recommend."

101. Lind [and Bentham], *Answer to the Declaration*, 107.

102. See Jensen, "Democracy and the American Revolution."

103. See Becker, *History of Political Parties in the Province of New York*, 22, stating that

two questions were at the forefront during 1765 to 1776: "The first was the question of home rule; the second was the question, if we may so put it, of who should rule at home."

104. See Wood, *Radicalism of the American Revolution*.

105. Perry, *Sources of Our Liberties*, 287–88.

106. McIlwain, *American Revolution*, 35–37.

107. See Tucker, *Treatise Concerning Government* (1781). Whether or not his intimate association of Priestly, Cartwright, and Locke and their common dedication to radical political ends is accurate, or rather something closer to exaggeration, is not a matter to be resolved here. See Breen, "Lockean Moment," 6, too readily accepting Tucker's assessment at face value.

108. Cited by Sheldon, *Political Philosophy of Thomas Jefferson*, 50.

109. Vattel, *Law of Nations*, 3.

110. Clark, *Massachusetts Election Sermon* (1781), 11.

111. Bland, *Inquiry* (1766), 116.

112. Berthoff and Murrin, "Feudalism, Communalism, and the Yeoman Free-holder," 282.

113. Farrand, *Records*, 1:440.

114. See Vattel, *Law of Nations*, 7–8, 19, 131, 225. His influential remarks apply this logic to civil war and find that those who revolt, once they enjoy sovereignty, deserve international standing. He provocatively wrote that civil war "gives rise, within the Nation, to two independent parties. . . . Of necessity, therefore, these two parties must be regarded as forming thenceforth, for a time at least, two separate bodies politic, two distinct Nations."

115. Wilson, *Works of James Wilson*, 2:589. Wilson was comparing Blackstone to Burke and finding them both wanting.

116. See Wright, *American Interpretations of Natural Law*, 187–88, noting that in the New York convention of 1821, many continued to hold "that all men are free and equal only in a state of nature, not after the establishment of civil government, 'for the many rights, flowing from natural equality, are necessarily abridged, with a view to produce the greatest amount of security and happiness to the whole community.'"

117. See Oakeshott, *Rationalism in Politics and Other Essays*, describing from a liberal conservative perspective a "new man's" confidence in "modern rationalism."

118. See Wright, *American Interpretations of Natural Law*, 92, pointing out that until the spring of 1775, any mention of natural rights was "invariably combined with a theory of the British constitution. It was not until after the war had been going on for some months that any very emphatic expression of the theory of natural rights in no way combined with an interpretation of the British or any man-made constitution is to be found. . . . [It should not be surprising then that] an Englishman but newly arrived in the land . . . [was] the first to state the theory of the natural rights of the colonists without reference to or reliance upon the laws or customs of England."

119. See Reid, "Irrelevance of the Declaration," 58–69; Reid, *Authority Of Rights*, 5–35; Reid, *Authority to Tax*, 24: "American whigs, in their quarrel with London, almost always sought recognition of English rights, or put more correctly, British rights of English origins. They certainly did not seek or want Irish rights. It is also likely that at least until the Declaration of Independence, if then, they never officially asked for or referred to a natural right. . . . 'It is,' the Stamp Act Congress asserted, 'from and under the English constitution, we derive all our civil and religious rights and liberties.'"

120. See McIlwain, *American Revolution*, 7–11.

121. Adams, *Works*, 1:160.

122. Lolme, *Constitution of England*, 377, explained one of the reasons the British Whigs and Americans seeking independence parted company was the fear that the former had of allowing the king to raise taxes in either Ireland or America without parliamentary mediation.

123. Among the leading lights of British radicalism urging a collapse of natural and civil rights were Sharp, *Declaration of the People's Natural Right to Share in the Legislature* (1774), Macaulay, *Address to the People of England* (1775), and Cartwright, *American Independence* (1774 and 1776). See McIlwain, *American Revolution*, 150, 158, concluding that after May 1776, the American position owed nothing to the British Whigs, but "rather to the Radicals than to the Whigs."

124. Smith, *Letters of the Delegates*, 1:46–49.

125. Locke, *Second Treatise*, sec. 87.

126. See Armitage, "Declaration of Independence and International Law," 61–62.

127. See Pound, "Rights of Englishmen and Rights of Man," 92: "Natural rights mean simply interests which we think ought to be secured . . . [and] it is fatal to all sound thinking to treat them as legal conceptions."

128. Reid, *Authority of Rights*, 73; see also Wright, *American Interpretations of Natural Law*, 146–47; Palmer, "Liberties as Constitutional Provisions," 62; Roche, "Curbing of the Militant Majority," 35.

129. See Hamburger, "Equality and Diversity," 313: Even though "the free exercise of religion might be 'exactly the same' under government as in nature, other inalienable rights were different under government and therefore were inalienable in a rather qualified way." Other individual rights, however, were occasionally claimed to be natural or inalienable. For a comprehensive listing of them by New England ministers, see Baldwin, *New England Clergy*, 82.

130. See Holmes, "Precommitment and the Paradox of Democracy."

131. Dry, *Anti-Federalist*, 70.

132. Schwartz, *Roots of the Bill of Rights*, 2:375. This was a position found in most of the other state declarations of rights. For another example, see the "North Carolina Declaration of Rights" (1776), ibid., 286–87.

133. Cited by Hamburger, "Equality and Diversity," 313. Much of the analysis here owes a great deal to Hamburger's prodigious research.

134. Stillman, *Massachusetts Election Sermon* (1779), 11; see also Stiles, *Discourse on the Christian Union* (1761), 28; Dorr, *Duty of Civil Rulers* (176)], 13; Patten, *Discourse Delivered at Hallifax* (1766), 13–14. Stillman was a minister deeply influenced by Locke, politically active, and at that time uniquely honored as a Baptist by having been asked to give the prestigious annual election sermon in Massachusetts. Nevertheless, he, too, limited his accounting of inalienable individual civil rights to that of religious conscience.

135. Hamburger, "Equality and Diversity," 312–13.

136. Smith, *The Occasional Reverberator* (5 Oct. 1753), cited by Leder, *Liberty and Authority*, 73–74.

137. Like the inalienable duty and non-negotiable obligation to worship God, and the corresponding right to do so, the comparable duty and responsibility for parents to care for and educate their children were tied to the inalienable right of parents to do so.

138. See Shain, *Myth of American Individualism,* 193–241.

139. Handlin and Handlin, *Popular Sources of Political Authority,* 374–75; see also ibid., 410–11, 423, 436.

140. See Palmer, "Liberties as Constitutional Provisions," 65–66.

141. Jefferson, *Writings,* 285.

142. Madison, *Mind of the Founder,* 9.

143. Clark, *Massachusetts Election Sermon* (1781), 8–9.

144. Whitaker, *Antidote Against Toryism* (1777), 12.

145. Hyneman and Lutz, *American Political Writing,* 100.

146. *Civil Liberty Asserted* (1776), 44–45; see also Canavan, "Relevance of the Burke-Paine Controversy," 166.

147. It is often overlooked that the language of natural rights, like the drive for independence, was most commonly advanced by New Englanders, that is, by many of the most religious among the colonists. As Wright, *American Interpretations of Natural Law,* has observed, "the New England writers seem to have been the leaders in spreading the gospel of the inherent rights deriving from the laws of nature" (75). This further suggests that the grounding for such claims, rather than being progressive and secular, is more likely to be reactionary in its naturalism and religiosity, for as Wright observed, "in many cases" the "'law of God' and 'law of nature'" were used interchangeably (43–44, 70).

148. See Lynd, *Intellectual Origins of American Radicalism,* 23–24. American thinking was in keeping with that of Locke in his defense of the same two inalienable rights, though surprisingly few authors took note of this shared understanding.

149. See Shain, "Afterword: Revolutionary-Era Americans: Were They Enlightened or Protestant? Does It Matter?"

150. See Jellinek, *Declaration of the Rights of Man and of Citizens;* Vossler, *Jefferson and the American Revolutionary Ideal;* Bainton, "Appeal to Reason," 126–27, for an introduction to the fascinating early twentieth-century German debate regarding whether the introduction of natural-rights discourse into modern political philosophy stemmed principally from the religious thought of Americans in 1776 or the secular thought of the French fifteen years later.

151. See Amar, "Consent of the Governed," 477, 480–83; Detweiler, "Changing Reputation," 557; Lence, *American Declaration of Independence,* 44; Lutz, *Origins of American Constitutionalism,* 113; Reid, "Irrelevance of the Declaration," 58, and *Authority of Rights,* 5.

152. Schmitt and Webking, "Revolutionaries, Antifederalists, and Federalists," 198.

153. Among many readings that rely more on faith than evidence, see Gerber, "Whatever Happened to the Declaration?" 218; Perry, *Puritanism and Democracy,* 146; Kenyon, "Republicanism and Radicalism," 319, and "Declaration of Independence," 115; Kulikoff, *Agrarian Origins of American Capitalism,* 113–16; Pencak, "Declaration of Independence," 228; Roelofs, "American Political System," 326; Skidmore, *American Political Thought,* 46; Webking, *American Revolution,* 107; Zuckert, *Natural Rights Republic.*

154. See Jellinek, *Declaration,* 17, citing the marquis de Lafayette in noting that the ideas that led American patriots to seek independence from Britain were "only the principles of the sovereignty of the people and the right to change the form of government."

155. See Lucas, "Rhetorical Ancestry," 150–51; Wills, *Inventing America,* 335: "Political declarations seem analogous to *declaration* in the stricter legal sense, which meant a jus-

tifying explanation for the bringing of a suit. First, one brought the action and identified its object. Then a declaration had to be filed"; Fliegelman, *Declaring Independence,* 151, citing John Quincy Adams in noting that "a 'declaration' was defined as 'the narration' inserted into a writ or indictment to which a defendant answers. Thus, in purely legal terms a declaration was a descriptive account of grievances, not a proclamation of principles, a declaration of injuries, not of independence."

156. Jefferson, *Writings,* 1501.

157. See Malone, *Story of the Declaration,* 86; Nicgorski, "Significance of the Non-Lockean Heritage," 177.

158. See Reid, "Irrelevance of the Declaration," 83; Wills, *Inventing America,* 323–24; Lind [and Bentham], *Answer to the Declaration,* devoting only three pages, 120–22, to the Preamble, but scathing in his indictment of it: Americans "perceive not, or will not seem to perceive, that nothing which can be called Government ever was, or ever could be, in any instance, exercised, but at the expence of one or other of those rights" to life, liberty, and the pursuit of happiness.

159. See Ginsberg, "Declaration as Rhetoric," 229: "The references to the Divinity are sufficiently varied and vague to permit anyone to make Him over into the image of his own God. *Laws of Nature and of Nature's God* is especially ingenious since it covers the cases of a mechanical universe actively run by God, a mechanical universe operating without God, or a God and nature independent but harmonious in operation in their operation."

160. Wills, *Lincoln at Gettysburg,* 38–39.

Bibliography

Adams, John, and Thomas Jefferson. *The Adams–Jefferson Letters,* ed. Lester J. Cappon. Chapel Hill, NC, 1959.

Adams, John Quincy. "An Oration Delivered Before the Cincinnati Astronomical Society," 10 Nov. 1843. In *Selected Writings of John and John Quincy Adams,* ed. Adrienne Koch and William Peden, 397–407. New York, 1946.

Adams, Randolph G. *Political Ideas of the American Revolution: Britannic-American Contribution to the Problem of Imperial Legislation, 1765 to 1775.* 1922. 3d ed. New York, 1958.

Adams, Willi Paul. *The First American Constitutions: Republican Ideology and the Making of the State Constitutions in the Revolutionary Era.* Trans. Rita Kimber and Robert Kimber. Chapel Hill, NC, 1980.

[Allen, John]. *The American Alarm . . . for the Rights, and Liberties, of the People: Humbly addressed to the King and Council, and to the constitutional sons of liberty, in America.* Boston: D. Kneeland and N. Davis, 1773.

Amar, Akhil Reed. "The Consent of the Governed: Constitutional Amendment outside Article V." *Columbia Law Review* 94 (March 1994): 457–508.

Armitage, David. "The Declaration of Independence and International Law." *William and Mary Quarterly,* 3d ser., 59 (Jan. 2002): 39–64.

Bainton, Roland. "The Appeal to Reason and the American Constitution." In *Constitution Reconsidered,* ed. Conyers Read, 121–30. New York, 1938.

Baldwin, Alice M. *The New England Clergy and the American Revolution.* Durham, NC, 1928.

Becker, Carl L. *The Declaration of Independence: A Study in the History of Political Ideas.* 1922. Rept. New York, 1958.

——. *The History of Political Parties in the Province of New York, 1760–1776.* 1909. Rept. Madison, WI, 1968.

Bemis, Samuel Flagg. *The Diplomacy of the American Revolution.* Bloomington, IN, 1935.

Berthoff, Rowland, and John M. Murrin. "Feudalism, Communalism, and the Yeoman Freeholder: The American Revolution Considered as a Social Accident." In *Essays on the American Revolution,* ed. Stephen G. Kurtz and James H. Hutson, 256–88. Chapel Hill, NC, 1973.

Black, R. M. "The Ethics of the Declaration of Independence." *Annals of the American Academy of Political and Social Science* 2 (July 1891): 138–44. Rept. in Ginsberg, *A Casebook on the Declaration of Independence,* 78–82.

Blackstone, William. *Commentaries on the Laws of England: A Facsimile of the First Edition of 1765–1769.* 4 vols. Chicago, 1979.

Bland, Richard. *An Inquiry into the Rights of the British Colonies.* 1766. In *Tracts of the American Revolution,* ed. Merrill Jensen, 108–26. Indianapolis, 1967.

[Boucher, Jonathan]. *A Letter From a Virginian, to the Members of the Congress.* Boston: Mills & Hicks, 1774.

Bradford, M. E. *Better Guide than Reason: Studies in the American Revolution.* La Salle, IL, 1979.

Breen, T. H. *The Lockean Moment: The Language of Rights on the Eve of the American Revolution.* Oxford, 2001.

Bryan, Frank, and John McClaughry. *The Vermont Papers: Recreating Democracy on a Human Scale.* Post Mills, VT, 1989.

Bryce, James. "Law of Nature." Chap. 11 in vol. 2 of *Studies in History and Jurisprudence.* 1901. Rept. Freeport, NY, 1969.

Burlamaqui, Jean Jacques. *The Principles of Natural and Politic Law.* 2 vols. 1763. Trans. Mr. Nugent. 5th ed. Boston, 1807. Rept. New York, 1972.

Butterfield, Herbert. *Whig Interpretation of History.* 1931. Rept. New York, 1965.

Calhoun, John C. "Speech on the Oregon Bill," 27 June 1848. In *Union and Liberty: The Political Philosophy of John C. Calhoun,* ed. Ross M. Lence, 539–70. Indianapolis, 1992.

Canavan, Francis. "The Relevance of the Burke-Paine Controversy to American Political Thought." *Review of Politics* 49 (Spring 1987): 163–76.

Cartwright, John. "American Independence, the Interest and Glory of Great Britain," 1774 and 1776. In *English Defenders of American Freedoms, 1774–1778,* comp. Paul H. Smith, 125–92. Washington, DC, 1972.

Chinard, Gilbert. *Thomas Jefferson: The Apostle of Americanism.* Boston, 1933.

Civil Liberty Asserted and the RIGHTS of the SUBJECT DEFENDED Against the Anarchical PRINCIPLES of the Reverend Dr. Price. London: J. Wilkie, 1776.

Clark, Jonas. *Massachusetts Election Day Sermon: A Sermon Preached before His Excellency.* Boston: Gill and Edes, 1781.

Commager, Henry Steele. "The Declaration of Independence." In *Thomas Jefferson: The Man . . . His World . . . His Influence,* ed. Lally Weymouth, 179–87. New York , 1973.

Conrad, Stephen A. "Putting Rights Talk in Its Place: The *Summary View* Revisited." In *Jeffersonian Legacies,* ed. Peter S. Onuf, 254–80. Charlottesville, VA, 1993.

Considerations upon the Rights of the Colonists to the Privileges of British Subjects. New York: John Holt, 1766.

Dana, William F. "The Declaration of Independence as Justification for Revolution." *Harvard Law Review* 13 (Jan. 1900): 319–43. Rept. as "Political Principles of the Declaration," in Ginsberg, *Casebook on the Declaration of Independence,* 102–26.

Detweiler, Philip F. "The Changing Reputation of the Declaration of Independence: The First 50 Years." *William and Mary Quarterly,* 3d ser., 19 (Oct. 1962): 557–74.

Dorr, Edward. *The Duty of Civil Rulers: A Connecticut Election Sermon.* Hartford, CT, 1765.

Dry, Murray, ed. *The Anti-Federalist.* Abridgment of Herbert J. Storing, ed. *The Complete Anti-Federalist.* Chicago, 1985.

Dull, Jonathan R. *A Diplomatic History of the American Revolution.* New Haven, CT, 1985.

Engeman, Thomas S., and Michael Zuckert, ed. *Protestantism and the American Founding.* Notre Dame, IN, 2004.

Evans, M. Stanton. *The Theme Is Freedom: Religion, Politics, and the American Tradition.* Washington, DC, 1994.

Farrand, Max, ed. *The Records of the Federal Convention of 1787.* 4 Vols. Rev. ed. New Haven, CT, 1937.

Fliegelman, Jay. *Declaring Independence: Jefferson, Natural Language, and the Culture of Performance.* Stanford, CA, 1993.

Friedenwald, Herbert. *The Declaration of Independence: An Interpretation and an Analysis.* 1904. Rept. New York, 1974.

Gerber, Scott D. "Whatever Happened to the Declaration of Independence? A Commentary on the Republican Revisionism in the Political Thought of the American Revolution." *Polity* 26 (Winter 1993): 207–32.

Ginsberg, Robert. "The Declaration as Rhetoric." In Ginsberg, *A Casebook on the Declaration of Independence,* 219–44.

———, ed. *A Casebook on the Declaration of Independence.* New York, 1967.

Greene, Jack *All Men Are Created Equal: Some Reflections on the Character of the American Revolution.* New York, 1976.

Grotius, Hugo. *The Rights of War and Peace.* 1625. Rept. 3 vols. Indianapolis, 2005.

Gurvitch, Georges. "Natural Law." In *The Encyclopedia of the Social Sciences,* ed. Edwin R. A. Seligman, 11:284–90. New York, 1933.

Guttridge, G. H. *English Whiggism and the American Revolution.* Berkeley, CA, 1963.

Hamburger, Philip A. "Equality and Diversity: The Eighteenth-Century Debate about Equal Protection and Equal Civil Rights." *Supreme Court Review* 1992 (1993): 295–392.

———. "Natural Rights, Natural Law, and American Constitution." *Yale Law Journal* 102 (Jan. 1993): 907–60.

Handlin, Oscar, and Mary Handlin, eds. *The Popular Sources of Political Authority: Documents on the Massachusetts Constitution of 1780.* Cambridge, MA, 1966.

Hawke, David Freeman. *A Transaction of Free Men: The Birth and Course of the Declaration of Independence.* 1964. Rept. New York, 1989.

Hazelton, John H. *Declaration of Independence: Its History.* 1906. Rept. New York, 1970.

Holmes, Stephen. "Precommitment and the Paradox of Democracy." 1988. Rept. in *Con-*

stitutionalism and Democracy, ed. Jon Elster and Rune Slagstad, 195–240. Cambridge, 1993.

Howard, Martin, Jr. *A Letter from a Gentlemen at Halifax.* 1765. In *Tracts of the American Revolution,* ed. Merrill Jensen, 63–78. Indianapolis, 1967.

Hutson, James H. "The Partition Treaty and the Declaration of American Independence." *Journal of American History* 58 (March 1972): 877–96.

Hyneman, Charles S., and Donald S. Lutz, ed. *American Political Writing during the Founding Era, 1760–1805.* 2 vols. Indianapolis, 1983.

Jaffa, Harry V. "Human Rights and the Crisis of the West." In *The Promise of American Politics,* ed. Robert L. Utley Jr., 53–77. Lantham, MD, 1989.

Jefferson, Thomas. *The Papers of Thomas Jefferson,* ed. Julian Boyd et al. Princeton, NJ, 1950–.

———. *The Portable Thomas Jefferson,* ed. Merrill D. Peterson. New York, 1975.

———. *Writings of Thomas Jefferson,* ed. Merrill D. Peterson. New York, 1984.

Jellinek, Georg. *The Declaration of the Rights of Man and of Citizens: A Contribution to Modern Constitutional History.* Trans. Max Farrand. 1901. Rept. Westport, CT, 1979.

Jensen, Merrill. *The Articles of Confederation: An Interpretation of the Social and Constitutional History of the American Revolution, 1774–1781.* Madison, WI, 1940.

———. "Democracy and the American Revolution." *Huntington Library Quarterly* 20 (1957): 321–41.

———, ed. *Tracts of the American Revolution, 1763–1776.* Indianapolis, 1967.

Johnson, Samuel. *Taxation No Tyranny.* March 1775. In *Political Writings of Dr. Johnson,* ed. J. Hardy, 100–132. New York, 1968.

[Johnson, Stephen]. *Some Important Observations, Occasioned by . . . the public fast . . . On account of the peculiar circumstances of the present day.* Newport, RI: Samuel Hall, 1766.

Kendall, Willmoore. "Equality: Commitment or Ideal?" *Intercollegiate Review* 24 (Spring 1989): 25–34.

Kendall, Willmoore, and George Carey. *Basic Symbols of the American Political Tradition.* Baton Rouge, LA, 1970.

Kenyon, Cecelia M. "The Declaration of Independence: Philosophy of Government in a Free Society." In *Aspects of American Liberty: Philosophical, Historical, and Political,* ed. George W. Corner, 114–25. Philadelphia, 1977.

———. "Republicanism and Radicalism in the American Revolution: An Old-Fashioned Interpretation." In *The Reinterpretation of the American Revolution,* ed. Jack P. Greene, 291–320. New York, 1968.

Kulikoff, Allan. *The Agrarian Origins of American Capitalism.* Charlottesville, VA, 1992.

Leder, Lawrence H. *Liberty and Authority: Early American Political Ideology, 1689–1763.* Chicago, 1968.

Lence, Ross M. "The American Declaration of Independence: The Majority and the Right of Political Power." In *Founding Principles of American Government: Two Hundred Years of Democracy on Trial,* ed. George J. Graham Jr. and Scarlett G. Graham, 29–59. Rev. ed. Chatham, NJ, 1984.

Lincoln, Abraham. "Speech in Springfield, Illinois," 26 June 1857. In *The Life and Writings of Abraham Lincoln,* ed. Philip Van Doren Stern, 414–27. New York, 1940.

Lind, John [and J. Bentham]. *An Answer to the Declaration of the American Congress.* London: T. Cadell, 1776.

Locke, John. *Second Treatise of Government* (1690), ed. C. B. Macpherson. Indianapolis, 1980.

Lolme, J. L. de. *The Constitution of England.* 1775. Rev. ed. 1821. Rept. Buffalo, NY, 1999.

Lucas, Stephen E. "Justifying America: The Declaration of Independence as a Rhetorical Document." In *American Rhetoric: Context and Criticism,* ed. Thomas Benson, 67–130. Carbondale, IL, 1989.

———. "Rhetorical Ancestry of the Declaration of Independence." *Rhetoric and Public Affairs* 1 (1998): 143–184.

———. "Stylistic Artistry of the Declaration of Independence." *Prologue* 22 (Spring 1990): 25–43.

Lutz, Donald S. *The Origins of American Constitutionalism.* Baton Rouge, LA, 1988.

———. *A Preface to American Political Theory.* Lawrence, KS, 1992.

Lynd, Staughton. *Intellectual Origins of American Radicalism.* New York, 1968.

Macaulay, Catharine. "An Address to the People of England, Ireland, and Scotland on the Present Important Crisis of Affairs." In *English Defenders of American Freedoms, 1774–1778,* comp. Paul H. Smith, 107–24. Washington, DC, 1972.

Madison, James. *The Mind of the Founder: Sources of the Political Thought of James Madison,* ed. Marvin Meyers. New York, 1973.

Mahoney, Dennis J. "The Declaration of Independence as a Constitutional Document." In *The Framing and Ratification of the Constitution,* ed. Leonard W. Levy and Dennis J. Mahoney, 54–68. New York, 1987.

Maier, Pauline. *American Scripture: Making the Declaration of Independence.* New York, 1997.

Maine, Henry Sumner. "Modern History of the Law of Nature." Chap. 4 in *Ancient Law.* 1864. Rept. Tucson, AZ, 1986.

Malone, Dumas. *Jefferson and His Time.* Vol. 1. *Jefferson the Virginian.* Boston, 1948.

———. *The Story of the Declaration of Independence.* New York, 1954.

Maxcy, Jonathan. *An Oration* (1799). In vol. 2 of *American Political Writing during the Founding Era, 1760–1805,* ed. Charles S. Hyneman and Donald S. Lutz. Indianapolis, 1983.

McDonald, Forrest. *Novus Ordo Seclorum: The Intellectual Origins of the Constitution.* Lawrence, KS, 1985.

McIlwain, C. H. *The American Revolution: A Constitutional Interpretation.* 1923. Rept. Ithaca, NY, 1962.

Miller, Perry. "From the Covenant to the Revival." In *The Shaping of American Religion,* ed. James Ward Smith and A. Leland Jamison, 1:322–68. Princeton, NJ, 1961.

Morgan, Edmund, ed. *Prologue to Revolution: Sources and Documents on the Stamp Act Crisis, 1764–1766.* New York, 1959.

Morris, Gouverneur. "Political Enquiries, 1776: An Essay by Gouverneur Morris." In "Several Essays on the Nature of Liberty—Natural, Civil, [and] Political," appended to "'The Spirit of Commerce Requires That Property Be Sacred': Gouverneur Morris and the American Revolution," by Willi Paul Adams. *Amerikastudien* 21 (1976): 327–31.

Mullett, Charles F. *Fundamental Law and the American Revolution.* New York, 1933.

Nicgorski, Walter. "The Significance of the Non-Lockean Heritage of the Declaration of Independence." *American Journal of Jurisprudence* 21 (1976): 156–77.

Oakeshott, Michael. *Rationalism in Politics and Other Essays.* 1962. Rept. London, 1977.

Paine, Thomas. *Common Sense.* January 1776. In *Tracts of the American Revolution, 1763–1776,* ed. Merrill Jensen. Indianapolis, 1967.

Palmer, Robert C. "Liberties as Constitutional Provisions, 1776–1791." In *Liberty and Community: Constitution and Rights in the Early American Republic,* ed. William E. Nelson and Robert C. Palmer, 55–148. New York, 1987.

Palmer, R. R. "A Neglected Work: Otto Vossler on Jefferson and the Revolutionary Era." *William and Mary Quarterly,* 3d ser., 12 (July 1955): 462–71.

Patten, William. *Discourse Delivered at Hallifax.* Boston: D. Kneeland for Thomas Leverett, 1766.

Pencak, William. "The Declaration of Independence: Changing Interpretations and a New Hypothesis." *Pennsylvania History* 57 (July 1990): 225–35.

Perry, Ralph Barton. *Puritanism and Democracy.* New York, 1944.

Perry, Richard L., ed. *Sources of Our Liberties: Documentary Origins of Individual Liberties in the Constitution and Bill of Rights.* 1959. Rept. Buffalo, NY, 1991.

Peters, Ronald M., Jr. *The Massachusetts Constitution of 1780: A Social Compact.* Amherst, MA, 1978.

Pole, J. R. "Loyalists, Whigs, and the Idea of Equality." In *A Tug of Loyalties: Anglo-American Relations, 1765–85,* ed. Esmond Wright, 66–92. London, 1975.

Pound, Roscoe. "The Rights of Englishmen and the Rights of Man." In *The Spirit of the Common Law,* 85–111. Boston, 1921.

Powell, H. Jefferson. "The Original Understanding of Original Intent." *Harvard Law Review* 98 (March 1985): 885–948.

Pufendorf, Samuel. *On the Duty of Man and Citizen According to Natural Law.* 1673. Rept. Cambridge, 1991.

Quarles, Benjamin. "Lord Dunmore as Liberator." *William and Mary Quarterly,* 3d ser., 15 (Oct. 1958): 494–507.

Randolph, Edmund. "Edmund Randolph's Essay on the Revolutionary History of Virginia, 1774–1782 [written between 1809–1813]." *Virginia Magazine of History and Biography* 43 (Oct. 1935): 115–38, 209–32, 294–315; 44 (1936): 35–50, 105–15, 223–31, 312–22; 45 (1936): 46–47.

Reid, John Phillip. *Constitutional History of the American Revolution: The Authority of Rights.* Madison, WI, 1986.

———. *Constitutional History of the American Revolution: The Authority to Tax.* Madison, WI, 1987.

———. "The Irrelevance of the Declaration." In *Law in the American Revolution and the Revolution in the Law,* ed. Hendrik Hartog, 46–89. New York, 1981.

Roche, John "The Curbing of the Militant Majority: A Dissent from the Classic Liberal Interpretation of Civil Liberties in America." *Reporter,* 18 July 1963, 34–38.

Roelofs, H. Mark. "The American Political System: A Systematic Ambiguity." *Review of Politics* 48 (Summer 1986): 323–48.

Schmitt, Gary J., and Robert K. Webking. "Revolutionaries, Antifederalists, and Federalists: Comments on Gordon Wood's Understanding of the American Founding." *Political Science Reviewer* 9 (1979): 195–229.

Schwartz, Bernard, ed. *The Roots of the Bill of Rights: An Illustrated Source Book of American Freedom.* 4 vols. New York, 1980.

Shain, Barry Alan. "Afterword: Revolutionary-Era Americans: Were They Enlightened or Protestant? Does It Matter?" In *The Founders on Faith and Civil Government,* ed. Daniel Dreisbach, Mark Hall, and Jeffry Morrison, 273–98. Lanham, MD, 2004.

———. *The Myth of American Individualism: The Protestant Origins of American Political Thought.* 1994. Rept. Princeton, NJ, 1996.

Sharp, Granville. *Declaration of the People's Natural Right to a Share in the Legislature; Which is the Fundamental Principle of the British Constitution of State.* London: B. White, 1774.

Sheldon, Garrett Ward. *The Political Philosophy of Thomas Jefferson.* Baltimore, MD, 1991.

Sigmund, Paul E. "Late Medieval Roots of Liberal Theory, with Special Attention to the Influence of Conciliar Thought on Liberal Constitutionalism." Paper presented at meeting of the American Political Science Association, Chicago, 1995.

Skidmore, Max J. *American Political Thought.* New York, 1978.

Smith, Paul H. ed. *Letters of Delegates to Congress.* 26 vols. Washington, DC, 1976–2000.

Stiles, Ezra. *A Discourse on the Christian Union.* Boston: Edes and Gill, 1761.

Stillman, Samuel. *Massachusetts Election Day Sermon.* Boston: T. J. Fleet, 1779.

Thacher, Oxenbridge. *The Sentiments of a British American.* 1764. In *Pamphlets of the American Revolution,* ed. Bernard Bailyn, 483–98. Cambridge, MA, 1965.

Tucker, Josiah. *A Treatise Concerning Civil Government.* London: T. Cadell, [1781]. Rept. New York, 1967.

Vattel, Emmerich de. *The Law of Nations, or the Principles of Natural Law.* 1758. Ed. James Brown Scott. Washington, DC, 1916.

Vossler, Otto. *Jefferson and the American Revolutionary Ideal.* 1929. Trans. Catherine Philippon and Bernard Wishy. Washington, DC, 1980.

Waldron, Jeremy. *God, Locke, and Equality: Christian Foundations in Locke's Political Thought.* Cambridge, 2002.

Warren, Charles. "Fourth of July Myths." *William and Mary Quarterly,* 3d ser., 2 (July 1945): 237–72.

Webking, Robert H. *The American Revolution and the Politics of Liberty.* Baton Rouge, LA, 1988.

Wesley, John. "Calm Address to the American Colonies," *Massachusetts Gazette,* 1 Feb. 1776.

Whitaker, Nathaniel. *An Antidote Against Toryism, or the Curse of Meroz.* 1777. In *Patriot Preachers of the American Revolution, 1766–1783,* ed. Frank Moore, 186–231. New York, 1860.

White, Morton. *The Philosophy of the American Revolution.* Oxford, 1978.

Wills, Gary. *Inventing America: Jefferson's Declaration of Independence.* Garden City, NJ, 1978.

———. *Lincoln at Gettysburg: The Words That Remade America.* New York, 1992.

Wilson, James. *The Works of James Wilson.* 1804. Ed. Robert Green McCloskey. 2 vols. Cambridge, MA, 1967.

Winthrop, Robert C. *The Centennial of Independence.* Boston, 4 July 1876. In *Old South Leaflets,* vol. 8, no. 191, pp. 289–308. Boston, n.d.

Wise, John. *A Vindication of the Government of New-England Churches*. Boston: J. Allen, 1717.

Wishy, Bernard. "John Locke and the Spirit of '76." *Political Science Quarterly* 73 (Sept. 1958): 413–25.

Wood, Gordon S. *The Radicalism of the American Revolution*. New York, 1992.

Wright, Benjamin F., Jr. *American Interpretations of Natural Law: A Study in the History of Political Thought*. New York, 1962.

Zuckert, Michael. *The Natural Rights Republic: Studies in the Foundation of the American Political Tradition*. Notre Dame, IN, 1996.

Zyskind, Harold. "The Declaration of Independence." In *Promoting Growth toward Maturity in Interpreting What Is Read*, ed. William S. Grey, 7–12. 1951. Rept. as "How to Read the Declaration of Independence," in Ginsberg, *A Casebook on the Declaration of Independence*, 177–83.

The Creation, Reconstruction, and Interpretation of the Bill of Rights

AKHIL REED AMAR

Perhaps the most striking feature of modern constitutional jurisprudence is the leading role that the Bill of Rights now plays both inside courtrooms and beyond. It was not always so.

The Creation of the Bill of Rights

A separate bill of rights was no part of James Madison's careful plan at the Philadelphia Convention of 1787, and the document that emerged from Philadelphia omitted an explicit bill of rights. When Anti-Federalist skeptics pounced on this omission during ratification debates, Federalists scrambled to defend the document with a jumble of counterarguments. Some Federalists claimed that the entire Constitution was a kind of bill of rights; others pointed to the specific rules limiting Congress in Article I, Section 9, as a functional bill of rights; and many also claimed (sometimes contradicting themselves or their allies) that a bill of rights would in fact prove useless or even dangerous. Madison himself promised to revisit the issue once the Constitution went into effect. Although he kept his promise, shepherding a set of amendments through the First Congress, many of his colleagues viewed the exercise as a "nauseous" distraction from more important and immediate tasks of nation building.[1]

Once ratified, the Bill of Rights played a remarkably small role during the antebellum era—at least in court. For example, no federal judge invalidated the Sedition Act of 1798, which in effect made it a federal crime to criticize President John Adams or his allies in Congress. Only once in the entire antebellum era did the Supreme Court use the Bill of Rights to strike down an act of the federal government: in *Dred Scott*'s highly implausible and strikingly casual claim that the Fifth Amendment's due process clause invalidated free-soil laws like the Northwest Ordinance and the Missouri Compromise.[2] Reviewing newspapers that were published in 1841, Dean Robert Reinstein could not find a single fiftieth-anniversary celebration of the Bill of Rights.[3]

Indeed, the Bill of Rights as it was conventionally viewed in the antebellum era looked profoundly different from the Bill of Rights as widely understood today. Born in the shadow of a Revolutionary War waged by local governments against an imperial center, the original Bill affirmed various rights against the central government, but none against the states, as the Supreme Court made clear in the landmark 1833 case of *Barron v. Baltimore*.[4] And the rights that the original Bill did affirm sounded more in localism than libertarianism. (We must recall that in large part Madison drafted his proposed amendments and the First Congress accepted a modified version of them in order to ease the anxieties of Anti-Federalists.) For example, while the First Amendment made clear that Congress could not establish a national church, it also forbade Congress from disestablishing state churches. Several of the states had government-supported churches in the 1780s, and many other "nonestablishment" states favored Protestant Christianity in some way or other. As of 1787, eleven states—nine in their state constitutions, no less—imposed explicit religious qualifications for public servants. Thus, as originally understood, the First Amendment rule that "Congress shall make no law respecting [that is, on the topic of] an establishment of religion" was less antiestablishment than it was pro–states' rights: religious policy would be decided locally, not nationally, in the American equivalent of the European Peace of Augsburg (1555) and Treaty of Westphalia (1648).

The Second Amendment celebrated local militias (the heroes of Lexington and Concord), and the Third Amendment likewise reflected uneasiness about a central standing army. Much of the rest of the Bill reinforced the powers of local juries. The Fifth Amendment safeguarded grand juries; the Sixth, criminal petit juries; and the Seventh, civil juries. Beyond these specific clauses, many other parts of the original Bill also championed the role of local and populist juries—who were expected to protect popular publishers in First Amendment cases, hold abusive federal officials liable for unreasonable searches in Fourth Amendment cases, and help assess just compensation against the federal government in Fifth Amendment cases. The only amendment endorsed by every state convention demanding a bill of rights during the ratification debates was the Tenth Amendment, which emphatically affirmed states' rights.

Madison himself wanted more—a Bill championing countermajoritarian individual rights and protecting them against states, too—but in the First Congress, he was swimming against the tide. His proposed amendment requiring states to respect speech, press, conscience, and juries passed the House (as the presciently numbered Fourteenth Amendment) but died in a Senate that championed states' rights.

The Reconstruction of the Bill of Rights

Only after the Civil War dramatized the need to limit abusive states would a new Fourteenth Amendment and a distinctly modern view of the Bill emerge—a view celebrating individual rights and preventing states from abridging fundamental freedoms. From the 1830s on, antislavery crusaders began to develop, contra *Barron*, a "declaratory" interpretation of the Bill of Rights that viewed the Bill, not as creating new or merely federalism-based rules applicable only against federal officials, but as affirming and declaring preexisting higher-law norms applicable to all governments, state as well as federal. According to this declaratory view, for example, although the First Amendment directly regulated Congress, it also affirmed a preexisting right to free expression. To *Barron* contrarians, when the amendment referred to "*the* freedom of speech" (italics mine), it thereby implied a preexisting legal freedom. Perhaps this legal freedom of speech could not be enforced against states in federal court, some contrarians conceded. But the First Amendment reference to "the freedom of speech" was itself evidence that a true legal right against all governments existed, a right that states were honor-bound to obey even in the absence of a federal enforcement scheme.

And what was true of the freedom of speech was also true of the other rights and freedoms explicitly declared in the remainder of the Bill of Rights: the First Amendment freedom of religious exercise, the Fourth Amendment right against unreasonable searches, the Fifth Amendment entitlement to just compensation, and so on. This declaratory theory took shape in a world where many Southern states had enacted extremely repressive laws to prop up slavery—censoring abolitionist speech and press, suppressing antislavery preachers, implementing dragnet searches against suspected fugitive slaves and slave sympathizers, imposing savagely cruel punishments on runaway slaves and their allies, and, indeed, violating virtually every right mentioned in the federal Bill of Rights.

With the passage of the Fourteenth Amendment, contrarians sought to write their views into the Constitution itself and to overrule *Barron*, just as they sought to overrule *Dred Scott*. By proclaiming, in Section 1 of the Fourteenth Amendment, that "No state shall make or enforce any law which shall abridge the privileges or immunities of citizens of the United States,"

Reconstruction Republicans tried to make clear that henceforth states would be required by the federal Constitution and by federal courts (and by Congress, too) to obey fundamental individual rights and freedoms—the "privileges" and "immunities" of American "citizens." Where would judges find these freedoms? Among other places, in the federal Bill of Rights itself. Inclusion in the Bill of Rights was strong evidence that a given right—free speech, free exercise, or just compensation, for example—was indeed a fundamental privilege or immunity of all American citizens.[5]

Of course, by seeking to enforce these rights against state governments, Congressman John Bingham and his fellow Reconstructionists were effectively turning the Founders' Bill of Rights on its head. The original Bill had reflected the localism and communalism of the American Revolution, whereas Bingham and company were animated by the nationalism and emerging individualism of the Civil War. Images of British imperial misbehavior and local heroism had inspired the eighteenth-century Bill of Rights, whereas images of slave-state misconduct and national heroism hovered over the Thirty-ninth Congress as it drafted the Fourteenth Amendment. For example, the original First Amendment was worded to emphasize that Congress simply lacked enumerated power to regulate religion or censor speech in the several states. Note how its language—"Congress shall make no law . . ."—echoed and inverted the language of the necessary and proper clause: "Congress shall have power . . . to make all laws . . ." in suitable federal domains. But Bingham's vision stripped away the First Amendment's veneer of states' rights, stressing instead that henceforth states must not "abridge" (a word borrowed from the First Amendment itself) the freedom of speech or of the press or of religion. What had initially been drafted as an amendment to protect state autonomy in religious matters became, in Bingham's revision, a basis for national restrictions on states insofar as their policies violated the individual rights of their citizens to the free and equal exercise of religion.[6] A similar story could be told about many other provisions of the original Bill of Rights, which were importantly reconceptualized during the Reconstruction.

The Judicial Interpretation of the Bill of Rights

Alas, the Supreme Court in the 1873 *Slaughter-House Cases* strangled the privileges or immunities clause in its crib, treating this key Reconstruction language as a mere reiteration of the principles underlying the Founders' supremacy clause.[7] As a result of this judicial coup de main, later generations of judges often turned instead to the due process clause, using it to accomplish many of the purposes originally intended for the privileges or immunities clause of the Fourteenth Amendment.

The first big step away from the regime fostered in 1833 by *Barron v. Baltimore* came in the 1897 *Chicago Burlington* case, which, like *Barron* itself, involved the norm of just compensation. Using language that nicely tracked the declaratory theory, the Court now held that states were indeed bound by the principle of just compensation laid down in the Fifth Amendment: "The [Fifth Amendment] requirement that property shall not be taken for public use without just compensation is but 'an affirmance of a great doctrine established by the common law for the protection of private property. It is founded in natural equity, and is laid down by jurists as a principle of universal law.'"[8] Standing alone, this case could be dismissed as a sport, reflecting the special solicitude for property on the turn-of-the-century *Lochner* Court. But over the course of the twentieth century, the justices made clear that this case did not stand alone. By the end of the century, almost all of the rights and freedoms specified in the Founders' Bill of Rights had come to be applied against state and local governments as well as the federal government.

The process began, inauspiciously, in the 1907 case of *Patterson v. Colorado*.[9] A newspaper had published material mocking the justices of the state supreme court. Unamused, the state court—sitting without a jury, proceeding without any specific statute authorizing punishment of nonlitigants, and in effect acting as judges in their own case—held the publisher in contempt and levied a fine on him. Writing for the Court, Justice Holmes proclaimed that "even if we were to assume that freedom of speech and freedom of the press were protected from abridgement on the part not only of the United States but also of the states," the newspaper publisher in the case would still lose because the state had not imposed a full-blown system of "prior restraint" involving formal press licensing and pre-publication censorship. The elder Justice Harlan (who had written the Court's majority opinion in *Chicago Burlington*) dissented, reiterating his view that the privileges or immunities clause encompassed First Amendment (and other Bill of Rights) freedoms, and construing those freedoms far more robustly than had Holmes.

By 1925, Holmes's assumption in *Patterson* had evolved into a stronger assertion, given voice by Justice Sanford writing for the Court in *Gitlow v. New York:* "For present purposes we may and do assume that the freedom of speech and of the press—which are protected by the First Amendment from abridgement by Congress—are among the fundamental personal rights and 'liberties' protected by the due process clause of the Fourteenth Amendment from impairment by the States."[10] Although Gitlow lost his case, over the next few years this assumption hardened into a series of holdings invalidating state laws that impermissibly restricted speech, press, and assembly rights.[11]

During this same period, however, the Court also held that other provisions of the federal Bill did not fully apply against states. Writing for the Court in the 1937 case of *Palko v. Connecticut*,[12] Justice Cardozo upheld a state law permitting the prosecutor to appeal from a legally erroneous acquittal in a criminal case. Assuming for the sake of argument that an appeal in a comparable federal case would be barred by the Fifth Amendment's double jeopardy clause,[13] Cardozo distinguished between those aspects of the federal Bill that were "of the very essence of a scheme of ordered liberty" and those that were not. Unlike rights of free expression, the right in the case at hand fell into the latter category and should not be imposed on states, Cardozo argued. Applying this "ordered liberty" framework over the next few years, the Court in *Cantwell v. Connecticut*[14] and *Everson v. Board of Education*[15] held that the Fourteenth Amendment made the First Amendment's free exercise and nonestablishment principles, respectively, applicable against states.

The scene was now set for a great judicial debate on the relationship between the Founders' Bill of Rights with its localist and communal assumptions and the Reconstructionists' Fourteenth Amendment with its more individualistic and nationalist underpinnings. In the 1947 case of *Adamson v. California*,[16] Justice Black's dissent put forth his now-famous theory of "total incorporation." Justice Douglas joined Black's dissent, and two other dissenters—Justices Murphy and Rutledge—agreed with Black that the Fourteenth Amendment incorporated the Bill of Rights. Unlike Black, however, Murphy and Rutledge suggested that courts might also use the broad language of the Fourteenth Amendment to protect additional unenumerated rights beyond the Bill of Rights. In this view, the Fourteenth Amendment "incorporated" all the rights and freedoms of the federal Bill and made them applicable against states in precisely the same way as against the federal government. In a separate concurring opinion, Justice Frankfurter vigorously disagreed. In his view, the Reconstruction amendment required that states obey principles of fundamental fairness and ordered liberty, principles that might occasionally overlap with the Bill of Rights but that bore no necessary logical or evidentiary relation to the Bill as such.[17]

Black may have lost the first battles, but he eventually won the war. With Frankfurter's retirement in 1962, the anti-incorporation logjam broke, and most of the previously unincorporated provisions of the Bill of Rights came to be applied against the states—though not following Black's theory. Rather, the Court pursued an approach championed by Justice Brennan, called "selective incorporation," by which the justices purported to play by Frankfurter's ground rules while reaching Black's results. Under this third approach, the Court's analysis could proceed clause by clause, fully incorporating every provision of the Bill deemed "fundamental" without deciding in advance (as Black would have had it) whether each and every clause would necessarily pass the test.

Methodologically, Brennan's approach seemed to avoid a radical break with existing case law rejecting total incorporation, and it even paid lip service to Frankfurter's insistence on fundamental fairness as the touchstone of the Fourteenth Amendment. In practice, however, Brennan's approach held out the possibility of total incorporation through the back door. For him, once a clause in the Bill was deemed "fundamental," it had to be "incorporated" against the states in every aspect, just as Black had insisted. And nothing in the logic of selective incorporation precluded the possibility that, when all was said and done, virtually every clause of the Bill would have been deemed fundamental. As things turned out, in applying this approach, the Warren Court almost always found that a given clause of the Bill did indeed set forth a fundamental individual right. Today, much of the Bill of Rights has come to apply with equal vigor against state and local governments.[18] The only major exceptions are the Second Amendment, the Third Amendment (which rarely arises in modern adjudication), the Fifth Amendment grand jury requirement, the Seventh Amendment's rules regarding civil juries, and, of course, the Ninth and Tenth Amendments.

The Supreme Court's approach to incorporation has generated a vast amount of academic commentary, some of it quite critical.[19] This is hardly surprising, given the enormity of the stakes: the process of incorporation has utterly transformed the original meaning of the Bill of Rights, and has come to define modern constitutional law. Mid-twentieth-century critics of the idea of incorporation—like Justice Frankfurter and the younger Justice Harlan—argued that applying the Bill of Rights against state and local governments would ultimately weaken American liberty. If judges were to use the Bill against states, the argument went, these judges would be tempted to water the Bill of Rights down to take into account the considerable diversity of state practice; and then in turn, these judges would hold the federal government to only this watered-down version. But as Justice Black and fellow incorporationists anticipated, extension of the Bill of Rights against the states has, in general, dramatically strengthened the Bill, not weakened it, in both legal doctrine and popular consciousness. Unused muscles atrophy, while those that are regularly put to use grow strong.

In area after area, incorporation enabled judges first to invalidate state and local laws, and then, with this doctrinal base thus built up, to keep Congress in check. The First Amendment is illustrative. Before 1925, when the *Gitlow* Court began in earnest the process of First Amendment incorporation, free speech had never prevailed against a repressive statute in the United States Supreme Court. Within a few years of incorporation, however, freedom of expression and religion began to win in the High Court landmark cases involving states.[20] These and other cases began to build up a First Amendment tradition,[21] in and out of court, and that tradition could then be used against even federal officials. Not until 1965 did the Supreme Court strike down an act of Congress on First Amendment grounds (in *Lamont v. Postmaster General*[22]), and when it did so, it relied squarely on doctrine built up in earlier cases involving states. Consider also the flag-burning cases of *Texas v. Johnson*[23] and *United States v. Eichman*.[24] In the first case, decided in 1989, the justices defined the basic First Amendment principles to strike down a state statute, and then, in the second case, handed down the next year, the Court stood its ground on this platform to strike down an act of Congress.

The large body of modern legal doctrine concerning the Bill of Rights has rolled out of courtrooms and into the vocabulary and vision of law students, journalists, activists, and, ultimately, the citizenry at large.[25] But without incorporation and the steady flow of cases created by state and local laws, the Supreme Court would have had far fewer opportunities to be part of the ongoing American conversation about liberty and rights.

Perhaps nowhere has the importance of incorporation in shaping American jurisprudence been more evident than in the field of constitutional criminal procedure. The overwhelming majority of criminal cases are prosecuted by state governments under state law. Only after the incorporation of the Fourth, Fifth, Sixth, and Eighth Amendments did federal courts develop a robust and highly elaborate—if also highly controversial—jurisprudence of constitutional criminal procedure.[26]

The centrality of race to modern conceptions of civil rights and civil liberties further confirms the significance of Reconstruction and its re-

reading of the communal aspirations embodied in the original Founders' Bill of Rights. Sometimes the role of the Fourteenth Amendment is explicitly acknowledged—as when the Court in *Bolling v. Sharpe*,[27] the 1954 companion case to *Brown v. Board of Education*,[28] read the Founders' Fifth Amendment's due process clause in light of the Reconstructionists' equal protection clause and held that segregation in federal schools was every bit as impermissible as in state schools. Other times, the influence of the Fourteenth Amendment on the jurisprudence of the Bill of Rights has been almost unconscious, as in the landmark 1964 case of *New York Times v. Sullivan*.[29] Although the facts of this case—involving an all-white local jury from an ex-Confederate state trying to shut down the speech of a Yankee newspaper and a national civil rights movement led by a black preacher—obviously call to mind images of Reconstruction, the Court tried to tell a Founding story starring Madison and John Peter Zenger rather than a Reconstruction tale touting Bingham and Frederick Douglass. But only the Reconstruction can explain why—contra Zenger—local juries are not always to be trusted to protect free expression.

What are we to make of the fact that our standard legal narrative has often exaggerated and misread the Founding and diminished the Reconstruction and still later periods? Perhaps many of us are guilty of a kind of curiously selective ancestor worship—one that gives too much credit to James Madison and not enough to John Bingham, that celebrates Thomas Jefferson and Patrick Henry but slights Harriet Beecher Stowe and Frederick Douglass. Great as men like Madison and Jefferson were, they lived and died as slaveholders, and their Bill of Rights was tainted by its quiet complicity with the original sin of slavery. Even as we celebrate the Founders, we must ponder the sobering words of Charles Cotesworth Pinckney in the 1788 South Carolina ratification debates: "Another reason weighed particularly, with the members of this state, against the insertion of a bill of rights. Such bills generally begin with declaring that all men are by nature born free. Now, we should make that declaration with a very bad grace, when a large part of our property consists in men who are actually born slaves."[30]

But the Reconstruction amendment did begin with an affirmation of the freedom—and citizenship—of all. The midwives of this new birth of freedom were women alongside men, blacks alongside whites. As twentieth-century judges increasingly came to realize, because of these nineteenth-century men and women, our eighteenth-century Bill of Rights has taken on a rather new life and meaning.

Concluding Observations

The foregoing account of the Bill of Rights seeks to correct several common misconceptions and misunderstandings, most of which suffer from one or another kind of anachronism—suffer, that is, from a basic failure to place the eighteenth-century Bill of Rights in its proper historical context. What follows are a few brief thoughts about my approach as distinct from the views of philosophical universalists, modern liberal nationalists, ultrapacifists, Madisonians, and Court watchers.

In contrast to philosophical universalists—those inclined to see the Bill of Rights as a timeless expression of universally applicable philosophical principles deducible directly from right reason or from careful reflection on famous philosophical treatises—I have tried to show how the Bill in fact has often meant different things to different generations. Even though some of the Americans involved in the struggle over the Bill of Rights saw themselves as enunciating universal truths, modern interpreters would do well to understand the historical context in which these enunciations occurred.

As against modern liberal nationalists, who celebrate today's Bill of Rights as enforced by national judges to protect individual and minority rights against majoritarian intolerance—especially at the state and local levels—I seek to point out that this vision of the Bill of Rights was not the dominant one at its creation. Madison may have had such a vision, but in this respect, he was way ahead of his time. Even as late as 1789, after a Revolutionary War that helped forge a strong continental identity for many American leaders, localism loomed large throughout America.[31] The thirteen separate colonies had distinct legal identities long before their troubles with the mother country in the 1760s and 1770s. Before the Revolution, Massachusetts and Virginia were as juridically distinct from each other as Ireland and India; they were tied to a common Crown, but not directly to each other. In the 1780s, the Virginia legislature had been meeting for over a century and a half; it was thus older for the Founders than the Fourteenth Amendment is for us today. Indeed, the profound nationalizing moment embodied by the drafting and ratification of the Constitution predictably generated a localist backlash, which left a visible trace in the original Bill of Rights, designed as it was by moderate Federalists seeking to soothe thoughtful Anti-Federalists/states' rightists. Only after the Civil War and the transformative Fourteenth Amendment did the Founders' Bill morph into what might be called a second Bill of Rights—

the strong nationalist and individualistic charter celebrated by today's liberal nationalists.

As I see it, the history of the Bill of Rights is thus inextricably intertwined with the larger history of America, and especially with the history of its two major constitutional wars: the Founders' Bill of Rights was the product of the American Revolution, and the Reconstructionists' revision of it was the product of the Civil War. Thus, the Revolution was itself a continental effort, and the Founders' Bill was itself a continental statement. But the Revolution was fought by an alliance of local governments against an imperial center, and in the Founders' Bill, we can see some of the residual skepticism of central governments, of the central government's professional standing armies as distinct from local militias, and even of central government–appointed judges as distinct from local citizen juries. (It is worth noting that most of the highest-ranking judges in colonial America were Tories during the Revolution: in ten of the thirteen colonies, the sitting chief justice or his equivalent ultimately chose George III over George Washington when the fighting broke out.)[32]

A very different—more nationalist, minority rights–oriented, individualistic, and judge-centered—vision prevailed in the aftermath of the Civil War, when Americans appreciated the need to empower federal judges to rein in abusive local governments. Local enforcement bodies like militias and juries were viewed with far more skepticism during Reconstruction than in the immediate aftermath of the Revolution. Thus, the Reconstruction Republicans and the twentieth-century Court that followed tended to recast and refine various Founding ideas in the course of "incorporating" various rights against states.

Ultrapacifists may find my emphasis on wars disconcerting. Like philosophical universalists who think that rights come directly from philosophical treatises or from the heavens, ultrapacifists may be uncomfortable with my insistence on the bloody history of the Bill of Rights' actual creation and reconstruction. But if it is far too crude to say simply that rights come from the barrel of a gun, it is equally simplistic to leave guns out of the story altogether. (Indeed, one of the most interesting stories in the entire Bill is how the Reconstruction generation recast the Founders' ideas about arms-bearing in light of the Civil War and post–Civil War experience.[33])

Nor is the influence of wars on rights limited to the Bill of Rights. For example, many of the expansions of America's franchise have been spawned by America's wars. Unpropertied militiamen who fought for the Revolution won the vote in that era; blacks in blue served the Union in the Civil

War and were rewarded with the Fifteenth Amendment; women won passage of the Nineteenth Amendment during World War I, with President Wilson explaining that the amendment was in fact a "vitally necessary war measure"; and young adults aged 18–21 got the vote during the Vietnam era because, as the slogan ran, if they were "old enough to fight," they were "old enough to vote."[34]

My account is thus more Marsian than Madisonian, focusing as I do on the larger themes of American history, including its wars, rather than on the brilliance of one man—James Madison, the driving force behind the Bill of Rights in the first House of Representatives. For all his influence and intellectual leadership, Madison had only one vote in the House, and no official role in the Senate that signed off on the Bill or in the state legislatures that ratified the Bill and thereby made it part of the law of the land. True, in some ways, Madison was very much ahead of his time, anticipating as he did the Reconstruction generation's insistence that a proper Bill of Rights needed to rein in abusive state conduct. But in other ways, the man who lived and died as a major slaveholder is not a good proxy for the fiercely antislavery men and women who reglossed the Bill in the 1860s. It thus matters whether modern interpreters seeking historical guidance in interpreting the basic principles of America's Bill of Rights dwell (erroneously, in my view) on Madison or focus instead (correctly, I would argue) on Reconstruction Republicans like John Bingham.

Court watchers—those who stress Supreme Court case law more than the Constitution's text and accompanying amendment history—may find my account flawed because I insist that the Civil War and the Fourteenth Amendment gave birth to the modern individualistic Bill of Rights that Americans now enjoy and celebrate. Court watchers may correctly point out that it was not until long after Reconstruction—not until the mid-twentieth century, in fact—that incorporation and associated changes in the interpretation of the Bill of Rights actually took hold in case law. As sophisticated Court watchers see the matter, the real wars to emphasize—in a sense, a third and a fourth one critical to the history and changing meaning of the Bill of Rights—may well be World War II and the Cold War, rather than the first two, the Revolutionary War and the Civil War. But what this seemingly realistic and sophisticated account of rights on the ground and in the Court misses is that the justices themselves generally did not say that they were devising new rights in response to twentieth-century developments like Nazi Germany. Rather, the twentieth-century Court insisted that it was the Fourteenth Amendment that warranted the Court's constitutional interpretations. In short, the twentieth-century

Court said that many of its older cases were wrong and that the Fourteenth Amendment really did mean what it said: equality for blacks and full civil rights for all against abusive state governments, with the Bill of Rights as a paradigmatic list of the sort of fundamental civil rights that states should never be allowed to abridge.

Thus, though the standard Court-watcher story of the Bill of Rights can account for when the Court changed its doctrine, in the aftermath of the horrors of World War II and in the face of the pressures of the Cold War, it cannot quite explain what the Court said: namely, that the Fourteenth Amendment calls for some sort of incorporation against states. By stressing the historical correctness of this modern judicial orthodoxy, I am in fact taking the Court far more seriously than some of the Court's supposed friends, who invite us to disregard the modern Court's own account of its actions.

One final thought: If the modern Court is basically right about the Fourteenth Amendment—and I think it is—then it follows that the Court was basically wrong about the Fourteenth Amendment during an earlier era. This, in turn, is a reminder that not all constitutional wisdom comes from courts, as some extreme Court watchers are wont to believe. Much of what is genuinely admirable about today's Bill of Rights case law derives from principles that the American people understood and embraced long before the Supreme Court finally saw the light.

Notes

1. James Madison, *Papers of James Madison* 12:346.
2. 60 U.S. (19 How.) 393, 450 (1857).
3. Reinstein, "Completing the Constitution," 361, 365n.25.
4. 32 U.S. (7 Pet.) 243 (1833).
5. At this point, an obvious question arises: If the privileges or immunities clause was designed to prevent states from abridging fundamental freedoms and rights such as those spelled out in the federal Bill of Rights, why did the Fourteenth Amendment go on to specifically ban states from depriving persons of due process of law? Wasn't due process (a right mentioned in the Fifth Amendment) a "privilege or immunity" already covered? Yes, but as the Fourteenth Amendment's leading drafters explained to their colleagues, the privileges or immunities clause speaks of the rights of "citizens," whereas the adjoining due process clause sweeps more broadly, including aliens in its protections of all "persons." Another question: If the framers of the Fourteenth Amendment meant to hold states to the Bill of Rights, no more and no less, why did they not say so more directly? My answer: Strictly speaking, Bingham and company meant both more and less than the first eight amendments as such. On applying the amendment to protect fundamental rights beyond those specified in the Bill of Rights itself, consider the views of Justices Murphy and Rutledge, discussed in the text accompanying note 16. And on the ways in

which the Fourteenth Amendment might incorporate something less than the Bill of Rights as such, see below in note 19 (discussing "refined incorporation").

6. For general theoretic discussions about how a given text or other sign can come to mean different things in different historical contexts, see Balkin, "Deconstructive Practice," 743; Balkin, "Ideological Drift," 869; Lessig, "Fidelity in Translation," 1165.

7. 82 U.S. (16 Wall.) 36 (1873). Justice Bradley's dissent in that case contained important language recognizing that this key clause was designed to overrule *Barron.* Ibid. at 114–18, 121–22.

8. 166 U.S. 226, 236 (1897).

9. 205 U.S. 454 (1907).

10. 268 U.S. 652, 666 (1925).

11. See, e.g., 283 U.S. 359 (1931); 283 U.S. 697 (1931); and 299 U.S. 353 (1937).

12. 302 U.S. 319 (1937).

13. Is this an attractive assumption? Why should our criminal justice system allow appellate courts to review and correct a legal error made by the trial judge if and only if that legal error leads to an erroneous conviction as opposed to an erroneous acquittal? If the defendant is entitled to appeal a legal error made against him, why should the prosecutor not have the same entitlement? Note that the issue here is arguably different from, say, rules concerning doubt about factual guilt; although reasonable doubts are to be resolved in the defendant's favor, are legal errors the same as factual doubts?

14. 310 U.S. 296 (1940).

15. 330 U.S. 1 (1947).

16. 332 U.S. 46 (1947).

17. Note that Frankfurter's test is, in essence, the same test that the Court has often applied generally to so-called substantive due process cases. This similarity should not be surprising once we recall that incorporation of the Bill of Rights was itself viewed by many as a kind of substantive due process, in which judges used the language of the due process clause to protect what were often substantive, nonprocedural rights such as freedom of expression and freedom of religion.

18. See, e.g., 333 U.S. 257 (1948) (Sixth Amendment right to public trial); 338 U.S. 25 (1949) (Fourth Amendment); 367 U.S. 643 (1961) (exclusionary rule); 370 U.S. 660 (1962) (Eighth Amendment right against cruel and unusual punishment); 372 U.S. 335 (1963) (Sixth Amendment right to counsel); 378 U.S. 1 (1964) (Fifth Amendment right against compelled self-incrimination); 380 U.S. 400 (1965) (Sixth Amendment right to confront opposing witnesses); 386 U.S. 213 (1967) (Sixth Amendment right to speedy trial); 388 U.S. 14 (1967) (Sixth Amendment right to compulsory process); 391 U.S. 145 (1968) (Sixth Amendment right to jury trial); 395 U.S. 784 (1969) (Fifth Amendment right against double jeopardy); and 404 U.S. 357 (1971) (Eighth Amendment right against excessive bail) (dictum).

Apodaca v. Oregon, 406 U.S. 404 (1972), offers an interesting counterpoint. In *Apodaca,* four Justices (White, Burger, Blackmun, and Rehnquist) argued that the Sixth Amendment does not require that a criminal jury be unanimous to convict, while four other Justices (Douglas, Brennan, Stewart, and Marshall) claimed that the Sixth Amendment does require unanimity. Justice Powell cast the deciding vote to uphold Oregon's law, on the theory that although the Sixth Amendment does require unanimity, this aspect of Sixth Amendment doctrine should not be incorporated against states jot-for-jot.

Note that in *Apodaca* a clear (5–4) majority believed that federal criminal convictions must be unanimous, and a strong (8–1) majority also accepted jot-for-jot incorporation treating state and federal governments identically, and yet these majorities did not "add up" to a Court majority requiring that state criminal convictions be unanimous. The case thus raises interesting social-choice theory questions about how votes are and should be aggregated on a multimember Court, and how the sequencing of issues—implicating concerns about "path dependence" and "agenda manipulation"—may sometimes influence outcomes. (Imagine, e.g., that well before *Apodaca* the Court had squarely held, 5–4, that federal nonunanimous juries violated the Sixth Amendment. Imagine further that prior to *Apodaca* the jot-for-jot incorporation issue also had been firmly settled in a series of cases involving other aspects of the Sixth Amendment, in which the Court had repeatedly held, 8–1, that states must be held to the same standards as the federal government. With these square holdings already on the books, would the *Apodaca* Court still have refused to "add up" these holdings?) For interesting discussion of these issues, see Easterbrook, "Ways of Criticizing the Court," 802; Kornhauser and Sager, "Unpacking the Court," 82; Kornhauser and Sager, "The One and the Many," 1; and Rogers, "Issue Voting," 997.

19. For famous commentary harshly critical of Justice Black's position, see Fairman, "Does the Fourteenth Amendment Incorporate the Bill of Rights?" 5. Fairman's scholarship was, in turn, sharply attacked in Crosskey, "Charles Fairman, 'Legislative History,' and the Constitutional Limitations on State Authority," 1; Curtis, *No State Shall Abridge;* and Aynes, "On Misreading John Bingham and the Fourteenth Amendment." Consider also the following effort to synthesize the three main positions in this modern debate:

> This synthesis, which I shall call "refined incorporation," begins with Black's insight that *all* of the privileges and immunities of citizens recognized in the Bill of Rights became "incorporated" against states by dint of the Fourteenth Amendment. But not all of the provisions of the original Bill of Rights were indeed rights of citizens. Some instead were at least in part rights of states, and as such, awkward to fully incorporate *against* states. Most obvious, of course, is the Tenth Amendment, but other provisions of the first eight amendments resembled the Tenth much more than Justice Black admitted. Thus there is deep wisdom in Justice Brennan's invitation to consider incorporation clause by clause—or more precisely still, right by right—rather than wholesale. But having identified the right unit of analysis, Brennan posed the wrong question: Is a given provision of the original Bill really a *fundamental* right? The right question is whether the provision really guarantees a privilege or immunity of *individual citizens* rather than a right of *states* or the *public* at large. And when we ask this question, clause by clause and right by right, we must be attentive to the possibility, flagged by Frankfurter, that a particular principle in the Bill of Rights may change its shape in the process of absorption into the Fourteenth Amendment. This change can occur for reasons rather different from those that Frankfurter offered. (He, more than Black and Brennan, diverted attention from the right question by his insistence on abstract conceptions of "fundamental fairness" and "ordered liberty" as the sole Fourteenth Amendment litmus tests, and by his disregard of the language and history of the privileges or immunities clause.) Certain alloyed provisions of the original Bill—part citizen right, part state right—may need to undergo refinement

and filtration before their citizen-right elements can be absorbed by the Fourteenth Amendment. And other provisions may become less majoritarian and populist, and more libertarian, as they are repackaged in the Fourteenth Amendment as liberal civil rights—"privileges or immunities" of individuals—rather than republican political "right[s] of the people," as in the original Bill. (Amar, *Bill of Rights*, xiv–xv)

20. See the cases cited above in note 11.

21. See, generally, Kalven.

22. 381 U.S. 301 (1965).

23. 491 U.S. 397 (1989).

24. 496 U.S. 310 (1990).

25. For an important argument expressing skepticism about the magnitude of impact of Supreme Court decisions generally, see Rosenberg, "The Hollow Hope."

26. Amar, *Constitution and Criminal Procedure.*

27. 347 U.S. 497 (1954).

28. 347 U.S. 483 (1954).

29. 376 U.S. 254 (1964).

30. Elliot, *Four Debates*, 316.

31. For an illuminating general discussion, see Murrin, "A Roof without Walls," 333–48. Murrin's reminder that "until [the 1774 Continental] Congress met, more of its members had visited London than Philadelphia" is particularly arresting. Ibid., 340.

32. Connecticut, Rhode Island, and Delaware were the exceptions. See Amar, *America's Constitution*, 207, 569n2.

33. I have told this story in detail elsewhere. See, e.g., Amar, *Bill of Rights*, 46–59, 216–18, 257–66, and Amar, "The Second Amendment," 889. For a brief synopsis, see Amar, *America's Constitution*, 322–26, 390:

> The Second Amendment gave rise to a particularly nice illustration of how the precise language of "privileges or immunities" incorporated core elements of the Bill of Rights while at the same time refining and redefining the Founders' text. At the Founding, the Second Amendment's affirmation of the people's right to bear arms intertwined with a strong commitment to local militias, a pronounced uneasiness about a federal army, and a tight focus on the political rights and responsibilities of voters/jurors/militiamen. Four score years later, this original vision had dissolved, thanks largely to the Civil War and to the very process by which the Fourteenth Amendment was to be ratified with the aid of the Union Army. Yet when filtered through the well-chosen language of "privileges or immunities of citizens," the Founders' Second Amendment could be refined into a rather different kind of right: a right/privilege to keep a gun at home for self-protection—a right of all citizens, female as well as male, acting individually rather than in a collective militia, wielding weapons in a private space rather than mustering on the public square.
>
> In 1866, the prevalence in the South of marauding bands of white thugs, terrorizing black families whom state governments were failing to safeguard via genuinely "equal protection" of criminal laws, made an individual right to keep a gun in his—or her—home a core civil right deserving federal affirmation. This transformation of a Founding-era political right into a Reconstruction-era civil right was exemplified by a key congressional enactment in 1866, which declared that "laws . . . concerning

personal liberty [and] *personal* security, . . . *including the constitutional right to bear arms,* shall be secured to and enjoyed by all the citizens."

34. For details, see Amar, *America's Constitution.*

Bibliography

Adamson v. California, 332 U.S. 46 (1947).

Amar, Akhil Reed. *America's Constitution: A Biography.* New York, 2005.

———. *The Bill of Rights: Creation and Reconstruction.* New Haven, CT, 1998.

———. *The Constitution and Criminal Procedure: First Principles.* New Haven, CT, 1997.

———. "The Second Amendment: A Case Study in Constitutional Interpretation." *Utah Law Review,* 2001, 889.

Apodaca v. Oregon, 406 U.S. 404 (1972).

Aynes, Richard. "On Misreading John Bingham and the Fourteenth Amendment." *Yale Law Journal* 57 (1993): 103.

Balkin, J. M. "Deconstructive Practice and Legal Theory." *Yale Law Journal* 96 (1993): 743.

———. "Ideological Drift and the Struggle over Meaning." *Connecticut Law Review* 25 (1993): 869.

Barron v. Baltimore, 32 U.S. 243 (1833).

Benton v. Maryland, 395 U.S. 784 (1969).

Bolling v. Sharpe, 347 U.S. 497 (1954).

Brown v. Board of Education, 347 U.S. 483 (1954).

Cantwell v. Connecticut, 310 U.S. 296 (1940).

Chicago, Burlington and Quincy Railroad v. Chicago, 116 U.S. 226, 236 (1886).

Consol. Rail v. Railway Labor Executives, 496 U.S. 310 (1990).

Crosskey, William Winslow. "Charles Fairman, 'Legislative History,' and the Constitutional Limitations on State Authority." *University of Chicago Law Review* 1 (1954): 22.

Curtis, Michael Kent. *No State Shall Abridge: The Fourteenth Amendment and the Bill of Rights.* Durham, NC, 1984.

De Jonge v. Oregon, 299 U.S. 353 (1937).

Dred Scott v. Sandford, 60 U.S. 393, 450 (1857).

Duncan v. Louisiana, 391 U.S. 145 (1968).

Easterbrook, Frank. "Ways of Criticizing the Court." *Harvard Law Review* 95 (1982): 802.

Elliot, Jonathan, ed. *Four Debates on the Adoption of the Federal Constitution.* New York, 1836.

Everson v. Board of Education of Ewing TP., 330 U.S. 1 (1947).

Fairman, Charles. "Does the Fourteenth Amendment Incorporate the Bill of Rights?" *Stanford Law Review* 2 (1949): 5.

Gideon v. Wainwright, 372 U.S. 335 (1963).

Gitlow v. New York, 268 U.S. 652, 666 (1925).

In re Oliver, 333 U.S. 257 (1948).

In re Smoot, 82 U.S. 36, 114–18, 121–22 (1873).

Kalven, Harry, Jr. *A Worthy Tradition: Freedom of Speech in America.* New York, 1988.

Klopfer v. North Carolina, 386 U.S. 213 (1967).

Kornhauser, Lewis A., and Lawrence G. Sager. "Unpacking the Court." *Yale Law Journal* 96 (1986): 82.

180   Akhil Reed Amar

———. "The One and the Many: Adjudication in Collegial Courts." *California Law Review* 81 (1993): 1.

Lamont v. Postmaster General, 381 U.S. 301 (1965).

Lessig, Lawrence. "Fidelity in Translation." *Texas Law Review* 71 (1993): 1165.

Madison, James. *The Papers of James Madison*. Vol. 12. Ed. Robert Allen Rutland et al. Charlottesville, VA, 1979.

Malloy v. Hogan, 378 U.S. 1 (1964).

Mapp v. Ohio, 367 U.S. 643 (1961).

Murrin, John M. "A Roof without Walls: The Dilemma of American National Identity." In *Beyond Confederation: Origins of the Constitution and American National Identity*, ed. Richard Beeman et al., 333–48. Chapel Hill, NC, 1987.

Near v. Minnesota, 283 U.S. 697 (1931).

New York Times v. Sullivan, 376 U.S. 254. (1964).

Palko v. Connecticut, 302 U.S. 319 (1937).

Patterson v. Colorado, 205 U.S. 454 (1907).

Pointer v. Texas, 380 U.S. 400 (1965).

Reinstein, Robert J. "Completing the Constitution: The Declaration of Independence, Bill of Rights, and Fourteenth Amendment." *Temple Law Review* 66 (1993): 361, 365n.25.

Robinson v. California, 370 U.S. 660 (1962).

Rogers, John M. "'Issue Voting' by Multimember Appellate Courts: A Response to Some Radical Proposals." *Vanderbilt Law Review* 49 (1996): 997.

Rosenberg, Gerald N. "The Hollow Hope: Can Courts Bring about Social Change?" *University of Chicago Law Review* 1 (1991): 139–42.

Schilb v. Kuebel, 404 U.S. 357 (1971) (dictum).

Stromberg v. California, 283 U.S. 359 (1931).

Texas v. Johnson, 491 U.S. 397 (1989).

Washington v. Texas, 388 U.S. 14 (1967).

Wolf v. Colorado, 338 U.S. 25 (1949).

The Dilemma of Declaring Rights

JACK N. RAKOVE

In the celebrated correspondence between James Madison and Thomas Jefferson over the value of adding a declaration of rights to the proposed Constitution, it was the minister to France who, as usual, claimed the best lines. It was Jefferson who unequivocally asserted "that a bill of rights is what the people are entitled to against every government on earth, general or particular, & what no just government should refuse or rest on inference." Madison's worry that "a positive declaration of some essential rights could not be obtained in the requisite latitude" also left Jefferson unmoved. "Answer. Half a loaf is better than no bread. If we cannot secure all our rights, let us secure what we can."[1] Here, as elsewhere in their exchanges, Jefferson reminds us what a wonderfully direct and trenchant writer he could be. Not for him the careful definitions, labored distinctions, and grainy qualifications that marked Madison's writings, public and private. Jefferson at his best can be a very modern writer: a master of short snappy sentences and vivid phrases, with a pronounced aversion to that talisman of eighteenth-century punctuation, the semicolon. At times, of course, his quick quill got him into trouble. As Madison noted many years later, "Allowances also ought to be made for a habit in Mr. Jefferson as in others of great genius of expressing in strong and round terms, impressions of the moment."[2] But the vigor and elegance with which Jefferson expressed many of his strongest impressions also explain his lasting hold on the American political imagination.

The conventional wisdom of that same political imagination is inclined to conclude that, on the merits of the question, Jefferson for once got the better of Madison. That is the lesson that the standard story of the adoption of the first ten amendments to the Constitution seems to impart. That story runs like this:

The issue of a bill of rights was raised belatedly at the Federal Convention, and the framers blew the answer by blowing off George Mason and Elbridge Gerry, the two premature Anti-Federalists who supported its addition to the Constitution. This was a capital error, as the Federalists soon learned. James Wilson sought to head off criticism of this omission in his widely publicized speech of October 6, 1787. Wilson argued that it would be dangerous to include explicit protection for particular rights if such statements could be interpreted as vesting greater power in the government than the Constitution in fact deposited. This casuistry proved vulnerable to easy criticism, and Anti-Federalists gained some support by making the omission of a bill of rights a leading count in their indictment of the danger of ratifying an unamended Constitution. In some of the closely contested states, Federalists agreed to recommend amendments to the consideration of the new Congress, and this recommendation sometimes embraced the addition of statements of rights. In the closely divided Virginia ratification convention, one such commitment was extracted from Federalists, captained by Madison, and he in turn took that pledge even more seriously during his tough race against James Monroe for election to the first House of Representatives. Madison issued public letters promising to take responsibility for pursuing the adoption of amendments if elected, and he honored that pledge during the first session of the First Congress, forcing his "nauseous project of amendments" down the craws of his reluctant colleagues.[3] Other Federalists begrudgingly yielded to Madison's appeal, and the Bill of Rights, as it came to be known, made its way through Congress, on to the states and eventual ratification. And even though it lay moribund for a century and a half, its inclusion in the text of the Constitution ultimately had a profound effect on modern American constitutionalism through the transmutative power of the Fourteenth Amendment and the incorporation doctrine.

With some qualifications—notably those concerned with whether Federalists believed they really had contracted to consider and deliver amendments—this story offers a passable political account of the adoption of the first ten amendments to the Constitution. It fails to do justice, however, to the framers' decision to slough off Gerry's and Mason's original suggestion to add a statement of rights to the Constitution. Political miscalculation that it might have been, that decision reflected two genuine problems raised by the progress of constitutional theory since 1776, especially as Americans had to consider the sources of the authority of rights and the appropriate means of expressing statements of rights as constitutional texts. These two problems can be described as the dilemmas of "enumeration" and "textualization." Far from being quaint artifacts of the debates of the 1780s, of mere antiquarian or scholarly interest, these two problems remain highly germane to our own ongoing debate over the merits and dangers of "rights talk."

To illustrate this point, we can consider two of the most highly charged controversies in the contemporary discourse of rights: the recognition of a woman's right to obtain an abortion, first declared in *Roe v. Wade,* and the Second Amendment, with its dense quarrels over the meaning and extent of "the right of the people to keep and bear Arms."

As a constitutional question, abortion illustrates the dilemma or difficulty of restricting the catalogue of fundamental rights to those explicitly enumerated in the text of the Constitution. The effect of *Roe v. Wade* was to elevate a woman's right to an abortion to the status of a fundamental constitutional right. As with many other rights, the attainment of that status did not place abortion wholly beyond the realm of legislative regulation. But by barring the states from the wholesale prohibition of abortion, *Roe v. Wade* and later decisions sustaining its essential holding gave that right a constitutional status equivalent to other rights explicitly mentioned in the Constitution. The authority for this decision was derived, in part, from the concept of the right to privacy recognized in the prior contraception case of *Griswold v. Connecticut* (1965). There, Justice William O. Douglas had held, in a famous if all-advised phrase, that "penumbras, formed by emanations" from other guarantees in the Bill of Rights, recognized the existence of "zones of privacy" into which the authority of the state could not intrude. The right of a married couple to use contraception, and by extension of a woman to decide whether to terminate a pregnancy, became a fair inference from this larger notion of privacy. The Court in both cases had the option, at least in theory, of relying as well on the Ninth Amendment as a reservoir of fundamental rights, with its declaration that "the enumeration in the Constitution, of certain rights, shall not be construed to deny or disparage others retained by the people." But in the absence of any substantive jurisprudence of that article, the Court declined to ask whether and how a general right of privacy or particular applications of that right might be located in the capacious if vague language of the Ninth Amendment.

That article was, of course, included in the original list of amendments proposed to the states because its framers took the issue of enumeration seriously. That is, they understood that a decision to include certain rights in a constitutional declaration could be interpreted as a decision to relegate other rights to a potentially inferior status or position. The plain meaning of the Ninth Amendment is that other rights equally deserving of protection still exist, somewhere, on some authority. The problem with this formulation is that it offers no clue as to how to identify or discover those other rights that we wish neither to deny or disparage. This defect lies at the heart of the modern debate over the idea that abortion should be treated as a constitutional right. In the absence of an explicit constitutional guarantee, something that can be readily found within the four corners of the text, the idea that a judicially discovered but unenumerated right can be deemed equivalent to one enumerated in the first eight amendments or in Section 1 of the Fourteenth Amendment is bound to remain controversial. The most persuasive writing of a Ronald Dworkin or a Laurence Tribe cannot wholly remedy the absence of an explicit constitutional provision. Omission thus implies disparagement—even when the Ninth Amendment paradoxically commands otherwise.

The Second Amendment poses a different problem. Whereas the Ninth Amendment states a broad principle, the Second seems to commit its putative interpreters to an exquisitely and demandingly precise exegetical exercise. "A well-regulated militia, being necessary to the security of a free state, the right of the people to keep and bear Arms, shall not be infringed." Where does one start with this text? Does "regulated" carry the modern connotation of regulated by the state, or a prior, now archaic, meaning synonymous with "effective"? Does the "militia" consist of the entire free adult body of the people? Or is it only a reference to the institutional militia that Congress can organize, arm, and discipline under its Article I, Section 8, Clause 16 power, and which it can also call into the national service to put down an insurrection presumably launched by the less formal, popular, indeed populist militia that can spontaneously mobilize itself against the threat of tyranny? Is "the people" synonymous with the sum of all the individual persons who comprise it? Or can it potentially be limited in the same way that the right of the people to be represented in the lower house of Congress is actually delegated to the subset of electors designated by the Constitution and the laws of the states? Is "keep and bear Arms" solely a military phrase, implying that the right so protected is restricted to service in the militia for public purposes? Or can it be extended to an individual right of self-protection against interlopers violating the sanctity of the family castle? And if this right, expansively defined, cannot be infringed at all, does that mean that all local laws and ordinances adopted for reasons of maintaining public health and safety should be subject to the strictest forms of constitutional scrutiny?

These questions are not mere cavils in the wars over the interpretation of the Second Amendment. Each of these possible interpretations has been the subject of close textual analysis and a variety of other interpretive moves that can be deployed to read the substantive right either narrowly or broadly. Can one use other antecedent formulas, as proposed by the state ratification conventions, as interpretive glosses on the amendment as eventually adopted? Or does the fact that Congress chose other language limit the interpretive valence of these prior statements? Was the Senate's deletion of the key modifying phrase, "composed of the body of the people" (following "militia") a mere editorial tinkering, designed to eliminate superfluous or redundant language? Or did it express the well-conceived desire of a strongly Federalist legislative chamber not to yoke future congresses to support a militia far larger than the country could possibly use?

The absurd textualism that surrounds the modern interpretation of the Second Amendment thus illustrates a different problem in the proper drafting of a bill of rights. Not only does every word matter; it must also be assumed that each word was deliberately chosen to achieve an exquisite degree of "perspicuity" (as Madison would say) to guide later interpreters. It is not enough to suggest that the Second Amendment may only have been contrived to state in some general way one or more principles: that a well-regulated militia should obviate the need for a standing army; that individuals have a strong natural right to self-defense; that Congress should feel duty-bound to maintain the militia in a well-regulated state. Somehow the precise definition and proper interpretation of every word are essential to deciphering the true and proper meaning of an amendment that, ironically, may number among the most obsolete clauses of the Constitution.

There are thus two dilemmas inherent in the composition of a fully constitutionalized bill of rights that is to be recognized as equally authoritative with any other clause of the constitutional text. One is the problem of enumeration: What happens if a right is left out, either because the political costs of including it are too high, or simply because its existence has not yet been recognized or fully perceived? The other is the problem of committing the concept of a right to a finite textual formula. What happens if the language chosen is confusing, or imprecisely vague, or unwieldy? Is one bound to interpret that language in the narrowest way possible, squeezing every drop of meaning from its literal text? Or are we entitled to render a free interpretation of the greater principle that the particular text could only partially and inadequately express? Indeed, one can legitimately ask whether it is linguistically possible to cabin any conception of a right within the terse textual formulas that the argot of American constitutionalism prefers. If so, then every interpreter has to act as a

Dworkinian Hercules, applying principles of moral philosophy to fashion a suitable interpretation of the right in question.

Federalist skepticism about the utility of including a bill of rights in the Constitution therefore deserves a more powerful explanation than the conventional story about oversight and political miscalculation provides. Or to put the point more directly: Madison's dismissal of bills of rights as so many "parchment barriers"—nice to look at, perhaps, but not something a serious constitutionalist and libertarian would rely on—has to be understood as the product of a closely reasoned analysis, and not a post hoc rationalization of a political error. Madison used that telling phrase in two places: in his reformulation of the fundamental problem of separating the powers in *Federalist* No. 48, and again, some months later, in his letter to Jefferson detailing his reservations about a declaration of rights. In both cases, Madison's analysis was predicated upon a recognition that the principal challenge of designing a proper constitution is to identify the sources of "real power" within the polity, whether resting within "the impetuous vortex" of the legislature or swirling unpredictably among the popular majorities in the larger society.

For the principal author of the first ten amendments to the Constitution, then, the dilemma of adding a declaration of rights to the original text lay both in the inherent inadequacy of such documents as formal statements of constitutional values and in their political inefficacy. The sources of the latter concern are familiar to everyone who has read and grasped Madison's writings on the nature and danger of faction in republican government. To explain his and other Federalists' reservations about the inherent inadequacies of bills of rights, however, requires examining the distinctive and not unproblematic place these documents occupied in the early history of the American constitutional experiment.

Historical examples of declarations or bills of rights were well known to the generation that made the American Revolution and adopted the first written constitutions. Magna Carta was such a document; and so were the parliamentary Petition of Right of 1628, foisted upon a reluctant Charles I to little effect, and the better-known Declaration of Rights of 1689, accepted with better grace by William and Mary as a condition of their accession to the throne abandoned by the new queen's father, James II. Similarly, various colonies possessed statements of rights included in their founding charters or other legislatively adopted documents.

To say that such documents were familiar in a general way, however, neither explains how they were meant to function constitutionally nor reveals much about their legal authority. Appeals to charters and other statements of rights were part of the arsenal to which colonists resorted after 1765 as they responded to the challenge posed by the new policies of the empire. But as John Phillip Reid has argued, such appeals represented only one of the ten distinctly identifiable kinds of arguments with which Americans justified their immunity from parliamentary legislation.[4] In explaining where their rights came from—what their sources were—Americans had an embarrassment of philosophical and polemical riches from which to choose. Few would have argued that charters or other legal documents were the sources of the rights they recognized, or whose existence they declared. To declare a right was not to create it or even to secure its protection through legally recognizable channels. Rather, it was to confirm its existence. Freedom of conscience, for example, did not exist because it had been formally recognized in the parliamentary Toleration Act or its colonial equivalents. Instead, such acts would be understood as confirming the existence of a right that had other sources.

The authority of the colonial charters dissolved, of course, during the Revolutionary interregnum of 1774–76. Late in 1775, and with accelerating momentum in 1776, the individual colonies began to emerge from the condition Locke had called a "dissolution of government" as, with the permission of the Continental Congress, they began drafting new constitutions of government. In the process, of course, they launched American constitutionalism on its distinctive path. In place of the antecedent British conception of a constitution as a descriptive term, the Americans began thinking of constitutions as concise written documents, adopted at precise moments of historical time. For a few precocious writers, such as the author of *Four Letters on Interesting Subjects,* these texts were also capable of acquiring the status of supreme fundamental law, thereafter regulating what the institutions of government could and could not do in their name. For most Americans, however, that strong definition of the authority of a constitution was something yet to be discovered and fully developed.[5]

In most, though not all, of the states, the adoption of new declarations of rights became part of this process of promulgating state constitutions. But the exact role or function they played in this process remained uncertain and ambiguous. For one thing, it was not wholly clear whether these bills of rights were themselves constitutional documents. They were freestanding texts, framed to accompany the adoption of constitutions, but not formally part of the documents they accompanied. In their literalminded, provincial way, Americans may have felt that adopting such statements of principles was something a people emerging from the condition of a "dissolution of government" or fashioning a new compact of government were naturally supposed to do. The Virginia provincial convention, for example, approved its Declaration of Rights on June 12, 1776. Another long fortnight passed, however, before the convention adopted, as a completely separate document, the actual constitution under which the legal authority of government would be exercised. That latter document made no reference to the prior declaration of rights. Moreover, it came encumbered by, or rather was introduced by, a long preamble which could be regarded, to some extent, as a bill of rights of its own. This was the long list of charges against George III for having "endeavoured to pervert [the Kingly Office in this Government] into a detestable and insupportable Tyranny." This bill of charges against the king explicitly enumerated all the violations of colonial rights that warranted the convention's decision to "ordain and declare the future Form of Government of Virginia." When Jefferson relied on the same compilation of charges in the Declaration of Independence, he, too, converted that document into a bill of rights, one that now evoked the right of revolution to enable a new American people "to assume among the powers of the earth, the separate and equal station to which the Laws of Nature and of Nature's God entitle them."[6]

To think of the Declaration of Independence as a bill of rights seems strange to us. But that is because we assume that the final form of a bill of rights represented by the federal constitutional amendments of 1789 is the sole and proper template for such texts. That clarity had not yet been attained in 1776. At the birth of American Revolutionary constitutionalism—when the distinctive American definition of a constitution was itself also still in formation—an array of documents could be regarded as declarations of rights, serving an array of functions.

The Virginia Declaration of Rights illustrates other sources of ambiguity and uncertainty in thinking of the original bills of rights as constitutional documents. Consider, for example, its fifth article: "That the Legislative and Executive powers of the State should be separate and distinct from the Judicative; and, that the members of the two first may be restrained from oppression, by feeling and participating the burdens of the people, they should, at fixed periods, be reduced to a private station, return into that body from which they were originally taken, and the vacancies be supplied by frequent, certain, and regular elections, in which all, or any part of the former members, to be again eligible, or ineligible, as the law shall direct." In addition to this statement of the principle of separated powers, Article 5 also endorses the idea of rotation in office. But this endorsement is only a principle, not a constitutional command. Nothing in the constitution adopted later in June imposed what we now call term limits on legislators. There was no "must" in the constitution to correspond to the "should" in the declaration.

This, in turn, illustrates another distinctive, if unsettling aspect of the first declarations of rights. In Gordon Wood's apt characterization, the bills of rights provided "a jarring but exciting combination of ringing declarations of principles with a motley collection of common law procedures."[7] "Motley" may be an unwise adjective to apply here, if read to disparage the importance of imposing routine but essential procedural restraints on the instruments of state power. These procedural guarantees are, in fact, what we find familiar in the early bills of rights. It is the statements of principles that now seem anomalous. What is the point of endorsing rotation in office if it is not simultaneously enforced by a constitutional rule or command? The confusion becomes more profound when we consider a provision like Article 15 of the Virginia declaration: "That no free Government, or the blessing of liberty, can be preserved to any people but by a firm adherence to justice, moderation, temperance, frugality, and virtue, and by frequent recurrence to fundamental principles." What right (as we use that term) is being protected by this injunction? What does it mean to say we have a right to adhere to "frugality"? (For a libertarian, would not "prodigality" be just as good?) And to whom, if anyone—or perhaps everyone—is the statement addressed?

To answer these questions requires realizing that the first bills of rights were not understood as legal or constitutional documents, guaranteeing citizens a right to initiate litigation to secure violated rights, or even requiring specific institutions to undertake particular actions. As the typical use of the monitory "should" rather than the mandatory "shall" strongly suggests, these documents were understood as broad statements of principle meant to guide everyone's behavior, rather than specific commands or rules requiring a particular course of legal action. A people had a right, indeed a duty, to declare the purposes and principles of the governments they were establishing. But that purpose was as much moral and political as legal and constitutional.

Moreover, as Leonard Levy and other commentators have noted, the early bills of rights were less than satisfactory when it came to identifying the range of fundamental rights meriting constitutional recognition.[8] If the existence of some optimal list of basic rights had truly depended on their inclusion in these declarations, the first American constitutionalists could be easily faulted as careless draftsmen. But of course few if any of the authors of the first declarations of rights were thinking in those terms. If a bill of rights was still regarded primarily or essentially as a statement of principles, rather than a set of legally enforceable claims, then particular omissions did not matter. Under the prevailing assumptions of 1776, the security of rights still depended on the workings of representative assemblies and juries, the two institutions historically charged with protecting the people against the abuse of power. The purpose and function of bills of rights were not to impose actual restraints or obligations on government. Rather, they were conceived as statements of principle meant to guide the behavior of officials and citizens alike. Nor were they the source of authority for the rights they professed to recognize. They simply affirmed the existence of rights whose deeper authority was rooted in nature and custom.

There was one noteworthy exception to this original understanding. It is found in the constitution that Jefferson drafted for Virginia in the spring of 1776, when he was stuck in Philadelphia having to write the Declaration of Independence, rather than where he would have much preferred to be, back in Williamsburg working on the new constitution. Jefferson's draft was exceptional in incorporating the statement of rights within the body of the constitution, under the heading "Rights Private and Public." The effect, of course, would have been to constitutionalize the rights therein enumerated, and not leave them as a freestanding set of principles. Jefferson's compilation of rights is interesting on other grounds. Consistent with concerns he had expressed two years earlier in his *Summary View of the Rights of British America,* Jefferson would have used this text to provide that the "unappropriated" lands the commonwealth would control— whether those taken from the Crown or those properly purchased from their "Indian native proprietors" by the legislature "on behalf of the public"—would be used to assure that "every person" should be entitled to own "in full and absolute dominion" an estate of fifty acres. "Person" as used here might even, conceivably, include women, because elsewhere in Article 4 Jefferson provided that "Descents shall go according to the laws of Gavelkind [equal division among heirs], save only that females shall have equal rights with males"—thereby demonstrating, as any lawyer would note, that Jefferson knew how to distinguish persons by gender when it seemed necessary to do so.[9] In effect, Jefferson's conception of rights was designed to assure the existence of a suitably republican citizenry by giving the mass of the free population the individual self-sufficiency—or competence, as it was often called—that in turn would provide them with the requisite independence.

There is further evidence of the precocity of Jefferson's thinking about rights in the bill for religious freedom that he included in the comprehensive revisal of Virginia laws that he helped prepare in the late 1770s. For a student of the history of rights, broadly defined, the critical passage in this remarkable text is the long, almost Faulknerian preamble, which justifies the quintessential liberal right of freedom of conscience in terms that anticipated his discussion of religion in the *Notes on the State of Virginia*. But, for a constitutionalist, the key passage is the seeming afterthought of the concluding paragraph: "And though we well know that this Assembly, elected by the people for the ordinary purposes of legislation only, have no power to restrain the acts of succeeding Assemblies, constituted with powers equal to our own, and that therefore to declare this act irrevocable would be of no effect in law; yet we are free to declare, and do declare, that the rights hereby asserted are of the natural rights of mankind, and that if any act shall be hereafter passed to repeal the present or to narrow its operation, such act will be an infringement of natural right." For Jefferson, the ultimate existence of freedom of conscience could not depend on this bill, which the legislature made a statute in 1786, for any subsequent meeting of the Virginia assembly could repeal its enactment. Instead, he specified (in my view, correctly) that "the rights hereby asserted are of the natural rights of mankind."

From the vantage point of 1776, a right secured by statute stood on firmer ground than a right affirmed as a matter of principle in a declaration of rights. But Jefferson stood at the leading edge of the incipient American movement to recognize and distinguish constitutions as supreme fundamental law. This, again, was a point he later developed in the *Notes on the State of Virginia,* arguing that merely calling a document a constitution would not make it fully or robustly constitutional. Presumably, the same reservations applied, a fortiori, to the sub-constitutional declarations of rights adopted in 1776.

Jefferson's criticisms of the defective authority of the first state constitutions had its parallel in the protests against the efforts of the Massachusetts General Court to promulgate a constitution on its own authority. Popular resistance to that claim finally led Massachusetts to develop the critical innovation that set a precedent for the procedures used in 1787–88. In 1779, the General Court provided for the calling of a special convention whose sole duty would be to draft a constitution that it would then submit for ratification by the people of Massachusetts, duly assembled in their town meetings. Here lay a critical development in the doctrine of American constitutionalism. To escape the trap of *quod leges posteriores priores contrarias abrogant,*[10] a constitution had to be drafted by a special body, acting non-legislatively, and it then had to secure the subsequent imprimatur of a sovereign people.

The Massachusetts precedent was significant in three respects. First, it established a doctrinal basis for distinguishing the authority of a constitution from that of other forms of law. Second, it illustrated the anti-legislative animus that best explains why this distinction was coming to be perceived as useful, even necessary. From the vantage point of an American theory of rights, that populist animus also helps to explain why Madison and other like-minded elite thinkers could reject the traditional view of representative assemblies as the principal institutional guardians of the rights of the people and instead recognize that the unjust misuse of the power to legislate, as Madison observed in 1787, was calling "into question the fundamental principle of republican Government, that the majority who rule in such Governments, are the safest Guardians both of public Good and of private rights."[11] But third, and for our purposes most important, Massachusetts also incorporated its Declaration of the Rights of the Inhabitants of the Commonwealth as Part the First of the constitution proper. The Massachusetts declaration, in other words, treated the bill of rights as a constitutional document in the full, modern sense of the term. That fact, in turn, helps to explain why the equality principle stated in Article I of the declaration played a significant role in the judicial abolition of slavery in Massachusetts that followed, not wholly coincidentally, in the early 1780s.

The idea that bills of rights could attain full constitutional status did not mean, however, that they could or should be relied upon as essential safeguards for the protection of rights. The Madisonian critique of bills of rights as "parchment barriers" clearly pointed toward the opposite conclusion. Though Madison believed that bills of rights could be used as limitations on the authority of the legislature, he was also increasingly skeptical that such formal restrictions on its power would prove efficacious against "the infinitude of legislative expedients" that could always be deployed to evade a black-letter prohibition. Further doubts about the efficacy of bills of rights came from Madison's efforts to gauge the real political forces that swirled through the republican body politic. Those real forces, the Madison of 1787–89 believed, lay in the people themselves, or rather in the popular majorities that threatened to form too often on the basis of interest, passion, and capricious opinion. They would not be deterred from imposing their will on disfavored minorities by the mere existence of a parchment barrier in the shape of a declaration of rights.

Moreover, because these majorities were more likely to coalesce within the narrower compass of individual states, where most daily governance would still occur, the adoption of a national bill of rights would do little to protect minority rights within the states.

The cursory discussion of the belated Gerry–Mason proposal for the inclusion of a bill of rights in the Constitution makes it impossible to say whether other framers shared Madison's concerns or agreed with his analysis. But the public debate that developed once the Convention adjourned indicates that both Anti-Federalists and Federalists were wrestling with the implications of incorporating or omitting statements of rights from a constitution that proclaimed itself "the supreme law of the land."

The logic of the Anti-Federalist position was deeply positivist. If the Constitution did not contain a satisfactory list of rights, they argued, the people would no longer know what their rights were. They would have no standard against which to judge the legitimacy of disputed acts of government, and accordingly would lack both the knowledge and confidence to challenge their overreaching, self-aggrandizing rulers. Given their mistrust of all three branches of the proposed national government, Anti-Federalists could not argue, as Jefferson did and we would, that the existence of a bill of rights was essential to empower and encourage the weakest department, the judiciary, to protect citizens against arbitrary government. The Anti-Federalist case for a bill of rights thus remained more political than legal. A bill of rights would operate, not by encouraging aggrieved Americans to run to the nearest federal court to file suit at the first sniff of tyranny, but rather by giving the people at large a standard against which to judge acts of power. The adoption of a bill of rights would thus operate within what Larry Kramer has called the tradition of popular constitutionalism, that is, the belief that the people themselves are the best guardians of their rights and liberties, and that they do so most effectively when they mobilize politically.[12]

In this sense, the Anti-Federalist notion of the function of a bill of rights remained faithful to the political traditions of 1776, leaving them vulnerable perhaps to the recurring charge that they had been left behind in the progress of constitutional theory since independence. But on the authority of rights they do not appear to have been laggards at all. The people's vague memories of their customary rights could never prevail against the explicitly enumerated powers of a "consolidated" national government fortified by the "sweeping" necessary and proper clause and an all-conquering supremacy clause. When compared to the starting position of 1776, the Anti-Federalist argument of 1787–88 thus presupposed that the existence and security of rights depended on their explicit inclusion in the constitutional text. If rights were omitted from that document, their authority would be diluted or relegated or rendered cloudy and uncertain. In place of the tenfold arguments for rights that Professor Reid ascribes to the incipient Revolutionaries of the 1760s and 1770s, the Anti-Federalists now seem to have recognized only one: the supreme authority of the black-letter text. They thereby attributed to the missing rights-bearing articles of 1787 an authority that no one in 1776 would have bestowed on the "motley" and unsystematic mélange of republican principles and common-law procedures compiled in the early state declarations.

The Federalist response to these positions began with James Wilson's Statehouse speech of October 6, 1787, which, coming as it did from a member of the Constitutional Convention and the intellectual heavy-weight among the Pennsylvania Federalists, immediately acquired a prestige and authority that could never be diminished. In the passages directed to the question of a bill of rights, Wilson did not discuss the risk of relegating some rights by enumerating others. Rather, he relied upon the more ingenious argument that the stipulation of some rights might be wrongly read to imply that powers had been granted to the new government which in fact the Constitution had not conveyed. But where, Anti-Federalists responded, had the national government been empowered to abrogate the "great writ" of habeas corpus, or to adopt bills of attainder or ex post facto laws—all of which were restricted in Article I, Section 9? Or, similarly, did not the positive provision for jury trial in criminal cases in Article III, Section 2, leave the right to jury trial in civil cases constitutionally unprotected?

But if Wilson's reply was vulnerable to criticism, the Anti-Federalists' "parade-of-horribles" mentality proved just as easy to lampoon. The point of departure was the inclusion in the published dissent of the minority Anti-Federalist members of the Pennsylvania convention of a clause endorsing as a potential, if hitherto overlooked, constitutional right the "liberty to fowl and hunt in seasonable times, and on lands they hold . . . and in like manner to fish in all navigable waters, and others not private property, without being restrained." If the list of rights had to be that inclusive, Federalists replied, where could it possibly end? Why not, a waggish Noah Webster asked, include this "restriction: 'That Congress shall never restrain any inhabitant of America from eating and drinking *at seasonable times,* or prevent his lying on his *left side,* in a long winter's night, or even on his back, when he is fatigued by lying on his *right*'"?

Beneath the overstatements and the humor, both sides were wrestling with a fundamental problem that directly reflected the development of American constitutional theory since 1776. Once one thought of written constitutions not as transition mechanisms, equivalent perhaps to what we now call super-statutes, but as supreme fundamental law, the advantages and drawbacks of incorporating statements of rights within the four corners of the text posed a genuine and profound problem. If one wanted to secure a particular right, its inclusion in the text was essential. But if the security of a right—or of rights more generally—was understood to depend on that inclusion, then the question of which rights made it into the text, or the exact language with which they were formulated—textualized—would have a lasting effect on their authority and scope. Omitted rights could indeed become relegated rights. And poorly or weakly formulated rights presumably could create interpretive problems that would complicate rather than facilitate their enforcement.

It was, I think, James Madison who saw these problems most clearly. Madison's reservations about the efficacy of a federal bill of rights, as I have noted, were grounded in his larger theory of faction: its greater propensity to form in smaller political units, its sources in popular passions and interests that would sweep aside mere statements of principle, and its capacity to work its mischief through a politically potent legislature that would overawe and intimidate the weaker branches. His preferred solution to the problem of rights would have been to empower the new Congress to negate state laws, a proposal that rested on his assumption that the real dangers to rights would arise provincially, not nationally, and that the mode of electing Congress would make it "sufficiently neutral" or "sufficiently disinterested" to exercise its awesome power as a "disinterested & dispassionate umpire" of disputes arising within the states.[13]

Madison restated his concerns about the efficacy of a bill of rights in his "parchment barriers" letter to Jefferson of October 17, 1788. In this rich document, several points deserve special notice. First, while indicating his willingness to support the adoption of a bill of rights, Madison also revealed that he still did not regard its "omission [as] a material defect." Second, Madison generally endorsed the Wilsonian argument that the form of delegating powers to the government would act to protect "the rights in question." Third, and in this analysis more important, Madison listed among his reservations the concern "that a positive declaration of some of the most essential rights could not be obtained in the requisite latitude." Here, in this brief observation, Madison encapsulates the problem that this essay has addressed.

For the force of Madison's reservation extends to the dual problem of

enumeration and textualization. A bill of rights could lack "requisite latitude" if it were too narrowly drawn: narrow both in terms of which rights
were enumerated and in how those rights were stated. Madison's own il-
lustration of this point suggests that the question of textuality was as serious as the problem of enumeration. "I am sure that the rights of conscience
in particular"—the rights to which he individually was most deeply committed—"if submitted to public definition would be narrowed much
more than they are ever likely to be by an assumed power." Madison could
draw on his own experience in this regard, both in turning back the General Assessment Bill in Virginia only a few years earlier, and in his success
in enlarging the statement of the principle in the Virginia Declaration
of Rights from the mere tolerationist language originally proposed to a
broader recognition of freedom of conscience. Those two personal suc-
cesses did not outweigh the risk that trusting the definition of a right to a
political process requiring approval from the majority of the polity might
have the consequence of diluting the desired statement in the name of securing its adoption. One might be left with a statement of the right in
question that would be less than satisfactory. It was one thing to "declare"
a right as a statement of a general principle. But the more one regarded
that statement as a definitive text—a precise legal formula—the more
careful one had to be to get that right, well, right.

This was a problem of the first order, and one that could not be easily
or perhaps ever solved within the emerging conventions of American constitutional draftsmanship. There is a genuine dilemma in declaring rights
that makes the Federalist position more defensible than the standard story
recognizes, and we are grappling with its consequences still, every time we
ask whether there can be other sources for fundamental rights than the text
of the Constitution itself, or whenever we visit that twilight zone of contemporary constitutional controversy known as the Second Amendment.

Notes

1. Madison, *Papers of James Madison*, 10:337, 12:14.
2. Madison to Nicholas Trist, 23 Dec. 1832, *James Madison: Writings*, 862.
3. Madison to George Eve, 2 Jan. 1789, to Richard Peters, 19 Aug. 1789, ibid., 427–
29, 471.
4. For the record, this list includes: "(1) their rights as Englishmen; (2) natural law;
(3) the emigration contract; (4) the original contract; (5) the original American contract;
(6) the emigration purchase; (7) colonial charters; (8) equality with other British subjects;
(9) principles of the British constitution; and (10) principles of the customary American
constitution." Reid, *Authority of Rights*, 65–66.

5. For a dissenting view on this point, see Kruman, *Between Authority and Liberty*.

6. Texts of all three documents (the Virginia Declaration of Rights, constitution, and the Declaration of Independence) can be found in Kurland and Lerner, *Founders' Constitution*, 1:6–11.

7. Wood, *Creation*, 271.

8. Levy, *Emergence*, 227.

9. Jefferson, *Papers of Thomas Jefferson*, 1:362–64.

10. Later laws that contradict earlier ones abrogate them. For further discussion of the key role this maxim of statutory construction played in the evolution of American constitutionalism, see Rakove, *Original Meanings*, 99–100, 129–30.

11. Madison, "Vices of the Political System of the U. States," in *James Madison: Writings*, 75.

12. Kramer, *People Themselves*.

13. Madison, "Vices of the Political System of the U. States," and Madison to Washington, 16 April 1787, *James Madison: Writings*, 79, 81–82.

Bibliography

Jefferson, Thomas. *The Papers of Thomas Jefferson*. Vol. 1. Ed. Julian Boyd. Princeton, NJ, 1950.

Kramer, Larry. *The People Themselves: Popular Constitutionalism and Judicial Review*. New York, 2004.

Kruman, Marc. *Between Authority and Liberty: State Constitution Making in Revolutionary America*. Chapel Hill, NC, 1997.

Kurland, Philip, and Ralph Lerner, eds. *The Founders' Constitution*. Chicago, 1987.

Levy, Leonard. *Emergence of a Free Press*. New York, 1985.

Madison, James. *James Madison: Writings,* ed. Jack N. Rakove. New York, 1999.

————. *Papers of James Madison*, ed. William T. Hutchison et al. Chicago and Charlottesville, VA, 1962–.

Rakove, Jack N. *Original Meanings: Politics and Ideas in the Making of the Constitution*. New York, 1996.

Reid, John Phillip. *A Constitutional History of the American Revolution: The Authority of Rights*. Madison, WI, 1986.

Wood, Gordon S. *The Creation of the American Republic, 1776–1787*. Chapel Hill, NC, 1969.

The Limited Horizons
of Whig Religious Rights

A. GREGG ROEBER

We are so far removed from the world of the Founders that recapturing their horizons that defined religion requires special effort on our part. Our difficulty is compounded by the fact that the Founders said little about religious rights and had no coherent shared philosophy they developed in order to instruct later generations. Moreover, as this essay argues, the Founders had a limited notion of what the "rights" of "religion" were, largely because their understanding had been shaped by the particular legacy of Protestant Christianity, of which they were heirs, but in which they were not always active participants. The essay begins by considering recent literature on the vexed issues of religion, state, and society, and on what the Founders did or did not think about these weighty matters. Next, we survey the unpleasant facts that challenge idealistic notions of the religious liberality that supposedly characterized the Founding generation and distanced them from their more openly Protestant neighbors. We then turn to look carefully at their complex notions about the rights of conscience. Finally, we reflect on just how remote, how different our understanding of "religion" is from theirs. Continual invocation of the Founders by partisans in America's culture wars obscures their distance, their accomplishments, and their limitations.

The outline sketched above runs counter to a number of accounts, both scholarly and journalistic, of how the Founders viewed religion. Many of these narratives have either intentionally or accidentally resurrected a "Whig" interpretation of the Founders' views on religious rights. In his classic essay, Herbert Butterfield concluded that "behind all the fallacies of the whig historian there lies the passionate desire to come to a judgment of values, to make history answer questions and decide issues and to give the historian the last word in a controversy." The "chief aim" of the historian, he argued, should rather be "the elucidation of the unlikeness between past and present and his chief function is to act in this way as the mediator between other generations and our own."[1]

Too often, however, as Americans debate about religion, their society, and the role of the state, the "unlikeness" of the Founding generation and their neighbors eludes us. Instead, the Founders' accomplishments have been subsumed under a banner that proclaims the triumph of fully familiar post-Christian individualism, secularism, and a general freedom from busybody religiosity. Many accounts locate the roots of this triumph in the Protestant Reformation. John Witte, for example, has suggested that the "Lutheran gene" in the "genetic code of Protestantism" consists of "an instinct for egalitarianism—for embracing all persons equally, for treating all vocations respectfully, for arranging all associations horizontally, for leveling the life of the earthly kingdom so none is obstructed in access to God."[2] More nervously, Witte admitted that, in looking at the Founders, John Adams's endorsement of a "mild establishment" seems irrelevant today, and Witte worried instead about the capacity of "secular prejudices to become constitutional prerogatives."[3] T. H. Breen and Timothy Hall have located the growth of a "modern" sense of a secular self in the "transatlantic commercial context" of pre-Revolutionary New England, and Frank Lambert, Derek H. Davis, Vincent Phillip Muñoz, Annabel Patterson, and Jon Meacham all have tended, in disparate ways, to celebrate a marketplace of both material and ideological goods that presented the triumph of individual choice to late eighteenth-century North Americans. The confident atmosphere of both material and ideological prosperity encouraged Americans, in these interpretations, to follow the noble, farsighted, and vaguely secular tradition of religious liberty of conscience dedicated to "separation" of church and state.

A vague species of "public religion" in these accounts apparently was foreseen by the Founders as a kind of comforting assurance for common aspirations. According to these authors, no mechanisms were envisioned for translating real religious conviction into public policy, for fear of relapsing into wars of religious conscience. American exceptionalism would put an end to the threat of religious sectarian violence that had marred the European experience. In not a few of these explorations, these elite gentlemen and their liberal defense of religious liberty are described as later falling among thieves on the road to a multicultural Jericho, bushwhacked by lurking evangelical bandits.[4]

This essay dissents from such interpretations and argues that we should not forget that the Founding elite worked with hidden assumptions and were not free of prejudices. We should also reject accounts of twenty-first-century critics who demonize the Founders as intentional creators of an aggressively secular polity and society. The Founders' dedication to limited religious rights operated within restricted horizons, horizons that now lie so far in a distant country that we can scarcely recognize the landscape they once defined. For that reason, careless invocation of the Founders as either hostile to Christianity or willing to "accommodate" it misses the nuances of eighteenth-century assumptions about who could belong in the social and political order of the new republic, and on what terms.

The Limited Religious Rights of the Founders: A Distant Country

The American Founders believed that liberty stood watch and ward over the pretensions of power. They also believed that religious factions had long served as the means by which power, the dread enemy of liberty, had wrought havoc in state and society. But the Founders did not talk very much about religious "rights" as such. We tend to think of "rights"—and indeed, of "religion"—as a personal, subjective, "moral power" over our own selves, that is, as a protected space into which others cannot legitimately intrude. The Founders, however, were much more inclined to think about rights within a much older perspective that included the linked concepts of duty and obligation—to God first, but to kindred, society, and nation as well.[5]

We take for granted the fact that the First Amendment to the federal Constitution removed the new government completely from determining the content, the application, and especially the definition of religion. But in coming to such sweeping conclusions, we overstate the case. What we know with confidence regarding what the Founders thought about the "rights" of religion is that they, along with the Protestant majority, were determined that the new republic would not have a national religious establishment. We also know that they accepted the demands emanating from various states that religious liberty must be protected. The terms used are also significant: "religious liberty" or "liberty of conscience"—not "rights" per se. Both the Founding elite and the more openly Protestant majority intended, in protecting religious liberty, that a personal conviction about the deity and the manner of worship should not be subjected to government scrutiny or control.

But we can easily draw two equally erroneous conclusions from what the Founders wrote. First, we need to avoid the temptation to attribute their determination to protect religious liberty to either religious indifference or hostility to Christianity. In actual fact, these men remained deeply influenced by the very Protestant world whose institutionalized churches and clergy they also criticized. Although they refused to allow the predominantly Reformed Protestant theology of their neighbors to dictate "officially" the character of society or the frame of government, they nonetheless counted on the persistence of a well-formed moral sense in a population steeped in the norms and memories of the Reformation. Second, against all myths to the contrary, the Founders were not committed to a set of philosophical views vaguely connected to a "secular Enlightenment," or a "liberal secularism" marked by an affinity for contract law and individualism.[6] Instead, they shared with the more biblically informed Protestant majority an inherited discourse, a set of cultural memories that allows them to appear to us as though they had thought through all the implications of what religious liberty would mean for society. In fact, however, they had not. Instead, they remained indebted to the definition of religion that had been created by Catholic–Protestant debates over the previous two and a half centuries. As a result, the limited horizons of their world only become clear when we view them from this inherited historical perspective.

The eighteenth-century American understanding of religious rights, even among elites, continued to be formed by a Reformed Protestant tradition that manifested itself in many local and regional variations. Seventeenth- and eighteenth-century Protestant European settlements in North America flourished in increasingly diverse forms, encompassing Anglicans, New England dissenters, Dutch and German Reformed and German Lutheran transplants, Scotch-Irish Presbyterians, some Native Americans, and most recently, African Americans. As the Founders deliberated in the late eighteenth century, both Methodist and Baptist movements began their rise to dominance in an overwhelmingly Protestant America. Whatever divided Protestant Christians (and much did), all these heirs of the Reformation nevertheless shared a common conviction about religious rights that had also shaped an understanding of the term "the rights of Englishmen."

Admittedly, though, the Founders, "a select group of the most influential political and military leaders . . . brilliantly successful men of affairs who were well informed about religion," were not, on the whole, "traditional" Christians.[7] Although most were Deists or liberal Protestants in doctrine, they were no less wary of Roman Catholicism than were their more biblically inclined neighbors. It is also true that many of them had laid aside the explicitly pessimistic views of human nature held by most

Protestant North Americans. Most of their neighbors continued to be shaped by the Reformation's reading of Augustine of Hippo and to believe in the very real possibility that a great portion of humanity was destined for Hell. Protestants still debated the exact number of the elect, the way in which conscience dictated the worship of this just God, and whether Catholics, Jews, or heathens could be saved.[8] Such questions did not interest the elite Founders.

Nevertheless, the Founders did subscribe to a belief in a world of future rewards and punishments. Indeed, "Americans of all religious persuasions . . . took what might be described as a macro and a micro view of the impact of religion on society. At the macro level, they believed that God tangibly exalted nations that were obedient to him; at the micro level, they perceived that religion, operating through the future state doctrine, transformed otherwise sinful individuals, creating good citizens who made an orderly society possible and who, when aggregated, made it prosperous."[9]

No one has satisfactorily explained exactly how and why the Founding generation of North America's political leaders came to adopt, in place of a straightforward, biblical, Reformed Protestant tradition, a more complicated "commonsense moral reasoning" that spoke a language of "self-evident truths." But they did. And because of their conviction that a universal human nature could be probed on the basis of reason, and that informed choices and duties could be identified to guide both individual and society, they were perhaps slightly more optimistic about the possibilities of political and social betterment than were their fellow citizens— but only slightly. Accordingly, before we are tempted to believe that their disdain for a narrow reading of God's judgments on human mischief implied that they envisioned a horizon of unlimited future possibilities, we should pause. In practice, not everyone fit, or indeed was thought capable of fitting, into their notions of how religious rights and liberty of conscience would produce a Protestant society where government would have no role in defining religious rights. What these leaders counted on was the judgment of a prevailing—but correctly informed—public opinion among their biblically oriented Protestant neighbors. That opinion was what they took for granted to sort out how convictions of conscience or "moral sense" would be allowed social and political expression beyond the narrow bounds of private belief and worship.[10]

John Adams, for example, in his "Dissertation on the Civil and Canon Law," proclaimed that liberty and Catholicism were irreconcilable. His personal religious beliefs surely lay far to the left of those of most of his

New England neighbors, but Adams knew that a majority of European Americans shaped by Reformed Protestant convictions saw religious rights in historically conditioned terms. Dejected at times about the lack of moral fiber in his fellow North Americans, Adams remained convinced that Christianity had an indispensable role to play in inculcating ethical standards among citizens of the Republic. And he meant Protestant Christianity. Liberty, he wrote, had been "everlastingly persecuted by the great, the rich, the noble, the Reverend." Here, he followed Paul Dudley's inestimable service to "unsullied liberty" that had taken the form of a quadrennial lecture heard by Adams and dedicated to "the detecting and convicting and exposing the Idolatry of the Romish Church, Their Tyranny, Usurpations, Damnable Heresies, fatal Errors, abominable Superstitions, and other crying Wickednesses in their high Places . . . the Church of Rome is that mystical Babylon, that Man of Sin, That Apostate Church spoken of, in the New-Testament."[11]

No less so in the eighteenth than in the sixteenth century, Protestant defenders of liberty, whether partisans of a militant biblical God or enamored of "moral sense," understood "the identification of the clergy with superstition and fornication, and the personification of the church as the whore of Babylon [that] had a significance . . . from the time of the corruption of the true religion in England by the introduction of monasticism."[12] The assault on the devisal of individual property, perverse sexual mores, and corrupt religious dogma followed in Catholicism's train, logically and inevitably.

Again, it is true that religious rights as envisioned by these Founders may not have been identical with the way their biblical Reformed Protestant, largely rural contemporaries thought of them. Indeed, the Founders did not care very much for the piety of the Protestant world that had created them. These men worried about religion because factional disputes based on religious conviction threatened property and public order. But still, both strains in this non-Catholic, vaguely Protestant culture shared enough of a common vision to ensure significant points of reference, a shared bank of religious and cultural memories that they never had to articulate explicitly. Thus, the Founders conceded, based on their formative (even if unacknowledged) Protestant heritage, the importance of religion as a duty to God, and with the singular exception of James Madison, believed it must serve as a necessary component in forming the consciences and sense of duty in citizens. In some but not all of the new states, some of the Founders also were willing to enlist religious groups to address, through trusts and incorporated societies, local and state problems of poor relief and reform. But their interest in religion largely ended there; it was clearly utilitarian.

Admitting, then, that the following argument runs counter to much of the received wisdom about religious rights and the Founders, we should resist the temptation to suppose that John Adams was unusual because he possessed a peculiarly sour disposition. Similarly, we must not assume that Massachusetts was unique when its new constitutional framers opted for a view of religious rights that promoted "religion in utilitarian terms, as morality ensuring social control." Skepticism about the goodness of humankind persisted as centerpiece in nearly all the Founders' anthropology, in spite of their being heirs of generations who had sought to overcome Augustinian pessimism about human society and politics. Thus, even though their intellectual predecessors had sought to rehabilitate the traditionally scorned passion for gain, and may have succeeded to a limited degree, few of the eighteenth-century merchants, lawyers, great planters, and speculators put much stock in overly optimistic or deeply theoretical views of human behavior.[13]

In this instance, Madison was typical in his reading of David Hume's essays that shaped his *Federalist* No. 10. Here, he took to heart Hume's twin warnings against both religious zealots and the voracious drive for accumulation of property and power. But Hume's essay delivered its brilliant payload because it was fired by engines burning with disdain for roseate views of human nature. In accord with this suspicion, Hume was especially cynical in his deep-seated loathing of Christian clergy.[14] Similarly, the Founders probably did intend that the adoption of the First Amendment should mark the "end of Christendom" in North America, because, like James Madison, many "saw religion as a source of faction." And taking their measure from the inherited fear of Catholicism bred in them, the Founders understood that "establishment always involved a government preference," a leading cause of faction. But this move away from religious establishment did not mark them as "secular liberals." The Founders preferred nothing; they intended to deny the federal government any competence in the entire area of "religion." But with this, agreement about what else they might have meant by "religious rights" ends, because they themselves were not willing to acknowledge their own indebtedness to Catholic–Protestant debates over religion, whose institutionalized forms that they had learned to fear.[15]

The robustly Protestant men and women in North America, living in villages and rural areas, shared the Founders' anxiety about clerical hierarchies and privileges, as well as their sense that religious rights, particularly inalienable ones, implied nonnegotiable duties owed to God and to fellow citizens. And based on their knowledge of the vastly different character of religious practices, laws, and customs in the pre-Revolutionary colonies, the Founders were content to maintain the vitality of local–regional understandings of "religious rights." Among these practices and customs was the conviction, shared by many Protestant groups with varied theological traditions, that correct belief implied social obligation. When Mary Fish in Connecticut, for example, drew up her 1773 "Portrait of a Good Husband," she expected him to provide his family with instruction "in the grand principles of religion," to exhibit a heart "open to the cries of the poor and needy," and to "owe no man anything but love."[16] German speakers in Pennsylvania asked that religious societies that had already been incorporated "for the Advancement of Virtue and Learning and for other pious and charitable Purposes" be guaranteed the same right of self-determination that they were used to under the old regime.[17] Ordinary believers' notions of religious rights were closely connected to communal and local senses of mutual obligation.

Not before the 1820s can we actually document a serious challenge to these values, in the "broad and chaotic surge of democratic principles . . . individual freedom, self-interested material striving, and the expansive liberty of both marketplace and mind."[18] Far from representing a completely distinct vision of religious rights, even Boston's Unitarian elite built upon a very old tradition of voluntary moralism that for generations had relied upon community and "familial moral oversight."[19] It was no surprise, therefore, that such people were comforted when leaders like Adams affirmed that "the churches had a role to play in making the moral calculus of republicanism actually work."[20]

More individualistic Protestant groups could dream dreams for the future of America, ones that guaranteed the success of Baptist and Methodist revivalists. The appealing idea of a nationally covenanted vision cherished by many "conservative" or "churchly Protestants" was too dangerous a remedy to secure a republic still very much conceived of in local and sovereign state terms. But even though elite and popular forces both opposed state or national hierarchies or establishments, what would emerge by the end of the eighteenth century would be a nation comprised of Protestant groups, and hence a Protestant, not a secular, society.[21]

At first, challenges to a vaguely Protestant society seemed geographically remote. That fact allowed the Founding elite to refuse to cast their own outrage over the actions of Barbary Coast pirates in the same terms as did their more biblically pious Protestant fellow citizens. When Islamic pirates took Christians captives, men as different in their personal and public views as Washington and Jefferson refused to describe enslavement and loss of honor as affronts to "Christianity"; they were, however, urged to do so.[22] Closer to home, however, the popular theology and intolerance that were never far from the Founders' minds provided far less room to maneuver and continued to shape their responses to Native Americans, African Americans, Catholics, and Mormons.[23]

A Protestant Society, a Minimal State

In actual, lived experience, only Protestants of varying sorts were likely to inhabit the landscape created by the Founders' religious horizons. Scattered evidence from the pre-Revolutionary decades might have warned them that "others" seeking admittance but not fitting within an admittedly vague but broadly defined Protestant world would not be welcomed. Postconstitutional public policies left little doubt of this. Among the issues that demonstrated the restrictive features of the Founders' understanding of religious rights were the federal funding of Protestant missionaries among Native Americans; the response to the unnerving rise of a Roman Catholic presence and hierarchy; a reinvigorated anti-Semitism that began to take shape in the 1790s; the manner in which the challenges raised by African Americans to the predominant conventions about religious rights were treated; and the repressive response to the rise of Mormonism. All of the conflicts that surrounded these issues might have been predicted had the limitations of the Founders' concept of religious rights been more freely admitted or recognized. The "free exercise" of religion among these groups clashed with the understanding of religious rights that flowed from their Whig tradition.[24]

Although already two centuries old, the debate over whether to Christianize or civilize Native Americans escalated in post-Revolutionary North America. Elizabethan optimism about the speed of the process by which "Gospel agency" would accomplish the task disappeared in seventeenth-century clashes between English and North American Indian cultures. And the cautionary conclusions eighteenth-century Scottish observers had drawn from Britain's own long story of Christianization were forgotten in a new burst of Protestant enthusiasm for Christian missions in the new republic.[25] The initial congressional resolution of February 5, 1776, swiftly moved in its language from a "friendly commerce" between the United Colonies and the Indians to "the propagation of the Gospel." Secretary of

War Henry Knox's vision of civilizing Indians rested explicitly on Christian missions that emerged "as the key to a successful policy."[26]

Scholars have repeatedly demonstrated that the inculcation of morals and civil obedience lay at the very heart of this vision of "religious rights." From Knox's tenure as secretary of war to the creation of the "Civilization Fund" in 1819, one can scarcely find any other understanding of the goals of religion, in particular, that informed U.S. relations with Native Americans. No serious protection or cultivation of indigenous religion and no patient waiting for an integration of Native American spiritual insight into Christian doctrine emerged in the Anglophone Protestant evangelizations of the antebellum era. Moravian efforts among the Delaware and Cherokee that had exhibited a willingness to take the longer view of such processes declined and faltered. They failed because public opinion within the dominant evangelical Protestant culture and its political sympathizers rejected this overly broad understanding of religious liberty. Of particular interest, this nexus of evangelical fervor and civic religion found support under Jefferson and his successors, though no one doubted that Protestant missionaries were to be the agents of religion. Importantly, civilizing projects did not include Roman Catholic participants.[27]

Not surprisingly, then, in eighteenth-century Maryland, Catholics had not found much reason to be confident about their rights of religion. The Seven Years' War had witnessed a serious proposal brought to the floor of the lower house of the Assembly to impose the full force of English penal statutes on Catholics, including confiscation of their property. The threat never materialized, but it provoked an inquiry by Charles Carroll of Annapolis into the possibility of selling his vast estates and moving to Catholic Louisiana. Forbidden by Maryland's government even to offer refuge and charity to exiled French Catholic Acadians, he was eventually persuaded by his son, Charles Carroll of Carrollton, to be cautious before abandoning hope for better treatment in Maryland.[28]

Catholic struggles to adjust themselves to the Founders' vision of religious rights ranged from apologetic responses to anti-Catholic suspicion to fierce local battles over trusteeships while pleading for Catholic participation in the moral education of youth. The memory of a French- and Spanish-Catholic menace to British North America, coupled with aggressive Catholic policies on the Continent during the eighteenth century, did nothing to alleviate Protestant fears of their historic enemy.[29] Unfortunately, just as North American Catholics reassured Protestant contemporaries that Rome and republicanism were compatible, papal condemnation of Febronianism (typified by the Synod of Pistoia), the nationalist church alternative to papal centralization, reignited Protestant suspicions. With such concerns in mind, the framers of the Massachusetts constitution effectively barred Catholics from office. Protestant defenders of liberty were certain that religious rights could not extend to Catholics, who were schooled in the "use of mental reservation and equivocation to conceal the truth from those the speaker reasonably believed were not entitled to the truth." Such an understanding of conscience might provide cover for outright assaults on the public good. The outbreak of conflict between local trustees of Catholic parishes and the new bishop of Baltimore, John Carroll, sparked a new wave of court cases and pamphlet warfare.[30]

The writings of the first American-trained priest ordained in the United States, Demetrius Gallitzin, pointed out where the conflicts over religious rights would occur: in the care and education of children and family in the context of property rights. A scion of the princely Golitsyns family of Russia, Gallitzin had come of age in liberal Enlightenment surroundings in the Netherlands before converting to Rome and emigrating to North America. Writing against a Presbyterian opponent fifteen years after his ordination in 1795, Gallitzin rejected the Enlightenment's reliance on "corrupted reason" and scorned theological toleration of Protestant errors as an unacceptable alternative to the Roman Catholic Church's sole possession of true doctrine. More ominously to local Protestants, he successfully used his independent financial position to construct a Catholic enclave, the town of Loretto in western Pennsylvania, with an eye toward building a community immune from baneful Protestant influence. Gallitzin brought the abstract issues of the inculcation of religious conviction, free exercise of religion, and the protection of both by propertied Catholics to the practical level: those who entrusted their children to Protestant-dominated schools, Gallitzin observed in one sermon, were no different from ancient Canaanites who had sacrificed their children on the altar of Baal.[31]

In South Carolina, although the new 1790 constitution allowed Catholics to hold office and own property, in practice Catholics were expected to remain "religiously circumspect and . . . [to] support the dominant racial and political order." Bishop John England learned this lesson in 1835 when a mob decided that the twin evils of abolitionist literature and Catholicism could be removed by burning the first and destroying the property of the adherents of the second. This bishop who had baptized slaves and agreed to represent the Vatican in Haiti thenceforth turned his back on education for freed blacks and wrote in support of slavery.[32] Ironically, five years after a mob had burned the Ursuline convent in Charlestown, Massachusetts, Protestant Britain's pressure on the papacy to denounce the slave trade produced cheers for the pope in neighboring Boston. Popular public opinion's capacity to dictate where religious conscience was permitted to express itself beyond private worship tended, as with America's Founding elites, to be liberal, but only at a distance.[33]

The survival of a Catholic identity protected by private endowments seemed to push the boundaries of religious rights in America as both Protestant and liberal Deists understood them. Jewish citizens of the new republic watched and learned. Jews were at one and the same time liberated from European constraints by American legal and constitutional rights and, paradoxically, doomed to experience that same liberty as the dissolvent of that "order and solidarity . . . they had had in the Old World." Faced with a renewed anti-Semitism in the 1790s that hinted darkly at Jewish economic influence behind both elite politics and banking schemes, American Jews confined themselves wholly to looking after their own. They eschewed making converts or in any way antagonizing the overwhelmingly Protestant religious culture of the early republic. Although the election campaign of 1800 revealed the dangers of appealing too overtly to anti-Semitic themes, the near hegemony of Jeffersonians outside New England did not signal the welcome of Jews into public life in the rest of North America, either.

As William Pencak has persuasively argued, the level of tolerance extended to Jewish Americans actually declined at the end of the eighteenth century. Nor were the promoters of intolerance bigoted evangelicals or backcountry folk who had never had personal dealings with Jews. Defense of Judaism's "rights" began and ended at the door of the synagogue. Although the "private" practice of Judaism as a matter of conscience could be freely exercised, no extension of Jewish convictions, rituals, or social conventions was ever seriously contemplated by even the most "progressive" of eighteenth-century religious liberals. The "inward" turn of Jewish communities toward charitable activities designed to protect the lives and fortunes of their own small numbers testified eloquently to the fact that they understood quite well where the boundaries of their religious "rights" lay.[34]

In certain respects, American Jews remained safely within the acceptable definition of religious rights because they were small in number and confined their exercise of religion to purely "private" benevolent organizations that sought little more than communal survival and the acceptable teaching of ethical behavior. Nevertheless, for the evangelical majority in America, they remained suspect, as non-Christians. Even among liberal observers from Deist quarters Jews incarnated a curious mixture of prop-

erly enlightened exercise of private religious opinion and respectable morals
with an antiquated and alien identity incompatible with expansive and
"progressive" visions of the Republic.[35]

In the overwhelmingly evangelical context of the early republic that
confidently blended biblical literalism with white male enfranchisement
and property rights, "the most radical alternative to Reformed [Protestant]
literalism was offered by the least noticed theological voices of the day,
African-Americans."[36] The most skeptical view of African American Christianity, advanced by Jon Butler, suggests that religious rights in this context were almost wholly absent. Butler's "spiritual holocaust" that putatively witnessed the evisceration of African religion, however, has elicited
protest and dissent from other scholars. In varying degrees and depending upon the local and regional example one studies, African American religion appears to have exemplified genuine conversion to Christianity in
both urban and rural manifestations. True Christianity, to borrow the famous title of the German theologian Johann Arndt, produced not revolutionary consciousness and assaults upon Europeans, but an astonishing
rebirth of the ancient ideal of Christianity as a long-suffering faith.[37]

But freed African Americans nonetheless insisted that their bearing
the cross of discrimination did not exempt the white Protestant majority
from respecting their religious rights. Despite the attention paid to slave
religion by recent historians, it was the African American cleric Richard
Allen's ability to found the African Methodist Episcopal Church and promote a mutual benefit society that earned W. E. B. DuBois's unbounded
admiration.[38] Allen's and the AME's attack on the American Colonization
Society stemmed from the free black conviction that despite a record of
enslavement and disenfranchisement, the free exercise of religion in the
American republic obligated the state to protect their rights to property
and religious association. Despite the explicit invocation of Jeffersonian
principles by Allen and Madison's presidency of the ACS, Madison's thinly
disguised contempt for free blacks (most of them devout evangelical Christians) and the spread of increasingly discriminatory state laws aimed at
driving out free black populations illustrate the true limits of Whig religious thought. The actual religious rights of African Americans would not
be allowed exercise beyond the conventional boundaries of separate worship as an expression of private religious conviction.[39]

Local and regional interpretations of religious rights had not preoccupied the Founders, and not only with regard to the issue of African Americans, freed or slave. As the last of the Founding generation passed away,
increasing incidents of anti-Catholic riots and the dismissal of the rights of

Cherokees, many of whom were also Christians, paled by comparison to the looming challenge to religious rights posed by the rise of Mormonism.

Although a definition of religious rights on the federal level lay in the post–Civil War decades, Mormon polygamy and the control over property and marriage by a church hierarchy elicited sharp local and regional reactions in the 1830s. Those reactions showed how supposedly "private" issues of religious conscience could quickly spill over into public areas where local and state authorities shaped the definition of religious rights according to majority opinion that reflected the dominant Protestant worldview—exactly as it had for centuries. Early opponents explicitly linked Mormon polygamy and slavery, the "twin relics of barbarism," to the traditional Catholic menace. Protestant secular control of property, marriage, and individual conscience were now threatened by twin perils, Mormonism and Romanism. As a result, what had been only implicit, given the Founders' unstated assumptions, now became explicit: democracy and Protestantism were indistinguishable, and the American government could be "neither heathen nor sectarian."[40]

"Liberty of Conscience" in Context

The Founders' concept of "religious rights," as the preceding controversies illustrate, cannot be probed by simple referral to "separation" of church and state. Moreover, "separation between church and state cannot be understood simply as the history of religious liberty and its protection by American institutions."[41] Rather, whether and how a person or group could apply "essential rights of religion" to public life remained one of the dilemmas skirted by the Founders. They could do so because they were confident that the Protestant majority's correctly informed opinions would tolerate neither a "national" religion nor non-Protestant religions. James Madison would have extended the First Amendment's prohibitions against government interference in the liberty of conscience to the states—especially states such as Massachusetts or Connecticut where an establishment had malformed the public opinion of citizens. But most of his contemporaries refused to go along. They were confident that Protestant public opinion would establish the horizons for "free exercise" of religion in a manner that would not depart significantly from the Protestant "civic ethics" model of "religious rights" and, in so doing, would maintain a recognizably Protestant society that nonetheless was not directed by an explicitly Christian state.

Did the Founders in truth, then, actually contemplate an absolute, unrestricted "liberty of conscience" as part of their definition of "religious rights"? The numerous proposals that poured into Congress from the states demanding protection for "liberty of conscience" at first glance suggest as much. So did James Madison's own proposal that "the full and equal rights of conscience" should not "be in any manner, or on any pretext, infringed." Madison, however, was out of step with his contemporaries. His "lost amendment" would have explicitly forbidden any state from violating "the equal rights of conscience." Similarly, he was also to lose his battle to provide that "no person religiously scrupulous of bearing arms shall be compelled to render military service in person."[42] What are we to make of these proposals, and what actually came to be adopted?

Madison assumed that the multiplicity of religious groups and a properly shaped and informed public judgment would ride herd on expression of religious conscience and keep both federal and state governments out of the business of defining religion. This, his public communal grounding of religious rights, however, did not survive in the final language of the First Amendment. But his original language that stated "the people shall not be deprived" reflects his conviction that "freedoms of thought and belief and 'conscience' and speech and writing and publishing and arguing and assembling to debate and organize do, to be sure, have their personal or private aspect . . . [but] they also have a public dimension . . . more likely to be overlooked: that the republic rests on public liberty, serving the public good."[43] What is not immediately obvious is that the long history of anti-Catholic fears in both Britain and North America informed both his and Jefferson's determination to rely upon a properly shaped public opinion to guard against temptations to relapse into religious opinions and practices that might endanger a free republic. They had no intention of leaving opinion's public expression to the chance operations of wrongly informed consciences.

But what, more exactly, did the Founders understand the term "conscience" to mean? English law and the specifically local and regional religious convictions about conscience that had flowed from Catholic–Protestant confrontations in Europe contributed to their understanding. Yet by the eighteenth century, both in North America as in Britain, "conscience" was conceived and defined in ways that are sometimes confusing and contradictory. When we think of "private conviction" or "subjective conscience," we identify with heroes of "religious liberty" like the seventeenth-century perfectionist Roger Williams of Rhode Island. So, too, did the many petitions that flowed into Congress from New England and Virginia Baptists and others who had suffered from assessments or bans on their ministers' performing marriages in states with Congregational or Anglican established churches. But did the Founders subscribe "literally" to this understanding of conscience as wholly subjective? It is hard to imagine that Madison, Jefferson, Washington, or any of the other liberal Christians and Deists actually did. Madison was indeed scandalized by maltreatment of Baptists early in his public career. But the political stances and commitments of the Founders demonstrate that they could not have sympathized with the radical subjectivism of "separatist" Protestantism. Historically, unlike the Founders, such perfectionists had demanded an absolute and total separation between the "spiritual" and the civic order because they regarded the domain of politics to be the realm of temptation, if not forthrightly demonic.

If the Founders were not acolytes of radically subjective notions of religious conscience, however, it is even less plausible to turn them into disciples of the Erastian skepticism of Thomas Hobbes or David Hume. These giants of the European Enlightenment had concluded that the prince or state alone could determine the manner in which religious convictions would shape the social and political norms of a people. Given American hostility to monarchical and, after the War for Independence, executive power in general, the Founders could hardly have found anything useful in this tradition to inform their notions of conscience.[44]

A concern to protect private subjective conscience undoubtedly grew in several corners of the eighteenth-century European and North American world. But we cannot afford to forget that subjective private conscience had been tempered in English legal and constitutional thought. It had been given a secondary, subordinate role to what was thought of as a "legal" or "judicial" conscience. This idea of conscience grew in proportion to the need for certainty about rights and liberties. And this notion of judicial conscience depended upon a profound respect for settled custom, case law, and statutes that were all deemed "rational" and tightly linked to the close reading of such materials by judges bound by more than their own subjective opinions and private consciences. This definition of legal or judicial conscience had been shaped by an English anti-Catholic history that the Founders knew well.

Beginning in the sixteenth century, English jurists had successfully bridled the dangers of purely subjective "religious conscience," harnessing it to serve the needs of the "legal conscience" manifested in English common law. Henry VIII had found the essay *Doctor and Student*, published between 1528 and 1530 by the barrister Christopher St. Germain, especially timely. The essay fortuitously appeared at just the right moment for arguing against those who had fled to religious conscience for protection in resisting the royal divorce. It also gave real force to the royal claim that no foreign body of law was superior to the law of England. The politically astute writer could reassure his readers that certainty was to be found "in the historical laws of England," and not in the dangerous and unpredictable arena of private religious conviction.

By 1600, John Selden confirmed and repeated St. Germain's teaching, as did Sir Matthew Hale and his contemporary, Lord Nottingham. By the 1670s, Nottingham confidently concluded that "conscience" was "not religious but 'civic and political.'" Hale, for his part, believed that historical evidence pointed to "legal, moral and political virtues" that had nothing to do with specific religious doctrine. They were part of a general, minimal "natural law" found in the laws given to Noah and to Moses, but accessible to all nations, not just ancient Israel.[45] This subordination of religious conscience to the glorious triumph of English law, with its predictable certainty that protected liberty and the defense of property, had instructed educated North American Europeans long before anyone thought about separation from Britain.[46] Indeed, Thomas Jefferson appealed to such a standard in an opinion on whether courts had the power to fix the fees of court officers.[47]

The shock that North Americans felt when they discovered that independent judicial conscience apparently did not guarantee them the rights of Englishmen went a very long way toward convincing many that the reliance upon this unwritten mixture of immemorial custom, statute, and settled case law was fraught with unacceptable levels of uncertainty. The explicit amendments to the new federal Constitution spelling out the need for the protection of religious liberty reflected that disillusionment. It was not, however, simply the memory of Protestant defenders of subjective conscience like Roger Williams or the heroes of international Protestantism who figured in Foxe's *Book of Martyrs* or the Mennonite *Martyrs' Mirror* that drove these proposals.

Rather, it was the long history of anti-Catholic legislation in England, begun under Elizabeth I—the Oath of Allegiance crafted in the wake of the Gunpowder Plot of 1605 that "floated in on a raft of fresh anti-Catholic legislation"; the fears of Catholic conspiracy in the late seventeenth century that had fed the Glorious Revolution: these threats, real and imagined, also still informed late eighteenth-century political leaders. To seek refuge in purely private religious conscience—that is, to have equivocated in saying what one truly believed as a cover while plotting against lib-

erty—this was the great threat that had demanded attention to the definition of "conscience" in England. Private conviction had been tempered
to a more legal/judicial definition of the term, the better to root it in the
predictable and rational rule of English law—and to guarantee the survival of the Protestant faith. Some historians have argued that the fluidity
of the late seventeenth-century English church was such that the move toward gradual toleration of dissenting Protestants ought not surprise us.
But James II's attempt to extend religious toleration to Roman Catholics
by his Declaration of Indulgence threatened the certainty about settled
statute, custom, and usage and provoked the Glorious Revolution, both
in England and in three of the North American colonies.[48]

Despite North Americans' eventual disillusionment with the British
constitution, however, they did not suddenly transform themselves into
idealistic, naive defenders of subjective conscience. James Madison's un-
happiness with British protections of liberty left him increasingly skeptical about relying upon improperly formed Protestant public opinion alone.
But neither did he trust malformed public opinion that imposed religious
tests in the states barring non-Christians and, in many cases, Catholics
from office. It is not, however, Madison's concern for Catholics or non-
Christians that explains his willingness to attack state sovereignty on issues
of religion. Rather, it is his underlying fear that these religious test acts reflected a possible relapse toward factionalism and a form of preferential establishment, especially in states with a prior history of such behavior.[49]

Most of his colleagues, however, were not prepared to dictate what the
rights of conscience in the particular states should be. Madison may have
been aware that relatively little debate about the issue of conscience and
its limits had surfaced in the pre-Revolutionary colonies. The most comprehensive survey of those debates concludes that they were remarkably
rare. Among them, Elisha Williams's 1744 pamphlet arguing for a "natural right" for persons to read Scripture for themselves but in a Protestant
context effectively reprised the arguments of the very English jurists just
named—Matthew Hale, John Selden, and Lord Nottingham. A decade
later, Jonathan Mayhew's defense of the happy marriage of religion and
reason did little more than "fight for elbow room within the Congregational Church for theological liberals like himself." Benjamin Gale's
Reply to a Pamphlet, written a year later, also defended religious rights,
conscience, and reason by explicitly excluding non-Protestants.[50] Liberty
of conscience in North America thus remained locked in visions of a
Protestant society and, at times, a neutral understanding of the state. The

Founders pushed the argument by intentionally eliminating the possibility of a Protestant national state, but they could do so because they assumed the existence of a Protestant society.

It requires some effort on our part to understand how inherited fears of Catholicism, the resolute defense of property and English common law, and a "reasoned" common-sense searching of Scripture and history all got bundled together in these notions of conscience. At the actual level of how cases were increasingly being decided by appeals to standards of evidence, English lawyers increasingly "sought a middle ground between an unattainable, absolute certainty and the reduction of all questions of fact to mere opinion that would have rendered the processes of justice meaningless." By the eighteenth century, English lawyers commonly confused the role of "custom" with that of "reason" in the law by drawing upon the settled case-law precedents that had served as a defense against assaults on property and liberty—even while appealing increasingly to witness testimony and reasonable standards of evidence. This confusion emanated from lawyers' attempts to keep decisions firmly grounded in real, historical cases—the "legal conscience" based on custom and settled law just referred to—but, at the same time, to insist that such decisions were part of a "natural law" grounded in rational principles.[51]

This conflation crossed the Atlantic. James Otis of Massachusetts believed that the purpose of the law was to do justice to all human beings, male and female, black and white, who were all equal by nature. Settled case law demonstrated both truths. Indeed, Otis's appeals to conscience and to a sense of obligation "retreat into the language of seventeenth-century Reform Protestantism." Otis took rhetorical aim at novel contract theories about social relationships that seemed to him altogether too abstract. The obligation of conscience took concrete forms for him and, not surprisingly, centered upon the protection of the family and familial property: "Who acted for infants and women, or who appointed guardians for them?" For Otis, the exercise of conscience flowed from the obligation to do justice to the weakest familial and co-religious dependents. These were obligations based in the law of God and illustrated by how the law had actually been decided, not by appeal to newfangled notions of contract. Otis did not have to be explicit in acknowledging his indebtedness to a specifically Christian definition of "doing justice," for he knew his audience would understand the biblical basis for his argument. Otis, as a Protestant lawyer, argued from the local traditions of New England society when he insisted that rights were tied to duties and were quite different from privileges and immunities.[52]

Madison and Jefferson understood what Otis meant because, like him, they believed that laws of nature existed that produced concrete consequences in legal decisions and political policy. These laws presupposed social duties and obligations, not just subjective or personal rights. When we look at religious rights, we can see in concrete fashion what they understood the term to mean. Jefferson, seeking to distance himself from the wars of religious conscience that had blighted the European past, was himself a product of a particular form of natural-law thinking. When he invoked the "laws of nature," he understood that very specific duties were to be performed. Concerning religious rights, Jefferson maintained that only a mature mind that had been strictly indoctrinated would ever come to the proper exercise of both religious rights and obligations that were anything but "self-evident." His appeal to a talented aristocracy properly trained in schools vigorously protected from the influence of the clergy (thus his desire to be remembered as the founder of the University of Virginia and his vigilant screening of who could lecture on the law in this institution) reveals Jefferson's indebtedness to the very Western Christian tradition's understanding of a correctly formed conscience.

Jefferson's conviction that one must execute the duties of one's station was, in this respect, not so very different from that of his more explicitly Protestant neighbors.[53] Not surprisingly, the later public school movement in the nineteenth-century United States was led by a Unitarian whose religion "was sympathetic to the rationalistic and moralistic idea of religion. Tolerance in this style was unaware of its own sectarianism."[54] Madison, too, agreed that fellow citizens be informed in their sense of conscience and obligation. In his correspondence with Jefferson, he provided his mentor with a "theological catalogue" as requested in 1824, noting that "altho' Theology was not to be taught in the University, its Library ought to contain pretty full information for such as might voluntarily seek it in that branch of Learning." Catholic and Protestant theological works constituted the majority of the titles, and "not a single book of infidelity or skepticism, no Voltaire or Hume or Paine was listed, no works loose in their principles or 'Enemies to Religion.'"[55]

What Madison intended by supplying these titles might well have fallen under the warning "Know thine enemies." Precisely because the notion of liberty of conscience implied more than just a defense of subjective conscience, Madison, even though he vigorously disagreed with northern jurists of the early nineteenth century in their concrete conclusions, shared their understanding that public opinion had to be properly shaped so that it could form the boundaries of the republican experiment.

No less than Thomas Jefferson, James Kent, or Joseph Story, he firmly believed that they were merely expositing inherited law, and not making it. But unlike Jefferson or Madison, these jurists affirmed that Christianity was part of the common law. They did so, not because they intended to lay down judicial principles that defined precisely the "rights of religion" or specified doctrinally just which Christianity they meant, but rather because attacks on Christianity threatened to become assaults upon property and public order. Given the demographic facts of North America, "intemperate attacks on Christianity could be illegal while similar attacks on Islam could not."[56] Kent and Story could believe without difficulty that they were obligated to defend what a properly informed public opinion held to be the appropriate and socially acceptable application of beliefs in a supreme being and the duties owed to that deity.

Catholicism had historically stood for assaults upon liberty, property, and the sanctity of the freeborn Protestant control of marriage and household. Blasphemous attacks by Mormons or freethinking editors in the 1830s assaulted religious rights in different guises, but with the same moral values as their targets. The majority of American Protestants still agreed with the definition of "rights of conscience" expressed in Article II of the Massachusetts constitution, as "the duty of all men in society" to worship a supreme creator God. Denial of this duty—defined by what the majority would tolerate—was not something the courts were willing to contemplate. In sentencing Abner Kneeland for having violated the state's act against blasphemy, after refusing to allow his appeal to the U.S. Supreme Court, Chief Justice Lemuel Shaw, a Unitarian, in 1838 recognized that the law of religious rights could extend only as far as an informed public opinion would allow. "Shaw, along with the Suffolk County prosecutor and all the judges who sat on Kneeland's case, knew that the governing elite of Massachusetts in 1838 would not accept the unconstitutionality of a statute protecting scriptural, Christian doctrine."[57]

These boundaries upon private conscience illustrate the nature of limited religious rights and explain why many could continue to view a vague kind of Protestantism as a useful mechanism for inculcating civic virtue. Such notions also allowed informal Protestant customs or rituals to surround political occasions. Most customs of this sort had been carried forward from the Continental Congress into the Federal era, creating the "unofficial" Protestant establishment, not only in various states, but even in some federal policies and assumptions about religious "rights." Beginning with opening prayers in the Continental Congress, but extending later to chaplaincies for both houses of the federal Congress and congressional subsides for Protestant missionary efforts among Native Americans, these practices seemed both "rational" and based on long-standing custom as well. They aimed neither at "establishment" nor at the curtailment of the free exercise of religion. That they might override individual subjective conscience in the case of Native Americans, Catholics, African Americans, and, by the 1830s, Mormons, did not necessarily contradict the understanding of religious rights that the Founders had exhibited.[58]

It seemed reasonable and customary, given the inherited notions about the Catholic threat and the role of conscience as vigilant guard over civil rights, liberties, and obligations, that the Protestant majorities in many states insisted upon education using a King James version of the Bible that did much to provide a memory bank of common language references for Protestant identity across a gamut of theological opinions. They did so in order to ensure that their children understood the connections that linked Protestantism to property and religious liberty, and the obligation to defend all three. If the majority of Protestant Americans took such relationships for granted, Alexis de Tocqueville knew why. He concluded that "religion . . . directs mores, and it is in regulating the family that it works to regulate the state."[59] Most of the Founders would have found unremarkable his observation on the interrelatedness that bound religion to the quality of society and the state's mere affirmation of both.

The Founders did not think alike on such issues, and individual states and localities struggled to find where the boundaries lay that would limit purely subjective conscience by tying it to a broader sense of obligation. These struggles reflected the intentions of the Founders, who were practical politicians, not political theorists.[60] Yet the understanding of conscience that acknowledged duties owed to God and doing right by one's neighbors, especially the poorest of them, merged with the emerging language of "natural rights" in shaping the public sphere. North Americans of the Founding era expected the public arena to reflect their respect for the older, inherited Protestant notions of religious rights, exemplified in their fitful romance with notions of "virtue."[61] Struggling to explain what the American fascination with "rights" really meant, John Adams concluded that Americans grounded their notions of rights "in their Religion."[62]

The Founders left to local and state constituencies the details of how these rights were to find social expression,[63] and in fact only partially endorsed the definition of religion found in Virginia's campaign to establish religious liberty. Religion, as Jefferson and Madison cast the term in the Act for Establishing Religious Freedom, was a purely "private," subjective arena of opinion where belief in some divinity and worship of that divinity—the "duties" owed a creator—were discharged. But the logic of Whig religious thought demanded something more than a merely abstract defense of subjective conscience. In the new republican experiment, no one could contemplate putting at risk "the safety of private property from arbitrary governmental requisition . . . part of the whig culture colonial Englishmen shared with most inhabitants of the realm." The obligation to encourage and inculcate correct religious principles had long been an inseparable part of English liberties that were summed up in the term "property." The accumulation of property in the wrong hands, however, might be used by the ill informed or unwary to advance a "false" notion of religion that might sabotage the republican experiment, returning North Americans to an institutional, state-sanctioned version of Christianity. Madison and Jefferson, in particular, worked hard to prevent this from happening.[64]

They attempted to impede what both regarded as "wrong" opinions about religious rights that included acquisition of property to advance the cause of an institutionalized religion. Property—historically thought of as the bulwark of individual and collective liberty against the tyranny of the prince or state—could not be allowed to fall into the hands of those whose improper use of it would endanger liberty itself. In this notion of property, religious rights were construed in the narrowest terms to mean solely private belief and worship. Yet the horizons of the Whig world that the Founders had taken for granted as they thought about rights, religious and otherwise, had already begun to fade as their generation itself passed into memory.

Conclusion

The de facto reading of the Fourteenth Amendment into the First, since the *Cantwell v. Connecticut* decision of 1940, so far distances us from the local–regional world of religious rights that the Founders and the Protestant majority shared that we scarcely recognize it. The vision of the Founders was one characterized by their deference to a mélange of diverse local and regional experiences and particular notions of both property and conscience that they used to define "religious liberty." They hoped to prevent the clash of particular convictions in the arena of public law by balancing "factions" against each other. But, in reality, the distance among those factions was never really very large, nor were the horizons of these elite Founders so very different from those of the biblically pious Protestant majority of citizens. Precisely because of the limited horizons shared by both, Americans in the twenty-first century should forgo the temptation to tame that alien, almost unrecognizable, country by applying "accommodationist" and "separationist" labels to supposed positions held by inhabitants of this long-vanished world's understandings of "religious rights."[65]

It is increasingly hard for us to recognize how interwoven were "dissenting Christianity and natural law," "the resilience of Christian habits of mind and sectarian modes of life," and "a continuity between heterodox Dissent, rationalist deism and Enlightenment reason." But if we do remember these connections, that were so real for eighteenth-century North Americans, we must realize that in invoking the Founders we then give up once and for all the "comforting belief that enlightened secularisation has definitively marked off our civilized 'modernity' from the passional moral violence of a communitarian Christian past."[66]

By leaving the disputes over religious rights to the states and a properly informed Protestant Christian public opinion, the Founders hid behind the very Protestantism whose formal establishment they rejected. Informally, this predominantly Reformed Protestant world provided the real arena where religious rights had to be carefully watched for potential threats to property and public safety—but also relied upon, regarded not just as desirable, but "even indispensable, as a foundation for a country ruled by law, not by men."[67] The Founders were men who had—they hoped—escaped from the traditions of a powerful institutional church and an accompanying state-centered model of political life. But they enjoyed the prospect of contemplating religious "liberty" where their predecessors had only been able to speak in terms of religious toleration because the Founders' immediate horizons really encompassed an overwhelmingly Protestant population. The conviction that "citizens must be willing to live with each other; they need not approve of each other's commitments, religious or otherwise,"[68] would prove in the long run far more daunting a challenge than they could have imagined.

Today, ironically, the very central government that the Founders intended never to have any competence in defining what constitutes religious belief and practice now does so on a regular basis. By contrast, the Founders' notions of religious rights existed in a world whose horizons had been created by Catholic and Protestant controversies and terms of engagement. Their understanding was one that took duties and obligations seriously enough to fight off both establishment and indifference. In the very long run, that contest in North America produced a version of Protestant religion that the Founders and their Protestant fellow citizens would have found wanting: "private, voluntary, individual, textual, and believed," but eventually lacking a real public voice. Religion associated with "public, coercive, communal, oral, and enacted religion . . . iconically represented historically in the United States, for the most part by the Roman Catholic Church (and by Islam today) . . . is the religion of most of the world"; in America, that religion has been "carefully and systematically excluded, both rhetorically and legally, from modern public space."[69] We succumb to mirages if we suppose that the collapse of the Whig horizons that defined the contest over religion in terms of property, conscience, and mutual obligation in shared cultural memories and language will ultimately prove to be a triumph for liberty. Claims laid today by partisans of the "moral power" of religious rights brook no such restraints, and have no such memories, nor does the twenty-first century state—to our increasing peril.

Notes

1. Butterfield, *Whig Interpretation of History*, 64–65, 10.

2. Witte, *Law and Protestantism*, 301.

3. Witte, "A Most Mild and Equitable Establishment of Religion," 31.

4. See Breen and Hall, "Structuring Provincial Imagination," 1438; Breen, "Lockean Moment"; Lambert, *Founding Fathers and the Place of Religion in America;* Muñoz, "James Madison's Principle of Religious Liberty"; Patterson, *Nobody's Perfect*, 221: "'whig' here meant in the largest philosophical sense, as someone who believes in progress"; Meacham, *American Gospel.* The most elaborate argument for the modernity and secularity of early modern America and the relative unimportance of religious influences is Butler, *Becoming America*, 185–224, 242–43. For a broader survey of the problems surrounding narratives of religion and law, see Roeber, "Law, Religion, and State Making in the Early Modern World," 199–227.

5. See Hutson, *Forgotten Features of the Founding*, 96.

6. Hence my disagreement with McGarvie's *One Nation under Law*, 11–16, 82–90, 190–91. For a searching examination of secular liberal individualism among the Founders, see Shain, *Myth of American Individualism.*

7. See Hutson, *Founders on Religion*, xvii.

8. For an example of such debates among German-speaking arrivals on the fate of Africans, Native Americans, and Jews, see Roeber, "What the Law Requires Is Written on Their Hearts."

9. Hutson, *Forgotten Features*, 32–33.

10. The best treatment of this curious development is Noll, *America's God*, 93–113. Students should be warned that the term "natural law" is unnervingly complex. One assessment suggests over 120 different constructions of what this term could mean. See Foriers and Perelman, "Natural Law and Natural Rights." I am indebted to David Konig for alerting me to this survey. See also the classic study by Wright, *American Interpretations of Natural Law*, 331–38, and his warning that "clearly thought out theories of natu-

ral law have not been common in this country" (338). He also noted that an emphasis on individual rights or "negative" defenses must be balanced against the Founders' interest in "theories of positive right" as well (340).

11. Adams, "Fragmentary Notes for 'A Dissertation on the Canon and the Feudal law,'" in *Papers of John Adams*, 1:106, 107.

12. On Adams's "irrelevance" and importance, see Wood, *Creation of the American Republic*, 567–92; see also Noll, *America's God*, 203–4; and on Protestant linkages of Catholic private behavior and menace to doctrine, see Parish, "Beastly Is Their Living and Their Doctrine," 138–52, quotation at 148, 149.

13. On the attempt to reread the Augustinian heritage, see Hirschman, *Passions and the Interests*, and on Hume's fear of religious factions and Smith's response, see Muller, *Adam Smith in His Time and Ours*, 54–60, 156–57.

14. See Adair, "'That Politics May Be Reduced to a Science'" 104–5.

15. See Curry, *Farewell to Christendom*, 33, 36–37.

16. Buel and Buel Jr., *The Way of Duty*, 80–81.

17. See Roeber, *Palatines*, 303–4.

18. Hanley, *Beyond a Christian Commonwealth*, 6.

19. Bernard, "Original Themes of Voluntary Moralism," 31.

20. Noll, *America's God*, 203.

21. See Roeber, "Migration of the Pious."

22. See Rojas, "'Insults Unpunished,'" 159–86, and for broader context, Marr, "Imagining Ishmael"; on the relative indifference of the British elite to the capture of their fellow countrymen, see Milton, *White Gold*, 18–31, 197–203, 268–79.

23. On the conservative nature of "popular" theologies up to the 1830s, see Noll, *America's God*, 145–57.

24. Noll cites several newer studies that show that Protestant groups were far from content to remain disconnected from social and political activity and relegated to a singular concern: "private" liberty of conscience. See *America's God*, 450–51, 561.

25. See Lucas, "Conquering the Passions."

26. Beaver, *Church, State, and the American Indians*, 57, 63.

27. See the summary and bibliography in McCarthy, *American Creed*, 126–33, 242, and Sheehan, *Seeds of Extinction*, 119–29; on the Moravian efforts, see Merritt, *At the Crossroads*; Smith, "Community of Women"; and McLoughlin, *Cherokees and Missionaries*.

28. See Carroll, *Dear Papa, Dear Charley*, 1:28, 30, 88, 130, 157, 169–70, 182, 225, 33–34; Hoffman, *Princes of Ireland, Planters of Maryland*, 272–78.

29. See Ward, *Protestant Evangelical Awakening*, 15–31.

30. Noonan, "Quota of Imps," 177, 194; Carey, *People, Priests, and Prelates*, 19–24, 207; Light, *Rome and the New Republic*, 18–39; Roeber, "Long Road to *Vidal*," 435–38.

31. See Murphy, *Gallitzin's Letters*, 96; Lemcke, *Life and Work of Prince Demetrius Augustine Gallitzin*, 209–10. Among many recent assessments of Catholicism in the early republic, see the insightful analysis of Protestant projections of various anxieties on Catholics offered by Franchot, *Roads to Rome*.

32. See Miller, "Roman Catholicism in South Carolina," 84, 95–96.

33. On Catholicism's changing views on slavery and the responses in America in the 1830s, see Noonan, *Church That Can and Cannot Change*, 104–9.

34. See Pencak, *Jews and Gentiles in Early America*, 247–68.

35. On the ambivalent status of Jews in Enlightenment Europe, see Sutcliffe, *Judaism*

and Enlightenment, 254–56. For the North American context, see McCarthy, *American Creed,* 60–67; Häberlein and Schmölz-Häberlein, "Competition and Cooperation," 409–36; Pencak, "Jews and Anti-Semitism in Early Pennsylvania," 365–408.

36. Noll, *America's God,* 404.

37. See Butler, *Awash in a Sea of Faith,* 129–63; for alternative views, see Morgan, *Slave Counterpoint,* 610–58; Frey and Wood, *Come Shouting to Zion,* xi, 35; on Moravians and African Americans, see Sensbach, *A Separate Canaan,* 245–70; and on black Methodism, see Roeber, "Migration of the Pious," 38–40.

38. See McCarthy, *American Creed,* 120.

39. On Madison and the ACS, see McCoy, *Last of the Fathers,* 281–86, 301–5.

40. Gordon, *Mormon Question,* 56, 8, and on the linking of Mormonism and Catholicism, 33–39, 142–45; see also Norgren, *Cherokee Cases.*

41. Hamburger, *Separation of Church and State,* 491. Readers familiar with Hamburger's work will recognize that I am in basic agreement with his arguments.

42. This summarizes Miller, *Business of May Next,* 247, quotations at 270, 256; see also Pfeffer, *Church, State, and Freedom,* 161–80; McGarvie, *One Nation,* 55–58.

43. Miller, *Business of May Next,* 270–71.

44. See Tuck, "'Christian Atheism' of Thomas Hobbes," 129–30; Murphy, *Conscience and Community,* 214–43.

45. Saunders, *Anti-Lawyers,* 24–29, 60–63.

46. See Colbourn, *Lamp of Experience,* 83–106.

47. See Dewey, *Thomas Jefferson, Lawyer,* 128. On both Sir Edward Coke and Hale, see Pocock, *Ancient Constitution and the Feudal Law,* 30–55, 170–81.

48. For the argument that religious toleration in North America actually stemmed from the unintended consequences of Stuart absolutism, see Haefeli, "Creation of American Religious Pluralism," chaps. 5–8.

49. On the history of equivocation, see Sommerville, "The 'New Art of Lying,'" 159–84; for the English context, see Hogge, *God's Secret Agents,* 185–88. On Madison's disappointment about New England support for the rights of conscience, see ibid., 76–77.

50. Curry, *First Freedoms,* 97, 101, 103.

51. On this transformation, see Shapiro, *Probability and Certainty in Seventeenth-Century England,* 272.

52. Whitman, "Why Did Early Modern Lawyers Confuse Custom and Reason?" 1–48; on Otis, see Wood, *Creation of the American Republic,* 8–10, 260–63; Breen, "Subjecthood and Citizenship," 385, 387, quoting Otis, *Rights of the British Colonies Asserted and Proved,* 419.

53. See Konig, "Principia Jeffersonia."

54. Strout, "Jeffersonian Religious Liberty and American Pluralism," 211.

55. Noonan, *Lustre of Our Country,* 87. I do not think on the basis of the list that Noonan is justified in thinking of Madison as a "traditional" Christian. For Madison to Jefferson, 10 Sept. 1824, see Madison, *Writings of James Madison,* 9:202–7.

56. Banner, "When Christianity Was Part of the Common Law," 29, 33.

57. Noonan, "Quota of Imps," 173, 175.

58. On some of the customs, see Davis, *Religion and the Continental Congress,* 133: "The Continental Congress essentially deferred to the states on all issues of establishment, aid to religion, freedom of belief, and sundry other religious matters." For a dissent

from the claim that the First Amendment enshrined this deference, see Curry, *Farewell to Christendom*, 121–22.

59. Tocqueville, *Democracy in America*, 278. On the irony of the "royal" translation's later success among Protestants in North America, see Nicolson, *God's Secretaries*, 225–30.

60. For a sample of varying opinions, see Hutson, *Founders on Religion*, 134–39, 189–94.

61. See Saunders, *Anti-Lawyers*, 118–23, and his suggestive observation that both John Witherspoon at Princeton and James Wilson at the College of Philadelphia struggled to reconcile religious and civic grounds for conscience and "rights."

62. Adams to Thomas Boylston Adams, 18 March 1794, cited in Hutson, "Emergence of the Modern Concept of a Right in America," 217.

63. Though Mark McGarvie's argument is correct in many respects, I find it unconvincing when he asserts that the inexorable logic of "separation" uniformly meant that the church "as a private corporation . . . was found to be an inappropriate institution to assume roles in governance and the shaping of public policy." The argument appears to rest upon a juxtaposition of a religious majority and a "secular enlightened" group of Founders. See McGarvie, *One Nation under Law*, 191.

64. See Adams, *First American Constitutions*, 311. For details comparing Virginia's opposition to incorporation of religious trusts to the encouragement given in Pennsylvania and New York, see Roeber, "Long Road to *Vidal*."

65. On the debates between "separationists" and "accommodationists," see Sandoz, *Government of Laws*, and Davis, *Religion and the Continental Congress*, 199–229.

66. Saunders, *Anti-Lawyers*, 115; see also Clark, *Language of Liberty*, 111, 305–90.

67. Sullivan, *Impossibility of Religious Freedom*, 154.

68. Murphy, *Conscience and Community*, 289. Murphy's critique of the "return of Whig history" is quite insightful; see ibid., 16–24, 276–94.

69. Sullivan, *Impossibility*, 8.

Bibliography

Adair, Douglass. "'That Politics May Be Reduced to a Science': David Hume, James Madison, and the Tenth Federalist." In *Fame and the Founding Fathers: Essays by Douglass Adair*, ed. Trevor Colbourn, 93–106. New York, 1974.

Adams, John. "Fragmentary Notes for 'A Dissertation on the Canon and the Feudal Law.'" In *The Papers of John Adams*, ed. Robert J. Taylor et al., 1:106, 107. Cambridge, MA, 1977.

Adams, Willi Paul. *First American Constitutions: Republican Ideology and the Making of the State Constitutions in the Revolutionary Era*. Expanded ed. Lanham, MD, 2001.

Banner, Stuart. "When Christianity Was Part of the Common Law." *Law and History Review* 16 (Spring 1998): 27–62.

Beaver, R. Peirce. *Church, State, and the American Indians: Two and a Half Centuries of Partnership in Missions between Protestant Churches and Government*. St. Louis, 1966.

Bernard, Joel. "Original Themes of Voluntary Moralism: The Anglo-American Reformation of Manners." In *Moral Problems in American Life: New Perspectives on Cultural History*, ed. Karen Halttunen and Lewis Perry, 15–39. Ithaca, NY, 1998.

Breen, T. H. *The Lockean Moment: The Language of Rights on the Eve of the American Revolution*. Oxford, 2001.

————. "Subjecthood and Citizenship: The Context of James Otis's Radical Critique of John Locke." *New England Quarterly* 71 (1998): 378–403.

Breen, T. H., and Timothy Hall. "Structuring Provincial Imagination: The Rhetoric and Experience of Social Change in Eighteenth-Century New England." *American Historical Review* 103:5 (Dec. 1998): 1411–38.

Buel, Joy Day, and Richard Buel Jr. *The Way of Duty: A Woman and Her Family in Revolutionary America.* New York, 1984.

Butler, Jon. *Awash in a Sea of Faith: Christianizing the American People.* Cambridge, MA, 1990.

————. *Becoming America: The Revolution before 1776.* Cambridge, MA, 2000.

Butterfield, Herbert. *The Whig Interpretation of History.* London, 1963.

Carey, Patrick W. *People, Priests, and Prelates: Ecclesiastical Democracy and the Tensions of Trusteeism.* Notre Dame, IN, 1987.

Carroll, Charles, of Carrollton and Charles Carroll of Annapolis. *Dear Papa, Dear Charley: The Peregrinations of a Revolutionary Aristocrat,* ed. Ronald Hoffman et al. Chapel Hill, NC, 2001.

Clark, J. C. D. *The Language of Liberty, 1660–1832: Political Discourse and Social Dynamics in the Anglo-American World* Cambridge, 1994.

Colbourn, H. Trevor. *The Lamp of Experience: Whig History and the Intellectual Origins of the American Revolution.* Chapel Hill, NC, 1965.

Curry, Thomas J. *Farewell to Christendom: The Future of Church and State in America.* New York, 2001.

————. *The First Freedoms: Church and State in America to the Passage of the First Amendment.* New York, 1986.

Davis, Derek H. *Religion and the Continental Congress, 1774–1789: Contributions to Original Intent.* New York, 2000.

Dewey, Frank L. *Thomas Jefferson, Lawyer.* Charlottesville, VA, 1986.

Foriers, Paul, and Chaïm Perelman. "Natural Law and Natural Rights." In *Dictionary of the History of Ideas: Studies of Selected Pivotal Ideas,* ed. Philip P. Wiener, 3:13–27. New York, 1973.

Franchot, Jenny. *Roads to Rome: The Antebellum Protestant Encounter with Catholicism.* Los Angeles, 1994.

Frey, Sylvia R., and Betty Wood. *Come Shouting to Zion: African American Protestantism in the American South and the British Caribbean to 1830.* Chapel Hill, NC, 1998.

Gordon, Sarah Barringer. *The Mormon Question: Polygamy and Constitutional Conflict in Nineteenth-Century America.* Chapel Hill, NC, 2002.

Häberlein, Mark, and Michaela Schmölz-Häberlein. "Competition and Cooperation: The Ambivalent Relationship between Jews and Christians in Early Modern Germany and Pennsylvania." *Pennsylvania Magazine of History and Biography* 126 (2002): 409–36.

Haefeli, Evan, "The Creation of American Religious Pluralism: Churches, Colonialism, and Conquest in the Mid-Atlantic, 1628–1688." Ph.D. diss., Princeton University, 2000.

Hamburger, Philip. *Separation of Church and State.* Cambridge, MA, 2002.

Hanley, Mark Y. *Beyond a Christian Commonwealth: The Protestant Quarrel with the American Republic, 1830–1860.* Chapel Hill, NC, 1994.

Hirschman, Albert O. *The Passions and the Interests: Political Arguments for Capitalism before Its Triumph.* Princeton, NJ, 1977.

Hoffman, Ronald. *Princes of Ireland, Planters of Maryland: A Carroll Saga, 1500–1782.* Chapel Hill, NC, 2000.

Hogge, Alice. *God's Secret Agents: Queen Elizabeth's Forbidden Priests and the Hatching of the Gunpowder Plot.* New York, 2005.

Hutson, James H. "Emergence of the Modern Concept of a Right in America: The Contribution of Michel Villey." *American Journal of Jurisprudence: An International Forum for Legal Philosophy* 39 (1994): 185–224 at 217.

———. *Forgotten Features of the Founding: The Recovery of Religious Themes in the Early American Republic.* Lanham, MD, 2003.

———, ed. *The Founders on Religion: A Book of Quotations.* Princeton, NJ, 2005.

Kan, Sergei. *Memory Eternal: Tlingit Culture and Russian Orthodox Christianity through Two Centuries.* Seattle, 1999.

Konig, David. "Principia Jeffersonia: Thomas Jefferson and the Natural Law Tradition." Paper presented at American Society for Legal History, Princeton, NJ, 21 Oct. 2000.

Lambert, Frank. *The Founding Fathers and the Place of Religion in America.* Princeton, NJ, 2003.

Lemcke, Peter Henry, O.S.B. *Life and Work of Prince Demetrius Augustine Gallitzin,* trans. Joseph C. Plumpe. London, 1940.

Light, Dale B. *Rome and the New Republic: Conflict and Community in Philadelphia between the Revolution and the Civil War.* Notre Dame, IN, 1996.

Lucas, Joseph R. "Conquering the Passions: Indians, Europeans, and Early American Social Thought, 1580–1840." Ph.D. diss., Pennsylvania State University, 1999.

Madison, James. *The Writings of James Madison.* Vol. 9. Ed. Gaillard Hunt. New York, 1910.

Marr, Timothy Worthington. "Imagining Ishmael: Studies of Islamic Orientalism in America from Puritan Millennialism to Melville." Ph.D. diss., Yale University, 1997.

McCarthy, Kathleen D. *American Creed: Philanthropy and the Rise of Civil Society, 1700–1865.* Chicago, 2003.

McCoy, Drew R. *The Last of the Fathers: James Madison and The Republican Legacy.* Cambridge, 1989.

McGarvie, Mark Douglas. *One Nation under Law: America's Early National Struggles to Separate Church and State.* DeKalb, IL, 2004.

McLoughlin, William G. *Cherokees and Missionaries, 1789–1839.* New Haven, CT, 1984.

Meacham, Jon. *American Gospel: God, the Founding Fathers, and the Making of a Nation.* New York, 2006.

Merritt, Jane T. *At the Crossroads: Indians and Empires on a Mid-Atlantic Frontier, 1700–1763.* Chapel Hill, NC, 2003.

Miller, Randall M. "Roman Catholicism in South Carolina." In *Religion in South Carolina,* ed. Charles H. Lippy, 82–102. Columbia, SC, 1993

Miller, William Lee. *The Business of May Next: James Madison and the Founding.* Charlottesville, 1992.

Milton, Giles. *White Gold: The Extraordinary Story of Thomas Pellow and Islam's One Million White Slaves.* New York, 2004.

Morgan, Philip. *Slave Counterpoint: Black Culture in the Eighteenth-Century Lowcountry.* Chapel Hill, NC, 1998.

Muller, Jerry Z. *Adam Smith in His Time and Ours.* New York, 1993.

Muñoz, Vincent Phillip. "James Madison's Principle of Religious Liberty." *American Political Science Review* 97 (2003): 17–32.

Murphy, Andrew R. *Conscience and Community: Revisiting Toleration and Religious Dissent in Early Modern England and America.* University Park, PA, 2001.

Murphy, Grace, ed. *Gallitzin's Letters: A Collection of the Polemical Works of the Very Reverend Prince Demetrius Augustine Gallitzin (1770–1840).* Loretto, PA, 1940.

Nicholls, Mark. *Investigating Gunpowder Plot.* Manchester, UK, 1991.

Nicolson, Adam. *God's Secretaries: The Making of the King James Bible.* New York, 2005.

Noll, Mark. *America's God: From Jonathan Edwards to Abraham Lincoln.* New York, 2002.

Noonan, John T., Jr. *A Church That Can and Cannot Change: The Development of Catholic Moral Teaching.* Notre Dame, IN, 2005.

———. *The Lustre of Our Country: The American Experience of Religious Freedom.* Berkeley, CA, 1998.

———. "Quota of Imps." In *Virginia Statute for Religious Freedom: Its Evolution and Consequences in American History,* ed. Merrill D. Peterson and Robert C. Vaughan, 171–99. Cambridge, 1988.

Norgren, Jill. *Cherokee Cases: The Confrontation of Law and Politics.* New York, 1996.

Otis, James. *The Rights of the British Colonies Asserted and Proved.* Boston, 1764. In *Pamphlets of the American Revolution, 1750–1765,* ed. Bernard Bailyn, 408–82. Boston, 1965.

Parish, Helen. "'Beastly Is Their Living and Their Doctrine': Celibacy and Theological Corruption in English Reformation Polemic." In *Protestant History and Identity in Sixteenth-Century Europe.* Vol. 1. *The Medieval Inheritance,* ed. Bruce Gordon, 138–52. Aldershot, UK, 1996.

Patterson, Annabel. *Nobody's Perfect: A New Whig Interpretation of History.* New Haven, CT, 2002.

Pencak, William. "Jews and Anti-Semitism in Early Pennsylvania." *Pennsylvania Magazine of History and Biography* 126 (2002): 365–408.

———. *Jews and Gentiles in Early America, 1654–1800.* Ann Arbor, MI, 2005.

Pfeffer, Leo. *Church, State, and Freedom.* Rev. ed. Boston, 1967.

Pocock, J. G. A. *The Ancient Constitution and the Feudal Law: English Historical Thought in the Seventeenth Century.* New York, 1967.

Roeber, A. Gregg. "The Law, Religion, and State Making in the Early Modern World: Protestant Revolutions in the Works of Berman, Gorski, and Witte." *Law and Social Inquiry* 31:1 (Winter 2006): 199–227.

———. "Long Road to *Vidal:* Charity Law and State Formation in Early America." In *Many Legalities of Early America,* ed. Christopher L. Tomlins and Bruce H. Mann, 414–47. Chapel Hill, NC, 2001.

———. "The Migration of the Pious: Methodists, Pietists, and the Antinomian Character of North American Religious History." In *Visions of the Future in Germany and America,* ed. Norbert Finzsch and Hermann Wellenreuther, 25–47. Oxford, 2001.

———. *Palatines, Liberty, and Property: German Lutherans in Colonial British America.* Baltimore, 1998.

———. "What the Law Requires Is Written on Their Hearts: Noachic and Natural Law among German-Speakers in Early Modern North America." *William and Mary Quarterly,* 3d ser., 58 (Oct. 2001): 883–912.

Rojas, Martha Elena. "'Insults Unpunished': Barbary Captives, American Slaves, and the Negotiation of Liberty." *Early American Studies: An Interdisciplinary Journal* 1 (Fall 2003): 159–86.

Sandoz, Ellis. *A Government of Laws: Political Theory, Religion, and the American Founding.* Baton Rouge, LA, 1990.

Saunders, David. *Anti-Lawyers: Religion and the Critics of Law and State.* London, 1997.

Scales, Len, and Oliver Zimmer, eds. *Power and the Nation in European History.* Cambridge, 2005.

Sensbach, Jon T. *A Separate Canaan: The Making of an Afro-Moravian World in North Carolina, 1763–1840.* Chapel Hill, NC, 1998.

Shain, Barry A. *The Myth of American Individualism: The Protestant Origins of American Political Thought.* Princeton, NJ, 1994.

Shapiro, Barbara J. *Probability and Certainty in Seventeenth-Century England: A Study of the Relationship between Natural Science, Religion, History, Law, and Literature.* Princeton, NJ, 1983.

Sheehan, Bernard W. *Seeds of Extinction: Jeffersonian Philanthropy and the American Indian.* New York, 1973.

Smith, Anna. "Community of Women: Cherokees and Moravians in the Early Nineteenth Century." Paper delivered at the conference "German Moravians in the Atlantic World," Wake Forest University, Winston-Salem, NC, 4–6 April 2002.

Sommerville, Johann "The 'New Art of Lying': Equivocation, Mental Reservation, and Casuistry." In *Conscience and Casuistry in Early Modern Europe,* ed. Edmund Leites, 159–84. Cambridge, 1988.

Strout, Cushing. "Jeffersonian Religious Liberty and American Pluralism." In *Virginia Statute for Religious Freedom: Its Evolution and Consequences in American History,* ed. Merrill D. Peterson and Robert C. Vaughan, 201–35. Cambridge, 1988.

Sullivan, Winnifred Fallers. *The Impossibility of Religious Freedom.* Princeton, NJ, 2005.

Sutcliffe, Adam. *Judaism and Enlightenment* Cambridge, 2003.

Tocqueville, Alexis de. *Democracy in America,* ed. and trans. Harvey C. Mansfield and Delba Winthrop. Chicago, 2000.

Tuck, Richard. "The 'Christian Atheism' of Thomas Hobbes." In *Atheism from the Reformation to the Enlightenment* ed. Michael Hunter and David Wooton, 111–30. Oxford, , 1992.

Ward, W. R. *Protestant Evangelical Awakening.* Cambridge, 1992.

Whitman, James. "Why Did Early Modern Lawyers Confuse Custom and Reason?" *University of Chicago Law Review* 31 (1991): 1–48.

Witte, John, Jr. *Law and Protestantism: The Legal Teachings of the Lutheran Reformation.* Cambridge, 2002.

———. "'A Most Mild and Equitable Establishment of Religion': John Adams and the Massachusetts Experiment." In *Religion and the New Republic: Faith in the Founding of America,* ed. James H. Hutson, 1–40. Lanham, MD, 2002.

Wright, Benjamin Fletcher, Jr. *American Interpretations of Natural Law: A Study in the History of Political Thought.* New York, 1962.

Wood, Gordon S. *The Creation of the American Republic, 1776–1787.* Chapel Hill, NC, 1969.

Looking Backward and Forward: A Nation of Rights | **3**

The History of Rights in Early America

GORDON S. WOOD

We Americans today talk all the time about rights—everyone has rights—and we believe that they trump all other claims and values. Much of the time we seem to regard our preoccupation with rights as something new, something recent, something that began, say, with the Warren Court and the civil rights movement. But our obsession with rights is not new at all. We have a long history of rights. The meaning of rights, however, has changed over time. Rights have meant different things to different generations of Americans, especially to those generations in the early part of our history.

Rights: English Historical Background

The history of rights in America extends far back in the past, back at least to the medieval period of English history. It is not very fashionable these days talk about the contributions of western Europeans to American culture, but in the case of our preoccupation with rights, we owe most of its importance to our English heritage. The English had a concern for rights and a Bill of Rights long before our Bill of Rights of 1791. As Chief Justice Thomas Hutchinson told a Massachusetts grand jury in 1769, "The bare Mention of the Word *Rights* always strikes an Englishman in a peculiar manner."[1] Englishmen valued their rights to their personal liberty and property—rights that were embedded in their medieval common law. The common law had deeply held principles, including, for example, the notions that no one could be a judge in his own cause and that no one, not even the king, could legally take another's property without that person's consent. These rights and liberties belonged to all the people of England, and they adhered in each person as a person. Their force did not depend on their written delineation; they existed in the customary or unwritten law of England that went back to time immemorial.

It was not just the people who had rights; the king did too, usually referred to as the king's prerogatives. These prerogatives or royal rights to govern the realm were as old and sacred as the privileges and liberties of the people. In that distant medieval world, the king had sole responsibility to govern: to provide for the safety of his people and to see that justice was done—that is, that the people's rights were protected both from each other and from the king's government. The king's courts were expected to adjudicate the law common to those courts and to the realm; hence the development of the term "common law."

The king's highest court of all—Parliament—arose sometime in the thirteenth century and was composed both of the feudal nobles that eventually became the House of Lords and of agents from the boroughs and counties of the realm that eventually became the House of Commons. Unlike the modern English Parliament, its medieval predecessor was convened by the king only sporadically and did not have as yet any direct responsibility for governing the country. Instead, its responsibility was mainly limited to voting supplies to the king to enable him to govern, presenting petitions to the king for the redress of popular grievances, and as the highest court in the land, correcting and emending the common law so as to ensure that justice was done and the people's rights were protected. This correcting and emending of the law was not regarded as legislation in any modern sense, for medieval men thought of law not as something invented but as something discovered in the customs and precedents of the past. The modern idea of law as the command of a legislative body was as yet inconceivable; indeed, law was equated with justice, and its purpose was to protect the rights of people from each other and from the king.

Thus the king had his rights to govern, and the people had their equally ancient and equally legitimate rights to their liberties and their property. Indeed, it is perhaps not too much to say that the whole of English constitutional history can be seen as a struggle between these two competing sets of rights. The courts, including the high court of Parliament, were supposed to adjudicate between these conflicting sets of rights. Because the king, in trying to fulfill his responsibility of governing the realm, often infringed upon the customary rights of the people, Englishmen periodically felt the need to have the king recognize their rights and liberties in writing. These recognitions in the early Middle Ages took the form of coronation oaths and assizes and charters issued by the Crown. In 1215, the barons compelled King John to sign what became the most famous written document in English history: the great charter, or Magna Carta. In it the king explicitly acknowledged many of the customary rights of the English people, including the right of a freeman not to be imprisoned, exiled, or executed "unless by the lawful judgment of his peers, or by the law of the land." This meant a judgment by the common-law courts or by Parliament, the highest court in the land.

The succeeding centuries of English history saw more struggles over rights and more attempts by the English people to place limits on their kings. These struggles came to a climax in the seventeenth century. When, in 1627, King Charles I attempted to raise money by forced loans, five English knights resisted, and Charles had the resisters arbitrarily imprisoned. This in turn led to the popular reinvocation of Magna Carta and the reiteration of the rights of a subject to his property and to no imprisonment without the legal judgment of his peers. In 1628, the House of Commons presented these grievances in a Petition of Right, which the king was compelled to accept.

Yet this hardly resolved the conflict between the rights of the king and the liberties of the people. Only after a bloody civil war, with one king beheaded and another driven from his throne, was the struggle between king and people finally settled in the Glorious Revolution of 1688–89, when the Convention-Parliament set forth a Declaration of Rights that quickly became enshrined in English constitutionalism. In this listing of rights, which became a statute or a bill of rights when the new king, William III, approved it, Parliament declared illegal certain actions of the Crown, including its dispensing with laws, using prerogative power to raise money, and maintaining a standing army without the consent of Parliament. At the same time, Parliament asserted certain rights and freedoms possessed by Englishmen, including the right to bear arms, to petition the king, to have free elections and frequent Parliaments in which speech would be free, and to have no excessive bail or fines.[2]

It is important to understand that this delineation of rights in 1689 was an act of Parliament consented to by the king. The English Bill of Rights was designed to protect the subjects not from the power of Parliament, but from the power of the king. Indeed, it was inconceivable that Parliament could endanger the subjects' rights. Only the Crown could do that. Parliament was the highest court in the land and was therefore the bulwark and guardian of the people's rights and liberties; there was no point in limiting it. Consequently, there were no legal or constitutional restrictions placed on the actions of the English Parliament; and despite the efforts of some British judges to invoke the declarations of the European Union, there are still none today, which makes the English Parliament one of the most powerful governmental institutions in the world.

So convinced were Englishmen in the decades following 1689 that tyranny could come only from a single ruler that they could hardly conceive of the people tyrannizing themselves. Once Parliament became sovereign, once the body that represented and spoke for them—the House of Commons—had gained control of the Crown authority that had traditionally threatened their liberties, the English people lost much of their former interest in codifying and listing their rights. Because the people themselves now controlled the government, charters defining the people's rights and contracts between the people and government no longer made sense. If the high court of Parliament represented or embodied the whole nation, then its judgments became in effect the sovereign commands of the whole nation, and what formerly had been adjudication now became legislation, binding everyone and encompassing everyone's rights. Because Parliament was the protector of the people's rights, it could be no threat to them.

American Rights—Part One: The People vs. the King

By the time of the American Revolution, most educated Englishmen had become convinced therefore that their rights existed only against the Crown. Against their representative and sovereign Parliament, which was the guardian of these rights, they existed not at all. Although the American colonists did not have quite the same confidence in Parliament that Englishmen at home did, they did equally fear the powers of the Crown and saw their own local representative assemblies as the bulwarks of their rights. Like Englishmen in relation to Parliament, very few colonists saw any need to protect their rights from their colonial assemblies. Following the Zenger trial in 1735, for example, no royal governor dared bring a case of seditious libel against anyone. But the colonial assemblies, which presumably spoke for the people, continued to punish individuals for seditious libel under the common law. In other words, liberty of the press existed against the Crown but not against the representatives of the people.[3]

In the 1760s and 1770s, during the crisis that eventually tore apart the First British Empire, the American colonists had the long English heritage of popular rights to draw upon. Like all Englishmen, they were familiar with the persistent struggle of the English people to erect written barriers against encroaching Crown power. Their own colonial past was littered with written documents delineating their rights. From the "Laws and Liberties" of Massachusetts Bay in 1648 to New York's "Charter of Liberties and Privileges" in 1683, the early colonial assemblies had felt the need to acknowledge in writing what William Penn called "those rights and privileges . . . which are the proper birth-right of Englishmen."[4]

As government and law stabilized in the eighteenth century, however, the need in the colonies for these sorts of explicit codifications of rights had declined, just as they had in the mother country. But the Englishman's instinct to defend his rights against encroachments of the governmental power of the Crown was always latently present and was easily aroused. And getting the ruler to recognize these rights on paper was part of that instinct. By the time of the imperial crisis, it was natural for colonists like Arthur Lee of Virginia to call in 1768 for "a bill of rights" that would "merit the title of the Magna Carta Americana."[5]

Indeed, as John Reid has reminded us, the colonial resistance movement of the 1760s and 1770s was all about the colonists' defense of their rights as Englishmen.[6] By the eve of the Revolution, the charters that the Crown had granted to many of the colonies in the previous century had come to be seen as just so many miniature magna cartas designed, as one New Englander declared, "to reduce to a certainty the rights and privileges we were entitled to" and "to point out and circumscribe the prerogatives of the crown." Their several charters (or, where these were lacking, "their commissions to their governors have ever been considered as equivalent securities") had become transformed into what, "from their subject matter and the reality of things, can only operate as the evidence of a compact between an English King and the American subjects." These charters, continued Joseph Hawley of Massachusetts, were no longer franchises or grants from the Crown that could be unilaterally recalled or forfeited: "Their running in the stile of a grant is mere matter of form and not of substance." They were reciprocal agreements "made and executed between the King of England, and our predecessors," contracts between ruler and people, outlining the rights of each but particularly the rights of the people.[7]

This imagined contract of rights between the king and the people was not Locke's contract, which was a contract among the people to form a society, but the "original governmental contract" that ran through much of eighteenth-century English thinking and justified the people's obeying the prerogative decrees and edicts of the king. This contract was an agreement, legal or mercantile in character, between rulers and people—equal parties with equal sets of rights—in which protection and allegiance were the considerations. "Allegiance," wrote James Wilson in 1774, "is the faith and obedience, which every subject owes to his prince. This obedience is founded on the protection derived from government: for protection and allegiance are the reciprocal bonds, which connect the prince and his subjects." This allegiance was not the same as consent. "Allegiance to the king and obedience to the parliament," said Wilson, "are founded on very different principles. The former is founded on protection: the latter on representation. An inattention to this difference has produced . . . much uncertainty and confusion in our ideas concerning the connexion, which ought to subsist between Great Britain and the American colonies."[8]

The Ambiguity of the Private and Public Realms: Part One

All of this contractual imagery between two equal parties, not to mention the familial imagery of a patriarchal king and the mother country, suggests that for many eighteenth-century Anglo-Americans the public and private realms were still largely indistinguishable. Indeed, the colonists never regarded the struggle between the rights of the Crown and the rights of the people as one between public and private rights. For even as late as the eve of the Revolution, the modern distinction between public and private was still not clear. The people's ancient rights and liberties were as much public as private, just as the king's rights—his prerogatives—were as much private as they were public. So-called public institutions had private rights, and private persons had public obligations. The king's prerogatives, or his premier rights to govern the realm, grew out of his private position as the wealthiest of the wealthy and the largest landowner in the society; his government had really begun as an extension of his royal household. But in a like manner all private households or families—"those small subdivisions of Government," one colonist called them—had public responsibilities to help the king govern.[9]

All of this meant that the colonists were used to a great deal of communal or "public" control and management of what we today would call "private" rights. Governments in this premodern colonial society regulated all sorts of personal behavior, especially the moral and religious behavior of people, without any consciousness that they were depriving people of their private liberty or rights. Of the nearly 2,800 prosecutions in the Superior and General Sessions courts of Massachusetts between 1760 and 1774, over half involved sexual and religious offenses, such as fornication and using profanity. Many of the other prosecutions involved drunkenness, slander, and various violations of decency and good manners. At the same time, the colonial governments spent very little time on what we today would call public matters. Royal governors did not have legislative policies, and assembles did not enact legislative programs. Many of the governments' activities were private, local, and adjudicative. The colonial assemblies still saw themselves more as courts making judgments rather than as legislatures making law. They spent a good deal of their time hearing private petitions, which often were the complaints of one individual or group against another. In William Nelson's survey of the Massachusetts General Court in 1761 ("as typical a year as any"), he could find "only three acts that were arguably legislative in the sense that they changed law or made new law."[10]

Indeed, to the colonists the separation of legislative, executive, and judicial powers that we value so greatly was far from clear. Because there was no modern bureaucracy and few modern mechanisms of coercion—a few constables and sheriffs scarcely constituted a police force—it was often left to the courts to exercise what governmental coercion there was and to engage in an extraordinary number of administrative and even legislative tasks, usually drawing on the communities for help.

Much of this judicial or magisterial activity—in fact, much of the government—was carried on without direct compensation. No one as yet conceived of politics as a paid profession or of a permanent civil service. Most office holding was still regarded, with varying degrees of plausibility, as a public obligation that private persons "serving gratis or generously" owed the community.[11] Every private person in the society had an obligation to help govern the realm commensurate with his social rank, the king's being the greatest because he stood at the top of the social hierarchy.

As Hendrick Hartog has written, all government in the colonial period was regarded essentially as the enlisting and mobilizing of the power of private persons to carry out public ends. "Governments," according to Hartog, "did not so much act as they ensured and sanctioned the actions of others."[12] If the eighteenth-century city of New York wanted its streets cleaned or paved, for example, it did not hire contractors or create a "public works" department; instead, it issued ordinances obliging each person in the city to clean or repair the street abutting his house or shop. In the same way, if the colony of Connecticut wanted a college, it did not build and run the college itself, but instead gave legal rights to private persons to build and run it, in short, creating what were called corporations. Most public action—from the building of wharves and ferries to the maintaining of roads and inns—depended upon private energy and private funds. Governments were always short of revenue and instead tended to rely mostly on their legal authority to mobilize the community and compel private persons to fulfill public obligations. They issued sanctions against private persons for failure to perform their public duties, and they enticed private persons into fulfilling public goals by offering corporate charters, licenses, and various other legal immunities together with fee-collecting offices.[13] Because the government, including the king, was only one property holder in a world of property holders, it could not take "private" property for "public" purposes without the consent of the owner of that property; in other words, it had no modern power of eminent domain.

The Revolution was designed to change all this dramatically. By creating republics, Americans brought into play the tradition of neo-Roman Whig thinking that emphasized the collective public liberty of the people.[14] In stressing the power of the republican commonwealth in this way, Americans suddenly became much more conscious of individual rights and interests as private ones that stood in opposition to the public good. Because the earlier mobilizing of "private" power for "public" ends was now viewed as "corruption"—that is, the exploitation of the "public" for "private" gain—it had to cease. It was now hoped that governments would no longer grant monopoly charters, licenses, and fee-collecting offices to private individuals in order to induce them to carry out public goals. Instead, the new republican leaders expected select individuals to become public servants working for the state and, generally, for a salary. State power in America began assuming some of its modern character as an autonomous entity capable of hiring agents to carry out public tasks. The Revolutionaries now claimed the primacy of the public good over all private individual rights and interests; indeed, they sought to separate the public from the private in a new manner and to prevent the former intrusion of private rights and interests into what was now seen as a distinct public realm. With such goals, Revolutionary Americans had to conceive of state power and individual liberty in radically new ways.

It would be difficult to exaggerate what this new idea of republican state power meant. No longer could government be seen as the exercise of someone's personal authority, as the assertion of prerogative rights or of the rights of those with economic and social superiority. Rulers suddenly lost their traditional personal rights to rule, and personal allegiance as a civic bond became meaningless. The long-existing Whig image of government as a contract between rulers and ruled disappeared virtually overnight. The Revolutionary state constitutions eliminated the Crown's prerogatives outright or regranted them to the state legislatures. These constitutional grants of authority, together with the expanded notion of consent underlying all government, gave the new state legislatures a degree of public power that the colonial assemblies had never claimed or even imagined.

Although the new state assemblies, to the chagrin of many leaders, continued to act in a traditional courtlike manner—interfering with and reversing judicial decisions and passing private acts affecting individuals—they now became as well sovereign embodiments of the people with legislative responsibility for exercising an autonomous public authority.

In republican America, government would no longer be merely private property and private interests writ large, as it had been in the colonial period. Public and private spheres that earlier had been mingled were now presumably to be starkly separated. Res publica became everything. The new republican states saw themselves promoting a unitary public interest that was to be clearly superior to the many private interests and rights of the people.

At the beginning of the Revolution, few Americans imagined that there could be any real conflict between this unitary public good expressed by the representative state legislatures and the rights of individuals. When, in 1775, a frightened Tory warned the people of Massachusetts that a popular Revolutionary legislature could become as tyrannical as the Crown and deprive the people of their individual liberties, John Adams dismissed the idea out of hand. That the people might tyrannize over themselves and harm their own rights and liberties was illogical, declared Adams. "A democratic despotism is a contradiction in terms."[15]

With their new heightened sense of the public good, the Revolutionary republican legislatures were determined to bring what were seen as the private rights of selfish individuals under communal control. Many Americans now viewed with suspicion the traditional monarchical practice of enlisting private wealth and energy for public purposes. Especially objectionable was the issuing of corporate privileges and licenses to private persons. In a republic, it was said, no person should be allowed to exploit the public's authority for private gain. Indeed, several of the states wrote into their Revolutionary constitutions declarations, like that of New Hampshire, that "government is instituted for the common benefit, protection, and security of the whole community, and not for the private interest or emolument of any one man, family, or class of men." And some of the states, like North Carolina, declared that "perpetuities and monopolies are contrary to the genius of a State, and ought not to be allowed."[16]

Because they wanted to avoid any taint of corruption by allowing private individuals to undertake public tasks, the new republican state governments sought to assert their newly enhanced public power in direct and unprecedented ways—doing for themselves what they had earlier commissioned private persons to do. The state assemblies began legislating—making and changing law—as never before. Indeed, as Madison complained in 1786, the states passed more laws in the single decade following Independence than they had in the entire colonial period. And these laws had less and less to do with private matters—with moral and religious issues—and more and more to do with public matters—with economic development and commercial convenience.

"Improvement" was on every Revolutionary's mind, and most leaders naturally assumed that the new state governments would take the lead in promoting it. The states now carved out exclusively public spheres of action and responsibility where none had existed before. They drew up plans for improving everything from trade and commerce to roads and waterworks and helped to create a science of political economy for Americans. And they formed their own public organizations with paid professional staffs supported by tax money, not private labor. The city of New York, for example, working under the authority of the state legislature, now set up its own public workforce to clean its streets and wharves, instead of relying, as in the past, on the private residents to do these tasks. By the early nineteenth century, as Hartog has told us, the city of New York had become a public institution financed primarily by public taxation and concerned with particularly public concerns. Like other post-Revolutionary governments, New York City acquired what it had not had before—the modern power of eminent domain: the authority to take private property for the sake of the public good without the consent of the particular property owner.[17]

Many thought that the new state legislatures, as the representatives of the people, could do for the public whatever the people entrusted them to do and that the needs of the public could even override the rights of individuals. Did not the collective power of the people expressed in their representative legislatures supersede the rights of the few? Of course, under monarchy, the people could legitimately defend their rights against encroachments from the prerogative rights and privileges of the king. But in the new republics, where there were no more prerogative rights, could the people's personal rights meaningfully exist apart from the people's sovereign power expressed in their assemblies? In other words, did it any longer make sense to speak of negative liberty where the people's positive liberty was complete and supreme? To be sure, as the Pennsylvania constitution and other Revolutionary constitutions declared, "No part of a man's property can be justly taken from him, or applied to public uses, without his consent," but this consent, in 1776 at least, meant "that of his legal representatives."[18]

American Rights—Part Two: Individuals vs. the People's Legislatures

In 1776 it was not at all clear that people had rights against their own representatives. Five states drew up bills of rights in 1776, and several other states listed the people's rights in the bodies of their constitutions. But because the Revolutionary constitutions so circumscribed the governors, many of the states felt no need any longer to protect the people's rights by separately listing them; their popular legislatures were surely no danger to the people's or individual liberties. This accounts for the confusion Americans in 1776 had in not being entirely sure against whom their bills of rights were directed. In English history, declarations of rights had been directed against the Crown and its prerogatives. But in republican America, where there was no longer any Crown or any prerogatives, did bills of rights make sense? What was the need of protecting the people's rights from themselves? Monarchies might become despotic, but democracies, when they ran to excess, could only become anarchical and licentious. Or so republican theorists since the ancient Greeks had assumed.

We know what happened. Within a decade the democratic despotism and the threat to individual rights from popular legislatures that had seemed so illogical and contradictory to John Adams and other American patriots in 1775–76 had become only too real—at least for many gentry leaders. Consequently, many of these leaders were faced with the new and great constitutional dilemma of limiting popular government and protecting private property and individual rights without, at the same time, denying the sovereign public power of the majority of the people.

This dilemma led some Americans to think freshly about Whig political theory and a number of constitutional issues, including those that justified the creation of a new federal constitution in 1787. Most difficult of all was the formulating of a defense of individual rights and liberties against the people themselves, against Parliament, so to speak. There were no precedents for this kind of discrimination between popular legislatures, the people, and individuals in English history or in their own colonial histories. And they had to do all this in the face of their own republican Revolutionary ideology—their belief in the autonomous power of the republican community to determine the public good.

It was not easy limiting the popular legislatures without denigrating the people and everything the republican Revolution of 1776 had been about. If the people were not capable of protecting their own rights and liberties, then what was the value of republican government? Many realized only too keenly that the violations of individual rights in the 1780s did not arise because the people had been forsaken by their legislative representatives; as a Boston newspaper declared, those violations occurred because the people's "transient and indigested sentiments have been too implicitly adopted." James Madison certainly agreed. The rampaging legislatures of the 1780s, he said in 1787, were not acting against the will of the people; they were acting on behalf of it. Unfortunately, the legislators were only too representative, only too democratic, reflecting only too accurately the narrow views and parochial outlooks of their constituents.

Good republicans had not expected this at the outset of the Revolution. "According to Republican Theory," said Madison, "Right and power being both vested in the majority, are held to be synonimous." But experience since 1776 had shown the contrary. "Wherever the real power in a Government lies," he told his friend Thomas Jefferson, then in Paris, "there is the danger of oppression. In our Governments the real power lies in the majority of the Community, and the invasion of private rights is chiefly to be apprehended, not from any acts of Government contrary to the sense of its constituents, but from acts in which the Government is the mere instrument of the major number of the constituents." That was why, for Madison, the crisis of the 1780s was truly frightening. For the legislative abuses and the many violation of individual rights, he said, "brought into question the fundamental principle of republican Government, that the majority who rule in such governments are the safest Guardians both of public Good and private rights."[19]

From his post in France, Jefferson scarcely grasped or understood what Madison was describing. His confidence in the people was too great for him ever to question their judgment. Instead, in his mind he drew a distinction between the representative legislatures and the people themselves. Jefferson had no doubt that all officials in government, even the popularly elected representatives in the lower houses of the legislatures, could act tyrannically. In fact, "173 despots would surely be as oppressive as one," he said of the Virginia House of Delegates in 1785. "An *elective despotism* was not the government we fought for."[20] But in discriminating between the people and a legislature, he held that this kind of tyranny was not really the people's fault. Jefferson always thought that the people themselves, if undisturbed by demagogues like Patrick Henry, eventually would set matters right. He saw little potential conflict between positive and negative liberty, between the people at large and individual rights. He was one of those who paid no attention to what Madison called that "essential distinction, too little heeded, between assumptions of power by the General

Government, in opposition to the will of the constituent body, and assumptions by the constituent body through the Government as the organ of its will."[21] For Jefferson, it could never be the people themselves, but only their elected agents, legislative or executive, that were in error.

Whatever doubts American leaders had privately about the virtue or good sense of the people, few of them by 1787 were willing to express such doubts publicly. Questioning the judgment of the people themselves had become too politically risky. Hence, publicly at least, they began drawing the same distinction between the people and their elected delegates as Jefferson had and to exploit it in their efforts to curb the state legislatures. Indeed, that distinction became the basis of all the major arguments mounted by the defenders of the new Constitution in 1787–88, the Federalists, as they called themselves. Confronted with arguments from the opponents of the Constitution, or as they were described by their opponents, the Anti-Federalists, that raised the question of where sovereignty— the final supreme indivisible lawmaking authority—would lie under the new Constitution, the Federalists denied that sovereignty would be taken away from the state legislatures and given to the Congress. Unlike Britain, where sovereignty rested with the king-in-Parliament, sovereignty in America, they said, belonged to no institution of government nor even to all of the institutions together; it belonged to and remained in the people themselves. In America, the notion that sovereignty rested in the people was not just a convenient political fiction; as experience since 1776 had demonstrated, the American people, unlike the English, retained an actual lawmaking authority. They could make fundamental laws or constitutions, whereas their legislative representative could make only ordinary statutes. In Britain, where the people out of doors were considered to be completely eclipsed by their representatives in the House of Commons, the laws or statutes made by Parliament were ipso facto constitutional.

By opening up and exaggerating the distinction between the sovereign people and their elected state governments, the Federalists tended to homogenize political power and turn all government officials, in both the state and federal governments, into equally mistrusted agents of the people, temporarily holding only bits and pieces of the people's sovereign power, out, so to speak, on always recallable loan. The various state houses of representatives lost their earlier exclusive representative character. The states' upper houses and governors, the federal congressmen, senators, and president all could be regarded as different kinds of agents of the people. Senates were now called a double representation of the people, and governors were labeled the best representative of the whole people in those states where they were elected by the whole people. In fact, if the chief magistrates could be called representatives of the people, why not also the lesser magistrates? So some now even began thinking of judges as representative agents of the people. All officials thus became the equally trusted or equally mistrusted agents of the people. But, unlike in Britain, their existence never eclipsed the people out of doors; the people always retained a political and legal existence even after electing all their various agents. Once this homogenization of all political power was grasped, once all governmental officials, whether executive, judicial, or even legislative were regarded, in Jefferson's words, as "three branches of magistracy," then it became possible to protect individual rights, if not from the people themselves, then from the popularly elected legislatures, without doing violence to republican theory.[22]

Leaders anxious about individual liberties and the rights of property could now identify the popular legislatures with the former monarchical or magisterial power (which is what Adams meant when he wrote of "democratic despotism") and could invoke the traditional language of the rights of Englishmen in these new republican circumstances. Not every American, of course, was willing to follow this line of thinking, and many opponents of the Constitution rose in defense of the peculiar popular character of the state legislatures and denied that their wills could be limited in any way. After all, they represented the people. But now the Federalists had a ready answer to this traditional argument. In *The Federalist,* Alexander Hamilton rebuked these defenders of the state legislatures by caustically observing that "the representatives of the people, in a popular assembly, seem sometimes to fancy that they are the people themselves." And he went on to suggest a way the people's rights embodied in the constitutions could be protected from the legislatures: by relying on other agents of the people, the courts. Because the people, not the legislatures, created constitutions, it could never "be supposed," he said, "that the constitution could intend to enable the representatives of the people to substitute their *will* to that of their constituents. It is far more rational to suppose that the courts were designed to be an intermediate body between the people and the legislature, in order, among other things, to keep the latter within the limits assigned to their authority."[23]

Already many others besides Hamilton had begun looking to the once-feared judiciary as a principal means of restraining the rampaging and unstable popular legislatures. They could, after all, legitimately argue that judges were just another kind of agent of the people, ideally situated to protect the people's rights against the oppressive actions of some other of their agents in the legislatures. As early as 1786, William Plumer, a future U.S. senator and governor of New Hampshire, concluded that the very "existence" of America's elective governments had come to depend upon the judiciary, for "that is the only body of men who will have an effective check upon a numerous Assembly."[24]

Thus was launched the massive rethinking out of which in a matter of decades emerged America's strong independent judiciary, a judiciary that became primarily concerned with protecting individual rights. In the years following the Revolution, judges shed their earlier broad and ill-defined political and magisterial roles and adopted ones that were much more exclusively legal. They withdrew from politics, promoted the development of law as a mysterious science known best by trained experts, and restricted their activities to the regular courts, which became increasingly professional and less burdened by popular juries. Many of those who were suspicious of democracy thought that this withdrawal from politics made the judiciary a far better protector of the rights of individuals than the popular legislatures could ever hope to be. As early as 1787, Alexander Hamilton argued in the New York Assembly that the state constitution prevented anyone from being deprived of his rights, except "by the law of the land" or, as a recent act of the assembly had put it, "by due process of law," which, said Hamilton in an astonishing and novel twist, had "a precise technical import": these words were now "only applicable to the process and proceedings of the courts of justice; they can never be referred to an act of legislature," even though the legislature had written them.[25]

The view expressed by Hamilton did not of course immediately take hold. The attorney general of North Carolina, for example, argued in 1794 that the clauses of the state constitution referring to due process and the law of the land were not limitations on the legislature; they were "declarations the people thought proper to make of their rights, not against a power they supposed their own representatives might usurp, but against oppression and usurpation in general . . . by a pretended prerogative against or without the authority of law." Thus the phrase stating that no one could be deprived of his property except by the law of the land meant simply, except by "a law for the people of North Carolina, made or adopted by themselves by the intervention of their own legislature." This view was accepted by the North Carolina Superior Court.[26]

It is not surprising that the argument Hamilton put forth in 1787 was opposed by others, for his argument was truly extraordinary, one of the first of many imaginative readings in our history to be given to that important phrase, "due process of law." Parliament, which included the

House of Commons, had always protected the rights of Englishmen, including their property rights, from the Crown's encroachments. That was what the Bill of Rights of 1688 had been all about. But Englishmen had never thought it necessary to protect these rights from the power of the people themselves, that is, from the legislative power of Parliament. Blackstone had agreed that one of the absolute rights of an individual was "the right of property: which consists in the free use, enjoyment and disposal of all his acquisitions, without any control or diminution, *save only by the laws of the land.*"[27]

Of course, for Blackstone the laws of the land included those laws enacted by the legislature, that is, Parliament. Not so any longer for Hamilton and many other Americans. As far as many Americans were concerned, the state legislatures (and even for some the federal body) had become legally or constitutionally no different from the former Crown. But as brilliant as some of the Federalists' arguments were, it was never easy to see these popularly elected governments as a threat to the people's or individual rights. And some of the Federalists or the traditional supporters of strong government themselves were confused. Because their opponents, the Jeffersonian Republicans, had so often invoked the "rights of man" against the oppressions of government, some Federalists could only conceive of retaliating in traditional terms—by seeking a strengthening of government against the licentiousness of the people, with their rights run amuck. But other, shrewder Federalists saw that they might be better off appropriating the "rights talk" of their Jeffersonian opponents and using it in their own behalf against the power of the state legislatures. Indeed, they perceived that the liberties of individuals could actually be turned against the political liberty or self-government of the people. In the United States, in defense sometimes of the people's rights and other times of individuals, the laws of the land were not just what the popular legislatures commanded.

The Ambiguity of the Private and Public Realms: Part Two

In fact, many Federalists now argued that the laws of the land concerning individual rights belonged exclusively to the courts. And the reason they belonged exclusively to the courts was that they involved private matters, not public, and private matters concerning individual rights required adjudication, not legislation. As William Nelson has pointed out, the courts now became eager to leave "to legislatures the resolution of conflicts between organized social groups," that is, conflicts of politics, and instead to concentrate on protecting the rights of individuals.[28]

Those Federalists and even those Republicans who were worried about democratic despotism and the legislative abuses of private rights argued that the popular state legislatures should stick to the great public responsibilities of being republics and not "take up private business, or interfere in disputes between contending parties," as the colonial assemblies had habitually done. The evils of such legislative meddling were "heightened when the society is divided among themselves;—one party praying the assembly for one thing, and opposite party for another thing. . . . In such circumstances, the assembly ought not to interfere by any exertion of legislative power, but leave the contending parties to apply to the proper tribunals [that is, to the judiciary] for a decision of their differences."[29]

These efforts to separate private issues from public ones, to remove some questions from legislative politics and transform them into contests of individual rights, contributed to the emergence of a powerful independent judiciary in the early republic. Almost overnight, the judiciary in America became not only the principal means by which popular legislatures were controlled and limited, but also the most effective instrument for sorting out individual disputes within a private sphere that the other institutions of government were forbidden to enter.

By carving out an exclusively public sphere for the promotion of republican state power, the Revolutionaries had necessarily created a private sphere as well—a private sphere of individual rights that was to be the domain solely of judges. The idea that there was a sphere of private rights that lay absolutely beyond the authority of the people themselves, especially in a republican government, was a remarkable innovation. Few colonists had ever believed that there were individual rights that could stand against the united will of the community expressed in its representative assemblies. But the Revolution had prepared Americans to accept this innovation in their conception of rights. And it had done so with its radical commitment to the right of religious freedom. Once Americans were able to limit state authority in religious matters—an area of such importance that no state had hitherto ever denied itself the power to regulate—they set in motion the principle that there were some realms of private rights and individual liberties into which executives and legislatures had no business intruding. If formerly public religious corporations created by the state became private entities immune from further state tampering, then why could not other formerly public corporations be treated in a like manner?[30]

Indeed, that is what happened as the economy of the early republic became privatized, which meant turning public responsibilities into private rights. As Oscar and Mary Handlin, Louis Hartz, and others pointed out over a half century ago, the new Revolutionary states had expected to involve themselves directly in the economy. But the states attempted to do more than they could handle. As Hartz wrote in reference to Pennsylvania, "The objectives of the state in the economic field were usually so broad that they were beyond its administrative powers to achieve."[31] And not just administrative powers, but fiscal powers as well. Because the new, democratically elected legislatures often were unwilling to raise taxes to pay for all that the governmental leaders desired to do, the states were forced to fall back on the traditional, premodern practice of enlisting private wealth to carry out public ends. Instead of doing the tasks themselves, as many devout republicans had expected, the states ended up doing what the Crown and all premodern governments had done—granting charters of incorporation to private associations and groups to carry out a wide variety of endeavors presumably beneficial to the public: in banking, transportation, insurance, and other enterprises. The states did not intend to abandon their republican responsibility to promote the public good; they simply lacked the money to do it directly. And, of course, there were many private interests that were only too eager to acquire these corporate privileges.

Yet because of the republican aversion to chartered monopolies, the creation of these corporations did not take place without strenuous opposition and heated debate. As a consequence, these corporations were radically transformed. The popular state legislatures began giving out these charter rights freely to a variety of clamoring interests, religious groups as well as business groups. If a group in Boston received a bank charter, then a group in Newburyport wanted one too; and then other groups in both cities requested and received bank charters as well. Before long there were chartered banks all over the state of Massachusetts. Not only did the number of corporations rapidly multiply, but their earlier monopolistic, privileged character changed as well. Whereas all the colonies together had charted only about a half dozen business corporations, the new states began creating them in astonishing numbers unmatched anywhere else in the world. From an exclusive privilege granted at the behest of the state to a few highly visible, socially distinguished recipients to carry out a public purpose, corporate charters eventually became an equal right available to virtually everyone. The states issued 11 charters of incorporation between 1781 and 1785, 22 more between 1786 and 1790, and 114 between 1791 and

1795. Between 1800 and 1817 they created nearly 1,800 corporate charters. With this multiplication, not only was the traditional exclusivity of the corporate charters destroyed, but the public power of the state governments was also dispersed. If "government, unsparingly and with an unguarded hand, shall multiply corporations, and grant privileges without limitation," then, declared Governor Levi Lincoln of Massachusetts, sooner or later "only the very shadow of sovereignty" would remain.[32]

At the same time, as these corporations increased in number and shed their exclusivity, they lost much of their earlier public character as well and were more and more regarded as private property. As private property, as rights vested by the legislatures in private individuals, these corporations now became exempt from further legislative interference. This idea that the corporate charter was a species of private property was expressed early. "In granting charters," declared William Robinson in the Pennsylvania Assembly in 1786 in defense of the charter of the Bank of North America, "the legislature acts in a ministerial capacity"; that is, it acted as the Crown had acted in mobilizing private resources for public purposes. This bestowing of charters, said Robinson, "is totally distinct from the power of making laws, and it is a novel doctrine in Pennsylvania that they can abrogate those charters so solemnly granted." There was a difference between laws and charters. Laws were general rules for the whole community; charters "bestow particular privileges upon a certain number of people. . . . Charters are a species of property. When they are obtained, they are of value. Their forfeiture belongs solely to the courts of justice."[33] This argument did not convince the Pennsylvania Assembly in 1786, but it was a brilliant anticipation of what was to come.

The more the state legislatures could be demonized as monarchy-like tyrants, the more their grants could be regarded as rights vested in individuals that could not be taken back by the legislatures. "The proposition that a power to do, includes virtually, a power to undo, as applied to a legislative body," wrote Hamilton in 1802, "is generally but not universally true. All *vested* rights form an exception to the rule."[34] This protection of vested rights, as Edward S. Corwin once pointed out, became "the basic doctrine of American constitutional law."[35] So much had legislative grants seemed to have become contracts that Senator Gouverneur Morris used the analogy to oppose the Jeffersonian Republicans' elimination of the circuit court positions created by the Federalists' Judiciary Act of 1801. When you give an individual the right to construct a toll road or bridge, said Morris, "can you, by a subsequent law, take it away? No; when you make a compact, you are bound by it."[36] This thinking prepared the way for the argument that corporations were actually contracts immune from state tampering under the contract clause in Article I, Section 10, of the Constitution, a position eventually endorsed by the Supreme Court in the *Dartmouth College* case in 1819.

Of course, many resisted these efforts to turn chartered corporations into a species of private property. Jefferson may have been especially dedicated to equal rights, but he did not believe that a corporate charter was one of those rights. To his dying day, he never accepted the idea that corporations were private property that could not be touched or modified by the legislative body that chartered them. That idea, he said, "may perhaps be a salutary provision against the abuses of a monarch, but is most absurd against the nation itself." Others agreed. "It seems difficult to conceive of a corporation established for merely private purposes," declared a North Carolina judge in 1805. "In every institution of that kind the ground of the establishment is some public good or purpose to be promoted."[37] This increasing stress on the need for a "public purpose" behind the state's activity, however, only worked to further privatize the business corporations. Eventually, people felt compelled to distinguish between corporations such as banks, bridges, and insurance companies that were now considered private because they were privately endowed, and those such as towns or counties that remained public because they were tax-based. Even in Massachusetts, which retained its established church until 1833, religious dissenters transformed religious corporations into private voluntary associations that acted beyond the state but were entitled to legal recognition and protection by the state.[38]

Conclusion

There was a curious paradox in these developments. Just as the public power grew in these years of the early republic, so too did the private rights of individuals. Those who sought to protect the rights of individuals did not deny the public prerogatives of the states. Instead, they drew boundaries around the rights of private individuals, including business corporations, which judges eventually transformed into private, rights-bearing "persons." In fact, the heightened concern for the private vested rights of persons was a direct consequence of the enhanced public power the republican Revolution had given to the states and municipalities. The bigger the public domain, the bigger the private domain of private rights had to be to protect itself. Although the power of the federal government certainly declined in the decades following Jefferson's election as president, the public authority and the police powers and regulatory rights of the states and their municipalities grew stronger.

Separating the political from the legal, the public from the individual, actually allowed for more vigorous state action as long as that action served what was called a "public purpose." Individuals may have had rights, but the public had rights as well—rights that grew out of the sovereignty of the state and its legitimate power to police the society. The state of New York, for example, remained deeply involved in the society and economy. Not only did the state government of New York distribute its largess to individual businessmen and groups in the form of bounties, subsidies, stock ownership, loans, corporate grants, and franchises, but it also assumed direct responsibility for some economic activities, including building the Erie Canal.[39] Even when the states, lacking sufficient tax funds, began dissipating their modern public power by reverting to the premodern practice of enlisting private wealth to carry out public ends by issuing increasing numbers of corporate charters, they continued to use their ancient police power to regulate their economies. Between 1780 and 1814, the Massachusetts legislature, for example, enacted a multitude of laws regulating the marketing of a variety of products—everything from lumber, fish, tobacco, and shoes, to butter, bread, nails, and firearms. The states never lost their inherited responsibility for the safety, economy, morality, and health of their societies.[40] The idea that there was a public good that could interfere with some private rights remained very much alive.

Despite all this state police power, legislation, and municipal regulation, however, it was usually left to the courts to sort out and mediate the conflicting claims of public authority and the private rights of individuals. The more the state legislatures enacted statutes to manage and regulate the economy, the more judges found it necessary to exert their authority in order to do justice between individuals and to make sense of what was happening. Following the lead of William Blackstone and Lord Mansfield in eighteenth-century England, American judges in the early republic interpreted the common law flexibly in order to mitigate and correct the harm done by the profusion of conflicting statutes passed by unstable democratic legislatures.[41] Judges were often able to play down the importance of precedents and to emphasize instead reason, equity, and convenience in order to bring the law into accord with changing commercial circumstances.[42]

They were able to do this and to expand their authority by transforming many public issues of the economy into private ones, turning political questions into questions of individual rights that could only be judicially determined. If an enterprising and improving society needed certainty in the law, then the courts seemed more capable than popular legislatures in assuring it. The success of the courts in promoting commercial and economic development in the early republic was due in large part to their ability to separate the legal issues of individual rights from the tumultuous and chaotic world of democratic politics. As Marshall said in his *Marbury* decision, some questions were political; "they respect the nation, not individual rights," and thus were "only politically examinable" by elected legislatures. But questions involving the vested rights of individuals were different; they were in their "nature, judicial, and must be tried by the judicial authority."[43] But these efforts to protect the rights of individuals from political abuse were not just Federalist-inspired. Even the strongly Jeffersonian Virginia Court of Appeals in 1804 took the position that the state legislature could do many things, but it could not violate private and vested rights of property.[44]

In the late 1780s, Madison had yearned for some enlightened and impartial men who would somehow transcend the interest-group politics that plagued the state legislatures. In *Federalist* No. 10 he had used judicial imagery in describing the problems of America's legislative politics. Madison accepted the fact that the regulation of different commercial interests had become the principal task of modern legislation. This meant, he wrote, that in the future, the spirit of party and faction was likely to be involved in the ordinary operations of government. Because, in traditional fashion, he continued to think of all legislative acts as "so many judicial determinations, not indeed concerning the rights of single persons, but concerning the rights of large bodies of citizens," he could only conclude pessimistically that legislators would become "both judges and parties at the same time." The best solution he could offer to prevent these parties from becoming judges in their own causes and violating the rights of individuals and minorities was to enlarge the arena of politics so that no party could dominate, thus allowing only disinterested and impartial men to exercise power and make decisions. Thus he hoped against hope that the new elevated federal government might assume a judicial-like character and become a "disinterested and dispassionate umpire in disputes between different passions and interests" within the individual states.[45] By the early decades of the nineteenth century, he, along with many other Americans, had concluded that the judiciary perhaps had become the only governmental institution that even came close to playing this role. It is a conclusion that in our history we have reached time and time again.

Notes

This essay is a much-revised version of my article, "Origins of Vested Rights in the Early Republic," *Virginia Law Review* 85 (1999): 1421–45, and that article is used with the permission of the Virginia Law Review Association.

1. Reid, *Authority of Rights,* 3.

2. Schwoerer, *Declaration of Rights,* 1689.

3. Levy, *Legacy of Suppression.*

4. Penn, *England's Present Interest Considered* (1675), 429.

5. Quoting Lee, Bailyn, *Ideological Origins of the American Revolution,* 189.

6. Reid, *Authority of Rights.*

7. Wood, *Creation of the American Republic,* 268–69.

8. Wilson, *Considerations on Authority of Parliament* (1774), in *Papers of James Wilson,* 2:736–37.

9. Wood, *Radicalism of the American Revolution,* 81.

10. Nelson, *Americanization of the Common Law,* 37–38, 14.

11. Douglass, *First Planting, Progressive Improvement,* 1:507.

12. Hartog, *Public Property and Private Power,* 62–68.

13. Seavoy, "Public Service Origins of the American Business Corporation," 30–36.

14. Skinner, *Liberty before Liberalism.*

15. Quoting Adams, Wood, *Creation of the American Republic,* 62–63.

16. Wood, *Radicalism of the American Revolution,* 188.

17. Hartog, *Public Property and Private Power,* 155; Scheiber, "Road to *Munn,*" 363.

18. Grant, "'Higher Law' Background," 70; Treanor, "Origins and Original Significance of the Just Compensation Clause," 694–716.

19. Quoting Madison, Wood, *Creation of the American Republic,* 410.

20. Jefferson, *Notes on the State of Virginia,* 120.

21. McCoy, *Last of the Fathers,* 115.

22. Jefferson, *Notes on the State of Virginia,* 121.

23. Cooke, *The Federalist,* nos. 71, 78.

24. Turner, *William Plumer of New Hampshire,* 34–35.

25. Hamilton, "Remarks in New York Assembly, 6 Feb. 1787," in *Papers of Hamilton,* 4:35.

26. Corwin, "Doctrine of Due Process of Law before the Civil War," 371–72.

27. Corwin, "Basic Doctrine of American Constitutional Law," 254.

28. Nelson, "Changing Conceptions of Judicial Review," 1176.

29. Philadelphia *Pennsylvania Packet,* 2 Sept. 1786.

30. See Shain, *Myth of American Individualism,* 193–240; Neem, "Politics and the Origins of the Nonprofit Corporation," 344–65.

31. Hartz, *Economic Policy and Democratic Thought,* 292.

32. Maier, "Revolutionary Origins of the American Corporation," 68–70.

33. Carey, *Debates and Proceedings of the General Assembly of Pennsylvania,* 11–12.

34. Hamilton, "Examination," 23 Feb. 1802, in *Papers of Hamilton,* 25:533.

35. Corwin, "Basic Doctrine of American Constitutional Law."

36. *Debates in the Senate of the United States on the Judiciary during the First Session of the Seventh Congress,* 39. I owe this citation to Kurt Graham.

37. Newmyer, *Supreme Court Justice Joseph Story*, 132; Scheiber, "Public Rights and the Rule of Law," 217–51.

38. Neem, "Politics and the Origins of the Nonprofit Corporation," 358.

39. Gunn, *Decline of Authority.*

40. Novak, *People's Welfare*, 15, 88.

41. Lieberman, *Province of Legislation Determined.*

42. Nelson, *Americanization of the Common Law*, 171–72.

43. Cranch, *U.S. Supreme Court Reports*, 165, 177.

44. Haskins, "Law versus Politics in the Early Years of the Marshall Court," 19–20.

45. Madison to Washington, 16 April 1787, *Papers of James Madison*, 9:384.

Bibliography

Bailyn, Bernard. *Ideological Origins of the American Revolution.* Cambridge, MA, 1967.

Carey, Mathew, ed. *Debates and Proceedings of the General Assembly of Pennsylvania.* . . . Philadelphia: Printed for Carey and Co. Seddon and Pritchard, 1786.

Cooke, Jacob E., ed. *The Federalist.* Middletown, CT, 1961.

Corwin, Edward S. "Basic Doctrine of American Constitutional Law." *Michigan Law Review* 12 (1914): 254.

———. "Doctrine of Due Process of Law before the Civil War." *Harvard Law Review* 24 (1911): 371–72.

Cranch, William, ed. *U.S. Supreme Court Reports.* Washington City: Published for John Conrad & Co, 1804.

Debates in the Senate of the United States on the Judiciary during the First Session of the Seventh Congress. Philadelphia: Printed by Thos. Smith, 1802.

Douglass, William. *Summary, Historical and Political, of the First Planting, Progressive Improvements, and Present State of the British Settlements in North America.* Boston: Printed and sold by Rogers and Fowle in Queen-Street, 1749.

Grant, J. A. C. "'Higher Law' Background of the Law of Eminent Domain." *Wisconsin Law Review* 6 (1930–31): 70.

Gunn, L. Ray. *The Decline of Authority: Public Economic Policy and Political Development in New York, 1800–1860.* Ithaca, NY, 1988.

Hamilton, Alexander. *The Papers of Alexander Hamilton,* ed. Harold C. Syrett et al. New York, 1961–87.

Hartog, Hendrick. *Public Property and Private Power: The Corporation of the City of New York in American Law, 1730–1870.* Chapel Hill, NC, 1983.

Hartz, Louis. *Economic Policy and Democratic Thought: Pennsylvania, 1776–1860.* Cambridge, MA, 1948.

Haskins, George L. "Law versus Politics in the Early Years of the Marshall Court." *University of Pennsylvania Law Review* 130 (1981): 19–20.

Jefferson, Thomas. *Notes on the State of Virginia,* ed. William Peden. Chapel Hill, NC, 1955,

Levy, Leonard. *Legacy of Suppression: Freedom of Speech and Press in Early American History.* Cambridge, MA, 1960.

Lieberman, David. *Province of Legislation Determined: Legal Theory in Eighteenth-Century Britain.* Cambridge, 1989.

Madison, James. *The Papers of James Madison.* Vol. 9. Ed. Robert A. Rutland et al. Chicago, 1975.

McCoy, Drew R. *The Last of the Fathers: James Madison and the Republican Legacy.* Cambridge, 1989.

Maier, Pauline. "Revolutionary Origins of the American Corporation." *William and Mary Quarterly,* 3d ser., 50 (1993): 68–70.

Neem, Johann N. "Politics and the Origins of the Nonprofit Corporation in Massachusetts and New Hampshire, 1780–1820." *Nonprofit and Voluntary Sector Quarterly* 32 (2003): 344–65.

Nelson, William E. *Americanization of the Common Law: The Impact of Legal Change on Massachusetts Society, 1760–1830.* Cambridge, MA, 1975.

———. "Changing Conceptions of Judicial Review." *University of Pennsylvania Law Review* 120 (1972): 1176.

Newmyer, R. Kent. *Supreme Court Justice Joseph Story: Statesman of the Old Republic.* Chapel Hill, NC, 1985.

Novak, William J. *The People's Welfare: Law and Regulation in Nineteenth-Century America.* Chapel Hill, NC, 1996.

Penn, William. *England's Present Interest Considered* (1675). In *The Founders' Constitution.* Vol. 1. Ed. Philip B. Kurland and Ralph Lerner. Chicago, 1987.

Philadelphia *Pennsylvania Packet,* 2 Sept. 1786.

Reid, John Phillip. *Constitutional History of the American Revolution: The Authority of Rights.* Madison, WI, 1986.

Scheiber, Harry N. "Public Rights and the Rule of Law in American Legal History." *California Law Review* 72 (1984): 217–51.

———. "Road to *Munn:* Eminent Domain and the Concept of Public Purpose in the State Courts." *Perspectives in American History* 5 (1971): 363.

Schwoerer, Lois G. *The Declaration of Rights, 1689.* Baltimore, 1981.

Seavoy, Ronald E. "Public Service Origins of the American Business Corporation." *Business History Review* 52 (1978): 30–36.

Shain, Barry. *The Myth of American Individualism: The Protestant Origins of American Political Thought.* Princeton, NJ, 1994.

Skinner, Quentin. *Liberty before Liberalism.* Cambridge, 1998.

Treanor, William Michael. "Origins and Original Significance of the Just Compensation Clause of the Fifth Amendment." *Yale Law Journal* 94 (1985): 694–716.

Turner, Lynn W. *William Plumer of New Hampshire, 1759–1850.* Chapel Hill, NC, 1962.

Wilson, James. *The Works of James Wilson,* ed. Robert G. McCloskey. Cambridge, MA, 1967.

Wood, Gordon S. *The Creation of the American Republic, 1776–1787.* Chapel Hill, NC, 1969.

———. *The Radicalism of the American Revolution.* New York, 1992.

Rights Consciousness in American History

DANIEL T. RODGERS

It is a truism of contemporary law practice that lawyers rarely spend much time kindling in everyday Americans a vivid sense of rights. Far more often, as legal anthropologists have shown, the exchange between clients and lawyers works the other way around. From the moment the injured and aggrieved cross the law office threshold seeking help in some tightly knotted relationship with their neighbors, bosses, public officials, or family, their talk is suffused with claims of rights and injustice. Anger, outrage, meanness, and naked self-interest are all poured into a flood of "rights talk." Into rights talk, too, flow just the opposite: altruism, hope, selflessness, and loyalty. Wading into this tide of legal and political abstractions, the lawyer's job is not to teach clients the language of rights. It is, rather, to talk them out of most of their rights claims, to nudge them toward mediation and compromise, to pare their cases down to the bare essentials that seem likely to form a successful suit in the courts.[1]

American civic culture has not always been saturated by rights consciousness of this sort, as several of the essays in this volume point out. But for well over two centuries, languages of rights have left a powerful mark on social and political relations in the United States. The negative effects of a political culture steeped in competing rights claims have often been noted.[2] Rights talk has destabilized politics, often at the expense of deliberation and compromise. It has sluiced complex issues of policy into narrow claims of personal and fractional interest. It has swept key issues of democratic politics into the undemocratic rule of the courts. It has helped to produce a society with more lawyers per person, it is said, than any other on the globe, and it has flooded every aspect of life with legalist argument. And yet rights talk has also been one of the most important ways in which Americans have infused their politics with a dimension beyond mere law or interests. Arguments about rights—and not just rights, merely, but essential, inalienable, human rights—have been among the key ways in which Americans have debated what a good society might look like, un-burdened of injustice and the dead hand of the past. In its messiness, power, and contradictions, it is one of the basic noises of American history.

Only a fraction of the historic contest over rights has taken place within the confines of courts and lawbooks. Scholarship on the Bill of Rights has consistently exaggerated the place of that document in the dynamics of rights history in the United States. The courts have never been as imagi-native producers of rights as were the litigants who pressed their argu-ments and cases on the justices, or raised them on the street corners or in the churches and the labor union halls. The law has delineated and institutionalized rights, sorted through the rights claims thrust upon it, siphoning off and defusing some, instantiating others. But the legal pro-fession's desire for control over the production of rights and the diffusion of rights consciousness has always been profoundly frustrated.

Rights talk in the American past has been not only the jargon of the courts, but also and more importantly a language of popular politics. It has been the talk of town meetings, political rallies, newspapers, volun-tary associations, religious assemblies, workmates, family gatherings, and electoral huckstering. In moments of crisis, the upshot of this broad diffu-sion of rights talk has been angry collisions of competing rights, as the rights of enslaved Americans have smashed up against the rights of other Americans to hold property in slaves, the breadline standees' right to a job against the rights of free enterprise, the rights of pregnant women against the rights of the unborn. Popular politics in America has not only been the site of extravagant rights assertion, but also of endemic rights viola-tions, perpetuated in the name of justice, security, patriotism, or racial pu-rity—even in the name of rights themselves. Rights have been invented and repudiated, expanded and violated, striven for and struggled over. The current emotionally charged and politically polarized furor over gay rights is no historical aberration; its dynamics are among the most famil-iar in American history. Yet it is from this ongoing, passionate, democratic debate over rights, often far from the dicta of courts, that the expansion of rights has drawn its primary historic energy.

Although an enduring feature of American political culture since the eighteenth century, rights consciousness has not been static. There are four key phases in its history. Each was marked by a moment of heightened rights talk and fertile, even audacious, rights invention. The first of these, extending from the beginning of the struggle over British imperial policy through 1791, witnessed an explosion of popular rights claims, the practice of thinking about rights with "natural" as a key modifier, and a passion for

rights declarations. From that movement's collision with a nervous coun-
terreaction against popular rights invention was to emerge, scarred and
truncated, the federal Bill of Rights. The period from the 1820s through
the Civil War saw a second eruption of rights claims, more radical than
the first in its focus on the social rights of workers, women, and slaves. A
quite different dynamic governed the third phase, from the mid-1870s
through the mid-1930s, as the movement of the courts into the creation
of rights, through a wholesale construction of new property and entrepreneurial rights, triggered a sharp reaction among many of those who
were the normal constituents of a rights-based politics. Then, out of the
changed mental landscape of the Second World War and grassroots struggles for racial justice, came yet a fourth era of rights invention—this time,
for a moment, with the courts and the outsiders in common cause. Its re-
verberations and counter-mobilizations still dominate the politics of the
contemporary United States.[3]

Rights invention in all these phases has not only been a response to
new adversities, as Richard Primus has described it, a way of pushing
back against novel forms of oppression; for what is most striking about
the history of rights talk is its capacity, at moments, to destabilize ancient
and deeply seated forms of power.[4] Rights invention has not only enabled
the construction of stories of peoplehood, as Rogers Smith emphasizes
in this volume; for rights talk, at other times, has fractured political discourse and splintered communities. Above all, the power in rights talk
has been a product of its openness, its democratic character, its capacity
to be grasped by outsiders. It has been one of the key languages in which
Americans have argued not only over substantive politics, but also, and
even more importantly, about whose voice should be heard. Its history, in
consequence, is not continuous, but episodic. Waves of massive rights invention—most of them from outside the structures of law and power—
passionate contest, partial incorporation, and retreat: these have been
the primary dynamics of rights in America. A messier history than the
Bill of Rights mythology permits, it is not without its own heroism and
inspiration.

Rights from Above and Below: The Emergence of a Language of Natural Rights

In 1776 there was nothing very remarkable about Jefferson's use of
the term "rights" in his phrase, "Certain unalienable rights." In a different
historical context, colonists' grievances over taxes and trade might have

coalesced around other claims than this: custom, for example, or justice, or (as some of the phrases of the 1770s had it) the people's general "happiness."[5] In the late eighteenth century, however, a multitude of factors conspired to press the fears and outrage of rebellious colonists into a language of rights. One was the precedent of 1688–89, the Glorious Revolution in which Parliament had deposed a king and forced the Declaration of Rights on his successor. Afterward, with each expansion of Parliament's powers, the American colonial assemblies had been quick to assert equivalent "rights" for themselves. Some of the colonies had won bodies of liberties and privileges from their governors, charters that the Americans had begun to imagine as local variations on the great English Carta. Not the least influential in shaping the language of rights was the common law, important not only for its specific bounty of legal rights, but for binding the notion of a body of traditional rights and immunities to the very concept of being a British subject.

Not surprisingly, then, when resistance heated up in response to the heavy-handed imperial reforms, colonial leaders were quick to denounce the new measures as violations of their "most essential rights and liberties." From the Stamp Act Congress's resolutions of 1765 through the Continental Congress's Declaration of Rights in 1774 and beyond, the patriot leaders and publicists drummed home the point that the new measures endangered their chartered and constitutional rights, the historical rights due to every British subject.[6]

What was much more remarkable in Jefferson's phrase was the adjective "unalienable"—abstract, indistinct, and still novel in the 1770s. At the beginning of the resistance, there had been little in the Anglo-American past to predict that the leaders of the rebellion would so quickly desert the safe ground of history and precedent for rights that were merely imaginary: natural and inalienable rights—rights that were not only basic, but primordial, antecedent to law, indeed, to history itself. The key to the rhetorical move was to think of rights, not by sorting through the precedents of the law, but by imagining what the human condition must have been at the moment of its birth, or had to be by its very constitution, or should have been if human history had not been bungled. As the argument over authority and taxes heated up, the new language gathered force. "The sacred rights of mankind are not to be rummaged for among old parchments or musty records," Alexander Hamilton declared in 1775. "They are written, as with a sunbeam, in the whole *volume* of human nature." John Adams had made the point a decade earlier: there were rights not to be found in any particular constitution, but "in the constitution of the intellectual and moral world," and hence could not be alienated without alienating liberty itself.[7]

As Rogers Smith points out, rights talk of this sort helped to construct an ethically constitutive language of peoplehood. But it was a risky course, and the danger of departing from legally established rights to rights grounded in the laws and original design of nature was not lost on the patriot leaders. Not the least of their fears was that it might allow the definition of rights to escape the control of lawyers and educated men and throw it open to any colonist with a philosophical bent. To the end of the Revolution, there were patriot leaders who resisted the open-ended adjectives. But the exigencies of argument pressed hard in the other direction, as escalating cycles of protest, repression, and outrage pushed the patriot demands beyond any sure foundation of precedent and constitution. To this was added the pressure of a mounting utopianism from below as the mobilization for resistance propelled new actors into the conflict: urban crowds, artisan radicals, and angry farmers and tenants. Nightmares of unrestrained official power and a utopian hope that the Americans might pin down freedoms no other people had successfully secured against the corruptions of history together conspired to destabilize an older, lawyers' discourse of historically situated rights.

Rights grounded in nature were rights that by definition constrained every government, even the emergency committees of safety that had begun to move into the revolutionary power vacuum by 1774–75. In practice, the American revolution, like all revolutions, suppressed a great many rights, as Loyalists experienced when their property was seized, or their buildings were burned, or they were silenced and harried out of their villages. There is "no *Loss of Liberty*, that court minions can complain of, when they are silenced," a South Carolina newspaper insisted; "no man has a right to say a word, which may lame the liberties of his country."[8] Yet coming on the heels of a decade of petitions and declarations, the same revolutionary fervor that made liberty seem so fragile that rights had to be smashed to preserve it also impelled the patriots to put rights on paper. In the now deeply politicized process of rights claiming, a flood of new ones was unloosed.

The first declaration of rights to bind a patriot government was Virginia's, debated at length in May and June 1776. Its philosophical untidiness was witness to the diverse pressures upon it. The Virginia Declaration of Rights was a compound of individual rights (freedom of the press, e.g., and the "free exercise" of religion), legal and procedural rights (trial by jury and protection from excessive bail and punishment), corporate rights (the right to a popular militia and the Revolutionary right to abolish any government faithless to the "publick weal"), together with general statements of political principles and pious statements of morality. In a gesture full of symbolic meaning, the Virginians claimed them not as grievances against the Crown, but as the "basis and foundation of Government" itself.

During the first years of independence, less than half the states followed Virginia's example of rights declaration. How deeply the new rights talk had lodged in popular politics, however, became clear as early as 1778, when the Massachusetts town meetings rejected a constitution drafted without a declaration of rights. Nowhere in late eighteenth-century America can one find so close a reading of public opinion as in the returns of the town meetings that discussed that constitution's failings. Some of them bear the marks of bookish lawyers; others have the spelling of little-schooled farmers. What is striking is the breathtaking inventiveness with which persons were now talking about rights: the inalienable right to follow the dictates of one's conscience (though it meant disestablishment of the clergy); the right to absolute property in oneself (though it meant the death of slavery); the right to make public officials stand for annual election; the right of even poor or black men to vote; the right "engraved in human nature" to a fairly apportioned legislature; the "unalienable right" of popular ratification of a constitution.[9] Unhinged from history and formal law, loosed from the monopoly of learned men, the business of imagining rights had grown from an argumentative strategy to a volatile popular movement.

Rights talk of this sort was still alive when the Constitutional Convention met in 1787, and it is in this context that its failure to propose a federal bill of rights must be understood. Prudence, to be sure, was against the project, given how fiercely the clauses of the state bills of rights had been debated and with what diverse results. So was the exhaustion of the delegates by the time George Mason, author of the Virginia Declaration of Rights, raised the issue in Philadelphia. The deeper instinct, however, was more conservative. The drafters had already carefully deleted every instance of the term "rights" from the Constitution in favor of a more cautious reference to "immunities" and "privileges." As the *Federalist*'s lame and belated treatment of the issue made clear, the Constitution's drafters were anxious to evade altogether the unpredictable popular talk of rights and to focus debate instead on constitutional mechanics and national pride.

When the Constitution came before the state ratifying conventions, it quickly became evident that the framers had miscalculated popular sentiment. The Anti-Federalists' objections to the Constitution only began with omission of a bill of rights. The sticking point was the power, scope, and elasticity of the proposed national government. By the time the ratification debate reached Virginia, however, the Anti-Federalists had made enactment of a bill of rights, prefixed to the Constitution, a condition of their acquiescence.

It fell to Madison in the First Congress to fulfill the bargain, though he was himself no partisan of bills of rights. When Jefferson wrote from France that "a bill of rights is what the people are entitled to against every government on earth," a skeptical Madison responded that "parchment barriers" like Virginia's rarely made much difference. In his opening remarks to an impatient Congress, Madison stressed not the philosophical value of a bill of rights, but the expediency of one in the current moment as "highly politic, for the tranquility of the public mind, and the stability of the Government."[10]

Finding that point of tranquillity was Madison's project, which he achieved through a combination of strategic compromise and equally strategic omission. Had he had his way, the guarantees of the first ten amendments would not have stood out as a separate bill of rights, but would have been woven unobtrusively through the body of the Constitution. Several of the rights that had gathered strong support in the ratifying conventions Madison let drop from his proposal altogether: the right of the people to "instruct" their representatives, a prohibition against chartered monopolies, and a constitutional limitation on peacetime armies. Other demands of the ratifying conventions succumbed to the caution of Madison's colleagues. In response to the demand that the Constitution begin with a clear statement of constitutional principle, Madison proposed prefixing a clause acknowledging the people's constitutional right to reform (though not abolish) their governments; but the proposal did not get past the House of Representatives. Following the language of the ratifying conventions, Madison proposed three substantial paragraphs elaborating the rights of free speech, assembly, and conscience. The House compacted them into two abbreviated clauses; the Senate bundled the personal rights language into a sentence. The House would have preserved most of those rights against both state and federal governments; importantly, the Senate restricted the First Amendment's scope to acts of Congress.[11]

It was no wonder that leaders of the bill of rights movement, like William Grayson, complained that their amendments had been "so mutilated and gutted that in fact they are good for nothing."[12] That turned out to be an exaggeration, colored by disappointment. In time, the amendments were to become, as Madison grudgingly admitted they might, "a good ground for an appeal to the sense of the community."[13] Unlike the Constitution, drafted in secret convention, the Bill of Rights was born as a demand from below. Politically, however, its enactment had been a holding action. It was not a speaking of the framers' mind, as partisans of pure "original intent" have imagined. The very act of enumeration, as Jack Rakove emphasizes, clouded the issue. It was a document born in debate, dissension, compromise, and contending power—born, in short, out of the usual processes of popular politics. The amendments proposed no new rights. Rather, they gathered up the fervor of rights invention that the struggle with Britain had loosed and filtered out a cautious sliver of it.

Rights from Below: The Expanding Universe of Social Rights

Rights consciousness in the late eighteenth century focused on official oppression: the tyranny of priests and kings, rapacious tax collectors, corrupt judges, and overbearing officeholders. Despite the efforts of a Thomas Paine or a Mary Wollstonecraft, domination that was rooted in social systems of property, class, racial subordination, or patriarchy proved hard to oppose with the existing language of rights. Power whose sources lay not in the state, but in custom and convention, had fallen largely outside the purview of the first bills of rights. When, in the middle years of the nineteenth century, Americans on the margins of politics began to think seriously about socially constructed forms of power, a second eruption of rights invention ensued.

The first hints of the new uses of rights appeared in the artisans' and workingmen's associations of the 1820s and 1830s. Urban artisans had been central to the struggle against Britain; it was their spokesmen who, in the debates over the Pennsylvania Declaration of Rights of 1776, had tried to incorporate a declaration: "That an enormous Proportion of Property vested in a few Individuals is dangerous to the Rights, and destructive of the Common Happiness of Mankind."[14] Now, in the early nineteenth century, as new forms of wage labor and capital organization began to erode the traditional props of artisan life and aspirations, workingmen's groups revived, recasting the Revolutionary language of rights to meet the changed class relations.

The workingmen's associations did not call for mere extension of rights already fixed in the law. As in the eighteenth century, the dynamic in rights talk lay in the utopian possibilities in the rhetoric of "natural" rights—the invitation to imagine those rights that, at the birth of a just society, must have preceded law, custom, and social convention. This was Locke's imaginative game (though he never imagined anything as radical as rights inalienable under any social circumstances), which he had played with property rights at its center. Now people in radically different social and economic circumstances seized on Locke's conjectures about the original relationship between labor and property and recast them in popular terms: the "natural and unalienable right" of "all who toil . . . to reap the fruits of their own industry," as the Philadelphia journeymen mechanics put it in 1828; the right to "just remuneration" for a worker's toil; the laborers' "natural right" to dispose of their own time as they saw fit.[15] Everywhere in the Euro-American world that the new class relations took hold, workers reached into the existing languages of politics for terms to express their sense of injustice. In mid-nineteenth-century America, the result was not only to revive, but also to sharply expand the domain of rights.

If rights talk could be turned from claims against governments to claims against private oppression, however, urban artisans were not the only potential users. By the 1830s, a burgeoning antislavery movement was spinning off incendiary claims to rights, among them the slavery-nullifying natural right of "every man . . . to his own body [and] to the produce of his own labor."[16] A decade later, a new women's rights movement was alive with utopian rights claims: a woman's right to property separate from her husband; to a "sphere of action" as broad as her conscience demanded; to the vote; to all the rights "integral" to her moral being.[17] Although sympathetic lawyers pressed these issues in the courts, the language of law and constitutions did not dominate the radical challenges of the mid-nineteenth century. More contagious were the abstract phrases of the Declaration of Independence. The workingmen's petitions were saturated with Jeffersonian borrowings. The women's rights convention at Seneca Falls in 1848 put its case into an elaborate paraphrase of the Declaration. Four years earlier, the antislavery Liberty Party had shoehorned Jefferson's "certain unalienable rights" passage into its platform, as the Republicans would do again in 1860. The dynamics of rights production were unleashed once more.

The rights innovators of the mid-nineteenth century formed no common movement. The abolitionist and women's movements, though historically allied, were not without mutual tension. In both movements, many preferred talk of duties and Christian obligations to the Revolution-descended claims of rights. As for the workingmen's movement, in an era of ugly mob attacks on free Northern blacks and their white allies, it was shot through with the surrounding racism. Many of the same political figures who championed the rights of white free labor succeeded in cutting down the civil freedoms of Northern black citizens and forcing them from the voting rolls. What joined the inventors of new rights was no common cause but a tactical and ideological contagion—a sense, passed from out-group to out-group, that the rhetorical legacy of the Revolution was ripe for reemployment, this time not against the grand tyranny of kings and despots, but against the customary, everyday tyrannies of capital, bosses, slave masters, and husbands.

The response at the political center to the new wave of rights demands was, as before, mixed and ambivalent. In the Virginia debate over slavery in 1829, some of slavery's defenders tried to scotch the idea that governments rested on any fundamental rights at all. Others tried to elaborate a politics grounded in loyalty and obligation. But as long as white Southerners clung to the ultimate right of secession; as long as owners felt the need to call their real and human property something other than a mere social convention; as long as husbands and slaveholders clung to their inviolable right to manage their own "domestic institutions" without interference—as long as all this remained, any general repudiation of natural-rights talk was unthinkable. The result was not a rhetoric of repudiation, but of circumlocution, compromises, silences, and strident reassertions, until—in a spectacular collision of competing rights claims—the nation broke into pieces in 1861.

The second wave of rights invention came to a more mixed end than the first. The death of slavery was its boldest, most sweeping achievement. With the defeat of the Confederacy, Northern Republicans went south to force into the Reconstruction constitutions phrases from Northern bills of rights. The radical workingmen's claim that all persons had an inalienable right to "the fruits of their labor" was injected into some of the Southern state bills of rights, in an effort to prevent slavery from rising up, phoenixlike, under another name. By 1868 the right of black men to vote had been temporarily forced on the South—although couched as a reward for their loyalty and character, the bills of rights drafters made clear, not as a right founded in their nature as men, as the African American delegates in Virginia and elsewhere had demanded. The Civil Rights Act of 1875 drew, for a moment, accommodations in private theaters, inns, railroad cars, and steamboats into the realm of rights. The right of women to vote, on the other hand, was abruptly set aside. The labor movement, raising the call for the eight-hour day as a basic right in the late 1860s, saw the antislavery Republicans flee the cause. On the margins of power, a new array of social rights had been elaborated and thrust against the center, a handful of them successfully.

Rights from Above: The Courts and Rights, and the Progressives' Rejection of Them

For the first century of independence, the strongest talk of rights had been found outside the courts. For a time, judges in the early republic had played with the principles of natural justice, usually to reaffirm property rights against invasion. But state and federal court judges quickly found their accustomed ground in the written words of statute and constitution.

Reconstruction marked, in this sense, a sharp and unprecedented turn. From the 1870s through the early 1930s—first in a trickle of dissenting opinions, then in a stream of majority decisions, and finally in a flood—the courts began to invent rights on their own. The first of these, pressed by Justice Stephen J. Field in 1873, was a direct offshoot of the Reconstruction debates over rights: the "sacred and imprescribable" right to choose one's occupation freely. In a different historical setting, Field's "right of free labor" might have focused on the plight of the ex-slaves, who were being rapidly constrained once more in tangles of tenantry, debt, and poverty. By the late 1880s and 1890s, however, in an atmosphere acrid as never before with labor disputes and fears of class warfare, the old antislavery slogan was reformulated as the "right of free contract" and thrust aggressively into labor law. With it, state and federal courts overturned laws that had banned scrip payment and payment in orders at the company store, laws setting maximum working hours, laws regulating the weighing of miners' coal output, laws preventing employers from firing union workers—all in the name of lifting "paternal" and "tutelary" burdens from wage earners and setting them free to make whatever employment contracts they had the will and "manhood" to make. Freedom of contract adjudication reached its high-water mark in 1923, when the U.S. Supreme Court invalidated a District of Columbia statute setting a minimum wage for women, on the grounds that the "individual freedom of action contemplated by the Constitution" mandated an unrestrained market of prices, the price of labor included.[18]

The sense of urgency in the courts' elaboration of these newly invented rights was manifest in the extraordinary expansion of cases of judicial review. Before the Civil War, the U.S. Supreme Court had struck down, on the average, a single state law each year. In the period from 1865 to 1898, the figure jumped to five a year; in the 1920s, it leaped to four-teen. State courts followed the same sharp upward slope in declaring state laws unconstitutional. Undergirding the innovations in constitutional practice was a reformulation of the courts as quasi-legislatures, censor-ing and policing the products of the popular branches of government. Ju-dicial review, the president of the American Bar Association declared in 1892, in articulating the new ambitions of the judiciary, was "the loftiest function and the most sacred duty of the judiciary." It was "the only break-water against the haste and passions of the people—against the tumul-tuous ocean of democracy."[19]

The two languages of rights, from above and below, competed for con-trol of many of the same terms, reappropriated from the antislavery move-ment and the eighteenth-century Revolutionary declarations. With a high eclecticism, the courts mixed formalistic Constitutional construction, elas-tic readings of the Reconstruction amendments, and a language of case precedent impenetrable to those outside the law, together with broad ap-peals to the "fundamental rights of liberty" in general, and the "sacred rights of property" in particular. But most post–Civil War judges realized that the inherited natural-rights line of argument was dangerously indis-tinct, and they picked their way through the eighteenth-century phrases with considerable care. The mental game that had proved so powerful an engine of democratic rights production, of thinking outside the bounds of time—either retrospectively to a vanished state of nature, or prospectively to human nature in its fulfillment—was not their project. Locke's specu-lations in retrospective anthropology did not tempt them. Cite though they did the bills of rights formula that "acquiring, possessing, and pro-tecting property" was a natural right, the judges were not interested in probing property's origins, much less in pursuing the workingmen's claim that their labor might be property's true and only legitimate foundation.

Rights that might have been construed as kinds of property, or essen-tial to property's protection, the courts let the legislatures annul. The 1875 Civil Rights Act's sections dealing with cases where the violation of a citizen's civil rights was done by a private firm or person were set aside as beyond the Constitution's reach. Also uncontested were the disfranchise-ment measures that swept African American voters off the Southern elec-toral rolls at the turn of the century, though it was patent to all that, with-out the vote, their property was all the more insecure. In an era of lynch mobs, red scares, and violently fought and violently suppressed strikes, the courts evinced little interest in what are now called personal liberties. The preoccupation of the courts was not with the basic ground of rights, or even property rights in general, but with the defense of particular sorts of entrepreneurial property claims. Theirs was a rights revival from above, defining, delimiting, and shoring up the ascendant powers of their day.

Although the court system was too complex to move in lockstep, the general drift of the era was clear. During the period of high industrial capitalism, massive immigration, business consolidation, and bitter and continuous labor conflict, the courts threw themselves into governance as never before. Legislatures—sometimes crudely and sometimes with care and sophistication—tried to forestall the worst exploitations of industrial capitalism. They defended their actions by citing the principles of protection, public health and safety, and the common good. At times, the courts adjusted and complied; as often, wielding the rhetoric of rights, they resisted.

In the face of these moves in the courts, other Americans remained free to make what they could of the language of rights. The Socialist Labor Party in the 1890s went to the polls with a platform appealing to inalienable rights. So did the advocates of women's suffrage, until shortly after the turn of the century, when they finally traded in the argument from rights for arguments about women's special gifts and character. The pacifists, socialists, and labor sympathizers who founded the American Civil Liberties Union in reaction to the strident patriotism of World War I included fervent Bill of Rights believers. But the more striking phenomenon of the late nineteenth and early twentieth centuries was the virtual abandonment of rights talk by most of the Americans who aligned themselves with the progressive movements of the day.

Some of the flight from rights rhetoric stemmed from a changed intellectual climate, dominated as never before by a sense of evolution and history. In that context, conservative and progressive thinkers alike worried that the concept of fixed, timeless rights was archaic: a throwback to ahistorical eighteenth-century reasoning. This was the ground on which Woodrow Wilson, at Princeton in the 1890s, dismissed Jefferson's natural-rights philosophizing as "false," "abstract," and "un-American." Wilson's counterpart at Harvard, summarizing the common wisdom of turn-of-the-century professional American political science, agreed; despite its "last despairing flicker in the courts of the United States," the concept of natural rights had been "abandoned by almost every scholar in England and America."[20] If the intellectuals' new consciousness of social evolution worked against the rights tradition, so did a general eagerness to extinguish the line of argument that had lured white Southerners in 1861 (and might lure others) into the folly of trying to implement the right to abolish a rights-threatening government. "The right of revolution does not exist in America," the state of Indiana instructed its schoolchildren in 1921. "One of the many meanings of democracy is that it is a form of government in which the right of revolution has been lost."[21]

Most powerful, however, was a sense that rights arguments were shackled to an archaic individualism, blind to historical circumstances, and oblivious to the larger good. "The doctrine of natural rights really furnishes no guide to the problems of our time," Charles Beard insisted in this vein in 1908.[22] Better to talk as Theodore Roosevelt and Woodrow Wilson did of the people's "will" and their "common interest." Amid "the ferocious, scrambling rush of an unregulated and purely individualist industrialism," as Theodore Roosevelt termed it, rights talk, unlinked to obligations and relationships, extracted from any broader sense of society and the public good, seemed futile and reactionary.[23] Early twentieth-century progressives made their ethically constitutive stories of peoplehood out of other ingredients. The Progressive Party in 1912, discarding every reference to rights from its platform, went to the people with a ringing case for "social and industrial justice" and the "public welfare." The Democratic Party platform of 1936 resounded with Jeffersonian appeals to "self-evident truths," but not with rights talk, pledging itself instead to secure the people's "safety," "happiness," and "economic security."[24] The Liberty League railed against the New Deal invasion of property and contracts with a rhetoric of rights; the core language of the New Dealers themselves, in contrast, turned on "the common good," the people's interdependent economic fates, the plight of the common man, and the "general Welfare" Preamble to the Constitution.

For almost two generations, from the 1890s through the mid-1930s, progressive activists' consciousness of social bonds and social-evolutionary processes combined with their deepening political contest with the courts to spur them away from the rights language of the judges. Rights talk was obfuscating talk. "More than anything else," Roscoe Pound summed up the legal realists' critique of the new adjudication in 1923, "the theory of natural rights and its consequence, the nineteenth century theory of legal rights, served to cover up what the legal order really was and what court and lawmaker and judge really were doing."[25] The language of the Revolution had been co-opted by the defenders of narrow entrepreneurial "liberty." To those struggling to bring industrial capitalism under public control, the eighteenth-century heritage was an impediment, an archaic word game, a set of "exploded" concepts.

The Progressive and New Deal eras present no monolithic face in this regard. Rights consciousness remained a protean and unpredictable force in American political culture. But at no other time has the very recourse to rights talk been so politically polarized or, in democratic circles, so deeply out of favor.

Rights from Below and Above: The Contentious Revival of Rights Talk

Then came the Second World War and, in its wake, a return to the more familiar pattern: vigorous, rights-based popular movements beating against a more cautious center. The precipitating event was the rise of Fascism: the ascendancy of political systems in which all rights seemed to have been swallowed up by a monstrously swollen state. In the late 1930s the dominant theme of Franklin Roosevelt's speeches had been "democracy"; by 1940 his speech writers were reaching back to eighteenth-century traditions to talk of "essential human freedoms" whose fate now hung in the balance. The New Dealers' war-accelerated rediscovery of rights culminated in Roosevelt's promulgation of a "second Bill of Rights" in 1944. A translation of the New Deal into claims that progressives had once spurned, it pledged the nation to an "economic bill of rights": the right to a useful job, adequate earnings, a decent home, adequate medical care, and protection from the economic fears of sickness, old age, accident, and unemployment.[26] The language of rights, joined to New Deal liberalism, had become protean and unpredictable once more.

The Supreme Court, beaten in its confrontation with the New Deal, took an equally momentous turn in the late 1930s and 1940s. Rejecting the political and economic program of their predecessors, the new appointees shifted their attention from property rights to the issues brought to a head by the specter of Fascism: rights of free expression, guarantees of fair criminal process against overbearing state power, and the festering double standards of racial inequality and segregation. The Court did not arrive at its new program of "preferred rights" without its share of backtracking, particularly during the war and the revived national security scare of the 1950s, but in the shadow of the European dictatorships its new course was clear.

Dismantling the elaborate edifice built on "freedom of contract" with the damning observation that the phrase was nowhere in the Constitution, the Supreme Court had reason to keep its distance from its predecessors' abstract reasoning about rights. Hugo Black was among those urging that course, plumping for a literalist Bill of Rights–based constitutionalism. But the needs of the moment, the enduring place of rights in the political culture, and the war and Cold War–revived talk of political fundamentals all pressed toward appropriation, rather than rejection, of the older lines of argument. By the 1940s, the Supreme Court was beginning to pick its way through rights again, establishing some of the sections of the Bill of Rights as so "basic" and "fundamental" as to be incorporated into state law through the Fourteenth Amendment. Before the decade was out, the Court had begun again to spin off inventions: rights nowhere specified in the Constitution, but so "fundamental" ("natural" by another name) that they were morally and logically entailed in the Bill of Rights itself. Sometimes through simple assertion, sometimes through ingenious argument, the rights of marriage and procreation, travel, association, the vote, education, and privacy had all been framed as "fundamental" by the end of the 1960s and through the process of "incorporation," laid beside the Bill of Rights as its modern addendum.

So centrally involved in policymaking did the new Court (like its predecessor) become that the rights revolution of the postwar years has often been misconstrued as a revolution from the top down. But this time, as before in the late eighteenth and early nineteenth centuries, the fuel came from below. Most important was the struggle for racial justice. Unlike their white counterparts, African American progressives had clung to the language of rights through the early twentieth century. In keeping with the mood of the times, the "Declaration of Principles," out of which the NAACP had emerged in the first decade of the century, ended with a list of the African Americans' social and civic "duties." But duties were only ancillary to assertions of political and "manhood" rights.[27] Rights claims mediated between the talk of "freedom," which had run so long and deep in African American culture, and the broken promises of Reconstruction. Given urgency by comparison of racial practice in the United States with Nazi racism and by the movement to enunciate new standards of universal human rights for a post-Fascist world, a civil rights movement remobilized vigorously during the war. It was this crusade from outside the racially protected institutions of power that supplied the courts, case by case, with the arguments that would eventually lead to *Brown v. Board of Education* and then, in the face of the massive resistance of Southern whites to that decision, to the intensified judicial activism of the 1960s.

The contagious example of the civil rights movement on other outside groups multiplied the effects of the new rights language. Through imitation, reaction, or rivalry, the tactics and rights claims of the black protest movement spread to others on the margins of power, slowly in the 1950s, then with snowballing effect in the 1960s and early 1970s. A women's rights movement was reborn in a consciousness-intensifying intersection with the civil rights protest. The American Civil Liberties Union mushroomed to its modern size in the 1960s, forming a powerful rights litigation lobby for the burgeoning liberation movements. By the mid-1970s, dozens of such movements had sprung up, holding deeply entrenched customs to the test of fundamental rights: movements for the rights of gay Americans, Native Americans, Chicano, and Asian Americans; movements for the rights of the young, the aged, the poor, the institutionalized, the homeless, and the handicapped. On the global scene, a powerful international human rights movement gathered force, loosed from its constraining Cold War categories, to try to bring new force to the human rights declarations of the late 1940s. Heightened by television and by the historic conjuncture of social movement organization with an activist judiciary willing to give a hearing to the rights claims roiling up from below, rights talk spread with unprecedented speed from out-group to out-group. Rights talk not only mobilized out-groups, but also, in some cases, created them, where group consciousness had barely had a public language before—the work of the National Welfare Rights Organization being a striking example.[28]

This eruption of rights claims and rights-claiming organizations generated resistance across a wide and fiercely contested front. Backlash movements proliferated, as the fury over racial desegregation or the courts' extension of free speech rights to obscenity and flag burning showed. In the state and federal courts, judges split with increasingly sharp discord over their receptiveness to the new rights claims; among the Reagan federal court appointees there was no mistaking their desire to curb the unpredictable, protean side of rights talk. And yet the language of rights was too powerful to be left only to the critics of the social status quo.

The framing of abortion policy as a contest between the "right to life" and the "right to choose" set a model for the battles to come. By the 1980s social and cultural conservatives who had reacted with alarm to the rights revolution of the 1960s were working hard all across the contested social terrain to defend their moral counter-crusade with new and counter claims of rights: parents' rights to keep the traditional family order in force and to shield children from the threatening messages of schools and commercial media, worshippers' rights to public prayer, taxpayers' rights to hold down public budgets, the tax-exemption rights of churches, the rights of the not yet born. Outsiders to power, they knew the resources other outsiders had drawn from rights language, both to mobilize themselves and to leverage their cause onto the dominant political discourse. In the early years of its existence, a Moral Majority organizer noted in 1990, "We framed the issues wrong." Framing school prayer as "good" did not win the day. "So we learned to frame the issue in terms of 'students rights.'. . . We are pro-choice for students having the right to pray in public schools."[29]

In this cacophony of competing rights, almost no one now talked, as eighteenth-century Americans had, of "natural rights." John Rawls's project of reimagining the social contract as it might have been made at a moment of original innocence, though it cut a powerful swath through the political philosophy seminars, never gained much popular traction.[30] The Catholic side of the right-to-life movement was rooted in a natural-law tradition—by which every social arrangement was ultimately accountable to its efficacy in fostering the essential purposes of human life—that never before had been as prominent in American political life. The bishops' attempts in the early 1980s to bring the morality of nuclear war and the moral underpinnings of the modern capitalist economy to the bar of judgment were rooted in it. But most cultural conservatives, including those who quickly quashed the hint of liberation theology in the bishops' report on the economy, were deeply suspicious of the utopian strain in natural-rights talk. The project of thinking one's way back beyond existing social arrangements, without the help of theological learning or a literally read biblical text to keep the experiment from running amok, ran counter to most cultural conservatives' instincts. As for the legal conservatives on the bench, in the *Bowers v. Hardwick* decision upholding state sodomy laws in 1986, a conservative Supreme Court majority, turning its back on the language of postwar rights invention, made clear its determination to get out of the business of instantiating any new "fundamental" rights.[31]

And yet, as the tumult of arguments through which *Bowers* was overturned in 2003 confirmed, the destabilizing element in modern rights talk remains, as in the eighteenth century, its openness to abstraction. What made the language of rights so powerful a political vehicle in the wake of the Second World War was not only its ability to focus a mass of grievances and aspirations into a sharply defined claim: to roll the messiness of pain and history and experience into a right. It was not only the close articulation between rights construction and the power of the courts, accelerated by the new institutions of public policy litigation. What made the language of rights so powerful in the last half of the twentieth century was, as before, its open-endedness, its invitation to think at cross-purposes to history, custom, and massively entrenched convention and to measure them against original principles of justice. The sheer volume of rights invention and rights dispute in the fifty years after *Brown* has no historic parallel. But the dynamics were familiar.

Conclusion: The Framers' Legacy

"None of the supposed rights of man," Marx objected in 1842, ". . . go beyond the egoistic man, man as . . . an individual separated from the community, withdrawn into himself, preoccupied with his private interest and acting in accordance with his private caprice."[32] The point, born in the conservative reaction to the French Revolution and a common coin of early twentieth-century progressive thought, cannot be dismissed. Rights claims are claims against others. They do not exist outside a situation of real or potential antagonism. From the beginning of American history, to talk of rights has been to specify tyrannies and hold them up to the bar of justice—the practical justice of the courts, when justice is to be found there, or the principles of justice itself, when the courts are blind. Like the Anglo-American legal system itself, rights claims invite sharp distinctions between the rights-invaded self and others. It is hardly an accident that a political culture repeatedly flooded by popular claims of rights has no easy time talking directly and sustainedly about common possessions, common interest, and entangled and interdependent destinies.

But rights consciousness in America has never been a simple vehicle for possessive individualism. From the Virginia Declaration of Rights through the New Deal's declaration of economic rights and beyond, strong rights claims have gathered individual and collective rights into a common fold. Some rights in the American polity are held by persons, others by groups, by the "community" (as the Pennsylvania Declaration of Rights of 1776 had it), or by the "people" as a whole. The rights of contemporary Americans include rights of possession and privacy, but they also include the right to assemble, organize, worship, vote, and strike—all collective or corporate rights capable of being held only by communities of persons.

That rights claims carry both public and private potential, that social democracy and laissez-faire can both be justified on rights-based foundations, is not due to the capriciousness of language. Rights consciousness contains its own peculiar collective dynamic. Translating pain and injury— a beating by a policeman, a "no Jews wanted" sign, or a compulsory religious oath—into claims of rights not only transfers personal wounds into the realm of justice; it simultaneously translates private experience into general claims and potentially universalizing language. This is the solidaristic dynamic in rights movements. This is likewise the dynamic of rights contagion, as universally stated rights slip past the adjectives (white, male, Christian, native-born, and the rest) constructed to hedge them in and move out in unanticipated ways and into the hands of other users.

Above all, what is most striking about the history of rights consciousness in America is its democratic character. Rights talk has not simply been an inheritance, a legacy from the nation's inception. It has not merely been an elaboration of what the framers had in mind, however inchoately or inexplicitly. Rights have been made, quashed, and remade at every level of American society, often by outsiders to the polity, far from the structures of power. The democratic character of rights talk has not precluded Americans from trampling massively on rights, not the least in the practice of slavery that bore so hard on the Constitution drafters' minds. But the utopian strain in rights consciousness remains—intellectually and sociologically—a powerful and unpredictable lever of change. Since the Revolution, rights talk has never been fully consolidated by the existing institutions of law, never separable from inquiry into rights as they ought to be, or may once have been. The result has been a widely diffused, often destabilizing, sometimes convoluted, often strident, but nonetheless inventive popular debate about the fundamentals of a just society.

The members of the First Congress who served as arbiters of the Bill of Rights' final language had far more narrow, immediate goals than this. Their project was to consolidate rights. As nervous as all centrists about the instability of rights arguments, they pruned the open-ended, natural-rights abstractions out of the document with the rigor of men determined to lock up that line of argument against the future and the external democratic clamor. Many of them hoped to make the language of rights routine and merely legalistic. The failure of their effort is one of American history's central events and American democracy's good fortunes.

Notes

An earlier version of this essay was published in *The Bill of Rights in Modern America: After 200 Years*, ed. David J. Bodenhamer and James W. Ely Jr. (Bloomington, IN: Indiana Univ. Press, 1993). I am grateful to Laura Weinrib for assistance in revision.

1. Merry, *Getting Justice and Getting Even*.
2. Glendon, *Rights Talk*.
3. For a fuller account, see Rodgers, *Contested Truths*.
4. Primus, *American Language of Rights*.
5. Handlin and Handlin, *Popular Sources*, 65.
6. Adams, *Papers of John Adams*, 1:137. More generally, see Breen, *Lockean Moment*.
7. Bailyn, *Ideological Origins*, 188; Adams, *Papers of John Adams*, 1:127.
8. Quoted in Wood, *Creation of the American Republic*, 63.

9. Handlin and Handlin, *Popular Sources*, 202–379.

10. Lloyd and Lloyd, *Essential Bill of Rights*, 320, 325, 341.

11. Veit, *Creating the Bill of Rights*.

12. Ibid., 300.

13. Lloyd and Lloyd, *Essential Bill of Rights*, 327.

14. Foner, *Tom Paine*, 133.

15. Commons, *Documentary History of American Industrial Society*, 5:86, 6:94.

16. Thomas, *Liberator*, 173.

17. Buhle and Buhle, *Concise History of Woman Suffrage*, 94–95; Grimké, *Letters*, 108.

18. Slaughter-House Cases, 16 Wallace 110 (1873); Adkins v. Children's Hospital, 261 U.S. 561 (1923).

19. Quoted in Paul, *Conservative Crisis and the Rule of Law*, 81. See also Gordon, "Legal Thought and Legal Practice in the Age of American Enterprise, 1870–1920."

20. Wilson, *Mere Literature and Other Essays*, 198; Lowell, *Essays on Government*, 193, 183.

21. Lynd and Lynd, *Middletown*, 198.

22. Beard, *Politics*, 31.

23. Quoted in Gable, *Bull Moose Years*, 125.

24. Johnson, *National Party Platforms*, 1:175–82, 360–63.

25. Quoted in Commager, *American Mind*, 375.

26. Roosevelt, *Public Papers and Addresses*, 13:41–42.

27. Broderick and Meier, *Negro Protest Thought*, 48–52.

28. Foner, *Story of American Freedom;* Cmiel, "Recent History of Human Rights."

29. Quoted in Bruce, "The Inevitable Failure of the New Christian Right," 230.

30. Rawls, *Theory of Justice*.

31. Bowers v. Hardwick, 478 U.S. 186 (1986).

32. Marx, *Essential Writings*, 62–63.

Bibliography

Adams, John. *The Papers of John Adams,* ed. Robert J. Taylor et al. Cambridge, MA, 1977–.

Adkins v. Children's Hospital, 261 U.S. 561 (1923).

Bailyn, Bernard. *The Ideological Origins of the American Revolution.* Cambridge, MA, 1967.

Beard, Charles A. *Politics.* New York, 1908.

Bowers v. Hardwick, 478 U.S. 186 (1986).

Breen, T. H. *The Lockean Moment: The Language of Rights on the Eve of the American Revolution.* Oxford, 2001.

Broderick, Francis L., and August Meier, eds. *Negro Protest Thought in the Twentieth Century.* Indianapolis, 1965.

Bruce, Steve. "The Inevitable Failure of the New Christian Right." *Sociology of Religion* 55 (1994): 230.

Buhle, Mary Jo, and Paul Buhle, eds. *The Concise History of Woman Suffrage.* Urbana, IL, 1978.

Cmiel, Kenneth. "Recent History of Human Rights." *American Historical Review* 109 (2004): 117–35.

Commager, Henry S. *The American Mind: An Interpretation of American Thought and Character since the 1880s.* New Haven, CT, 1950.

Commons, John R., et al., eds. *A Documentary History of American Industrial Society.* Cleveland, 1910–11.

Foner, Eric. *The Story of American Freedom.* New York, 1998.

———. *Tom Paine and Revolutionary America.* New York, 1976.

Gable, John A. *The Bull Moose Years: Theodore Roosevelt and the Progressive Party.* Port Washington, NY, 1978.

Glendon, Mary Ann. *Rights Talk: The Impoverishment of Political Discourse.* New York, 1991.

Gordon, Robert W. "Legal Thought and Legal Practice in the Age of American Enterprise, 1870–1920." In *Professions and Professional Ideologies in America,* ed. Gerald L. Geison. Chapel Hill, NC, 1983.

Grimké, Angelina E. *Letters to Catherine E. Beecher.* Boston, 1838.

Handlin, Oscar and Mary, eds. *The Popular Sources of Political Authority: Documents on the Massachusetts Constitution of 1780.* Cambridge, MA, 1966.

Johnson, Donald B., ed. *National Party Platforms.* Urbana, IL, 1978.

Lloyd, Gordon, and Margie Lloyd, eds. *The Essential Bill of Rights: Original Arguments and Fundamental Doctrines.* Lanham, MD, 1998.

Lowell, A. Lawrence. *Essays on Government.* Boston, 1889.

Lynd, Robert S., and Helen Merrell Lynd. *Middletown.* New York, 1929.

Marx, Karl. *Karl Marx: The Essential Writings,* ed. Frederic L. Bender. 2d ed. Boulder, CO, 1986.

Merry, Sally Engle. *Getting Justice and Getting Even: Legal Conciousness among Working-Class Americans.* Chicago, 1990.

Paul, Arnold M. *Conservative Crisis and the Rule of Law: Attitudes of Bar and Bench, 1887–1895.* Ithaca, NY, 1960.

Primus, Richard A. *The American Language of Rights.* Cambridge, 1999.

Rawls, John. *A Theory of Justice.* Cambridge, MA, 1971.

Rodgers, Daniel T. *Contested Truths: Keywords in American Politics since Independence.* Cambridge, MA, 1998

Roosevelt, Franklin D. *The Public Papers and Addresses of Franklin D. Roosevelt,* ed. Samuel I. Rosenman. New York, 1938–50.

Slaughter-House Cases, 16 Wallace 110 (1873).

Thomas, John L. *The Liberator: William Lloyd Garrison.* Boston, 1963.

Veit, Helen E., et al., eds. *Creating the Bill of Rights: The Documentary Record from the First Congress.* Baltimore, 1991.

Wilson, Woodrow. *Mere Literature and Other Essays.* Boston, 1896.

Wood, Gordon S. *The Creation of the American Republic, 1776–1787.* Chapel Hill, NC, 1969.

The Diversity of Rights in Contemporary Ethical and Political Thought

LEIF WENAR AND STEPHEN MACEDO

Rights are the language in which Americans assert their weightiest political claims. The deepest disagreements in American history have been expressed in the language of rights: states' rights, property rights, labor rights, the rights of communities, and, increasingly, individual rights of all sorts. Moreover, the enormous changes in Americans' worldviews over three centuries have been matched by changes in the rights Americans have asserted and the grounds supporting their confident assertions. As this volume of essays argues, Americans' understanding of their entitlements has continually shifted, sometimes subtly and sometimes seismically. Whatever their ideological differences, Americans have used the language of rights as a channel for the moral outrage of the aggrieved, "a way of pushing back against novel forms of oppression."[1] "The language of rights," as Richard Primus has aptly written, "has proved extremely flexible, flexible enough to be used in the service of every significant agenda in American politics."[2]

How should we understand these changes? Does this fluidity suggest that the rhetoric of rights is altogether opportunistic: that any claim might be dressed up and trotted out as a rights claim? And does this plasticity mean that rights claims in general should not be taken seriously? There is no denying that rights can serve many purposes, and that assertions of rights need to be approached with a critical eye. Any and every political program—justifiable or not—is liable to lay claim to the moral urgency of "rights talk." If the Bill of Rights was originally formulated so as to protect local communities against newly invigorated national political institutions, and if in the minds of eighteenth-century Americans rights claims in general were more closely aligned than today with duties and with communal rather than individual interests, nevertheless, the idea of morally imperative limits or claims on power is an important point of continuity. Rights function not as requests or recommendations, but as moral demands.

We argue in this essay that the elasticity of rights claims, their capacity to serve many different purposes over time—a feature observed by the historians in this volume, and bemoaned by critics of rights—is philosophically defensible and, indeed, is increasingly the leading view among those who study rights. By necessity, the language of rights is historically malleable, and the contemporary shape of rights is complex and multifaceted.

Rights are not nowadays conceived of solely as negative in character, severed from duties, and claimable by individuals as opposed to groups. If ever true, this is simply not the dominant view of the last fifty years in American, let alone in Western, moral thought. Of course, a static, essentialist, and negative understanding of rights has long been popular in some philosophical and political circles in the United States.[3] Indeed, the last thirty years have witnessed a resurgence of claims of property rights and free-market individualism. Some regard this as a return to the "classic" conception of Americans' rights—of God-given, individualistic claims of property owners against interference by the state, unconnected with commensurate duties.[4] But it would be a mistake to accept the claim of today's libertarians as accurately representing some original idea of American constitutional rights. As Akhil Amar has shown, this "classic" conception of rights is itself more recent than often thought; it is the progeny not of the "first" Bill of Rights of the Founding era, but of the "second" Bill of Rights, whose ascendance spanned the aftermath of the Civil War up to the New Deal.[5] The ideas that buttressed laissez-faire economics in the United States—according to which property rights and individual freedom of contract were understood to impose severe limits on government power—owed as much or more to the Social Darwinist views of Herbert Spencer and William Graham Sumner as to the natural-rights philosophy of John Locke or the free-market liberalism of Adam Smith, ideas in fact not readily embraced in the United States until the early nineteenth century.[6] A revived Lockean natural-rights philosophy was one ingredient in the ideological mix after World War II, but it was in no way the predominant position.

This essay focuses on the practice and the theory of rights since the middle of the twentieth century. We discuss two sets of materials. On the one hand, we draw content for the discussion from the legal instrument that spurred a wide and potent political movement to establish human rights as practically efficacious global standards in the latter half of the twentieth century: the Universal Declaration of Human Rights (1948). On the other hand, we survey some of the recent English-language theoretical reflections on basic rights. We believe that this instrument and these moral reflections are important aspects of the legacy of the American Bill of Rights of 1791. The main contribution of this essay is to emphasize that the best understandings of contemporary rights claims do not accord with any strict and narrow philosophical formulations. The plasticity of rights claims—noted by the historians who precede us—is itself an important legacy of the Bill of Rights. It is a legacy embodied in the Universal Declaration of Human Rights, and a legacy increasingly embraced by philosophers of rights as a sign of robust health rather than incoherence.

The Universal Declaration and the American Debate over Rights

The first article of the Universal Declaration of Human Rights, adopted in 1948, reads: "All human beings are born free and equal in dignity and rights. They are endowed with reason and conscience, and should act toward one another in a spirit of brotherhood." This language echoes the universal declaration of rights that was among the first words written by Americans acting as a newly separate people: "All men are created equal . . . endowed by their Creator with certain unalienable Rights." The Universal Declaration is in its origins and spirit effectively an American document.[7] Eleanor Roosevelt worked ceaselessly to generate an international instrument based on her husband's "four essential human freedoms." Two of the three dominant intellectual forces behind the Universal Declaration's construction were American-trained: P. C. Chang was a Chinese ambassador who had studied at Columbia with John Dewey, and Charles Malik was a Lebanese professor at the American University in Beirut, who was educated at an American mission school and who studied with Alfred North Whitehead at Harvard. If the Universal Declaration seems familiar to Americans reading it for the first time, this is because it was crafted from conceptual resources drawn from within their diverse, sometimes contested, national inheritance.

The immediate stimulus for Roosevelt and her contemporaries to draft and enact the Universal Declaration was the shock of confronting Fascism in World War II. The framers were especially concerned that aggressive and avaricious dictators would again rise to power and thrive on menacing their neighbors. As Michael Ignatieff has observed, "It was Hitler the warmonger, not Hitler the architect of European extermination, who preoccupied the drafters."[8] In this way the Universal Declaration resembles Amar's "first Bill of Rights," being an attempt to secure communities (here peaceful nations) against distant powers (aggressive totalitarian empires).[9] However, there were also farsighted drafters who saw the potential for interpreting the Universal Declaration as analogous

to the "second Bill of Rights"—as a resource for all individuals everywhere to call on when they needed assistance from distant champions
(here the "international community") to resist the oppression of local
powers (here tyrannical national authorities).

Indeed, the Universal Declaration is intended to be promiscuous in
the interpretations it attracts. As a political document aimed at gaining
the widest possible acceptance, the Declaration self-consciously sets out a
menu of justificatory concepts from which different audiences can select
to suit their normative commitments. The drafters wanted to include something to please almost everyone, and in assembling a roster of concepts,
they caught a great many themes that would come to dominate the postwar American debate. In the Universal Declaration we find several proto-
answers to the questions about rights that dominated American moral
and political theory after the war: Why do people have basic rights, which
rights do they have, who is a rights holder, and what is the relation between rights and duties? We will draw from the Universal Declaration to
organize the often-conflicting answers that philosophers and practitioners have given to these questions over the past sixty years.

Here is its Preamble:

Universal Declaration of Human Rights
PREAMBLE

Whereas recognition of the inherent dignity and of the equal and inalienable rights of all members of the human family is the foundation of
freedom, justice and peace in the world,

Whereas disregard and contempt for human rights have resulted in bar-
barous acts which have outraged the conscience of mankind, and the advent of a world in which human beings shall enjoy freedom of speech and
belief and freedom from fear and want has been proclaimed as the highest
aspiration of the common people,

Whereas it is essential, if man is not to be compelled to have recourse, as
a last resort, to rebellion against tyranny and oppression, that human rights
should be protected by the rule of law,

Whereas it is essential to promote the development of friendly relations
between nations,

Whereas the peoples of the United Nations have in the Charter re-
affirmed their faith in fundamental human rights, in the dignity and worth
of the human person and in the equal rights of men and women and have
determined to promote social progress and better standards of life in larger
freedom,

Whereas Member States have pledged themselves to achieve, in cooperation with the United Nations, the promotion of universal respect for and observance of human rights and fundamental freedoms,

Whereas a common understanding of these rights and freedoms is of the greatest importance for the full realization of this pledge,

Now, therefore,

The General Assembly

proclaims

This Universal Declaration of Human Rights

as a common standard of achievement for all peoples and all nations, to the end that every individual and every organ of society, keeping this Declaration constantly in mind, shall strive by teaching and education to promote respect for these rights and freedoms and by progressive measures, national and international, to secure their universal and effective recognition and observance, both among the peoples of Member States themselves and among the peoples of territories under their jurisdiction.

Why Do People Have Basic Rights?

The Universal Declaration contains elements of several political theories that have contended since the Second World War to answer the most fundamental questions about rights. The first question addressed is why humans have the basic rights that they do.

Some theories prominent in American intellectual life have attempted to lessen the pressure of this "Why?" question simply by avoiding it. Robert Nozick's libertarian theory of basic rights, set forth in his well-known 1974 book, *Anarchy, State, and Utopia,* exemplifies this strategy of avoidance. Nozick's theory is in its content closest to the "classic" Lockean account of strong, prepolitical rights of life, liberty, and property. Yet it is, in the main, silent concerning the reasons we should think that individuals have the rights on that list. Beyond stirring prose linking individual inviolability to nearly absolute property rights, references to the philosophies of both Locke and Immanuel Kant, and an occasional gesture toward the benefits of capitalism, Nozick did not do much to justify the basic rights that he favored. His hope seems to have been that the intrinsic appeal of the normative framework he deployed would be so compelling that his audience would not be tempted to test the soundness of his assumptions. Nozick's radically anti-statist conclusions are, however, quite controversial (he portrayed taxation as akin to slavery), so many readers have wanted to know more about why humans have all and only the rights on his list.

Nozick gave us "libertarianism without foundations," as a critique put it, and the lack of deeper grounding has kept even Nozick's spectacular argumentation from attracting widespread assent.[10]

The postwar American theorists who actually have attempted to answer the "Why?" question fall into five main groups. The first two groups emphasize different (though potentially complementary) ways of understanding natural rights by elaborating different aspects of Locke's argument.

NATURAL RIGHTS I: DIVINE CREATION. These authors emphasize the thick strands of natural-rights language in the Universal Declaration, such as the passages in the Preamble and Article 1 that speak of the inherent dignity and worth of the human person, and that declare all people to be endowed with reason and conscience, so that each person is owed respect as a free and equal being. The grounding theory suggested by these statements is that there is something in the nature of humans—in their constitutions or their distinctive attributes—that explains their having the basic rights that they do. Rights are natural to humans in something of the same way that gravity is natural to matter, and fully formed adult humans are owed respect for the full range of basic human rights.

This first group of theorists emphasize that a religious grounding for these rights is essential. In this they accord with many of their fellow citizens, for much of popular American discourse about rights—far more than in Europe—asserts a religious grounding for natural rights. The Declaration of Independence speaks of men being "endowed by their Creator with certain unalienable Rights."[11] Similarly, George W. Bush in his second inaugural address asserted that, "From the day of our founding, we have proclaimed that every man and woman on this earth has rights and dignity and matchless value because they bear the image of the maker of heaven and earth."[12]

Most contemporary philosophers would say that the human capacity for reason is what distinguishes humans from other mammals and makes adults of certain levels of cognitive abilities possessors of the full array of basic human rights. But there are exceptions to this broad consensus, including, recently, Jeremy Waldron. Waldron has argued that one of Locke's accounts of human equality—that God made men capable of reasoned and responsible self-direction—is the best one available in the political tradition, and that the strength of that account depends on rights holders' relationship to God. In Waldron's account the religious element is crucial: the possession of a degree of rationality holds central significance in Locke's theory because it allows us to understand God and God's law and to relate these to our own conduct. "There is no reason for the atheist to recognize such a threshold, and there is no reason to believe that he could defend it if he did."[13] For Waldron, without God's law, human equality is much less securely grounded.

It is not at all clear, however, why we need find this argument compelling. For one thing, the possession of a measure of reflective capacity is obviously an important ground of human equality and dignity: normal adult humans can develop conceptions of their own good and recognize others as capable of the same. Humans are moral creatures capable of self-reflection, and capable of complex emotions like resentment. The moral significance of the normal human capacities for reason, self-consciousness, and sophisticated communication is denied by virtually no one—even those who think we should treat animals far better than we do.[14] In addition, there are simply no powerful arguments for withholding the most basic human rights from normal adult human beings, at least under reasonably favorable conditions. There are plenty of arguments about which rights are basic and, at the margins, who has rights (e.g., fetuses, humans who have experienced brain death), and also about the conditions, if any, under which even basic rights (e.g., the right not to be tortured) might be suspended or overridden. But the invocation of a religious basis for rights does not help us settle any of these controversies; religious people are on both sides of all of these issues. We think that Waldron has simply assumed—without argument—a partisan account of what it means for rights to be securely grounded.

NATURAL RIGHTS II: MAN'S RATIONAL NATURE. Philosophers have been much less willing than American politicians to accommodate God in their justifications of rights. Few postwar theorists would agree with James Hutson that to separate rights from Christian norms is likely to divorce rights from morality (Waldron, e.g., would not say that).[15] Thus, we find a second group of theorists that picks up the other aspect of Locke's theory, resting the basis of human dignity on man's capacity for reflective self-direction.

Theorizing about natural rights as based in human rationality has flowed mostly in the Kantian tradition of the categorical imperative, which requires that rational beings be treated as ends in themselves and never merely as means. Warren Quinn exemplified the modern Kantian derivation of human rights from human nature in stating: "A person is constituted by his body and his mind. They are parts or aspects of him. For that very reason, it is fitting that he have primary say over what may be done to them. . . . Any arrangement that denied him that say would be a grave indignity. In giving him this authority, morality recognizes his existence as an individual with ends of his own—an independent *being*. Since that is what he is, he deserves this recognition."[16]

Here, the general injunction to give each individual primary say over his body and mind follows straight on from the individual's constitution as a self-guided, embodied, and thinking being. Frances Kamm, following Quinn, has explained specific rights—here, free speech—in the same mode: "The right to speak may simply be the only appropriate way to treat people with minds of their own and the capacity to use means to express [them]."[17] The appeal to human nature to ground rights is straightforward here, although the skeptic may wish to ask again just why is it "fitting" or "appropriate" that beings like this should have rights like that. That skeptical question has not received a deeper answer in this kind of modern Kantian theory of rights; perhaps it does not need one. Beyond a few infertile exceptions, theorists of this school have not attempted to go further in searching for a more systematic reply.[18]

CONSEQUENTIALIST JUSTIFICATIONS FOR RIGHTS. The third principal approach to answering the "Why rights?" question contrasts markedly with the natural-rights approach and in the past sixty years has been a good deal more lively. This is the consequentialist approach to basic rights, which continues the English utilitarian tradition of J. S. Mill, Henry Sidgwick, and Francis Edgeworth.[19] The Preamble of the Universal Declaration points toward a consequentialist approach when it states that human rights are the foundation of peace in the world; that they are essential to promoting friendly relations between nations; that observing them promotes social progress and better standards of life; and that disregarding them results in barbarity and rebellion. Here, essential rights are justified, not because they are suited to the nature of individuals, but rather because respect for these rights will result in maximal human flourishing.

To accommodate this different approach to justification it is useful to switch from the terminology of "natural rights" to that of "human rights." The new terminology of human rights commits one only to the thought that all humans have rights and not, as the old terminology suggests, to their having these rights because of something about their nature. For consequentialist moral theorists, rights are justified by their effects: they do not simply flow from the attributes of their bearers.

In America, the utilitarian approach has been remarkably vibrant since the Second World War, taking over large parts of the legal academy and establishing itself firmly in judicial reasoning about rights (especially, but not only, concerning the rights of "private law": property, contracts, and torts). The "law and economics" movement, as it is called, has enjoyed several decades of innovation and growth under the leadership of able and fearless exponents, including Ronald Coase, Gary Becker, Guido Calabresi, Richard Posner, and Richard Epstein.[20]

Whereas utilitarians measure rights against their standard of "maximum utility," adherents of the law and economics approach aim at "wealth maximization" and use the tools of economic analysis to determine exactly which rights will best engender optimal social outcomes. They have used their formal techniques to explain why free-speech rights are efficient while slavery would not be. (They have also delighted in being provocative, suggesting, for example, that more aggregate well-being might be produced if we allowed human organs and even babies to be bought and sold.) Their justificatory trajectory pushes these legal economists perhaps not surprisingly toward laissez-faire public policies concerning both market and personal rights. As Posner has put it, "The only basis for interference with economic and personal liberty is such a serious failure of the market to operate that the wealth of society can be increased by public coercion, which is itself costly."[21] These legal theorists carry on the tradition of classical liberalism, though their approach is often more narrowly economic than the greatest of classical liberals, such as Adam Smith.[22] And these legal economists are far from being pure libertarians: if the collective good requires government regulation or a restraint on freedom, many have proved quite willing to argue that brief.

Natural-rights theorists see rights as incidents of human nature, and so as pre-political constraints on legitimate political arrangements. Consequentialist theorists regard no right as having that sort of priority; all rights are instrumental, and any given right can become undeserving of our endorsement if circumstances change radically. Both approaches insist upon the authority of critical normative standpoints outside of political practice: in the one case human nature, in the other a utilitarian calculus, serves as the authoritative yardstick to gauge morality's demands. Both views offer a philosophical foundation for moral judgment, and each provides an account of political morality grounded in philosophical truths.[23]

RIGHTS WITHOUT PHILOSOPHY? In the 1980s a variety of philosophers and political theorists questioned the idea that judgments of political morality should be seen as depending on a prior philosophical conception of human nature or the nature of morality. Michael Oakeshott, a British conservative, was a forerunner of this line of thought with his insistence that political action and political judgment are always embedded within a particular tradition. The error of modern politics and much modern political philosophy is its "rationalism": its overreliance on self-conscious ideologies and rationally formulated principles that little attend to time and place. In Oakeshott's phrase, politics is properly the "pursuit of intimations."[24] Richard Rorty, Alasdair MacIntyre, and Michael Walzer, among others, have also advanced the idea that abstract political and moral philosophies—rationally constructed systems of thought—fail to provide useful guidance to political practice. MacIntyre argued that healthy political judgments are necessarily embedded in inherited practices.[25] Rorty argued that moral justification in politics "is mostly a matter of historical narratives . . . rather than philosophical metanarratives."[26] Walzer urged that political criticism is the work of "connected social critics" rather than academic armchair philosophers.[27]

This miscellaneous collection of criticisms of important contemporary moral and political theories provides several valuable reminders. Actual human beings are rarely moved by philosophical arguments as such. And it is certainly true that moral insight comes from many sources, including reflections on history, social movements, literature, investigative journalism, social science, and the arts, not to mention personal experiences of all sorts. In general, however, these lines of criticism seem to neglect the ways in which ordinary political practices are informed by expectations of reason-giving and articulate criticism. Principled political criticism is an important aspect of political practice across much of the world, characterizing the arguments that take place in courts most particularly, but not only there. We expect public actors at all levels—political parties and legislators, presidents, agency officials, and city councilors—to lay out the grounds for the proposals they advance and to defend them in public as the soundest interpretations of our basic political values: as the best versions of our shared ideals of freedom, equality, and the common good.[28]

The most basic claims in political morality need not, however, be grounded in any one particular account of philosophical or religious truth. We have already seen that the claims asserted in the Preamble of the Universal Declaration are compatible with a variety of deeper, or foundational, sources. The point is that people operating from many different ultimate philosophical and religious standpoints may converge on similar principles of political morality. Indeed, given the great plurality of philosophical and religious traditions in the world, it is essential that any human-rights regime that seeks to furnish a common standard of political legitimacy for all the world's peoples must be able to fit into a wide variety of deeper foundations. Given the job that we want human rights to do in the world—to serve as universal standards setting bounds on the acceptable conduct of all states—it would be self-defeating to base human rights on a particular philosophical or religious theory, for no one theory is capable of commanding the assent of the peoples of the world (none, for that matter, could command even the assent of all Americans). As Amy Gutmann has aptly put it, "The several foundations of human rights, taken together, are likely to be agreeable to more people than any single foundation, and no single foundation has a monopoly on reasonable claims to be made in its favor."[29]

These considerations point in the direction of a fifth approach to the "Why?" question, one that sees rights as neither pre-political nor post-political, but as broadly formulated and justified in light of a conception of their practical political role.

PUBLIC JUSTIFICATION AND REFLECTIVE EQUILIBRIUM. John Rawls's account of basic political rights exemplifies this fifth approach. Like the natural-rights theorists, Rawls described rights as appropriate to persons characterized in a certain way. Yet Rawls's conception of the person is a political conception: it is the citizen of a modern liberal state. The familiar civil and political rights, Rawls said, are the most defensible fundamental rules of political morality for persons understood as free and equal citizens who wish to cooperate with their fellow citizens on fair terms. Basic rights spring from a certain political self-conception, and this self-conception, Rawls believed, is one of the most powerful ideals in a richly diverse American political tradition.

Asked to go deeper, to explain why, ultimately, individuals should assume this political conception as their own, Rawls responded with a principled demurral. The reason is captured in a phrase in the Universal Declaration that contains the germ of Rawls's view: ". . . a common understanding of these rights and freedoms is of the greatest importance." The justifiability and stability of a scheme for enforcing rights rests on those who are bound to observe those rights having a common understanding of what the scheme of rights will come to in political terms. Rights need to be justified—critically justified in light of the best that is to be said for and against them—but the justifications should be articulated in terms that can be widely appreciated by persons from a broad range of world faiths and cultures. Rawls's vision is that adherents of diverging spiritual and philosophical views will form an overlapping consensus that will support the "common understanding" of basic political rights and justice. And this may not be implausible. The pope adopted the dignitarian language of free and equal persons enjoying basic rights in his encyclical *Pacem in Terris* (1963), and the Catholic rationale for supporting these ideas and rights is just one of many rationales that citizens in a pluralistic society might accept.[30]

What Rawls had to say about the deepest justification for each individual is more formal: that in the ideal case the political conception that each person favors will be part of that person's "reflective equilibrium." Reflection on political morality is a process that begins not with the construction and defense of a philosophical standpoint outside of politics, but with those "considered convictions" for which we think there is most reason for confidence (e.g., that religious intolerance and racial discrimination are unjust).[31] Each of us is fairly confident that we adhere to these principles sincerely, and not out of bias or self-interest. We then ask what broader principles and ideas help to elaborate and render coherent the intuitions underlying these and other particular convictions of political morality. We work back and forth from both sides, seeking to accommodate our considered judgments and intuitions about justice within a scheme of coherent and defensible principles, sometimes revising on one side or the other, so that the full scheme seems most defensible. The aim is not simply to smooth out certain inconsistencies, but to examine critically the articulated principles in light of all available alternatives, seeking the account of political morality that is strongest overall.[32] Rawls believed that his favored conception of society as a scheme of fair cooperation among free and equal citizens, and the principles that he derived from this conception, would be plausible to many people as central organizing ideas for achieving greater reflective equilibrium about what constitutes a just social order.

The survey above shows that the answers that American theorists have offered since the Second World War to the question of why humans should enjoy basic rights have been quite varied. Natural-rights views (either religious or Kantian) have maintained a persistent presence in philosophy departments and seminaries. Consequentialist approaches have gained a great deal of territory among judges and jurists wrestling with specific issues of policy. The Rawlsian approach—roughly speaking—has come increasingly to dominate the discussions of political theorists, but also of many law professors. A growing tendency common to all of these schools has been to avoid reaching for abstruse theological or metaphysical doctrines in attempting to find an answer to the question "Why rights?" It is quite unlikely that we will find an American Hegel justifying basic rights by their place within an all-embracing philosophical *Weltan-*

schauung. Rights are an important political practice; they furnish public standards for the acceptable use of power and widely accepted protections for individuals and communities. For rights to do the work we expect them to do in the world, foundational pluralism seems to work best.

Which Rights Do We Have?

The first specific rights proclaimed in the Universal Declaration are in Article 3: "Everyone has the right to life, liberty and security of person." The succeeding articles add on familiar prohibitions against slavery and arbitrary arrest, the standard guarantees of free association and assembly, and familiar endorsements of free thought, conscience, and religious practice. The libertarian tradition of negative individual rights, represented in postwar American thought by Nozick, Milton Friedman, and F.A. Hayek, had no trouble getting its rights on the list. The question for the postwar era has been whether additional rights—and especially those securing Roosevelt's "freedom from want"—should also be added to the list as well. As a matter of historical fact, the national delegates who drafted the Universal Declaration hardly argued about the inclusion of "welfare" rights such as the right to an adequate standard of living (Article 25). And many of the world's newer constitutions contain a variety of positive rights. The same consensus cannot be found in recent American intellectual debate. Throughout the liberal ascendancy in the third quarter of the twentieth century and the conservative or libertarian resurgence beginning in the fourth quarter, the rights of citizens to state provision have been rarely been off the public or the intellectual agenda.

One locus of contention in these debates has been the right of private property. On the libertarian right, Nozick argued that taxation is on a par with slavery, Friedman that robust capitalism is necessary to sustain freedom in a democracy, and Hayek that the main reason to grant welfare provision to the disadvantaged is to keep them from making desperate raids on the property of the well-off. On the liberal left, by contrast, there is agreement that property rights are crucial for human flourishing and freedom—but also that property rights are so important that, as Waldron has put it, "everyone must have property."[33] The Great Society programs that work toward this liberal ideal are well known; some academics have proposed even more progressive schemes, such as an assured basic income[34] or a large, onetime grant for each citizen upon coming of age.[35]

This debate across the political spectrum is poorly cast in terms of the contrast between "civil and political rights" on the one hand and "economic and social rights" on the other. Conservatives and libertarians have attempted to portray civil and political rights as "real" rights, while characterizing economic and social rights as expressing merely "aspirations" for a good society. However, property rights are the main point of contention between Right and Left—and property rights belong more naturally in the "economic" than in the "civil and political" category. A better division of the terrain separates out those who support "positive" as well as "negative" rights. "Negative" rights are the classic rights against interference: rights to the free enjoyment of life and property, and the unregulated liberty of contract. "Positive" rights go beyond the right to be left alone: positive rights require provision of specific goods and services. The Universal Declaration's rights to provision of unemployment benefits, medical care, and free education are canonical examples of the positive rights that many liberals endorse.

It is worth noting that America's politics of rights has never been about securing negative rights only. The rights to habeas corpus and procedural due process are not negative rights: they furnish positive claims, and require that the political community should establish and maintain fair, predictable, and competent courts of law. The right to vote requires the maintenance of fair elections and a wider political process. As Stephen Holmes and Cass Sunstein put it in the context of citizens' rights to state enforcement of their entitlements, all rights—even those to life, liberty, and property—are ultimately positive.[36] A politics of rights requires the creation of institutions and an appropriate prevailing mind-set among citizens. As Henry Shue and others have emphasized, a politics of rights today is often understood as being about securing the basic interests of free and equal individuals against possible abuses by powerful public and private actors.[37] Individual and collective interests are complexly combined in the modern politics of rights protection, as are negative immunities, positive entitlements, and duties of various sorts.

A "purist" libertarian position on negative rights cannot dodge the objection that the state is expected by many to provide positive protection for even negative rights. A theoretical propensity toward negative rights does have, however, at least one virtue: parsimony. One feature of the postwar political debates has been what has been described by many as a "rights explosion."[38] The flexibility of "rights talk" to express nearly any concern, combined with the privileging of rights in American political discourse, has resulted in a vast proliferation of rights assertions in the public domain—including many rather dubious ones. Article 24 of the Universal Declaration notoriously proposes that all humans have "the right to rest and leisure including . . . periodic holidays with pay." Other fragments of the explosion have been the bizarre assertion of the right of unborn children with birth defects not to exist, of the right of every American to a good pair of glasses, and even the difficult-to-specify rights of each person to sunshine and "a sex break."[39]

It would be fruitless and likely impossible to organize this profusion by trying to impose a rigid conceptual sorting system, such as "negative but not positive." Moreover, it is one thing to assert a right, and another thing actually to secure its protection. In sorting out the serious question of which rights should be recognized, there is no avoiding fundamental normative questions that require moral judgment. If rights are now about securing fundamental human interests against the abuses or neglect of the powerful, it is hardly surprising that as political societies become richer and more capable, the list of fundamental guarantees continues to grow. All sorts of abominations—including infant abandonment—were tolerated in those millennia of human history when dire poverty was the rule. It would be strange to regard it as a conceptual confusion when increasingly affluent societies raise the floor below which no one is allowed to fall.

Who Is a Right Holder?

In the debate over "Which rights?" there is a general consensus that the progressive left has had more brilliant theorists but the conservative right has been more successful in the political arena. When faced with a liberal argument that the vulnerable need the protection afforded by some novel right, conservatives have tended to argue mostly strategically: the interests of even the most vulnerable, broadly understood, will be better secured if the novel right is denied to them. (Conservatives have tended to argue, for example, that a very lightly regulated market regime—instead of an enforced right to redistribution—is the best way to maximize the incomes of the poorest.) These kinds of arguments have had a good deal of appeal to the generally pragmatic and center-right American public; whether they are demonstrably sound is of course a matter of cases and debate.

By contrast, on questions concerning who is a right holder, the progressives have generally had the better of the political battles. In particular, the postwar era has seen a great expansion of the legal rights enjoyed by women and racial minorities. Nor were these simply formal rights against discrimination in housing, employment, and business—as important as such protections are. Racial minorities gained much stronger protections for their rights to vote and even some measure of affirmative action in higher education and awards of government contracts. Women—though narrowly losing the Equal Rights Amendment—won significant victories in areas from divorce law to sexual harassment. Moreover, several groups previously unheard in the public forum—from gays to the aged—raised banners of rights to protest against discriminatory treatment and abuse. Few could have imagined forty years ago that gay marriage would so quickly make it to the cutting edge of rights claims.

Nor has Americans' generosity concerning right holders been limited even to human beings. As late as 1954, H. L. A. Hart could write that non-human animals "are not spoken or thought of as having rights."[40] Today, a well-established animal rights movement, whose central figure is the philosopher Peter Singer, has put hundreds of anti-cruelty laws on the statute books and is working toward securing rights, for at least "higher-order" mammals, not to be eaten or imprisoned in zoos.

Yet the biggest challenge to the nineteenth- and twentieth-century picture of rights as individual protections against interference has been the extension (or re-extension) of rights to groups. Even when women gained rights against, say, workplace discrimination, they were still ascribed rights as individuals who happen to be members of some ascriptive group. As previous chapters have shown to have been true in earlier American history, since World War II rights have been ascribed again to groups themselves, and this with a minimum of scholarly fuss.

The most striking, and now best-established, postwar ascription of rights to groups was also the least innovative. The Genocide Convention was unanimously passed, with strong American support, by the U.N. General Assembly in 1948 (although because of concerns over enforcement, it took the U.S. Senate almost forty years more to ratify a weakened version of it). The convention ascribes national, ethnic, racial, and religious groups the right not to suffer acts committed with intent to destroy them. Here, we see an older negative right against interference transposed so that the right holder is not a single person but rather a group. This right of groups to be safe from genocidal attack is now strongly affirmed by all sides on the American political scene (even though, as Samantha Power has shown, the United States has never actually intervened to stop a genocide in progress).[41]

Another and more robust set of group rights has been revived in North American political discourse, as a domestic reflection of the decolonization movement that swept the postwar world and that increased the number of U.N. member states from fifty-eight when the Universal Declaration was signed, to almost two hundred today. This is the corporate right of a people to self-government that Barry Shain shows earlier in this volume to have been central to the logic of the Declaration of Independence,[42] and that is now asserted by minority national groups and, especially, indigenous populations. Canada has led the way in both theory and practice here, with Will Kymlicka as the most eloquent theoretician of minority group rights, and vast areas of formerly sovereign Canadian territory turned into semiautonomous, native-controlled regions.[43] The United States has followed more cautiously on this path, yet has also granted limited territorial and economic group rights to tribes of native peoples.

Rights and Duties

The essays in this volume suggest that rights are nowadays considerably far more loosely linked to correlative duties than was once the case. We think there is an important element of truth here, but that this thesis should not be exaggerated.

By logic, every claim-right of a right holder correlates to at least one duty in someone else: a worker's right to be paid his wages, for example, correlates to his employer's duty to pay these wages. In general, it is common to say nowadays that there is no logical requirement that right holders must themselves be duty-bearers. Students of American history would seem to be correct in arguing that we have come a long way from the colonial America that Gordon Wood describes, in which "every private person in the society had an obligation to help govern the realm commensurate with his social rank,"[44] and all rights, corporate and individual, were correlatively tied to duties. The Universal Declaration, for example, contains only an anemic article on citizens' duties (that "everyone has duties to the community in which alone the free and full development of his personality is possible").[45] A recent UNESCO-sponsored "Universal Declaration of Human Duties and Responsibilities" made no progress in this area. Even Rawls's theory of justice, the most famous of the past half century, seems to require of citizens few duties beyond obeying the law, paying their taxes, serving, if called, on juries or in the armed forces, and occasionally voting.[46]

The impression of the modern rights-bearing but duty-free citizen is, however, far from representing the whole truth. We should not mistake a change in content for a simple decline. As our understanding of the content of basic rights claims has shifted, so too has our understanding of citizens' correlative duties: our expectations about the virtues that citizens ought to cultivate and that society ought to promote. Duty and virtue have not simply fallen off the map as correlates to rights. Many contemporary rights are joined to duties to perform certain actions. Americans may believe that the right to drive an automobile is the foundation of nearly every other right, but we are far less tolerant of drunk driving than we once were. Home and real property ownership remains widespread, but zoning laws require property owners to guard against degrading the environment, harming endangered species, and even causing certain kinds of offense or economic damage to their neighbors (e.g., by painting their houses very bright colors).

Many duties and obligations associated with parenthood and family life have been beefed up as well. No doubt, the duty of children—even adult children—to defer to their parents' authority has been attenuated; family relations are far more egalitarian than they once were.[47] Arguably, society is more willing to intervene in the affairs of family life—relations between parents and children and also relations between spouses—than was once the case. Parents have rights to raise and form their children, but they also have many duties to care for and educate their children. The modern "children's rights" movement is partly about using the law to heighten awareness of the duties of adults toward children.[48] Modern feminism, similarly, has been concerned with arguing against the notion that family life should be understood as a realm of "private rights" shielded from the inspection of the political community. In effect, we can understand one prominent strand of modern feminism as standing for the proposition that social and economic institutions should be redesigned so as to bring about women's empowerment as equals: that is, that the political community has a collective duty to intervene, protect, and empower women as equals capable of participating in public and private life.

With respect to civic life, it is possible that the language of obligations and duties has declined, but the only thing that is certain is that we think of civic duties less in terms of social rank than we once did ("my station and its duties"). The language of civic duty and obligation has been democratized, but it remains prominent. Nothing is more common than to bemoan the lack of civic virtue in America: we decry ordinary Americans' apathy and disengagement, and there are very many scholarly and practical educational programs devoted to promoting greater civic engagement and civic competence. "National service" programs have been supported by the current as well as the previous two presidential administrations. One would have to be politically deaf to miss the frequency of expressions of anxiety about (supposedly) declining civic virtue. We would also note that with respect to political office holding, our standards in regard to conflicts of interest and corruption have risen appreciably.

A complex pluralistic society cannot support the vast range of rights it aspires to guarantee without the active engagement of its citizenry. Living well among people who look different, think differently, and subscribe to religious and moral values different from one's own often takes a great deal of effort. The language of "duties" may be less apt than the language of "virtues" here. Using the latter, we can say that modern citizenship requires tolerance and civility, patience, an effort to search for sources of solidarity, a willingness to join with others in upholding and defending just institutions, and a readiness to accept others' words in good faith. Political elites often exercise moral leadership in modern mass democracies. But if rights are secured and progressively extended, it is, ultimately, because they eventually gain the support of ordinary citizens. And so it is clear in the work of the most prominent liberal political philosophers of the last half century, including John Rawls and Ronald Dworkin—precisely where one might expect to find rights to the exclusion of duties—that citizens are expected to exercise their share of political power by participating with others in a process of public justification.[49]

Conclusion

Americans' understandings of rights have changed over the course of time. There was no simple original "Lockean consensus" in the public mind at the time of the framing of the Constitution and the Bill of Rights. Nor is there now, in the new millennium, any simple consensus on who has which rights and why. Americans have always used the fluid language of rights to express their most urgent demands that power must be limited, and that certain interests must be secured for those under the umbrella of particular rights claims. Today Americans reach for the language of rights to support political reforms at all points along the political spectrum, and they do so from a wide range of perspectives, from the religious to the militantly secular. The language of rights in America has never been the language of a single group or movement. Rather, rights have been the language in which Americans have conducted their vigorous, often fractious debates about how to lead their common life together.

Notes

1. See Richard Primus, "An Introduction to the Nature of American Rights," in this volume.
2. Ibid.
3. See, e.g., Barnett, *Restoring the Lost Constitution*.

4. Unconnected, we might say, with "perfect" duties, that is, duties enforceable by the state.

5. See Akhil Reed Amar, "The Creation, Reconstruction, and Interpretation of the Bill of Rights," in this volume.

6. There are many accounts of the rise and fall of laissez-faire constitutionalism, sometimes referred to by the name of the leading case of that era, *Lochner v. New York.* See, e.g., Gillman, *Constitution Besieged;* for a contemporary defense of libertarian constitutionalism, see Epstein, *Takings.* For the classic account of the centrality of Locke to the American political tradition, see Hartz, *Liberal Tradition in America;* and for a contrary view, Smith, *Civic Ideals.*

7. See Glendon, *World Made New;* Lauren, *Evolution of International Human Rights.*

8. Ignatieff, "Human Rights, Sovereignty, and Intervention," 53.

9. See Akhil Reed Amar, "The Creation, Reconstruction, and Interpretation of the Bill of Rights," in this volume.

10. Nagel, "Libertarianism without Foundations," 137–49.

11. The Constitution is virtually silent on the subject of religion. When asked why the framers did not mention God in the Constitution, Alexander Hamilton replied— with a grin no doubt—"We forgot." Chernow, *Alexander Hamilton,* 235.

12. Bush, "Second Inaugural Address."

13. Waldron, *God, Locke, and Equality,* 81.

14. See, e.g., Singer, *Animal Liberation;* and more recently, Waal, *Primates and Philosophers.*

15. See James H. Hutson, "The Emergence of the Modern Concept of a Right in America: The Contribution of Michel Villey," in this volume.

16. Quinn, *Morality and Action,* 170.

17. Kamm, "Rights," 10. See also Nagel, "Concealment and Exposure."

18. An exception is Gewirth, *Reason and Morality.*

19. Utilitarianism is one species of consequentialism. Consequentialist justifications of rights need not be limited to a narrow utilitarian or economistic version of the values to be promoted; as Philip Pettit has explained, there are two separate parts to the relevant moral theories: the first is an account of value or values, and the second is an account of the proper stance toward those values, whether to honor or respect them or to promote their realization overall; see Pettit, "Consequentialism." For the purpose of this essay, we leave these important issues aside and focus on the utilitarian version of consequentialism.

20. For several of the classic papers by leading theorists, see Katz, *Foundations of the Economic Approach to Law.*

21. Posner, *Economics of Justice,* 78.

22. On Smith's thought, see Rothschild's *Economic Sentiments.*

23. See Wenar, "Rights."

24. Oakeshott, "Rationalism in Politics."

25. MacIntyre, *After Virtue.*

26. Rorty, "Postmodernist Bourgeois Liberalism," 586–87.

27. Walzer, "Philosophy and Democracy"; Walzer, *Company of Critics.*

28. For a critique of these critics and a defense of the role of public justification in our political practices, see Macedo, *Liberal Virtues.*

29. Gutmann, "Introduction."

30. The reasons justifying basic rights often need not go very deep because the ques-

tion is whether states can have good reasons for failing to guarantee rights claims. Those who abuse the most basic rights—the prohibitions on torture, genocide, etc.—typically deny doing so. Plausible defenses of these practices as normal instruments of governance are lacking. At the margins of course, there are real controversies: Are certain "coercive" interrogation techniques torture? Do "ticking time bomb" scenarios constitute real exceptions? These controversies are conducted in terms that are accessible to a wide variety of religious, philosophical, and cultural traditions.

31. Rawls, *Theory of Justice*, 19.

32. This is the idea of "wide reflective equilibrium"; see ibid., 48–51.

33. Waldron, *Right to Private Property*, 10.

34. Parijs, *Real Freedom for All.*

35. Ackerman and Alstott, *Stakeholder Society.*

36. Holmes and Sunstein, *Costs of Rights,* 46.

37. Shue, *Basic Rights.*

38. See Wellman, *Proliferation of Rights.*

39. Berger, *Rights*, 33.

40. Hart, *Essays on Bentham*, 185.

41. Power, *Problem from Hell.*

42. See Barry Alan Shain, "Rights Natural and Civil in the Declaration of Independence," in this volume.

43. Kymlicka, *Multicultural Citizenship.*

44. See Gordon S. Wood, "The History of Rights in Early America," in this volume.

45. Universal Declaration of Human Rights, art. 29.

46. Rawls, *Theory of Justice.*

47. For one interesting historical account, emphasizing the influence of John Locke's seventeenth-century educational writings and eighteenth-century novels on changes that continued into the nineteenth century and beyond, see Fliegelman, *Prodigals and Pilgrims.*

48. See, e.g., the essays gathered in Macedo and Young, *Child, Family, and the State.*

49. For an account of the importance of civic virtue to liberalism, see Macedo, *Liberal Virtues.*

Bibliography

Ackerman, Bruce, and Anne Alstott. *The Stakeholder Society.* New Haven, CT, 2000.

Barnett, Randy E. *Restoring the Lost Constitution.* Princeton, NJ, 2003.

Berger, Nan. *Rights: A Handbook for People under Age.* Harmondsworth, UK, 1974.

Bush, George. "Second Inaugural Address," Accessed online at http://www.washingtonpost.com/wp-dyn/articles/A23747-2005Jan20.html.

Chernow, Ron. *Alexander Hamilton.* New York, 2004.

Epstein, Richard A. *Takings: Private Property and the Power of Eminent Domain.* Cambridge, MA, 1986.

Fliegelman, Jay. *Prodigals and Pilgrims: The American Revolution Against Patriarchal Authority, 1750–1800.* Cambridge, 1985.

Gewirth, Alan. *Reason and Morality.* Chicago, 1978.

Gillman, Howard. *The Constitution Besieged: The Rise and Demise of Lochner Era Police Powers Jurisprudence.* Durham, 1995.

Glendon, Mary Ann. *A World Made New: Eleanor Roosevelt and the Universal Declaration of Human Rights.* New York, 2002.

Gutmann, Amy. "Introduction" to *Human Rights as Politics and Idolatry,* by Michael Ignatieff. Princeton, 2001.

Hart, H. L. A. *Essays on Bentham.* Oxford, 1982.

Hartz, Louis. *The Liberal Tradition in America.* 2d Harvest ed. New York, 1991.

Holmes, Stephen, and Cass Sunstein. *The Costs of Rights: Why Liberty Depends on Taxes.* New York, 1999.

Ignatieff, Michael. "Human Rights, Sovereignty, and Intervention." In *Human Rights, Human Wrongs,* ed. Nicholas Owen, 49–88. Oxford, 2002.

Kamm, Frances. "Rights." In *The Oxford Handbook of Jurisprudence and Philosophy of Law,* ed. Jules Coleman and Scott Shapiro, 476–513. Oxford, 2002.

Katz, Avery, ed. *Foundations of the Economic Approach to Law.* Oxford, 1998.

Kymlicka, Will. *Multicultural Citizenship: A Liberal Theory of Minority Rights.* Oxford, 1995.

Lauren, Paul. *The Evolution of International Human Rights.* Philadelphia, 1998.

Macedo, Stephen. *Liberal Virtues: Citizenship, Virtue, and Community in Liberal Constitutionalism.* Oxford, 1990.

Macedo, Stephen, and Iris Marion Young, eds. *Child, Family, and the State.* NOMOS: Yearbook of the American Society for Political and Legal Philosophy, vol. 44. New York, 2003.

MacIntyre, Alasdair. *After Virtue: A Study in Moral Theory.* London, 1997.

Nagel, Thomas. "Concealment and Exposure." *Philosophy and Public Affairs* 27:1 (1998): 3–30.

———. "Libertarianism without Foundations." In *Other Minds,* 137–43. Oxford, 1995.

Oakeshott, Michael. "Rationalism in Politics." In *Rationalism in Politics and Other Essays,* 5–42. London, 1991.

Parijs, Philippe van. *Real Freedom for All: What (If Anything) Can Justify Capitalism?* New York, 1998.

Pettit, Philip, ed. *Consequentialism.* Aldershot, NH, 1993.

Posner, Richard. *The Economics of Justice.* Cambridge, MA, 1981.

Power, Samantha. *A Problem from Hell: America and the Age of Genocide.* New York, 2002.

Quinn, Warren. *Morality and Action.* Cambridge, 1993.

Rawls, John. *A Theory of Justice.* Cambridge, MA, 1971.

Rorty, Richard. "Postmodernist Bourgeois Liberalism." *Journal of Philosophy* 80 (1983): 583–89.

Rothschild, Emma. *Economic Sentiments: Adam Smith, Condorcet, and the Enlightenment.* Cambridge, MA, 2002.

Shue, Henry. *Basic Rights: Subsistence, Affluence, and US Foreign Policy.* Princeton, NJ, 1996.

Singer, Peter. *Animal Liberation.* London, 2001.

Smith, Rogers M. *Civic Ideals: Conflicting Visions of Citizenship in U.S. History.* New Haven, CT, 1999.

United Nations General Assembly. Universal Declaration of Human Rights, art. 29.

Waal, Frans de. *Primates and Philosophers: How Morality Evolved.* Princeton, NJ, 2006.

Waldron, Jeremy. *God, Locke, and Equality: Christian Foundations of Locke's Political Thought.* Cambridge, 2002.

———. *The Right to Private Property.* Oxford, 1988.

Walzer, Michael. *The Company of Critics: Social Criticism and Political Commitment in the Twentieth Century.* New York, 2002.

———. "Philosophy and Democracy." *Political Theory* 9:3 (1981): 119–30.

Wellman, Carl. *The Proliferation of Rights: Moral Progress or Empty Rhetoric?* Boulder, CO, 1998.

Wenar, Leif. "Rights." In *Stanford Encyclopedia of Philosophy.* Accessed online at http://plato.stanford.edu/entries/rights/.

The Politics of Rights Talk, Then and Now

ROGERS M. SMITH

Politics makes strange bedfellows, even among scholars. Though many Americans celebrate their nation's Founding era as one that for the first time made universal principles of human rights central to the values and goals of a political society, some scholars on both the right and the left see these claims as fatuous. During the bicentennial of the Declaration of Independence, for example, most of the left-leaning scholars in a volume that sympathetically explored radicalism in America argued that the Founders fell far short of pursuing equal rights for all. Francis Jennings wrote that it was "a huge embarrassment to ideology" that the universal rights principles of the American Revolution did not apply to Indians. Joan Hoff Wilson argued that "the increased benefits of Lockean liberalism" during the Revolutionary period "accrued to a relatively small percent of all Americans" and were accompanied by "increased sexism and racism exhibited by this privileged group both during and after the Revolution."[1] Many have since agreed.

But other writers have argued for substantively similar views in ways that are far more congenial to American conservatives. In particular, developing a theme of Russell Kirk, John Phillip Reid has long contended forcefully that scholars have been wrong to argue that in the course of the Revolution, the American leaders abandoned claims to English rights and relied instead on "the natural rights of man rather than those peculiar to Englishmen." He has maintained (and reiterates in this volume) that throughout, the Revolutionaries "asserted their rights as 'Englishmen' and only as Englishmen." To Reid, it is neither surprising nor contradictory that Indians, African-descended slaves, and women did not successfully claim protection from Revolutionary ideology or the rights proclaimed in the Declaration of Independence. They were not Englishmen.[2]

Yet for many other scholars, it is not convincing to say that, for one reason or another, the American Revolutionaries did not really mean anything like what their talk of natural, equal rights suggests to us today. Words do change their meaning, so this thinking goes, but not that completely. So the questions remain: What role did the language of rights, particularly natural rights, actually play in the American Revolution? What role or roles has "rights talk" played since then?

Several very different answers are prominent. First, many patriotic Americans, whether conservative or liberal, view the universalistic, egalitarian phrases that begin the Declaration of Independence and various other documents of the Founding era as expressions of sincere convictions, even if Americans were not able to realize their implications fully for many years.[3] But again, many on the left find this account far too sanguine. They see the Founders largely as hypocrites, a few of whom subsequently felt obliged to live up to their rhetoric, but most of whom resisted doing so until and unless powerful political pressures compelled greater compliance. In contrast, more Burkean American conservatives incline in a third direction. They contend that we should accept that the Revolutionaries upheld only what they perceived as their legal rights as Englishmen, so that whatever the merits of arguments for universal, egalitarian human rights, the aims of the Founders should figure in that debate to a very limited degree, if at all. Whichever view we take, some common questions remain. Should we see the logical implications, or perhaps the rhetorical resonances, of the framers' "rights talk" as powerful ideological elements driving American political development over the next two centuries? Or should we see both the logic and rhetoric of the Founders' language as having played but a minor role in those transformations?

The answer I advance here does not fit wholly into any of the options listed above, though it has points in common with each of them. Like various other contributors to this volume, I conceive of rights as political instruments that political actors advocate and sometimes institutionalize chiefly to accomplish certain immediate purposes in their specific political contexts.[4] But those contexts sometimes can prompt them to articulate broader aims, going beyond their immediate goals, that the rights are said to serve. The rights themselves may then be defined in broader, grander terms, such as "eternal," "natural," "divine." Some political actors adopt these terms sincerely and reflectively, some sincerely and unreflectively, some insincerely and reflectively, and some insincerely and unreflectively.

Regardless of their motives or thoughtfulness, once those broader aims and grander conceptions of rights are announced, and especially if the rights thus defined are institutionalized in some way, they are available as political instruments for other political actors to deploy for causes going beyond the concerns that gave rise to the initial advocacy of the rights. As Daniel Rodgers has written, the Revolutionary era made talk of "natural rights" one of "the basic tools of politics" in America, a tool that has been especially "sharp with subversive possibilities."[5] But rights nonetheless have remained merely available as weapons that actors might or might not use in what have been uncertain, contingent political contests. The inner logic and rhetorical power of rights have assisted, but they have not compelled or guaranteed, the further elaboration of rights either to support or to attack the status quo—in politics, in law, and in everyday life.

Thus, though Reid is right to say that the Revolutionaries always thought they were claiming their rights as Englishmen, he is wrong to suggest that they did not feel politically impelled to rely increasingly on claims that their English rights were also universal natural rights. And though most Revolutionaries either did not see or did not accept the logical implications of universalistic, egalitarian, natural-rights talk, some did. Many more were willing to institutionalize those principles in part. Their actions created a political landscape in which other Americans could use these ideological and institutional legacies to push for a variety of other causes, and in the course of U.S. history, many did so, often to their benefit. Still, many did so unsuccessfully. They failed partly because it was always possible to argue that universalistic, egalitarian rights principles either were not what the framers meant or they were intrinsically undesirable. They also failed because many political struggles in America as elsewhere have been settled not so much by who had the better argument, but by who had the most overall power. In that calculus, having a good argument has always played a real but minor part.

Rights Talk in the Revolutionary Era

For several reasons, many scholars have not accepted John Phillip Reid's insistence on "the Englishness" of the rights that Americans invoked to give constitutional legitimacy to their revolution.[6] Reid's argument rests partly on his decision to focus only on "*official* claims to rights in actual controversy," made in "official colonial petitions, resolutions, or declarations," rather than widely read but unofficial statements like John Adams's 1765 "Dissertation on the Canon and Feudal Law," Jefferson's 1774 *Summary View of the Rights of British America,* and Tom Paine's 1776 *Common Sense* (or works with fewer but important readers, like James Otis's 1762 pamphlet, *The Rights of the British Colonies Asserted and Proved*).[7] Reid acknowledges that one can find in such "political pamphlets and anonymous newspaper articles claims made to rights on the authority of nature alone"—as Adams put it in 1765, "RIGHTS . . . antecedent to all earthly government,—Rights, that cannot be repealed or restrained by human laws—Rights, derived from the great Legislator of the Universe."[8] But though Reid's contrast between official documents and rabble-rousing pamphlets has force, there are Revolutionary-era documents that blur the distinction. In 1772, taking what Benjamin Franklin called "the unanimous act of a large American city," the Boston town meeting adopted Samuel Adams's *A State of the Rights of the Colonists,* which begins with an extensive discussion of the "Natural Rights of the Colonists as Men."[9] The document is hard to classify as a purely "private pamphlet" or a fully "official act."

Even if the distinction works on the whole, *pace* Reid, it is in fact neither surprising nor decisive that official documents largely emphasized claims that imperial authorities were violating the colonists' legal rights. In 1774, while serving on a committee in the First Continental Congress, John Adams, like his cousin Sam, continued to champion appeals to the laws of nature and natural rights. In so doing, he was undoubtedly sincere: though Adams was not a perfect man, few have questioned his candor or integrity. Still, others, like Joseph Galloway and James Duane, successfully argued that natural-rights arguments were "feeble." They insisted that claims made in terms of the British constitution would be more persuasive to imperial authorities.[10]

Their position made much sense. As Rodgers notes, to change the minds of ministry officials or members of Parliament, resistance leaders needed "a soberer language of charter precedents," and of at least "implicit" constitutional guarantees.[11] I have argued that political leaders often face related but distinguishable tasks of inspiring a sense of trust in themselves and their intentions, and a sense of the worth of their policies and plans.[12] In their official communications, the colonial leaders sought to maintain the trust of British imperial authorities that colonial Americans would remain loyal if their pleas were heard. Arguing primarily in terms of English constitutional rights rather than natural rights provided assurance that despite their disagreements with British policies, colonial officials could be trusted to continue to think and act as law-abiding Englishmen.

Accordingly, when the First Continental Congress issued its "Declaration of Rights," in October 1774, it largely heeded Duane and Galloway and referred only briefly to "the immutable laws of nature." Instead, its members stressed their rights as "English colonists" entitled to the "English liberty" that was the birthright of all "free and natural-born subjects."[13] When the Second Continental Congress issued its "Declaration of the Causes and Necessity of Taking Up Arms," on July 6, 1775, its members similarly claimed to be contending for "that freedom which we received from our gallant ancestors, and which our innocent posterity have a right to receive from us." Though they invoked divine justice, they did not speak of divine or natural rights.[14]

Yet as even Reid concedes, within a year the leading official documents were echoing the natural-rights language of the angry pamphleteers. In June 1776 the Virginia Declaration of Rights, chiefly drafted by George Mason, proclaimed in its first article, "That all men are by nature equally free and independent, and have certain inherent rights, of which, when they enter into a state of society, they cannot, by any compact, deprive or divest their posterity; namely, the enjoyment of life and liberty, with the means of acquiring and possessing property, and pursuing and obtaining happiness and safety." Because men could never properly divest themselves or their progeny of their original natural rights, colonial Americans and all their descendants were entitled to assert those rights, whatever lawyers might say about the evolving English constitution. The next month, the Continental Congress's Declaration of Independence simply announced that the American Revolutionaries held "these truths to be self-evident, that all men are created equal, that they are endowed by their Creator with certain unalienable Rights, that among these are Life, Liberty, and the pursuit of Happiness." Both documents would soon be echoed in state declarations of independence and early bills of rights, including those in Massachusetts, New Hampshire, Vermont, and Pennsylvania.[15]

Scholars like Rodgers and Hamowy therefore maintain that, in the latter's words, "as open rebellion with Great Britain approached, the colonists increasingly resorted to arguments based not on the prerogatives peculiar to Englishmen but rather on man's natural rights."[16] But Rodgers stresses that many Revolutionaries did so "slowly, hesitantly," both because they were aware of the "subversive" potential of rights talk to be used against some of their own hierarchical privileges, and because seventeenth-century doctrines of the state of nature, natural rights, and an original social contract had long been disparaged by many eighteenth-century British political and intellectual leaders. He contends that the "need for precedents" nonetheless drove many American writers to merge their historical pasts with state-of-nature doctrines in ways that helped them conjure up rights existing prior to the English constitution that they could deem both historical and natural.[17] Reid's answer to such arguments is to insist that apart from the odd "rhetorical flourish," official documents invoked natural and natural rights, if at all, only as "alternative authority" for what were still recognized to be at bottom positive rights under the English constitution.[18]

He is surely right to argue that most Revolutionaries never gave up their beliefs that the substantive rights for which they contended were properly theirs as part of the unwritten English constitution, nor did most ever alter the basic list of rights to which they felt entitled. Throughout the Revolutionary era, they demanded recognition of their property rights, their rights to representation and to taxation only with consent, their right to be governed under the rule of law, and their right to resist a government that persistently violated their legal rights, among other themes.[19] Both the Virginia Declaration of Rights and the Declaration of Independence's list of grievances stressed such familiar points, long argued in terms of English constitutional law, and they did not suggest that their authors now viewed these rights as purely natural.

Yet though Reid is persuasive in arguing against the view that the Revolutionary leadership ever conceded that their rights had no English constitutional foundation, he cannot deny that over time the official documents as well as the pamphlets began to feature nature as the ultimate basis for these substantive rights. He tries to insist instead that throughout, "natural rights were the reflection, not the essence; they were the confirmation, not the source of positive rights." But even his quoted sources say just the opposite, that natural rights "are *the only Foundation* of all just Authority, and *the sole Reason* for all Laws," so that "civil rights are, or ought to be, a confirmation of natural rights."[20]

The question I want to focus on here, however, is why the Revolutionaries came to give greater emphasis to nature as the source of rights that they did still hold to be their rights as Englishmen. Hamowy and Rodgers suggest that it was because, though they never admitted it, the Revolutionaries came to recognize that the English precedents were actually against them, that they were only "British subjects on the outposts of a ramshackle empire" over which the king-in-Parliament had come to be officially established as absolutely sovereign—after their ancestors had left England, true, but in ways that still bound all loyal and true British subjects such as they professed themselves to be.[21] I have previously endorsed this explanation for the new stress on natural rights.[22] I do not rule it out now; but I no longer think it was the major factor at work. The best indicator of their main motive is a fact that Reid observes but does not explain. He is right that the language of natural rights appears primarily in the "rhetorical" preambles of Revolutionary documents. But why is that?

What led the Revolutionaries to feature these claims instead of their specifically English ones, if the latter were at the core of their thinking?

Their motives may well have been the same as those of most of the Revolutionary pamphleteers. When the colonial leaders wrote the preambles or the first articles of the documents that definitively declared independence from Britain and founded new governments, their primary audiences were no longer imperial ministers or parliamentary members. They chiefly wrote for domestic consumption, as Pauline Maier has stressed— for the fellow colonists whom they sought to inspire to join the highly uncertain and dangerous Revolutionary cause.[23]

For this purpose, they needed what I have termed an "ethically constitutive" political story—an account offering morally compelling reasons for their fellow British American subjects to embrace a new vision of their proper political community, one in which they would be American citizens.[24] The Revolutionaries needed such an account because, whatever the strength or weaknesses of their constitutional arguments, they were not likely to persuade many to support their cause out of purely legalistic or even predominantly prudential, materialist considerations. Though they could and did appeal to the economic grievances and denials of political power many colonials were experiencing under British rule, the Revolutionary leaders could not credibly promise the colonists greater benefits in terms of either economic prosperity or political clout in the foreseeable future. Instead their course held out the prospect of long, hard struggles and great sacrifices. Yet they needed somehow to inspire potential supporters with a sense of the transcendent worth of this demanding endeavor. Under such circumstances, leaders throughout history have found that they could best win adherents by presenting their cause as morally right, as divinely supported, and as true to the highest, noblest features of their people's intrinsic nature. Those are exactly the themes that, at the point of greatest crisis and risk, the American Revolutionaries chose to stress to their potential compatriots. Rhetorical flourishes their talk of natural rights may well have been. But rhetorical flourishes are usually made for serious reasons: they generally represent efforts to robe their authors' themes in the most attractive garments available.

Still, the reluctance of many Revolutionaries to adopt the language of natural rights, and their continuing specification of those rights largely in terms of what they also saw as their rights as Englishmen, indicate that both Rodgers and Reid are largely right. Many did perceive talk of natural rights as dangerously hard to contain, in need of delimitation if those at the margins or at the bottom of society were not to invoke them on behalf of radical transformations. Though the American leaders trumpeted such rhetoric in their hour of Revolutionary need, they soon turned away from it again as they began in earnest to construct political systems that could endure. To do so, many undoubtedly felt they had to ensure that their new governments would serve the interests of the most privileged members of the new states and nation. Any emphasis on types of rights talk that could be used to challenge those advantages may well have seemed inadvisable.

Again, however, attention to the community-building roles played by what I have termed "stories of peoplehood" suggests another factor that may have been at work. "Ethically constitutive" appeals to God and nature can be uniquely useful during times of political and economic hardship, but they are, after all, at best inspiring intangibles—arguably, only pretty words. If they are not reinforced by the enjoyment of other benefits, their appeal to all constituents is likely to pale with endless repetition. What once rang sonorously begins to clank. In contrast, the provision of things of tangible worth, such as economic goods, physical security, and a share of political power, is likely to cement allegiances as these benefits repeat and accumulate.[25] Not merely to reassure the privileged, then, but to retain the support of all Americans, it probably made sense for the leaders of the new governments to emphasize in their words and deeds how their new regimes would promote the "general Welfare" and provide for the "common defence" and not simply pursue grand moral principles discerned in the state of nature.

Whatever the reasons, changes in these more mundane directions did occur. Rodgers notes that though state bills of rights established in the late 1770s often used the language of natural law and natural rights, by the 1790s, as states continued to modify their constitutions and to add bills of rights, such phrases fell out of fashion.[26] Nowhere was this shift more evident than in the new federal Constitution of 1787 and the Bill of Rights added to it in 1791. Though the Preamble spoke of "Justice" and the "Blessings of Liberty" along with "Welfare" and "defence," and the first nine amendments specified rights that were largely versions of time-honored English constitutional guarantees, talk of nature was altogether absent. Only the Ninth Amendment's reference to other rights "retained by the people" still hinted that there might be rights not arising from any foundation in positive law—a hint that almost all American judges have ignored through all subsequent history. Though many Americans have since become accustomed to interpreting the Constitution as a means to realize the principles of the Declaration of Independence, when read by itself the text of the 1787 Constitution provides no explicit indication that its

framers believed that governments are instituted among men chiefly to secure rights of any kind, much less inalienable, divinely endowed, natural
rights. Unlike the white-hot core of the Revolutionary era, the early constitutional period was not a time when invocations of rights shone brightly
in the discourses radiating from the new nation's centers of power.

The Rebirth of Rights Talk

Though not long after launching their new nation Americans began
to hold Independence Day commemorations, most scholars believe that
it was especially worker associations in the 1820s who revived the language
of rights, often via adaptations of the Declaration of Independence.[27] In
1829, George Henry Evans of the New York Working Man's Party published *The Working Men's Declaration of Independence,* which asserted the
"natural and inalienable rights" of "one class of a community" in "opposition to other classes of their fellow men" who denied them a political
"station of equality." In 1834, the Boston Trades' Union declared that,
"With the Fathers of our Country, we hold that all men are created free
and equal, endowed by their Creator with certain unalienable rights," and
that "Laws which have a tendency to raise any peculiar class above their
fellow citizens, by granting special privileges, are contrary to" these rights.[28]
Many more examples could be added.

Why was it American workers who seized on the Declaration and its
invocations of natural rights to champion their cause? Was it because the
logic of putatively universal rights obviously could be extended to encompass their demands? Perhaps, but if so, why did not other groups use
rights language sooner? Ironically, workers may have first found natural-
rights rhetoric a plausible vehicle for their endeavors because of what they
had in common with the distinctive traits of the original American Revolutionaries, rather than what they had in common with all humanity.
True, they were Americans, not Englishmen (though Evans was an English immigrant). Many were not even of English descent. But they were
overwhelmingly men of Northern European ancestry, like most of the
Revolutionaries. At least some could credibly claim the Founding Fathers
as their biological ancestors, supporting their identification with them.
Probably more importantly, the American workers, too, felt driven by circumstances to challenge the legitimacy of the unequal class structure under which they labored. For the Revolutionaries, the oppressive class structure had been a governmentally enforced hereditary aristocracy that they
felt they had to repudiate in the name of egalitarian republicanism. For

the workers, it was an aristocracy fostered by other sorts of governmental special privileges, such as grants of corporate charters, monopoly rights, public business, and public lands to the already advantaged, accompanied by preferential judicial treatment. Yet it was still an aristocracy inconsistent with a republic based on equal rights.

And like the Revolutionaries, the workers faced a steep uphill fight with few immediate rewards and great dangers of punishment from authorities claiming to be enforcing the law. Though many working-class leaders believed as fervently as the colonists that constitutional law, properly understood, was on their side, many courts believed that vested legal rights legitimated the privileges of the financial and employer elites against whom the new labor associations fought.[29] The workers, too, needed the moral legitimation, the psychological uplift, the sense of the compelling worth of their cause that the language of natural rights and divine support had provided to the Revolutionary insurgents, men who in so many ways seemed like themselves.

But if their ascriptive and situational similarities to the Revolutionaries aided American workers in turning the language of natural rights to their own purposes, their words and deeds then dramatized for all how this language could be deployed in new ways. In an era marked by renewed fervent religiosity and moral crusades, others soon followed suit. None did so more dramatically or radically than the great abolitionist, William Lloyd Garrison. Still, the radicalism of his stance should not be overstated. If Jacksonian wage laborers could proclaim themselves a class subjugated by a governmentally supported economic aristocracy, it was logically no great leap to say that slave laborers were far more oppressed— if only one accepted that slaves were human beings with equal basic rights. In the first issue of the *Liberator* in 1831, Garrison declared accordingly his commitment to "the great cause of human rights" based on assent to the self-evident truth "maintained in the American Declaration of Independence, 'that all men are created equal, and endowed by their Creator with certain inalienable rights.'" For Garrison, these principles demanded "the immediate enfranchisement of our slave population."[30]

Garrison's consistently religious rhetoric leaves little doubt that he was drawn to the language of rights not so much from a desire to invoke nature or reason or to gain any political advantage, as from his wish to express faithfully the moral edicts of the God in whom he passionately believed. He felt impelled to devote himself to abolition above all to satisfy his own conscience.[31] Yet he surely knew that many white workers had recently been using "rights talk" much the way he was attempting to do. He also knew that religious defenses of such rights were best suited to discomfort at least some of those deeply invested in slavery or simply content with the status quo. This was a familiar language that could win the trust of potential allies and their confidence in the worth of the abolitionist cause, while at the same time condemning as hypocrites those who professed the same religion but supported slavery.

By speaking ceaselessly of human rights and attracting equally pious and idealistic women activists, the abolitionist movement helped generate the nineteenth-century women's rights movement, commonly dated to the Seneca Falls Convention of 1848. In their "Declaration of Sentiments," again modeled on the Declaration of Independence, Elizabeth Cady Stanton, Susan B. Anthony, and their allies gave the language of rights still more expansive scope. They defined themselves not as an oppressed "class" or "people," but as "one portion of the family of man," seeking the "position" to which "the laws of nature and of Nature's God entitle them." The truths they held to be "self-evident" included the claim that "all men and women are created equal" and "endowed by their Creator with certain inalienable rights," among which they included "her inalienable right to the elective franchise." They, too, sought to turn working-class claims to rights to their advantage, though in a rather impolitic way: they noted that they were being denied rights, including voting rights, now conferred on "ignorant and degraded men."[32]

They also knew that, even more than American workers and almost as much as American slaves, they had little shelter in the structure of positive rights built into American law. They sought to use Blackstone, the great proponent of the common-law doctrine of coverture that subordinated women to their fathers or husbands, as authority for their higher-law appeals, noting that "Blackstone . . . remarks, that this law of Nature being coeval with mankind, and dictated by God himself, is of course superior in obligation to any other."[33] They dismissed the fact that, for Blackstone, the law of nature also mandated gender inequality—an inconvenience that hampered any reliance on the great Commentator in legal briefs for women's suffrage. But for women, as for workers, abolitionists, and the American Revolutionaries, proclamations of the natural and divine basis of the rights they claimed were not chiefly devices to persuade governing authorities. They were primarily means to override arguments about formal legality and to inspire (or shame) constituencies from whom they sought support, under circumstances in which they could not promise immediate material benefits.

Many making these proclamations were sincere. But like the American

Founders, when they spoke of universal human rights, they did so with particular groups claiming particular rights chiefly in mind. Sometimes they did not show much ardor for natural-rights contentions advanced by others. White male workers often did not champion the rights of slaves or women. Women suffrage advocates sometimes treated the rights conferred on foreign-born immigrants as improvidently granted. Their shared language of rights helped promote some alliances, but far from anything resembling a united front.

Rights talk had greater efficacy when deployed by the middle- and upper-class white male spokesmen for the new "mainstream" political party that rose on the ashes of the Whigs, the Republicans, led after 1860 by Abraham Lincoln. Though his record, too, displayed some inconsistencies and significant personal evolution, from the early 1850s on, Lincoln was one of the most consistent antebellum advocates for guaranteeing the basic rights delineated in the Declaration of Independence, though not necessarily more, to all persons, regardless of color or gender. He wrote in 1855 against Know-Nothing nativists who would read the Declaration to hold, "All men are created equal, except negroes and foreigners and Catholics." He contended in 1857 that in regard to the Declaration's rights, especially "her natural right to eat the bread she earns with her own hands, without asking leave of anyone else," a black woman "is my equal and the equal of all others."[34] He then made this view of the Declaration, and the contention that it required Congress to outlaw slavery in the territories, the centerpiece of his campaigns against Stephen Douglas for the Senate in 1858 and the presidency in 1860. Many scholars agree that Lincoln and what Americans came to make of Lincoln did more than perhaps anything else to foster beliefs that America as a political community somehow rested on the Declaration and natural-rights talk.[35]

Yet Lincoln's example only underlines that though rights talk could serve to help build American political coalitions, the inner logic of universal natural-rights claims was far from sufficient to bring about political transformations, regardless of who invoked them. The Illinois state legislature preferred Douglas to Lincoln for the Senate in 1858, and in the presidential election of 1860, Lincoln garnered just over 39 percent of the vote. Over 60 percent went to three other candidates who all in one way or another championed the extension of slavery. Only the fragmentation of the pro-slavery vote allowed Lincoln to be elected.[36] And though women and workers sometimes organized and mobilized impressively and even won a few legislative battles in the antebellum period, for the most part their talk of natural rights did not greatly alter the judicial rulings and the other structures of public policy and power that continued to enforce class and gender inequalities in American law and life.[37]

It was only under the extraordinary circumstances of the Civil War, when Southern Democrats first left Congress, then returned bowed by defeat, that the Republicans and more radical equal-rights advocates gained enough support to pass statutes and constitutional amendments providing new national guarantees of basic rights. Even then, national lawmakers largely followed the framers of the original Constitution by avoiding natural-rights language. In the Thirteenth Amendment, they banned slavery and involuntary servitude, and in the Fourteenth, they committed the national government to upholding the "privileges and immunities of citizens of the United States," along with guaranteeing due process when states dealt with the "life, liberty and property" of persons. But they officially referred to natural rights only in the 1868 Expatriation Act, which echoed the Declaration of Independence by terming expatriation "a natural and inherent right of all people, indispensable to the enjoyment of the rights of life, liberty, and the pursuit of happiness."[38] Outside the context of the specific right that had been at the heart of the American Revolution, U.S. lawmakers still treated natural-rights language as something more appropriate to political agitators than to major legal documents. After some three decades of worker, abolitionist, and women's rights movements regularly invoking natural rights as justifications for radically transformative changes, it is likely that at least some legislators preferred not to encode into the nation's basic laws terminology that they saw as dangerously hard to control.

Thus, as the late nineteenth century proceeded, egalitarians returned to the Declaration of Independence, rather than the postwar amendments, to invoke "higher-law" authority for their positions. Labor leaders and socialists probably did so most frequently, while adding that "inalienable rights" included a claim to the economic "means" to realize those rights.[39] The opponents of Chinese exclusion in the Congress also insisted that race-based immigration restrictions would violate the natural-rights principles of the Declaration, which had made the United States "the recognized champion of human rights" in the world.[40] The National Woman Suffrage Association continued to call the nation to honor "the broad principles of human rights proclaimed in 1776," as did proponents of African American rights.[41] But all these very reasonable arguments from natural-rights premises were made in losing causes. Opponents successfully derided them as "Utopian," as "sentimentalist," even saying that the Declaration's espousal of equality was "absolutely false."[42]

Indeed, the most politically potent uses of natural-rights language in the late nineteenth century came on behalf of the legitimacy of economic inequalities, in defense of the property rights and economic liberties of the employer and capitalist classes. The pattern was set by Justice Stephen Field in his influential dissent in the 1873 *Slaughter-House Cases,* which on the whole served to limit the capacity of the postwar amendments to protect the rights of American citizens, especially, as it turned out, African American citizens. Field protested that the Fourteenth Amendment had given the federal courts new authority to protect "the natural and inalienable rights which belong to all citizens," with economic liberties first and foremost among those.[43] Though his views did not carry the day then, they were later embraced by Supreme Court majorities that opposed many economic regulatory laws from the Progressive era through the early New Deal.

Such uses of the language of natural rights exemplify a different type of occasion in which, I have argued, political leaders find "ethically constitutive" accounts valuable. These are times when economic and political benefits are being obtained, as they were by leading business interests in the late nineteenth century, through means that are questionable in terms of prevailing moral discourses.[44] Assurances that nature and God approved the rights of the wealthy gave an aura of legitimacy that could impress even many who were experiencing severe hardships under the prevailing arrangements.

Nonetheless, the subversive potential of natural-rights talk remained. So while judges sometimes spoke briefly of natural law and natural rights and cited authorities who had elaborated them, most chose officially to ground economic rights on the positive-law authority of vague and permissive clauses providing for "due process" and, to a lesser degree, "equal protection." At times, conservative advocates of economic freedoms also argued for a range of other civil liberties, but usually with the understanding that these could reasonably be confined to white men, preferably those of Anglo-Saxon or at least Northern European ancestry, who were, after all, uniquely fit for lives of liberty.[45] Even so, by the dawn of the twentieth century, after natural-rights claims had been employed to support colonial revolution, abolitionism, workers' rights, women's rights, rights of immigrants, rights of employers, and more, everyone recognized that the language was expansive enough to be used to valorize almost any cause. Yet, by the same token, while Americans across the spectrum often argued in terms of rights, including natural rights, their shared language did not generate any shared trajectory in regard to the protection of basic freedoms. Many eminently logical rights claims came to naught. The rights that could be meaningfully enjoyed in practice as well as in law were generally the rights favored by those who could wield other forms of power.

Contemporary Rights Talk

Partly as a result of this often dispiriting reality, many left-leaning Progressive intellectuals and activists rejected natural-rights discourses, seeing them fundamentally as means to block egalitarian economic and social reforms. The greatest American thinker of the era, John Dewey, proclaimed that "natural rights and natural liberties" existed "only in the kingdom of mythological social zoology." Claims of individual rights, especially those of the owners of property rights, "must yield to the general welfare."[46] Progressive legislators and judges agreed, though their views remained mostly in the minority until the Depression brought Franklin D. Roosevelt and large majorities of New Deal Democrats to the presidency and the Congress. They, in turn, repopulated and transformed the obstructionist Supreme Court. Many Progressives and New Dealers did champion individual rights in certain contexts, and some still spoke of natural rights. But in contrast to the late eighteenth century and the first half of the nineteenth century, in the first half of the twentieth century, the language of nature and natural rights predominantly served to justify existing or new systems of inequality in America, while proponents of egalitarian change spoke most often of democracy, science, progress, and the common good.

Those patterns changed with World War II, the Cold War, and especially the modern civil rights movement. The impact of the struggles against racist Nazism and Fascism on political discourse, not just in the United States but in the rest of the world, is discernible in the founding documents of the United Nations. The Preamble of the U.N. Charter affirms "faith in fundamental human rights, in the dignity and worth of the human person, in the equal rights of men and women and of nations."[47] Subsequently, the Universal Declaration of Human Rights, adopted by the United Nations on December 10, 1948, spoke in its Preamble of "the equal and inalienable rights of all members of the human family," words especially reminiscent of the 1848 Declaration of Sentiments. Its Article 1 also announced that "All human beings are born free and equal in dignity and rights," using phrases not too different from those of George Mason's in 1776; and the list of particulars that follows also echoes many found in his Declaration of Rights, in the Declaration of Independence, and in the

Bill of Rights and the postwar amendments, along with more novel elements.[48] Yet these are not first and foremost restatements of traditional positive-law guarantees. Though in these documents the language of "natural rights" gave way to the term "human rights," perhaps due to the philosophic and political assaults on the forms of natural-rights talk common in the first half of the twentieth century, there can be no doubt that "human rights" are also seen as inherent, inalienable, fundamental rights that rest on the "dignity and worth of the human person," as the Universal Declaration states.

In this international environment, which included threats of U.N. investigations of American segregation, the United States faced new external pressures to address its massive systems of civic inequality. Returning black soldiers, many joining the movement of American blacks from southern farms to northern cities, added domestic pressures as well. Collectively, these circumstances helped incubate the modern American civil rights movement, which in turn made "rights talk" central to American political life once again.[49] The talk was now of human rights and, especially, God-given rights. But civil rights leaders like the Reverend Martin Luther King Jr. regularly traced these back to the "unalienable Rights" proclaimed in the Declaration of Independence, a document that King called a "promissory note" that the nation had yet to fulfill for "black men as well as white men."[50]

First the courts, then the president and the Congress responded to these pressures by banning racial segregation and passing the momentous 1964 Civil Rights Act and the 1965 Voting Rights Act, among other measures. The Supreme Court in the 1960s also extended most of the Bill of Rights guarantees to the states, especially rights of the accused; and in 1965 it discerned a new constitutional "right of privacy" that in 1973 proved capable of supporting broad rights for women to choose to have abortions. These developments helped spur related movements for women's rights, rights of religious minorities, welfare rights, consumers' rights, rights of the disabled, rights of indigenous peoples, gay rights, rights of immigrants, children's rights, animal rights, and much more. Scholars describe the resulting era as a "Rights Revolution,"[51] a new "Age of Rights,"[52] an era dominated by "rights talk."[53] As political opposition to many of the changes initiated in the civil rights era grew in the 1980s and 1990s, many debated whether all rights talk, whether it concerned "natural" or "human" rights, tended to be too absolutist, too conducive to selfishness, too dismissive of community responsibilities to be healthy.[54] Yet even efforts to limit the transformations thus initiated often appealed to doctrines of property rights, seen once again as natural rights,[55] as well as the less individualistic doctrine of states' rights.[56]

These modern political controversies over the scope and character of personal rights, human and sometimes now also animal, have plainly played a role in the different scholarly depictions of the scope and character of rights doctrines at the nation's Founding and in subsequent history that I noted at the outset. By and large, it is more middle-of-the-road scholars supportive of most modern changes, particularly the overthrow of official racial segregation, who have tended to agree with King and other activists that those developments are bringing to fruition promises advanced in the rights language adopted at the nation's inception. It is generally conservatives, viewing modern movements for personal rights as having gone much too far in ways that have damaged key social and political institutions, who tend instead to hold that the framers held more bounded conceptions of rights, that activists are now unduly expanding. And it is those at the opposite end of the political spectrum who, believing that U.S. political, economic, and social systems require far more radical egalitarian transformations than have occurred or been seriously considered, contend like conservatives that early American conceptions of rights were in fact quite narrow. Left scholars see those early rights doctrines as containing too many built-in class, race, gender, and religious biases to be any kind of guide to social justice.

The evidence and arguments about the place of rights talk in U.S. history advanced here cannot decide between these different characterizations. They do raise doubts about claims that there is anything inherent in the language of rights that makes governmental policies and citizen practices necessarily more individualistic, litigious, inefficient, or irresponsible, on the one hand, or more concerned for the disadvantaged or the victims of injustice, on the other. Discourses featuring rights, including natural rights, have been advanced for many different purposes, individualistic and communitarian, egalitarian and inegalitarian. And they have never been by themselves enough to ensure success for any endeavor. Rights talk has served to inspire support for precarious, sometimes desperately serious, sometimes eccentric causes on the part of the weak, and it has also provided bulwarks for the estates of the powerful, yet never to a degree that made any particular political outcome inevitable.

Does that mean that doctrines of rights, especially the early language of natural rights and the now-prevalent terminology of human rights, have never really mattered very much politically? That conclusion is unwarranted. The very ubiquity of resort to these discourses suggests that political actors have found them useful, and American history suggests why. Though rights talk has not been enough to determine the course of human events, in its different forms it has helped political leaders and government officials to forge coalitions of support for their movements and policies. It has been an often enticing, sometimes irresistible invitation for those who might otherwise be unlikely companions to get into the same political bed. When other factors have conspired to help each resulting coalition to endure and to enact the policies its members could agree upon, much has been achieved that might not otherwise have occurred—such as success for a revolution of backwater colonies against the world's greatest empire; success for those who resisted the expansion of forms of servitude deemed essential by much of the electorate; success for the disfranchised targets of gender and racial discrimination; and, yes, success for the wealthy few in resisting the redistributive impulses of democratic majorities, even in periods of great economic hardship. The politics of rights talk has indeed made for strange political bedfellows; and in politics as in life, the couplings of strange bedfellows often give rise to unexpected, sometimes grotesque, but sometimes inspiring new births. In the case of the politics of rights, more than once, those offspring have been new births of freedom.

Notes

1. Jennings, "Indians' Revolution," 322; Wilson, "Illusions of Change," 387.

2. Reid, *Authority of Rights*, 5, 13–14.

3. See, e.g., West, *Vindicating the Founders*.

4. Richard Primus, e.g., elaborates a broadly similar view in his essay, "An Introduction to the Nature of American Rights," in this volume, and more fully in Primus, *American Language of Rights*, 2–3.

5. Rodgers, *Contested Truths*, 45–46. In his essay, "Rights Consciousness in American History," in this volume, Rodgers stresses that rights talk can therefore be divisive. I concur, but would note that it is divisive on behalf of building some alternative form of community or "peoplehood."

6. Reid, *Authority of Rights*, 9; Hamowy, "Rights," 685–86.

7. Adams, *Political Writings of John Adams*, 3–21; Jensen, *Tracts of the American Revolution*, 19–40 (Otis), 256–76 (Jefferson), 400–446 (Paine).

8. Reid, *Authority of Rights*, 18, 91; Adams, *Political Writings of John Adams*, 4–5.

9. Jensen, *Tracts of the American Revolution*, 235.

10. C. F. Adams, *Works of John Adams*, 370–74.

11. Rodgers, *Contested Truths*, 48–49.

12. Smith, *Stories of Peoplehood*, 56–60.

13. Declaration of Rights.

14. Ver Steeg and Hofstadter, *Great Issues*, 449.

15. Maier, *American Scripture*, 165.

16. Rodgers, *Contested Truths*, 55–56; Hamowy, "Rights," 686.

17. Rodgers, *Contested Truths*, 46, 51–52, 54–56.

18. Reid, *Authority of Rights*, 91–92.

19. Ibid., 16.

20. Ibid., 94–95, citing James Otis and "a London writer in 1775."

21. Rodgers, *Contested Truths*, 54.

22. Smith, *Civic Ideals*, 77.

23. Maier, *American Scripture*, 130–31.

24. Smith, *Stories of Peoplehood*, 64–69.

25. Ibid., 93, 103.

26. Rodgers, *Contested Truths*, 60–64.

27. Foner, *We, the Other People*, 1–7; Rodgers, *Contested Truths*, 72; Maier, *American Scripture*, 197.

28. Foner, *We, the Other People*, 48, 53.

29. Orren, *Belated Feudalism*, 68–121; see also the essay by Gordon S. Wood, "The History of Rights in Early America," in this volume.

30. Ver Steeg and Hofstadter, *Great Issues*, 321–22.

31. Ibid., 322.

32. Foner, *We, the Other People*, 78–79.

33. Ibid., 81.

34. Lincoln, *Writings of Abraham Lincoln*, 247, 299.

35. Rodgers, *Contested Truths*, 77–78; Maier, *American Scripture*, 207–8; see also the essay by Barry Alan Shain, "Rights Natural and Civil in the Declaration of Independence," in this volume.

36. Smith, *Civic Ideals*, 271.

37. Orren, *Belated Feudalism*, 122–44, 173–82; Smith, *Civic Ideals*, 23–35.

38. Cited in Smith, *Civic Ideals*, 313.

39. Foner, *We, the Other People*, 85, 100, 121, 131.

40. Smith, *Civic Ideals*, 359–60.

41. Foner, *We, the Other People*, 107; Smith, *Civic Ideals*, 376.

42. Smith, *Civic Ideals*, 361.

43. Cited and analyzed in Graber, *Transforming Free Speech*, 30.

44. Smith, *Stories of Peoplehood*, 118.

45. Graber, *Transforming Free Speech*, 17–36.

46. Cited in ibid., 67–68; see also the essay by Daniel T. Rodgers, "Rights Consciousness in American History," in this volume.

47. Preamble, United Nations Charter.

48. United Nations General Assembly, Universal Declaration of Human Rights.

49. Klinkner with Smith, *Unsteady March*, 161–241.

50. King, "I Have a Dream," 305.

51. Sunstein, *After the Rights Revolution*.

52. Henkin, *Age of Rights*.

53. Glendon, *Rights Talk*.

54. Ibid.; Holmes and Sunstein, *Cost of Rights*.

55. Epstein, *Private Property*.

56. Klinkner with Smith, *Unsteady March*, 300, 329.

Bibliography

Adams, Charles Francis, ed. *The Works of John Adams, Second President of the United States, with a Life of the Author, Notes, and Illustrations*. Vol. 2. Boston, 1850.

Adams, John. *The Political Writings of John Adams*, ed. George A. Peek Jr. Indianapolis, 1954.

Declaration of Rights. 1774. Accessed online on 24 Aug. 2006 at http://earlyamerica.com/earlyamerica/milestones/decofrights/text.html.

Epstein, Richard A. *Takings: Private Property and the Power of Eminent Domain*. Cambridge, MA, 1985.

Foner, Philip S., ed. *We, the Other People: Alternative Declarations of Independence by Labor Groups, Farmers, Woman's Rights Advocates, Socialists, and Blacks, 1829–1975*. Urbana, IL, 1976.

Glendon, Mary Ann. *Rights Talk: The Impoverishment of Political Discourse*. New York, 1991.

Graber, Mark A. *Transforming Free Speech: The Ambiguous Legacy of Civil Libertarianism*. Berkeley, CA, 1991.

Hamowy, Ronald. "Rights." In *The Blackwell Encyclopedia of the American Revolution*, ed. Jack Greene and J. R. Pole, 682–87. Oxford, 1991.

Henkin, Louis. *The Age of Rights*. New York, 1990.

Holmes, Stephen, and Cass R. Sunstein. *The Cost of Rights: Why Liberty Depends on Taxes*. New York, 1999.

Jennings, Francis. "The Indians' Revolution." In *The American Revolution: Explorations in the History of American Radicalism*, ed. Alfred F. Young, 319–48. DeKalb, IL, 1976.

Jensen, Merrill, ed. *Tracts of the American Revolution, 1763–1776*. Indianapolis, 1967.

King, Martin Luther, Jr. "I Have a Dream" (1963). In *From Many, One: Readings in American Political and Social Thought*, ed. Richard C. Sinopoli. Washington, DC, 1997.

Klinkner, Philip A., with Rogers M. Smith. *The Unsteady March: The Rise and Decline of Racial Equality in America*. Chicago, 1999.

Lincoln, Abraham. *The Writings of Abraham Lincoln*, ed. A. B. Lapsley. New York, 1905–6.

Maier, Pauline. *American Scripture: Making the Declaration of Independence*. New York, 1997.

Mason, George. The Virginia Declaration of Rights. 1776. Accessed online on 28 Sept. 2004 at http://www.gunstonhall.com/documents/vdr.html.

Orren, Karen. *Belated Feudalism: Labor, the Law, and Liberal Development in the United States*. Cambridge, 1991.

Primus, Richard A. *The American Language of Rights*. Cambridge, 1999.

Reid, John Phillip. *Constitutional History of the American Revolution: The Authority of Rights*. Madison, WI, 1986.

Rodgers, Daniel T. *Contested Truths: Keywords in American Politics since Independence*. New York, 1987.

Smith, Rogers M. *Civic Ideals: Conflicting Visions of Citizenship in U.S. History*. New Haven, CT, 1997.

———. *Stories of Peoplehood: The Politics and Morals of Political Membership*. Cambridge, 2003.

Sunstein, Cass R. *After the Rights Revolution: Reconceiving the Regulatory State*. Cambridge, MA, 1990.

United Nations Charter. Preamble. 1946. Accessed online on 24 Aug. 2006 at http://www.un.org/aboutun/charter/preamble.htm.

United Nations General Assembly. Universal Declaration of Human Rights. 1948. Accessed online on 24 Aug. 2006 at http://www.un.org/Overview/rights.html.

Ver Steeg, Clarence L., and Richard Hofstadter, eds. *Great Issues in American History: From Settlement to Revolution, 1584–1776*. New York, 1969.

West, Thomas G. *Vindicating the Founders: Race, Sex, Class, and Justice in the Origins of America*. Lanham, MD, 1997.

Wilson, Joan Hoff. "The Illusion of Change: Women and the American Revolution." In *The American Revolution: Explorations in the History of American Radicalism*, ed. Alfred F. Young, 383–445. DeKalb, IL, 1976.

CONTRIBUTORS

AKHIL REED AMAR is Southmayd Professor of Law and Political Science at Yale University. His notable books include *The Bill of Rights: Creation and Reconstruction* (1998) and *America's Constitution: A Biography* (2005).

JAMES H. HUTSON is Chief of the Manuscript Division at the Library of Congress. His most recent book is *The Founders on Religion* (2005).

STEPHEN MACEDO is the Laurance S. Rockefeller Professor of Politics and the University Center for Human Values and Director of the University Center for Human Values at Princeton University. He writes and teaches on political theory, ethics, public policy, and law, especially on topics related to liberalism, democracy, diversity, and civic education. His books include *Diversity and Distrust: Civic Education in a Multicultural Democracy* (2000) and, as coauthor, *Democracy at Risk: How Political Choices Undermine Citizen Participation, and What We Can Do about It* (2005).

RICHARD PRIMUS is Professor of Law at the University of Michigan and the author of *The American Language of Rights* (1999). His work focuses on the relationship between history and constitutional law.

JACK N. RAKOVE is the William Robertson Coe Professor of History and American Studies and Professor of Political Science at Stanford University. He is the author of four books, including *The Beginnings of National Politics: An Interpretive History of the Continental Congress* (1979) and *Original Meanings: Politics and Ideas in the Making of the Constitution* (1996), which received the Pulitzer Prize in History. His edited books include *The Unfinished Election of 2000* (2001) and *James Madison: Writings* (1999).

JOHN PHILLIP REID is Russell D. Niles Professor of Law emeritus at New York University School of Law, where he teaches a course and co-teaches a colloquium in American legal history. He is the author of twenty-two books, including *Constitutional History of the American Revolution* (1995); *In a Defiant Stance: The Conditions of Law in Massachusetts Bay, the Irish Comparison, and the Coming of the American Revolution* (1977); and *Controlling the Law: Legal Politics in Early National New Hampshire* (2004).

DANIEL T. RODGERS is the Henry Charles Lea Professor of History at Princeton University, where he teaches American cultural and intellectual history. He is the author of *The Work Ethic in Industrial America* (1978); *Contested Truths: Keywords in American*

Politics since Independence(1987); and *Atlantic Crossings: Social Politics in a Progressive Age* (1998).

A. Gregg Roeber is Professor of Early Modern History and Religious Studies and Codirector of the Max Kade German-American Research Institute at Pennsylvania State University. Among the books he has written are *Faithful Magistrates and Republican Lawyers: Creators of Virginia Legal Culture, 1680–1810* (1981) and *Palatines, Liberty, and Property: German Lutherans in British America* (rev. ed., 1998). He is also the editor of *Ethnographies and Exchanges: Native Americans, Moravians, and Catholics in Early North America* (forthcoming, 2008). His published articles, reviews, and review essays have appeared in the *William and Mary Quarterly, Law and Social Inquiry, Zeitschrift für neuere Rechtsgeschichte, Pietismus und Neuzeit,* the *Journal of Interdisciplinary History, Reviews in American History, Church History,* the *Journal of American History,* and the *American Historical Review.*

Barry Alan Shain is an Associate Professor of Political Science at Colgate University. He is the author *The Myth of American Individualism: The Protestant Origins of American Political Thought* (1994) and *Man, God, and Society: An Interpretive History of Individualism* (2000), as well as numerous book chapters and essays. He is the recipient of four teaching awards and two National Endowment for the Humanity Fellowships, the most recent for the "We the People Project for the Understanding of American History and Culture."

Rogers M. Smith is the Christopher H. Browne Distinguished Professor of Political Science at the University of Pennsylvania. He is the author or coauthor of five books analyzing American political and legal traditions, including *Civic Ideals: Conflicting Visions of Citizenship in U.S. History* (1997). His essays have appeared in the *American Political Science Review,* the *Western Political Quarterly, Studies in American Political Development,* and other journals.

Leif Wenar received his Ph.D. in Philosophy from Harvard University. His work has appeared in the *Columbia Law Review; Ethics; Philosophy and Public Affairs; Mind; Analysis; Politics, Philosophy, and Economics; Ethics and International Affairs;* and the *Philosopher's Annual.* He has been a Laurance S. Rockefeller Fellow at the Center for Human Values at Princeton University, a Faculty Fellow at the Murphy Center of Political Economy at Tulane University, and a Fellow of the Program on Justice and the World Economy at the Carnegie Council on Ethics and International Affairs. He is currently Professor of Philosophy at the University of Sheffield.

Gordon S. Wood is Alva O. Way University Professor and Professor of History at Brown University. He is the author of many works, including *The Creation of the American Republic, 1776–1787* (1969), which won the Bancroft Prize and the John H. Dunning Prize in 1970, and *The Radicalism of the American Revolution* (1992), which won the Pulitzer Prize for History and the Ralph Waldo Emerson Prize in 1993. *The Americanization of Benjamin Franklin* was awarded the Julia Ward Howe Prize by the Boston Authors Club in 2005. His latest book, *Revolutionary Characters: What Made the Founders Different,* was published in 2006. Professor Wood is a Fellow of the American Academy of Arts and Sciences and the American Philosophical Society.

INDEX

Abingdon, Earl of, 71–72
abolitionist movement, 266, 312–13
abortion, 18, 183–84, 259, 274, 318
accused, rights of the, 318
Act for Establishing Religious Freedom (Virginia), 190–91, 219–20
Adams, Amos, 80
Adams, John, 202, 305; on British versus natural rights, 137, 138; on definability of rights, 50; on inalienable rights, 261–62; individual and community rights in writings of, 23; on liberty and Catholicism as incompatible, 202–3; on mild establishment, 199; on natural rights, 306; on religion and republicanism, 205; on rights and religion, 48, 219, 306; and Sedition Act of 1798, 163; skepticism about human nature of, 204; on sources of expertise on rights, 52; tyranny of legislatures dismissed by, 241, 243, 246
Adams, Samuel, 72–73, 123, 138, 144, 306
Adamson v. California (1947), 168
African Americans: civil rights movement, 273, 317, 318; Declaration of Independence appealed to by, 315; disfranchisement of, 269; Field's *Slaughter-House Cases* dissent and, 316; Fifteenth Amendment gives vote to, 173–74; post–Civil War economic constraints on, 268; Protestantism of, 201; racism in nineteenth-century workingmen's movement, 266–67; in white Protestant society, 206, 210, 219. *See also* racial equality; slavery
Alexander, James, 49
Allen, Richard, 210
Amar, Akhil Reed, 1, 8–9, 177n19, 281, 282
America: eighteenth-century language of rights in, 48–53; English historical background of rights in, 233–36; history of rights in early America, 233–57; individual rights versus state legislatures in early republic, 243–48; nature of rights in, 15–24; private–public distinction transformed in, 238–42; rights as existing against the Crown, 236–38; rights consciousness in history of, 258–79; seventeenth-century language of rights in, 42–48. *See also* American

Revolution; Civil War (American); colonial assemblies; colonial charters; Constitution of the United States; First Continental Congress; Founders; Second Continental Congress; Supreme Court; *and states by name*
American Revolution: developments in American approach to rights due to, 52–53; natural-rights discourse in, 3, 8, 9, 306, 308–10; rights talk in era of, 305–11; rights violated during, 262; universalist rights language emerges in period of, 5. *See also* Declaration of Independence
Andros, Sir Edmund, 46
animal rights, 295, 319
Anti-Federalists: on Bill of Rights, 9, 163, 164, 172, 182, 193–95, 264; question of sovereignty raised by, 245
anti-Semitism, 206, 209
Apodaca v. Oregon (1972), 176n18
Argall, Samuel, 44
Aristotle, 28, 30–31

Bacon, Anthony, 96
Bacon, Francis, 36
Bacon's Rebellion (1676), 45
Baptists, 201, 205, 212–13
Barron v. Baltimore (1833), 164, 165, 167
Beard, Charles, 271
Becker, Carl, 134
Bentham, Jeremy, 133, 149n62, 155n158
Berkeley, William, 44
Bill of Rights (1689), 41, 47, 91–92, 186, 248, 261
Bill of Rights (1774). *See* Declaration of Rights (1774)
Bill of Rights (1791): in antebellum era, 163–64, 182; Civil War and reinterpretation of, 4, 8–9, 165–66, 173, 281; as consolidation of rights, 277; creation of, 163–65, 263–65; dilemmas of declaring rights, 181–97; first phase of rights claims results in, 260, 263–65; Fourteenth Amendment in reinterpretation of, 4, 8, 165–66, 168–73, 273; historical evolution of, 163–80; incorporation by Supreme Court, 8–9, 167–71, 174–75, 273, 318; judicial interpretation of,

Constitutionalism and Democracy